What Others Say —

Bill Carter has lived a life like no other. From serving in John F. Kennedy's Secret Service to shepherding the Rolling Stones through their tumultuous first U.S. stadium tour and their myriad legal problems, he witnessed first-hand and participated in massive shifts in American history.

> Chet Flippo, Former Editor of *Rolling Stone* Magazine
> Editorial Director of CMT.com

Since November 22, 1963, JFK has been a household name for a whole generation of Soviet baby-boomers, that is my generation. That's why Bill Carter's history is so fascinating for me and for many people back in Russia. On a more personal note: Bill is a man who has once introduced me to the enchanting world of the gospel music.

> Vladimir Kiklo, ITAR-TASS UN correspondent

Bill Carter has been my friend, business associate and confidante for many years, but after reading his book, I realized that I really didn't know Bill. The man has traveled many roads and led an incredibly interesting life. This is an exciting story about a fascinating man and one everybody should read.

> Bob Eubanks, TV Personality
> National Speaker
> Author

The legendary NBC news anchor Tom Brokaw said, "It's easy to make a buck. It's a lot tougher to make a difference." That phrase can certainly be applied to William (Bill) N. Carter who through his intelligence, patience, vision and compassion has resolved a lot of problems for his famous clients. I like books. This is one of the most interesting I've read. *Backstage in History from JFK's Assassination to the Rolling Stones* reveals new, intimate, information about some of the most powerful public personalities of the past 50 years, with new insights into the life of Lee Harvey Oswald and other key events surrounding the assassination of President John F. Kennedy. This book is an electric page turner. *Backstage in History* covers Bill's close relationship with the Rolling Stones rock band and how he saved their career. Having known Bill for over the last twenty years, I have personally observed his building the career

of Reba McEntire and making her a super star. I watched as he did the same for Tanya Tucker. I also credit Bill Carter for the major success of Gospel music magnate Bill Gaither and his massive organization. There is MUCH MORE about some of the most important people and mores of our culture. It's a roller coaster read that will keep you up late at night with the light on.

Ralph Emery, TV Personality and Host
Author

Bill Carter is one of the best storytellers I have ever met. I loved sitting in his office listening to him tell us stories about his adventures. He has a broad range of friends, acquaintances and enemies and now I can read about all of them in one book!! Working with Bill taught me so many things that I continue to use today. This should be one heck of an interesting, entertaining book. I can't wait!

Reba McEntire, Country Artist
Actress

Carter and I have been good friends since we first met, back in the '70s. When we first met, he was living in Little Rock and just getting his feet wet in the music business. Our association continued after he moved to Nashville and became a personal manager to several country music artists. If you wanted something done that was complicated, tough to do and had a short timeline, Carter was THE person to call. He handled delicate matters for my friend and client, Steve McQueen and other industry people in Los Angeles, and he never failed in what he set out to do and he never complained. More importantly, he has been consistently honest and forthright in his dealings, something too seldom found in the entertainment industry in LA. He really is one of a kind, and I am proud to call him a friend through thick and thin.

W.J. (Bill) Maher
Formerly Senior Executive with CMA and ICM talent agencies
Primary Advisor to actor Steve McQueen

When I first met Bill Carter and started associating with him (on his mundane cases) he was representing the Rolling Stones, Tanya Tucker and other luminaries. His brilliant and exciting career as an adult contrasts with the days of his youth when he spent much of his time out of school picking cotton in the hellish hot fields of northeast Arkansas. If you want to get it from the inside from a charismatic, bright, unbelievably energetic figure, read Billy Neal Carter's memoirs.

Billy Roy Wilson
Little Rock, Arkansas

I consider myself normal. Bill Carter isn't. For instance he differs with "normal people" in that he embraces reincarnation and is a Democrat! But still he is one of the most unforgettable characters I'll ever meet. This book will tell a story and a good one, but it's the storyteller who is the real story. He's stubborn and determined, but has a tremendous sense of humor, he's tough but still a romantic and he is loyal yet is inclusive. He's a friend of mine and you will be his, as well, after you have read this book. Or at least an admirer.

> Jay Dickey
> Former Member of Congress 1993-2000, Arkansas - R

Bill Carter and I have been friends since law school in the early '60s and have shared many unusual experiences, from arresting and prosecuting forgers and counterfeiters, to defending murderers and other criminals, to springing Keith Richards and Ron Wood from jail in Fordyce, AR, and through several political campaigns. Bill has put these and his many other experiences into an interesting and readable account. It is a must read for anyone with an interest in a look behind the scenes at contemporary U.S. history, the legal system and the entertainment industry and how they work.

> Lindsey J. Fairley
> Retired Municipal Judge and U.S. Magistrate

Bill Carter has been my mentor and forceful advocate since the late '70s. Beginning with the Stones '81 tour, Carter helped me to elevate the business aspects of my craft and how lighting designers were perceived. I was too young and naïve to understand the nuances myself, so he taught me the ropes, employing a Broadway-style approach to our deal-making that only one other designer was using at that time. He became my "go-to" guy. His belief in me gave me a lot of confidence, and through him, other doors were opened, especially in television. Bill Carter is larger than life—like a character in an Elmore Leonard novel. (He would always be the good guy.) The word authentic comes to mind, he's uniquely and authentically himself—a real force of nature. He's honest and guileless, and he holds his friends close. Had I not met Bill, I literally would not have the career I enjoy today.

> Allen Branton
> TV, Concert and Broadway Lighting Designer

Bill Carter is an American in the *John Wayne* tradition. He made something out of himself. His story is one of a man who made things happen for his friends and clients, whether in politics, business or the entertainment arena. In one of his endeavors he helped one of America's great businesses, *Federal Express*, get off the ground!

Frank Watson, Former Law Partner
Member of the Original Board of Directors of Federal Express

GET CARTER

Backstage in History from
JFK's Assassination to The Rolling Stones

---◆---

Bill Carter
and Judi Turner

FINE'S CREEK
PUBLISHING

Nashville

Get Carter
Backstage In History From JFK's Assassination To The Rolling Stones

© 2006 by Bill Carter. All Rights Reserved

Printed in the United States of America

Fine's Creek Publishing
2525 West End Avenue, Suite 1100, Nashville, TN 37203
www.BillCarterOnline.com

ISBN 10: 0-9774604-2-8

ISBN 13: 978-0-9774604-2-7

Also available in hard cover, ISBN 0-9774604-0-1

No part of this book may be reproduced or transmitted in any form
or by any means, electronic or mechanical, including photocopying,
recording or by any information storage and retrieval system, without
permission in writing from the publisher.

If you wish to contact Bill Carter, you may do so through the Fine's
Creek Publishing website, www.BillCarterOnline.com.

Library of Congress Control Number: 2005938741

First Edition

DEDICATION

To my parents Henry and Faye Richardson Carter who always tried to provide me with guidance to select the right path in life, and to the brave men and women of the United States Secret Service.

Contents

List of Illustrations

FOREWORD

𝕴 RECKON EVERYONE WHO EVER met Bill Carter remembers vividly that first meeting. Mine was at Tavern on the Green, the ritzy restaurant in Manhattan's Central Park, at a reception for William Lee Golden of the Oak Ridge Boys, shortly after I moved to New York in 1982.

I was introduced to Bill by Kay West (she was publicist Kay Shaw then, now she's a terrific journalist) who told me he represented William Lee.

"So who else do you represent?" I asked. I'm sure I was already struck by Billy's deceptively relaxed demeanor (and yes, some of us *do* call him Billy, if not just plain *Carter*). I know he had that customary gleam in his eye and that good old boy grin that might have been completely disarming had he not also flashed his extraordinary sense of self-awareness and confidence. And I'm sure my jaw dropped when he replied so casually, as if they were some local boys from Little Rock, "Oh, the Rolling Stones."

By then, Carter was more of a ticket master for the Stones than the guy who got Keith Richards out of Canada when he was busted there on a heroin charge, as our friend Chet Flippo recounted in his classic rock book *On the Road with the Rolling Stones*. But he still looked bigger than life, as he has ever since, the only man I've ever known—or ever will know, I'll bet—who could be described that way.

I would later learn of his Secret Service background and JFK (I love telling people how I know with certainty that Oswald acted alone, since my friend Bill Carter told me so!), not to mention his experiences with the likes of Steve McQueen and Peter Tosh and how he took Reba McEntire to stardom—which I witnessed first-hand. I also saw him take two of my favorite artists, Jo-El Sonnier and Rodney Crowell, to the peaks of their careers. Much later Bill helped me with my own book (a biography of the pioneering punk band, the Ramones) and introduced me to Bill Gaither and his southern gospel organization—one of the most spiritually rewarding professional relationships I've enjoyed, though I remain a devout atheist, much to Bill's and especially his wonderful daughter Joanna's unending dismay.

But you shouldn't necessarily read too much into that—my atheism, that is. We were celebrating Joanna's birthday at lunch some years ago, and as so often happens, everyone present expressed their concern over my spiritual shortcoming. "I can't understand how you don't believe in a higher power," said Joanna, flustered as ever. "But I do believe in a higher power, my dear," I said reassuringly, then paused dramatically for effect before looking at her father and testifying thusly: "Bill Carter!" His response? That customary gleam in his eye and that old boy grin.

One last thing I remember about Billy that bears relating. Judi Turner once said how he doesn't show everyone his extraordinary kindness and compassion, and I know, more than most, how true that is. God knows, he can have a gruff, intimidating exterior—and he's probably the last person you want to get on the wrong side of. Indeed, there have been way too many times he's shook his head at me with his fearsome glare of disapproval. Yet there is no man I've ever known—or ever will know, I'll bet—with a bigger heart than Bill Carter.

—Jim Bessman, Music Journalist
Author

Preface

I NEVER INTENDED TO WRITE a book about my life. People who were familiar with things I had done always expressed fascination with my life and told me I should write a book about my experiences. Two of the most persistent of those friends were Chet Flippo and John Harricharan. Finally in the '90s, young people seemed to discover JFK and upon hearing of my association with that part of history, began to seek me out with questions.

My daughters, Julia—born in April 1963 just before JFK's death and Joanna—born in 1965, both began to inquire of my past since I rarely spoke of my Secret Service days. I was their hero because of my association with the Rolling Stones and that was not the way I preferred to be remembered.

Finally, in 1999 I decided to write a book for my family only, to preserve the important historical events I witnessed. I never intended for the book to be published.

Events surrounding the assassination had been blocked out of my mind for so long I had a difficult time recalling specific facts. I called the National Archives, which housed the Warren Commission files on the assassination of JFK. I asked to speak to the person in charge of the documents, and a young lady, named Martha Murphy, came on the phone. I expected to be given a difficult time. Instead, when I told her my name, she replied that she knew exactly who I was. I asked to examine the files that I had participated in, and she said they would be ready for me when I arrived.

My friend John Bennett, a retired Washington, D.C. political journalist, agreed to assist me in the research, and when we arrived at the Archives they rolled out fifteen file boxes on a cart for my examination. The Archives staff was helpful and allowed me to examine any evidence I wished. John Bennett held my hand through several long days of tedious research, and for that I am thankful and indebted to him. The photos and exhibits relating to the assassination that are reproduced in this book are courtesy of the National Archives. I believe they are a vital link to the events of that tragedy.

Because I was living events and had no real overview about their historical significance, I have relied heavily on the words of such authors as William Manchester, Ted Sorensen, Ben Bradlee, Arthur Schlesinger, Jr., Nina Burleigh, and others who provided a far broader scope of the events around the assassination and the landscape of the '60s than I ever could. We have attempted to be diligent in giving proper credit to these authors for their material. Over the years, friends have given me numerous books on Kennedy, most of which I never read until we began this book project. Because we are attempting to paint an accurate picture of the landscape of the era, we would, on occasion, include facts taken from books without remembering their exact source. If we have inadvertently failed to properly acknowledge words taken from other authors, I sincerely apologize.

By the same token, my friend Chet Flippo tells the story of the Rolling Stones so eloquently that I have borrowed liberally from his fascinating book. Chet is one of the greatest storytellers I know, but I still can't believe I did all the things he credited me with in his saga of life on the road with the Rolling Stones.

Reliving these events was excellent therapy for me as I now began to open up and talk about the subject of the assassination for the first time without breaking down emotionally.

As I began to dig through the JFK and Rolling Stones files, it occurred to me the interest others might have in some of the historical events of my life. A call to Bill Maher, formerly Steve McQueen's financial advisor and an old friend of mine, provided even more encouragement to write a book for public consumption. Not all the events are as much of historical significance as they are humorous. Whatever, it's just my life as I lived it!

Ruth Montgomery, a White House reporter during the Kennedy years, best-selling author, and later my treasured friend, used to tell me I was one of the most spiritually open persons she had ever met. She suggested my openness invited kindred spirits to seek me out. I write of some of these experiences. Through prayer I have always opened my soul to spiritual guidance. John Harricharan taught me to pray all the time, on an elevator, when bored on an airplane, driving, or any time I had a moment to focus on prayer rather than waste that time on idle thoughts. It worked for me, and I began to pray more and always end by asking for spiritual guidance.

Try not to be too judgmental as you read about some of the things I have done. I have simply tried to represent myself to the best of my ability. I am not Yale or Harvard educated—I wish I was. I always felt at a disadvantage and simply had to use the gifts God provided me. I'm sure there is a reason for the obstacles God placed before me, and I hope I have passed some of the tests. I remember once a client calling me at 3:00 a.m. When I answered, he paid me the supreme compliment a lawyer could receive when he said he knew that he could always depend on me being there when he had that one phone call. My uneducated parents taught me no prejudices and to treat everyone with respect and dignity. However, the most important things they taught me were honesty, integrity, hard work, and dependability. I hope I have not failed in these endeavors.

Acknowledgments

Throughout my life I have been richly blessed to know extraordinary people, but never more so than in putting this book together. It was a six-year odyssey, and during those years, I experienced a number of life-altering experiences. But through the years, those involved in helping me assemble this book have been a constant source of friendship, love, and support, and for that I am deeply appreciative. I used to tell artists who were nominated for awards not to try and thank a laundry-list of people if they won, because in the excitement of the moment, they were certain to leave off someone who had been crucial in their career success. The same applies to this book. There were so many people who generously shared their memories with me and encouraged me to write this book, that I cannot possibly mention everyone by name. You know who you are, and you have my heartfelt thanks. There are a few people I feel compelled to mention, though:

Judi Turner—what can I say? I don't know whether to thank her or not. But I can say the book would not have been written without her. She encouraged me to write this book, and when I became frustrated and would want to give up, she literally made me forge ahead. Through the years, she has been a true friend and kept me focused and nudged me when necessary. I very much appreciate her dedication to this project, and will always be grateful to her.

Also, my faithful assistant, Darlene Fort for her organizational skills and for putting up with me all these years. Special thanks to my former law partner Kathy Woods, who survived most of the events of this book and sometimes had a better memory than I. Also, thanks to Jim Bessman for all the encouragement through the years. Bruce Phillips provided legal assistance and friendship, and I appreciate his assistance. Jacqueline Landis did a masterful job in editing the book and really made it sing. Leland F. (Lee) Raymond of CyPress Publications (Web site http://cypress-starpublications.com) took the rough manuscript and really created the book. Every author needs professionals such as Jackie and Lee to make their words come alive in readable form. Karen Cronin has my gratitude for her usual expert job in designing the cover. Mike Vaden has been my business manager for two decades and a valued friend as well. Judi Turner and I spent a Saturday afternoon in Little Rock with my long-time friend, Judge Lindsey Fairley, laughing at his recollections of the Keith Richards' incident in Fordyce, Arkansas, and he was very helpful in providing his own insight into that hilarious event. Other friends from Arkansas such as my former law partner, Paul Henson, and Judge Bill Wilson, also helped fill in gaps in stories.

I am deeply indebted to my long-time friend and advisor, John Harricharan, and his assistant of many years, Anita Bergen. Because John is the author of several best-selling books, he was invaluable in helping me navigate the tricky waters of the publishing world. He spent countless hours counseling me, working on polishing the finished product, finding people who are tops in their fields to assist us, and being endlessly patient with the million questions of a novice author.

I have to thank Jan Carter for our wonderful years together, for being my friend, and for raising my two daughters, Julia and Joanna, while I ran around the world experiencing the events of this book.

I am so grateful for the opportunity to work with Bill and Gloria Gaither and Barry Jennings. Thanks to you for having confidence in me and providing an environment for spiritual growth.

Lastly, I am especially grateful for my angels for sending me a Polish lady on a white horse (literally) who I recognize as a soul mate who became my wife and I look forward to sharing an eternal life of love.

Part I

Introduction

L ADIES AND GENTLEMEN, we have begun our final approach into the Dallas/Fort Worth Airport . . ."

The announcement from the flight attendant startled me from a light, fitful sleep, and I eased my seat into an upright position, rubbing my knuckles over my eyes to remove the last traces of the weariness that never fails to overtake me on the four-hour LA to Dallas flight.

I stretched my cramped legs into the aisle in an attempt to remove the kinks and felt for the ends of my seat belt.

"Mr. Carter," a man's voice accompanied the brief touch of a hand on my shoulder. My Secret Service training leaves me a little suspicious when I unexpectedly encounter the captain of an aircraft singling me out as this one just had. "You are Mr. Carter, aren't you?" the captain repeated.

"I am," I affirmed, somewhat warily.

"We've been contacted by the ground crew in Dallas," he began. "As soon as we're on the ground, you have been asked to call your home in Little Rock. This is an emergency, but they asked me to assure you that it's not a family emergency."

Even with the captain's reassurance, there is still something alarming about receiving an emergency message from home when you're 30,000 feet in the air with no recourse but to endure the interminable wait until the plane lands, taxis to the gate, and all preparations for landing are completed. And on my best day, I am not a patient man.

Ignoring the polite requests from the flight attendant to wait until the plane had taxied safely to the gate before rising, I shot out of my seat as soon as we stopped moving and was first in line when the gate agent swung open the door to the cabin. I practically sprinted up the gateway, and spying a pay phone to the left of the gate desk, I raced to it. My wife, Jan, answered on the second ring. "What's wrong?" I barked.

"There's some kind of emergency at the office, and Kathy wanted you to call the minute you landed in Dallas," Jan replied.

I slammed the phone down on Jan and checked my watch to see how much time I had to get to the gate for my connecting flight home to Little Rock before placing a collect call to my legal assistant, Kathy Woods. Since it was after business hours, I reached Kathy at home, and she immediately answered.

"Bill, Keith and Anita have been arrested in Canada in connection with drugs," she said. Although it wasn't pleasant news, it didn't exactly constitute an emergency. My celebrated clients, the Rolling Stones, the most famous rock and roll band in the world in that year of 1977, had been plagued with run-ins with the law before, especially Keith Richards. Any time rock and roll was mentioned, it was always rounded out with "drugs, sex, and rock and roll." This was nothing we hadn't dealt with for the past five years, and I reminded her of that. Cops around the world laid in wait for the Stones to see who could bust them first.

Her next words, however, chilled me to the bone. "It's really bad this time," she stressed. "They had enough heroin that the Mounties got them for intent to distribute. They're talking prison, Bill, and you know what that means.

"Peter Rudge called," she was almost whispering. "They're scared, Bill. If Keith goes to prison, there is no more Rolling Stones. Rudge said Mick Jagger had two words to say: 'Get Carter!' "

Damned if that wasn't the story of my life.

"And so, my fellow Americans: ask not what your country can do for you—ask what you can do for your country."

Inauguration Address of John Fitzgerald Kennedy
January 20, 1961

Chapter I
Good Morning, Mr. President!

Y OU'VE HEARD THE SAYING, "Man makes plans, and God laughs." Well, God didn't spend a lot of time laughing at me, because I never planned for much of anything in my life. I'm either really lucky or fate had great plans for me. Things have fallen in my lap at the most opportune times and sent me reeling in a totally different direction from where I was headed. A fine example is how destiny snatched me from the brink of a potentially fatal career misstep and plunked me squarely down in the middle of history. Even I sometimes can't quite believe the way my life played out.

I wasn't headed anywhere in particular, when one day politics came calling. In 1958, when I was still in college at Arkansas State University, in Jonesboro, Arkansas, Henry Alstadt approached me. Henry was a pillar of the community and very active politically. He was a friend of E.C. "Took" Gathings, the congressman from our district. Any time a congressman or other major politician came to town, he sought out Henry Alstadt. Henry told me he wanted my help in a political campaign. Lee Ward, who was originally from my hometown of Rector, was a lawyer and judge in Jonesboro, and he was running for the governorship held by Orval Faubus. Henry thought I could be of help to him. Faubus was enormously popular in Arkansas, but at that time I didn't have any particular political leanings or allegiances, so I agreed to help.

Despite my lack of political knowledge or experience, I was hired to work in the Ward campaign; I was paid little to nothing—mainly just expenses. I traveled around the state for Lee, putting up signs, attending rallies and helping to organize. At different events, I would see both Judge Ward and Faubus speaking, and I remember thinking that, in spite of the fact that he was my candidate, there was no way Ward was going to beat Faubus. Although he was very controversial over his civil rights stance, the public thought Faubus was doing a great job as governor, enough to elect him to six terms. I was right to be concerned because, of course, Ward got trounced, but I got some valuable experience and found I really liked politics. In fact, I met some of Faubus' people in traveling around the state, and they told me that I should consider working with them in the next election.

During my summer break from college, Henry got me involved in another campaign—a local race for Leon Beaton, who was running for, and eventually won, the sheriff's race in Clay County. I literally went house to house all summer, talking to people about Leon Beaton. I got to know everybody in the county. I would go into their homes, leave them a card, shake hands, sit on the front porch with them, drink ice tea, and jaw with them about a little of everything. I was truly developing a talent for politics.

I think it's unusual that I never consciously planned to do anything specific in life, allowing things to just kind of fall into place at the time I needed them to. One year, when I was taking a break from college and working at the Irby Funeral Home in Rector, my boss, Dan McBride, told me I would make a great funeral director. He praised me when I left there and tried to get me to stay. I never had a job where I didn't do well or one where my employers didn't want me to stay and make a career out of that job. The circumstances that caused me to leave my jobs—with the Missouri Pacific Railroad, the Air Force, and then later the funeral home—were just that, circumstances. But the circumstances always prompted me to make a direction change. I didn't plan to go to college; circumstances led me there. I never planned a serious event in my life until much later in life. So now, for the first time, I found myself developing some direction. I was thinking, boy, I like this political gig—this is for me. I even thought I might major in political science—whatever that meant. I only knew it had something to do with politics and the government, and I thought maybe that was where I was headed.

Through Henry, I had met a guy named Harold Jenks, the postmaster at Piggott, Arkansas. Harold was also very active in the Democratic Party. In fact, he went to the Democratic Convention every year and was an officer in the National Democratic Party. Harold and I became friendly, and he served as a mentor to me through the years. Mostly at the suggestion of Henry or Harold, I became engaged in a number of political campaigns, including one for Jack Hurst, who was running for the Arkansas State Senate. I helped him get elected, and we later became good friends. Then Joe Harden ran for governor two years later, and I ended up working for him—again, traveling around the state and, again, running against Governor Faubus.

I was becoming a familiar face on the Arkansas political front, and I think I was being sought out for a number of reasons: I was an Air Force veteran, a college student, a mature guy, twenty-three years old, and made a good impression. I was well mannered, had a good personality, and I fit in well with these politicos.

Unfortunately, like Lee Ward before him, Joe Harden got trounced by Faubus, but it worked to my advantage because the Faubus people were beginning to notice me. In Lee Ward's race for governor, my name appeared in the campaign ads, and I was popular in Rector and in Clay County, where everybody knew me. I had been all over the state campaigning, and people were beginning to recognize me. Even though I was always working to defeat Faubus by supporting his opposition, it wasn't because I necessarily disagreed with the governor; in fact, I was coming to respect the fact that Faubus was a great politician. I didn't necessarily always agree with him philosophically or politically, but I observed what a talented politician he was, and I learned a lot by watching him make speeches. Back then, television was not yet effective in reaching the masses, so politics was carried out on a very personal level. Candidates traveled all over the state making speeches, holding rallies, and meeting the people face-to-face. Faubus, a real man of the people, was a master at meeting the masses. Finally, Faubus' people offered me a job in 1960, but I didn't take it; I was already involved in another campaign, which reached far beyond the Arkansas state line.

In 1960, when I was a senior at Arkansas State University, John F. Kennedy was running for president against Vice President Richard Nixon. Although I was aware of the campaign and found myself admiring the things Kennedy represented, I was not actively involved in his campaign. Then one day Harold Jenks called me out of the blue. "Bill," he started, "I've just been made the regional campaign chairman for the National Democratic Party for the western district of the United States. I'm now based out of Denver, but Arkansas is my region." I congratulated him but didn't understand why he was calling to tell me this. Then came the clincher. "I guess you know that Jack Kennedy is running for president on the Democratic ticket, and I'm having a little trouble getting anybody to run his campaign in the First District," he explained. "Then I remembered that you were in school in Jonesboro, and since that's in the First District, I thought you might consider coordinating the campaign efforts."

Wow! I thought, this was an incredible honor. They wanted me to coordinate Kennedy's campaign in my district! But why me? Harold had known me from the time he was a postmaster in Piggott, which was near Rector, and he also knew me through Henry Alstadt. I guess the fact that I had worked in two losing statewide gubernatorial races didn't make much difference to Harold. He had seen me at dozens of campaign rallies and meetings throughout the state, working on a losing cause, and something about me must have obviously caught his attention. I didn't even have to think about it; I agreed without hesitation.

The first thing Harold asked me to do was attend this "big" Kennedy meeting, supposedly to be attended by all the state Democrats. I showed up, but very few others did. Still, I left the meeting with an armful of Kennedy campaign material and a list of all the Democratic county chairmen in the First District. Then it was time for my national political baptism. Harold sent me first to Blytheville, in

Mississippi County, to meet with the county chairman. Now, this man was just about what you'd expect from an old politico from east Arkansas. He welcomed me into his office, and then I explained that I was there to ask him to support Jack Kennedy in his bid for the presidency. That old county chairman reared back and said, "You know, Bill, you seem like a fine young man, and I'm sure you'll do well, but you're on the wrong horse here, boy. He, uh, John Kennedy's kin to the Pope and the Catholics, so if I were you I would get out of this campaign. You're going to ruin your reputation getting associated with this bunch." With that, he invited me *not* to put up a single Kennedy sign in the Mississippi County of Arkansas, or I would be in trouble.

That was a harsh dose of reality, and I was fairly disillusioned, but I went around the district diligently and responsibly, and in the process had little success in securing help from old-line Democrats. About the only people in my district for JFK were the young idealists. This was the '60s South, and there was an incredible amount of prejudice against Catholics. It was unbelievable! I didn't understand that. Granted, I didn't know a lot about theology, and I have to admit I didn't know much of anyone but Methodists and Baptists in Arkansas, but I had met Catholics while I was in the Air Force, stationed in Minnesota and elsewhere, and I saw few differences between Catholics and Protestants.

I was excited about working for Jack Kennedy—not because I was a Democrat—because he was young, with fresh ideas for our country. There was an air of excitement everywhere he appeared. Prior to his candidacy, most young people had no interest in politics. Kennedy encouraged young people to participate, and the Young Democrats organization accepted his invitation, unless their parents prohibited their involvement. I was kind of glad the old dogs of the Democratic Party boycotted Kennedy's campaign; otherwise, I would probably never have had the opportunity to be so involved. And in spite of the prejudice against Catholics, Kennedy got elected. I didn't know at the time what a large part Kennedy's election was going to play later in my own life.

I was about to graduate from college in 1961, and up to that point I had done nothing really for most of my life but play tennis and work on political campaigns. I made good grades, but I still had a good time. Strange how once again events intervened to change the course of my life.

I had been persuaded by one of my professors to major in economics rather than political science, and he submitted my name for a scholarship worth $1,500 to Southern Methodist University, in Dallas, to pursue a master's degree in economics. I didn't have any other plans, so I figured, why not? My wife, Jan, and I had been married two years by then, and everything was going fine. My sister Doris' husband, Stan, was now assistant plant manager at the Dallas Ford plant, so Jan and I packed up my '56 Ford and headed to Dallas. We stayed with Doris and Stan, who got me a job as a security guard at the Ford plant.

In the fall of 1961, I went out to SMU to claim my scholarship and see about enrolling. Arkansas State was a blue-collar environment—it was just a state university, and everyone dressed casually, usually in blue jeans, long before they were hip. I arrived at SMU, driving my little '56 Ford, still receiving my GI bill of $135 a month, thanks to my stay in the Air Force, and it was a total culture shock. The students were all in blazers and creased slacks and driving new cars—they were rich kids. As I said, this was long before the hippies made blue jeans acceptable fashion, and these kids were dressed immaculately. Right away I was intimidated by the differences. More importantly, the scholarship didn't even pay the full tuition; the tuition was $1,750 a semester, and my scholarship was only $1,500. But I really think, more than anything, I was intimidated by the difference in social class between me, a small-town boy from Rector and Arkansas State, and the students at SMU. I didn't fit in, and I just knew I couldn't go to SMU. By now, it was September and classes were starting for that semester.

I figured that since I was interested in politics at the time, and most of the politicians were lawyers and judges, then law school would be the natural place for me. Some of my friends were going to law school at the University of Arkansas, so I called the Dean of the UA Law School, Dean Barnhardt, and explained that I was in Dallas, planning on attending SMU on an economics scholarship, but I didn't want to enroll. I told him that although I hadn't applied for law school, I would be forever grateful if he would accept me as a student starting that week. To my surprise, he agreed. He said to come up to Fayetteville and they'd enroll me. The tuition was $75 a semester. I figured I could make it somehow on my GI bill.

Once again, Jan and I packed up the old '56 Ford and headed back to Arkansas.

We couldn't get into student housing at the university at that late date, so Jan and I moved into an old, junkie garage apartment in Fayetteville. This apartment didn't have much but a bed, and it was filthy. I knew I had to get out of there somehow. That's when I got my first real lesson on how beneficial the right connections can be. Among the first people I met in law school was Lindsey Fairley, who would become a treasured lifelong friend. Lindsey's father-in-law, Harold Ohlendorf, was a wealthy Oseola farmer who was also a friend of Governor Faubus. I met others in law school who have become lifelong friends—Richard Earl Griffin, Burl Anthony (who became a congressman from Arkansas), Jay Dickey (also a congressman), and Farrell Faubus, the governor's son. Most of the people I was meeting in law school, in fact, were well-to-do and connected.

Through Lindsey I met E.J. Ball, a prominent lawyer in Fayetteville, who was Harold Olandorf's tax attorney. One day when I was talking to E.J., it came up in conversation that I was living out in this dump. He immediately called the university and arranged for us to get into university housing. It was totally a political move because he knew exactly who to call and how to get things done.

Jan and I moved into Carlson Terrace, which was really nice, new, modern university housing, and I made the discovery that anything can happen through the right connections. I thought back on how things had already developed in my life through networking—Henry Alstadt introducing me to Harold Jenks and Lindsey introducing me to E.J. I began to realize that since I didn't have money and my family didn't have any prestige or connections, then I had to attain these things through people I knew. I don't think I ever deliberately set out to meet anyone or cultivate a friendship strictly because a person was well connected, but I did recognize that influential people would help me get somewhere in life. I've had people tell me I seemed driven, but I was never specifically driven about anything. I think God blessed me with a sense of direction.

There was one thing, however, that influenced me.

When I was growing up in Rector, I had a reputation for being mischievous and forever getting into trouble. I can remember people in Rector saying I would never amount to anything. That stuck with me and hurt. I was determined to prove them wrong.

Strangely, it wasn't law school or political connections, but a bizarre twist of fate that determined my course in life.

During the brief time we lived in Dallas, my brother Richard had also moved down there from St. Louis, looking for a job. He decided to take a civil service test, hoping for a government job, and since I had nothing better to do at the time, he suggested I keep him company. Richard went in to take the test, and I was hanging around the hallway with nothing to do. The registrar at the civil service office noticed me and asked what I was doing. When I told her, she said, "Do you realize this is a two-hour exam? That's a long time to just hang around this hall with nothing to do." Since I didn't know I had any other options, I asked what she meant. "You can go in and take the test," she said. I told her I was about to go back to Arkansas to law school and wasn't really interested in a civil service job. But she wasn't going to give up easily. "It'll be good experience for you, and you never know when you might need a government job," she cajoled. I saw the wisdom in what she was saying, so I joined my brother and took the test. Then I left Dallas and promptly forgot about it once Jan and I had moved to Fayetteville and I started law school.

I had attended law school for a year and a half when suddenly my GI Bill was up. Just like that, I ran completely out of money. My mother and father could barely support themselves, and I had no other source of income. Plus, I had a young wife to support. I was out of options, so I quickly came to the conclusion that it just wasn't meant for me to be a lawyer. I could see no other recourse but to drop out and get a job. The buzz around campus was that State Farm Insurance was hiring law students who were leaving school to train as insurance adjusters. They were paying $450 a month and would give you a car to drive. That sounded like pie-in-the-sky money, so I applied to State Farm, knowing full well that if they offered me a job, I was theirs. And they did. Then I received a fateful phone call, which, once again, changed the direction of my life.

Destiny was calling.

It was 1962 when I received a phone call one day from a man who identified himself as Leroy Letteer with the United States Secret Service in Little Rock. "I understand you're looking for a job," he said. To begin with, I didn't know what the Secret Service was, and I thought it was pretty strange that someone from an organization unfamiliar to me knew I was looking for a job. I thought he'd reached a wrong number. So I asked him how he got my name and phone number. "I took your name from a civil service roster in Dallas," he explained. I knew for sure then that he'd made a mistake.

"You've got the wrong Bill Carter," I told him, "There's no way my name could be on any civil service roster." Then he really spooked me because he had my correct Social Security number, my phone number and address. I still wasn't making the connection, and it wasn't until some time later that I remembered taking the exam in Dallas.

But he was persistent. "Are you interested in a job?" he asked again. I told him I was just about to go to work for State Farm. "Is that a 'no,' or would you be interested enough in hearing about the Secret Service for me to come up there and talk with you?" Letteer kept on.

I thought it wouldn't hurt to talk to him, so he came to our little apartment in Fayetteville one afternoon and met with me. Mr. Letteer was probably in his early forties at that time, but he seemed older because he wore a hat, like most men did in those days. He was not a flashy guy; in fact, he often favored bow ties and was very soft-spoken and very bright. I must say, he was a good recruiter for the Secret Service. He didn't try to talk me into making a decision, and he made a very good impression. He put me totally at ease and simply outlined the career benefits of the job. I pursued the job primarily because I liked Mr. Letteer so much.

After Mr. Letteer left, I called my old friend and political mentor, Henry Alstadt. I said, "Henry, the Secret Service has talked with me about a job. What do you think about that?" I explained that I was about to take a job with State Farm, but what Mr. Letteer said had intrigued me, and I needed some advice.

"Well, Bill," Henry said, "being in the Secret Service would be real prestigious, and it would be a good opportunity for a young man with your background. I think you should give it some serious consideration." Then Henry did a really wonderful thing for me.

E.C. "Took" Gathings was the congressman from our district, and Henry thought Congressman Gathings could advance my case, so he telegraphed Took on my behalf. In the early '60s, other than the telephone, there were only two methods of communication: letters and telegrams. If you needed to reach someone hastily, you would send a telegram. Henry told the congressman I had worked on several statewide political campaigns, had served my country in the Air Force, and had recently been in law school at the university. Henry asked Took if there was anything that he, as my congressman, could do to help me. Congressman Gathings threw his support to me, gave me a good reference, and I got the job.

Again, I was completely ignorant about the Secret Service, and I never really considered it a particular compliment that I was chosen; at the time, I thought I was just getting a much-needed job. But I happened to fit the profile of the ideal Secret Service agent. The Secret Service was looking for six-foot-tall men who were healthy specimens, inconspicuous in a crowd, with a military background, from rural America, who were patriotic and willing to die for their country. I had all those qualifications. I said later there certainly is a God who kept me from becoming an insurance adjuster. I would not have been happy for long chained to a desk. But that's typical of how events have taken place in my life.

After my initial meeting with Mr. Letteer, I was asked to come down to Little Rock and submit to a formal oral interview. The process didn't take very long; I think I was hired within a month. I said adios to the State Farm offer, and just like that, I was in the Secret Service. I had personal interviews, took some psychological tests, and submitted to a background check.

I was sweating that background check because I felt sure they would turn up the fact that I had burned down a house in Rector as a teenage prank. It wasn't intentional, but it got me in a world of trouble. There was an old abandoned house where my friends and I went to drink beer, play poker, and just generally screw around. It was really cold in that old house, so one day we built a fire in an attempt to keep warm. Well, the flames got out of control and the house caught on fire. I guess we could have put it out, but we opted to let her burn, and we just left. Someone had apparently seen us, and they called the law. We were arrested and expelled from school.

We were locked up, but that wasn't all the punishment Sheriff Geraine Wolfe planned to inflict on me. He sat me down and set me straight. He pointed out that I was on the brink of disaster, what with always getting in way too much trouble and really pushing the limits. He said, "I'm going to tell you what you're going to do. Even though you've been expelled from school, I'm gonna help you get back in school and you're going to clean up your act. From now on, you're gonna walk the straight and narrow."

From that day on, in spite of the fact that I was getting plenty of punishment at home, Sheriff Wolfe took charge of me. He took me to the school board and had them review my case and reinstate me in school. I was a junior at that point, and after that incident, I was pretty much a model student. I was never again in any kind of trouble, but Geraine kept a close eye on me all the same.

Despite my checkered past, there was not one negative comment from the citizens in Rector or anywhere else about me when the Secret Service checked. I had completely erased any negative images of my high school shenanigans by the time the Secret Service got around to asking questions.

By then I must have been perceived as a patriotic person who would follow orders and be obedient.

The first thing the Secret Service did was send me to Washington for an initial training course, consisting of classroom instruction, judo, and weapons training. There were actually two six-week courses; the first six weeks consisted of a basic course, and then I went back later and took an advanced six-week course. Ironically, I completed the advanced course the day Kennedy was assassinated. Nevertheless, in between training courses, I was privileged to serve President Kennedy. Even though my time serving him would be short, I did have the opportunity to stand before him in the White House and say, "Good morning, Mr. President."

Chapter 2
Counterfeiting, Forgery, and Threats Against the President

WHEN I WAS ABOUT TO GRADUATE from high school, long before the Air Force, politics, and the Secret Service would enter my life, my Uncle Joe asked if I would consider coming up to live in St. Louis if he could get me a job with the Missouri Pacific Railroad. I had already been thinking about becoming a railroad engineer, and he said he could start me off with a job in the general offices. Uncle Joe was as good as his word, and he got me a job in the public relations department of the Missouri Pacific in St. Louis, right after graduation. My big boss was a guy named Raymond Maxwell, and his assistant was Bill Stuart.

A strict disciplinarian, my dad had instilled certain manners in me so that if I was out with strangers, I was most polite. I always said "yes, sir" and "no, ma'am," but for the most part I kept my mouth shut. My dad taught me that you talk only when you're spoken to, or you don't ever open your mouth. When I was with family at any kind of gathering, I didn't say a word. If I did, I got my dad's hand upside my head.

My manners served me well when I got the job at Missouri Pacific. One of my responsibilities was to get the mail and open it, and then I would distribute it. Basically that was my job—errand boy. But I was a polite errand boy. Bill Stuart was the office manager, and I was lucky that he took a real liking to me. Eventually, Bill and others in the office got together and decided that I should attend college at Washington University in St. Louis. Well, at that time I hadn't planned to go to college, and I certainly didn't have very good grades. I had been too busy having fun instead. In fact, I think the caption under my class picture in my high school annual said, "Away with the books—let's have some fun." I had no desire to go to college then and hadn't prepared myself to go. But Bill insisted that while I worked for the railroad, he wanted me to go. I later realized that maybe he saw something in me I couldn't see in myself.

Bill called Washington University and sent me out there to enroll in night school. Washington University in St. Louis is like Vanderbilt—very prestigious—and is ranked with Ivy League schools like Harvard and Yale. It's an old school with ivy on the walls—a very exclusive school. This was 1953, and the Korean War was winding down. My brother Richard had just been discharged from the Air Force. I was so scared of attending college that I ran down and enlisted in the Air Force. It was the only thing I knew to do that would keep me out of college. Of course, Bill and everyone in the office were all really disappointed, but they gave me a nice going away party anyway.

I chose the Air Force because I had visited Richard when he was stationed at Scott Air Force Base, and I thought it was a really cool environment. Plus, several of my high school buddies were joining the Air Force at that time, and it seemed like the logical place for me. For basic training, I was assigned to Lackland Air Force Base, in San Antonio, Texas. This was really tough, but I did well because, hell, the toughest drill sergeant in America was nothing compared to my old man. It was a piece of cake. When I entered the service, I was five feet seven inches tall and weighed 135 pounds. I was no physical specimen—I wasn't even shaving yet—but I was in great shape. I don't remember much about basic training other than it was grueling, and I learned never to volunteer for anything. Most of the problems other people encountered in basic were from smarting off or talking back. I didn't have that problem, because my dad instilled in me that you never spoke unless you had something to say, and I knew he would knock me silly if I popped off. The drill sergeant was no different from my dad.

So, having been through military basic training, Secret Service basic training was not that difficult for me, except for the lifesaving part. I can barely swim, so when I had to go through lifesaving, I had to learn to swim fairly well, and that was hard for me—I barely got through that. Right away I knew I was not one of the guys who would be jumping off a boat to save the president. Other than the swimming part of the training, I excelled. Again, thanks to my military training, I was expert with a weapon.

The weapons we were trained to fire were a .38-caliber Colt revolver, a high-powered rifle, the Thompson .45-caliber submachine gun, and a riot shotgun. Colt had just invented the AR-15, which was a .223 rifle (it later became the M-16 for the military). It was still in the testing stages, but the Secret Service usually had advanced weaponry before anyone else. We fired the gun, but it was not issued—it was not a part of the Secret Service arsenal when I entered, but it became so before I left the Service.

The training also involved classroom instruction, and during this time I finally began to get an inkling of what kind of organization I had become part of, and I have to say, I was pretty impressed. The Secret Service had not even been around for one hundred years when I took the oath—it was formed right after the Civil War. At that time there was no central bank in the United States, and all the states had their own currency, which was essentially worthless. They had bills that were for 3½ cents, or some such nonsense as that, and counterfeiting was rampant. Secretary of the Treasury Hugh McCullough became concerned about this and urged President Abraham Lincoln to organize an elite body of men whose sole purpose was to investigate counterfeiting. That organization, which became known as the Secret Service, was formed on April 14, 1865, as Lincoln's last official act before his assassination ("Secret Service," 1995).

I was especially impressed—and quite reassured—that in almost one hundred years, only one Secret Service agent had been killed in the line of duty, and only one Secret Service protectee had been assassinated during that time. In addition to investigating counterfeiters, after the Civil War the Secret Service investigated the violence surrounding the new Ku Klux Klan rallies, and their success in this area greatly enhanced the reputation of the agency. The Service also gained notoriety by capturing a renowned counterfeiter, Capt. William Brockway.

Then, in 1894, during Grover Cleveland's administration, his family was plagued by kidnap threats, especially against their youngest daughter, Ruth (of Baby Ruth fame). Mrs. Cleveland went behind her husband's back and asked the Secret Service to keep an eye on the family during a vacation in Massachusetts. She was the First Lady, so Chief William B. Hazen complied with her request, and for his actions he was promptly fired. The first president to be assassinated in office was President McKinley, in 1901, but this was before the Secret Service was assigned to protect the president. But because McKinley's assassination was the first big media event of the twentieth century, his successor, Teddy Roosevelt, became the first president to employ the protection of the Secret Service. The most legendary figure in the early days of the Secret Service was Col. Edmund Starling, a soft-spoken Kentucky gentleman who became chief of the White House detail in 1912, under Woodrow Wilson.

The number of threats against the president increased dramatically with the outbreak of World War I, in 1914, and by the next year, the Secret Service had begun investigating all neutrality violations against the United States by foreign countries. Col. Starling gained his fame chiefly for saving the life of the president of France during a visit by President Wilson to France in 1917. Col. Starling was a passenger in the car following that of President George Provinco when he witnessed an assassin level his gun and prepare to fire. An expert marksman, Starling fired his own weapon and hit the assassin in his firing hand. As a result, he was acclaimed a hero in France.

The Secret Service was also responsible for bringing down the Interior Secretary during a major scandal of the twentieth century—the Teapot Dome Scandal. Agents followed the trail of telegraphed correspondence to trap Secretary Albert B. Fall and prove his involvement in illegal oil field leases at Teapot Dome, WY.

In 1932, at the height of the Great Depression, the job of the Secret Service detail became more complex when the number of threats against the president reached a new high. Demonstrations against the president were held—a new phenomenon—and for the first time the Service had to protect the president against the American public. The election of Franklin D. Roosevelt as president presented its own special challenges. Because of the great measures he took to conceal the extent of his paralysis during the campaign (and through most of his presidency), the American people were never really aware that Roosevelt could not stand or walk under his own power. Although he used special braces and canes when appearing in public, Roosevelt was largely confined to a wheelchair as a result of his bout with polio.

Advance work took on new meaning during the Roosevelt administration, when the Secret Service was charged with building special ramps and elevators to compensate for his limitations. When war was declared in 1941, Roosevelt was determined to travel as much as possible to inspire the troops and factory workers who supplied them, so the Secret Service designed many special transportation devices that were used to move the president around the world. These included a Pullman railroad car—which was bulletproofed and armored and was the heaviest railroad car ever built—and an airplane, both of which were equipped with elevators and aisles wide enough to accommodate his wheelchair. During the war, the Secret Service also extended coverage to the First Lady, the young Roosevelt grandchildren, and visiting international dignitaries such as Winston Churchill, a frequent White House visitor who was much beloved by the Service. Roosevelt also traveled internationally, making the job for the Secret Service more difficult by war and a president who couldn't use his legs. It's said that the agents' resourcefulness in the face of extreme challenges proved the true mettle of the Secret Service.

A story I found particularly intriguing, and one that demonstrates the extraordinary lengths to which the Service will go for their protectee, happened during Roosevelt's campaign for a historic fourth term in 1944. A former governor of New York, Roosevelt had decided to end his campaign by conducting a tour of the five boroughs of New York City in an open touring car. The Secret Service was horrified not only by how this would affect his health but also at the security nightmare presented by a president touring the largest city in America in an open car during wartime. Roosevelt was visibly ill by late 1944, and a cold late-fall rain was predicted for the day of the tour. So concerned were they about his health that the Service commandeered garages along the route for pit stops. They would pull off into the garage, where there would be a mattress waiting on the floor. Then they would lift Roosevelt from the car, lay him on the mattress, and strip him of his clothes, after which they would thoroughly dry him with towels, wrap him in a blanket to warm him, give him a shot of brandy, re-dress him, and lift him back into his car, resuming the tour in ten minutes without any of the five million people gathered to see their much-loved president being the wiser.

Former Agent Jim Griffith relates a funny story about this tour of the boroughs. "We had arrived in Brooklyn when I saw an object fly through the air and land at the president's feet. I had no idea what it was, but I made a headlong dive over the president's head, landing in the floorboard of the car with my feet over the president's shoulders. It turned out to be one of New York's famous bagels. All that for a bagel! The president just howled with laughter; he thought it was hilarious" ("Secret Service," 1995).

There was a major shake-up in the Secret Service in 1942, when Col. Starling was removed in favor of thirty-six-year-old Mike Riley, signaling the beginning of the modern Secret Service protective detail. From this point on, agents would be younger, more aggressive, and better trained. Three years later there was another shake-up when Truman assumed the presidency upon Roosevelt's death, in April 1945. All of Roosevelt's agents were drafted into the Army as buck privates, and Truman got a whole new detail. During the war the Service had been charged with combating a new kind of counterfeiting—that of rationing coupons—and after the war yet another kind of counterfeiting became popular—Social Security cards and GI Bill checks. I guess it goes to show that criminals can copy anything that's printed on paper—or at least try—and it was our job to stop them. After the war counterfeiting specialists in the Secret Service were sent to Europe to investigate the numerous cases of bogus currency circulating throughout the continent.

But what happened on November 1, 1950, may have been one of the proudest days in the history of the Secret Service, as well as one of the two saddest.

President Truman had been living in Blair House while the dilapidated White House was being gutted and renovated. On a hot November afternoon (the hottest November day on record, eighty-five degrees), at 2:15, the president was taking a nap before going to a dedication ceremony at Arlington. Two Puerto Rican nationalists from New York, Griselio Torresola and Oscar Collazo, had devised a plot to kill Truman to draw attention to their fight for independence in Puerto Rico. Agents Vince Mroz and Stuart Stout, each heavily armed, were on duty inside Blair House, rotating their posts every half hour, while Secret Service uniformed officers Donald Birdzell, Joseph Davidson, and Leslie Coffelt were on duty outside. Agent Floyd Boring was outside, talking to Davidson. Officer Joseph Downs, who had just been relieved of his duty by Coffelt, was in the basement. Torresollo, armed with a German Lugar, entered the west gate and paused, speaking to Coffelt in a loud voice, hoping to draw attention from Collazo. Torresola then quickly drew his weapon and opened fire on Coffelt, point blank, before spinning and shooting Downs, who was emerging from the basement, three times. Collazo walked quietly by Davidson and Boring in the east booth and headed for the Blair House stoop. He spun around, aimed his German Walther P-38 and shot Birdzell in the leg. Although wounded, Birdzell had the presence of mind to run out into Pennsylvania Avenue, without even trying to return fire, in an attempt to draw the danger away from the house and the president. Collazo pivoted and kept firing, hitting Birdzell again. Torresollo took up the assault on Birdzell, who was lying in the streetcar tracks on Pennsylvania Avenue. Dying from his own massive wounds, Coffelt was still able to shoot Torresollo and, with a single shot, kill him. Collazo was on the front steps when Mroz opened the door. Boring and Davidson started up the steps at the same time and opened fire on Collazo; shots clipped his ear and hat, and then Boring's shot hit his chest. If Collazo had made it up the steps, Stout, armed with a Thompson submachine gun, would have been waiting for him in the entrance hall. Twenty-seven shots were fired in two minutes (McCullough, p. 811). Leslie Coffelt died at the hospital, but the two wounded officers and Collazo recovered from their wounds.

"I went to see Oscar Collazo in the hospital," recalled Jim Griffith. "I asked him if he was sorry his partner and a Secret Service agent had been killed and the White House officers wounded. He said he was only sorry he had failed" ("Secret Service," 1995).

The Secret Service had never dealt with a terrorist attack before, and from then on, a special bond developed between Truman and his agents. They adored him as a down-to-earth common man who looked after them. And Truman liked the Secret Service agents who watched over him, most of whom came from small towns or backgrounds much like his own and none of whom ever asked anything of him (McCullough, p. 808). Truman was friendly, considerate, and interested in them individually. He was also quite different from his predecessor in one major way—he actually walked, and that presented another challenge for his agents. "See, with President Roosevelt, he was a man you had under control," remembered Agent Floyd Boring. "He couldn't move without you . . . . Now, here's a guy, you had to move when he moved. And he moved fast! He was a whiz, just like that! He'd go—and went! And you had to go with him. So, we had to revise our thinking, and the whole strategy of the place changed because of his ability to be in movement and motion" (ibid., p. 364).

Truman delivered the eulogy for Coffelt and wept at his graveside. A plaque on the fence at Blair House pays tribute to Coffelt. Although Collazo was sentenced to die in the electric chair, as a gesture of goodwill to the people of Puerto Rico, in 1952 Truman commuted the sentence to life imprisonment (ibid., p. 812).

I was fortunate enough to meet Truman on two occasions, and it was easy for me to see why his agents liked him so much. The first time I met him, I was with a senior advance agent who had also served under Eisenhower. Truman was in the hospital in Kansas City, recuperating from a fall in his bathtub, and we went to visit him during our advance for a pending visit by President Johnson. He was a fiery, salty little man, but Mrs. Truman, "Bess," could keep him in line. When Ike's name was raised, the former president left little doubt how he felt about his successor, peppering his sentences with numerous four-letter words. He was silenced by two words from his wife, "Now, Harry!" On that occasion he asked my name, and before the end of the visit, he was calling me by my first name. I visited with him again during Lyndon Johnson's trip to the Muehlebach Hotel, in Kansas City, in June of 1965. I didn't advance the visit; I was a supplemental agent for that trip. Johnson was signing Medicare legislation, and Truman, who was beginning to show his age, was walking with the aid of a cane. When he saw me, he immediately remembered who I was and, again, called me by my first name. It was a gracious and flattering gesture, and I never forgot it.

In the wake of the attack on Truman, Congress unanimously passed legislation making Secret Service protection a permanent part of their duties and increasing the size of the force.

I found out that being in the Secret Service could often be a dirty business. Former Agent Vince Mroz explained. "In his reelection campaign in 1948, Truman initiated a whistle-stop campaign. We were out for two or three weeks at a time, traveling from Seattle to San Diego and back to Washington, and the agents were unable to take proper baths. Several times we'd pull off onto a siding for the night, and the agents would run for the hotel for a regular shower" ("Secret Service," 1995).

In 1953 Secret Service protective coverage was expanded to include the vice president. Jack Sherwood and Rex Scouten were assigned to Vice President Richard Nixon as his first two agents. Former agent Clint Hill remembers that in the 1960 campaign, neither candidate received Secret Service protection, even though Nixon, as vice president, was entitled to it. "On election night, I was assigned to vice-presidential candidate Ambassador Henry Cabot Lodge," he recalled. "The next morning, when Kennedy had won the election, I was assigned to Georgetown to head Mrs. Kennedy's detail" (ibid.).

Clint also relates that there was an assassination attempt on President-elect Kennedy. "The Kennedys were staying in Palm Beach and would go to mass on Sunday. They had to walk down a long path to get to the car. On December eleventh, a would-be assassin, armed with a homemade bomb, was waiting in the car behind the president-elect's car. For whatever reason, he changed his mind at the last minute." Clint also pointed out the difference between Eisenhower and Kennedy. "Being a former general, Eisenhower was very punctual. If we told him ten o'clock, he'd be there at nine fifty-nine. With Kennedy, if you told him ten o'clock, it might be twelve o'clock. We also needed to protect two young children, which was a whole new situation to adapt to. We just played it by ear." Mrs. Kennedy also roamed the world considerably, so agents had to accompany her (ibid.).

I was overwhelmed to be part of such an elite force, and I was fascinated by all the training I was undergoing, but the part that made the most lasting impression on my life was the psychological training. As part of our overall training, we were required to attend psychological training at St. Elizabeth's mental hospital on how to deal with the mentally impaired and deranged, and potential assassins. I remember clearly a female psychiatrist walking into class one day and writing on the blackboard, "Everyone in this room is crazy. It's just a matter of degree." That made such an impression on me that I never forgot it. In fact, on the many occasions when I've lost my temper since that time, I've thought about those lectures—about how craziness is relative and that we all suffer from emotional disease. The difference between most of us and those who are insane is the degree to which we're able to control our insanity. It's like when you get sick, you take an aspirin to control your fever. The same is true with an emotional disorder; if you can control it, then you can live with it. If you don't control it, and you let your temper or your emotions get out of control, it becomes a disease. I learned that, yes, I'm crazy. But I have to control that craziness so I can live a normal life. That's something that really stuck with me in maturing and becoming an adult.

I never forgot those lectures. I think those courses taught me that, even though we may be normal, we all have tendencies toward losing control of our emotions, and that's not acceptable. A person can't get mad and just shoot another person; people can't lose their temper and deliberately hurt somebody—they have to exercise some degree of control. I can lose my temper just like anyone else—and still do—but I know there's a little voice inside me that tells me to get control of myself. Furthermore, every person needs to understand that there is nothing wrong with getting mad or having emotional ups and downs.

And my natural inclination toward positive thinking prepared me well for my time in the Secret Service.

A&E, in conjunction with the History Channel, produced a very detailed documentary on the history of the Secret Service, from which we derived much of the preceding background information. If you are interested in further information on the Secret Service, I suggest you purchase the boxed set or check with A&E to see if it will be aired again.

Chapter 3
On Duty with the Kennedys in Virginia

UPON MY ACCEPTANCE INTO the Secret Service, I went right to work in the office with Mr. Letteer, even before going through my official training course. There weren't enough recruits to send a new agent to DC immediately upon hiring, so they waited until there were a sufficient number of new agents before convening a class. On completion of my training, I was assigned to the Little Rock field office of the Secret Service. Even though I was in Little Rock, I was told I was being groomed to serve on the White House detail.

As I've said, when Roy Letteer called me to offer me a job, I didn't even know what the Secret Service was. It wasn't until Henry Alstadt impressed upon me what an important and prestigious job it was that I even began to get an inkling of what I was getting into. I still don't think I had an appreciation for it until I actually got into the Secret Service and realized what an elite group my classmates were. Most had served in the military or been policemen, and they were very disciplined. I became aware of them as a special group, one I fit in well with. I am still friends with some of my classmates today.

I can't say enough about the profound influence Roy Letteer had on my life, either. Everyone should be as fortunate to have a Roy Letteer in their life. Not only was he a wonderful man and a superb teacher, but he became my mentor as well. He was a great supervisor and a great investigator, and he encouraged me in everything I did. If there was an arrest in a case we were working on, he might let me do the press interview so I could gain that experience. He would constantly put me out front when he didn't have to, because he was teaching me how to handle situations. Many of the things I've learned in life, I learned from him.

As with many agents who served in field offices throughout the United States, the Secret Service withdrew me from time to time and assigned me to supplement the White House detail. Any time the president moved around the country, they'd call us up. And it was through this on-the-job training that we learned how to protect the president. Prior to Kennedy being assassinated, the Secret Service was a lot different. For one thing, there weren't that many agents. The White House detail served the president full time, but if the president traveled around the country, there were always agents from the field offices who supplemented the White House detail. I looked back at my logs, and I was gone about six months of each of the four years I was in the Secret Service, many times traveling with the president.

A typical event would involve the president going to, let's say, Des Moines, Iowa, and Roy Letteer would get a call telling him they needed me in Des Moines. I would report to the advance agent in charge and be assigned where needed. There'd usually be a motorcade to wherever the president was speaking, a motorcade back to the airport, and then he'd fly on to his next destination. If it was a multicity trip, I might not always go on with the president to the next city. I might leapfrog ahead to another city on the itinerary.

There was one trip I remember particularly; it might have been Chicago. The cities don't really mean that much to you when you're traveling so much, so it's easy to lose track. But this time we'd had a large number of serious threats from suspicious people, and we decided to bring them all in and lock them up until the president left town. There were an enormous number of threats against Kennedy—I don't know if the threats necessarily had to do with his Catholicism—but people either loved John Kennedy or they hated him. He was a very strong personality. I remember years later, during the Nixon years, calling a friend of mine at the Secret Service and asking him how many serious threats there were that day against Nixon. He looked in his records and said there were 305. There were more than three hundred people in the United States who might carry out an assassination attempt on the president on that day. And this was twenty-five years ago, long before the days of terrorist attacks. But with Kennedy there were even more threats than that.

Among his staff, Kennedy inspired unusual devotion. He was the type of person whom I, personally, would lay down my life for. When you serve someone like Kennedy—and I've talked with other retired agents about this—there's a bonding that goes beyond anything I know, that I'm not sure ever goes away. I didn't get to know Mrs. Kennedy very well, although I was assigned to the Kennedy's house at Middleburg for a couple of months. I had very little contact with her; therefore, I was not close to her at all, but I still mourned her when she died. I had bonded with her without even realizing it, and because that bond remained even thirty years later, it was like losing a member of my family when she died. That was especially true of President Kennedy because I held him in such high esteem.

I have to say that while I didn't always agree with everything Kennedy did, he had a certain dignity about him. I think he had a great respect for the office, and I don't think he would ever have done anything to compromise it. He protected his conduct so that if he had an intimate encounter, he did so with only the most senior agents around. It's important to understand that Kennedy grew up in an environment where men had affairs. Nobody I knew in Rector, Arkansas, had mistresses, but they did in Georgetown and other places where the powerful and rich hung out. Kennedy was also a product of his times. I'm not sure I can put this into words, and I'm certain to offend most of the women today, but women in the early '60s were not treated as equals to men. With few exceptions, they did not serve in prominent positions within the government or big business; for the most part, women were homemakers, secretaries, and, occasionally, journalists. And they saw nothing wrong with that—if they were unhappy with their "Donna Reed" worlds, you would never have known it. An excellent book about one of Kennedy's alleged mistresses, Mary Meyer, is called *A Very Private Woman* by Nina Burleigh. As much as anyone I've ever read, Ms. Burleigh captures the morality of the '60s.

She says: "Washington has always attracted ambitious men absorbed in competition with each other. The cold warriors, possessed of atomic-era 'ballsiness' and wearing their machismo like World War II officers' epaulets, were consumed with power. They styled themselves after James Bond or the Rat Pack, men adorned with numbers of women. If their women did not find this attractive, they were very unhappy women. 'The husbands just overshadowed us completely,' said June Dutton, long divorced from Kennedy administration official Fred Dutton. 'Most of the men felt too important to involve their wives in what they were doing. There was no room for partners in it. We were just decorations and isolated. The men all gathered and talked, and women were left to talk about children and schools. The wives were just wives' " (p. 25). That's just the way it was. The majority of men in power in Washington at that time saw nothing wrong with having flirtations or affairs with women other than their wives.

I've heard it said that the press protected Kennedy, but I'm not sure the press even knew the extent of his activities, although Ms. Burleigh does describe an incident in which *Washington Post* publisher Phil Graham supposedly "outs" Kennedy's closeness to Mary Meyer before a convention of American journalists. I find it as interesting as she that not one word ever appeared in print about the incident. They either did not find it interesting or informative, or even credible, or they just thought nothing of it. Kennedy was a flirt; he seemed to genuinely appreciate women. I could name a lot of names I did hear about, but I won't. Some of the guys witnessed specific events and described them to the other agents. But I think the thing that made Kennedy stand out was that here was a person of dignity who respected the office of president, and he would never have allowed his indiscretions to become public knowledge during his presidency. Kennedy's friend Ben Bradlee wrote, "My friends have always had trouble believing my innocence of his activities, especially after it was revealed that Tony's [Bradlee's wife] sister, Mary Meyer, had been one of Kennedy's girlfriends. So be it. I can only repeat my ignorance of Kennedy's sex life, and state that I am appalled by the details that have emerged, appalled by the recklessness, by the subterfuge that must have been involved" (p. 217). Ben Bradlee was one of JFK's closest friends during the five years they were acquainted, and even he was unaware of any sexual misconduct. Women would have been attracted to John Kennedy no matter what he did in life. Men were attracted to him, too—not sexually—but they wanted him to be their buddy.

Arthur Schlesinger Jr., a writer, historian and former special assistant to President Kennedy, makes this point:

> Vague rumors about JFK did waft about Washington from time to time, but, as one who worked in the White House, I never saw anything untoward. Kennedy was a hard-working fellow, concentrating intently on the problems at hand. At no point in my experience did his preoccupation with women (apart from Caroline crawling around the Oval Office) interfere with his conduct of the public business . . . . Ben Bradlee, then head of the *Newsweek* bureau in Washington, in later years the brilliant editor of *The Washington Post*, was not only at the center of Washington news gathering; he was also Kennedy's closest friend in the press. "It is now accepted history," Bradlee writes in his 1995 memoir, *A Good Life*, "that Kennedy jumped casually from bed to bed with a wide variety of women. It was not accepted history then . . . . [I was] unaware of this proclivity during his lifetime." Nor can insiders ever pronounce on the inwardness of a marriage. My own impression, shared by others from the Kennedy White House, is that JFK, for all his adventures, always regarded Jacqueline with genuine affection and pride. Their marriage never seemed more solid than in the later months of 1963 (Schlesinger, p. 161).

I love the romantic picture Schlesinger paints of the president we both served so proudly: "He was easy, accessible, witty, candid, enjoying the clash of ideas and ripples of gossip, never more relaxed than when sitting in his rocking chair and puffing away on a fine Havana cigar. He was, in his self-description, an 'idealist without illusions.' He was the best of my generation. It is good for the country that he remains so vivid a presence in our minds and hearts" (ibid.).

Another writer I respect, Bruce Catton, said:

> What John F. Kennedy left us was most of all an attitude. To put it in the simplest terms, he looked ahead . . . . President Kennedy personified youth and vigor—and perhaps it was symbolic that both his friends and his foes picked up his Boston accent and began to say "vigah." He went about hatless, he liked to mingle with crowds and shake the hands of all and sundry, for recreation he played touch football, and for rest he sat in an old-fashioned rocking chair as if in sly mockery of his own exuberance. He seemed to think that things like music and painting and literature were essential parts of American life and that it was worthwhile to know what the musicians and artists and writers were doing. Whatever he did was done with zest, as if youth were for the first time touching life and finding it exciting. With all of this, there was a cool maturity of outlook. By itself, vigor is not enough. Courage is needed also, and when youth has courage

it acquires composition. In the most perilous moments President Kennedy kept his poise. He challenged the power of darkness at least once, and during the hours when his hand had to stay close to the fateful trigger he was composed and unafraid. Once in a great while a nation, like a man, has to be ready to spend itself utterly for some value that means more than survival itself means. President Kennedy led us through such a time, and we began to see that the power of darkness is perhaps not quite as strong as we had supposed . . . . It was his attitude that made the difference. (New York Times, p. 4)

In spite of the fact that I had served on some advance teams for presidential visits and had seen Kennedy on those occasions, I had not met him yet. For that reason, I vividly remember the first time I saw Kennedy at the White House and actually spoke with him. I was not on duty at the time but was just hanging out at the Secret Service office. Kennedy was walking down the hall with Jerry Behn, head of the White House Secret Service detail. With his incredible memory, he spotted a face with which he was not familiar, and being the kind of person he was, the president came right up to me, smiled, and introduced himself. I thought, what a slick guy this is! He just stopped and said, "I'm Jack Kennedy."

I could barely respond, "Good morning, Mr. President." He then asked where I was from. I was so taken aback, I was shaking. My heart almost stopped!

Here I was at the White House, working for the President of the United States and talking with him! Never in my wildest imagination, growing up in Rector, Arkansas, had I dreamed of ever even walking in the door of the White House, and certainly not serving the President of the United States—it was beyond comprehension. But here I was!

I'd never even been to Washington, DC until I joined the Secret Service, and I was staying, I might point out, in one of the most historic hotels in the entire city for weeks at a time. When I was on assignment at the White House, I stayed at the old Willard Hotel, which dated back to before the Civil War. In spite of the fact that it was the premier hotel in Washington during Civil War days, entertaining the likes of Abraham Lincoln and General Grant, it was just a ratty old hotel in the '60s, but it was cheap and only a block from the White House. I could stay there for $8 a night, and, when on assignment, I'd have to stay there for thirty to sixty days at a time. A full-day's per diem was only $16, and I had to pay for my meals and hotel out of that. Now the hotel's been completely renovated and is a very luxurious, exclusive hotel once again. But I liked it then; you have to remember that I wasn't accustomed to the finest accommodations at that time.

By this time I had been exposed to enough of the Secret Service and Washington that I was becoming a little awestruck about the whole thing. I was within an eyelash of the leader of the entire free world, and to me Kennedy was larger than life. Jack Kennedy, with his East Coast veneer and incredible magnetism, was so far removed from where I grew up; he was simply unlike anyone I had ever encountered before. What an incredible set of circumstances that I happened to end up being there!

To this day, I still retain my old daily reports from my Secret Service tenure. In researching for this book and delving back into that period of time, I still remember the stress of the Bay of Pigs and the Cuban missile crisis, which were portrayed in the movie *Thirteen Days*. I was in the Secret Service at that time, and it's hard to emphasize emphatically enough the enormity of those events. The Cuban missile crisis literally could have meant the destruction of the world.

I didn't ever get really close to Kennedy or spend any quality time with him—I was too junior in status— but that didn't stop me from forming a deep respect and admiration for him. He displayed such incredible courage and grace under pressure. He was a very casual person who always spoke to you; he was very nice and cordial. The senior agents who were assigned to Kennedy adored him. He was the type to punch you in the ribs and make some kind of light joke and treat you like you were his equal. He didn't keep any distance at all. Even though I wasn't close to him, the other guys were, and they would swap stories back and forth in my presence, so I developed a great affection and admiration for him. It was this very friendship with Kennedy that brought the agents under fire later after the events in Dallas had transpired.

In May of 1963, I was on one of my temporary assignments to the White House. President Kennedy was going to Berlin in June—this was the trip during which he delivered his famous Berlin Wall speech. All the senior agents were accompanying the president, but being as junior as I was, I remained back in the States with the First Lady. Jackie was, at that time, pregnant with their third child, Patrick, who was born in August, just a few months prior to the assassination but, tragically, lived only forty hours. Mrs. Kennedy was having some problems with her pregnancy, so she was not going to make the trip. The Kennedys had built a retreat out at Rattlesnake Mountain in Atoka, Virginia, near Middleburg, and I was assigned to stay back with her at the house.

Her background and culture were very different from mine and, for that reason, I didn't understand her very well. I felt she treated me more like a servant, not speaking to me unless she needed something. She always called me "Mr. Carter" and never called me by my first name. I'm sure it was a class thing with her. However, her chief agent, Clint Hill, was good friends with her, and Dick Keiser, one of my best friends in the Secret Service, later served on her detail and got along with her quite well. I always volunteered for the night shift when I was in Atoka, so I seldom saw her.

There was one particular incident involving the First Lady that I specifically remember because Jackie called my supervisor at the White House and complained, and I was called on the carpet about it. There were these big old tree snakes up at the Virginia house, and they were so bad that we carried .410 gauge pistols to shoot them. The gate to the property was down a narrow wooded lane that was covered with trees. When I was making my security rounds, I'd get out of the jeep at the gate to check certain points. These snakes would move from tree to tree like squirrels, and frequently at night, I wouldn't want to get out of the jeep, because you could hear them hissing but you couldn't see them in the dark. I couldn't stand those snakes, so many times I'd fire my .410 "snake gun," hoping to greatly reduce the snake population with each shot. I was on duty one day and had killed a bunch of them, but it never occurred to me to do anything about disposing of them. Jackie had been out somewhere, and when she drove up on her return, she saw all the dead snakes lying around, so she called the White House and complained. My supervisor called me and said, "Are you dumb, or what? You know Mrs. Kennedy doesn't believe in killing anything, and here you go leaving dead snakes all over the driveway!" He said he wasn't going to order me not to kill any more snakes, but he warned me to hide the snakes when I killed them.

President Kennedy came out occasionally with the kids for day trips, but by all accounts, he never formed the attachment to the property that Jackie did. Prior to building at Atoka, Mrs. Kennedy had wanted to find a refuge from their new fishbowl existence—some quiet country hideaway, secluded yet accessible, where they could relax and the children could play without being watched by curious tourists (Thayer, p. 225). The Kennedys had been leasing a house in Glen Ora, Virginia, for a couple of years, but the owner of that property, Mrs. Raymond Tartiere, had refused to extend the lease on Glen Ora. It was after this that the Kennedys, searching for a substitute retreat, bought thirty-nine acres less than twenty miles from Glen Ora. Initially called Atoka, Jackie rechristened the house "Wexford" (after Kennedy's County Wexford roots) to please the president (ibid). The cost of building, furnishing, and decorating the Virginia house did not endear it to JFK. He far preferred Camp David. Jackie, however, loved the property. One day, shortly after the foundations had been dug but little other building progress made, President Kennedy took his good friend Charles Bartlett to see the site. The president, who passionately loved the sea, was dubious about being closed in by the mountains. As he looked out over the brown grass on the surrounding hillsides, he turned to Bartlett with a shrug: "Imagine my ending up in a place like this!" (ibid) he exclaimed.

Although Mrs. Kennedy was an avid horsewoman, she did not keep horses on their property; she instead kept her horses at a neighboring horse farm. She was pregnant, however, for most of the spring and summer and did little, if any, riding when I was there. The kids weren't always with her—they stayed at the White House during the week but often came out on the weekend. John Jr. was very small, and Caroline was a very cute little girl, about five years old then. They'd put her on her little pony, Macaroni, and she'd ride around. The kids had their own agents, but I was never assigned to their detail. Jackie was always polite, graceful. I now think I may have been wrong in my early opinion of her—I was just immature and didn't understand her. I ended up having the greatest respect for her.

This was 1963, and I was there for two months that spring and early summer, just as the house was being completed. The house itself was a "modest" ranch-style house. Although it had fourteen rooms and six baths, the rooms were small. I hadn't been exposed to a lot of luxuries at that time, so I thought it was the height of luxury. It was the nicest house I'd ever seen. There was a master bedroom and several much smaller bedrooms for the children and servants. The president's bedroom was the largest room, of course, and was about sixteen feet by twenty feet. Off that was his study, in which he had displayed lots of photos from his Navy days. The dining room would seat about ten people comfortably. The nicest feature of the house was that each room opened out onto a veranda that looked out over the beautiful Blue Ridge Mountains. There was also a three-acre pond on the property for swimming and fishing.

The master bathroom had an item that exposed how naïve I was. We had to check the house routinely, and my first time in the bathroom I saw something whose purpose I couldn't quite figure out—it was a bidet. One of the other agents on the detail, Jim Plichta, didn't know what on earth that contraption was, either. We were too embarrassed to ask anyone, and I didn't find out until much later what it was used for.

The Kennedys were never there long enough to entertain guests; in fact, they never really got moved in. The president apparently spent four weekends at the property in the fall, after the death of Patrick, when he and Jackie were, from all accounts, rediscovering their love for each other. All those surrounding the couple had noticed a new closeness between them since the loss of the baby, a loss that devastated both the president and Mrs. Kennedy. In the last few months of his life, he seemed quite intent on pleasing Jackie.

The tent where the agents stayed while on duty was a large military tent, which had two good-sized rooms and a wooden floor. It was pretty well-equipped for the early '60s, with air-conditioning, a television, and radio. The area surrounding the house was heavily wooded and fairly remote. Access to the property was extremely difficult; the president actually had to helicopter in because the road could barely accommodate cars, especially in inclement weather. We had to rely on jeeps for our access.

The agents lived in Middleburg, about three miles away; we rented rooms from a nice couple in their forties.

It was a strange and funny situation, but a telling commentary about the times back then, that the Soviets—specifically the KGB—had rented a big stone house right down the road from the Kennedy's property. They were operating surveillance out of that house and trying to gain access to the Kennedy house to install bugs and that sort of thing. It was like playing Keystone Cops with the Russians' intelligence elite, trying to ensure that the Soviets didn't penetrate our security. They would play games with us, often even approaching the perimeter of the property. Our motion and audio detectors would, of course, pick up their every move, and we would ride down to see what they were up to. When they would see us coming, they would just walk away. There was no real subterfuge—we knew what they were up to, and they knew we knew.

I preferred pulling the midnight shift most times because that would give me time during the day to explore Middleburg, which is a beautiful part of Virginia, rich with historic thoroughbred horse farms. If the family was not in residence, there would be only four agents assigned to watch the property—one agent for each eight-hour shift and one extra. On my tour of duty, the other agents included Plichta, John Gorman, and Carroll Hamilton. But at night I would be the only person on duty. This was long before the technology revolution, so electronic surveillance equipment was not very sophisticated—there was no video surveillance. The Bendix Corporation had devised a special system for the house; we had the control monitor in our security hut.

At the time the house was being built, the agents' office and control center were located in a big Army tent at the front edge of the property. Of course, we had enough artillery to hold off an army, but it was just one agent at a time sitting in that lonely tent. If someone approached the fence anywhere around the property, the sensor would pick it up and a light would go on. I would know what area of the property had been compromised, but I would never know if it was a human or one of the animals that lived in the surrounding woods. We had microphones hidden around the property, so if more than one person was approaching the fence, I could flip a switch and listen to their conversation or at least detect their voices. When someone or something would come near the fence at night—which happened several times—I had to go down there in the jeep to check it out. I felt so vulnerable because they could see and hear me coming. If they wanted to shoot me, it would have been relatively easy because I was completely out in the open.

It was really spooky out there at night, and I'd make it worse by watching scary movies on TV. It was so quiet that you'd hear everything that moved. Several times I'd be reared back in my chair, about half asleep, with a machine gun across my lap, and an animal would rub up against the tent and scare me half to death. One time, it was about three o'clock in the morning, and a pack of wild dogs ran inside the tent. I looked up, but it scared me so much that I didn't even have time to react. I looked at them, they looked at me, and then they ran out of the tent again.

The Bendix people had assured us that their equipment was so sophisticated that the alarms absolutely could not be tripped by the weather. They warned us that if an alarm went off in a particular part of the house, it was unquestionably because someone was breaking in. It was stressed that in that event, we should assume the worst and immediately call the Virginia State Police for assistance. One night we were having a typical summer thunderstorm, and the fog had settled on the mountain so thickly it was like a curtain. Luckily for me one of the off-duty agents was hanging around killing time with me. Suddenly, the alarm went off, indicating that someone was breaking into Mrs. Kennedy's bedroom. We both immediately assumed the KGB had penetrated us and entered the house. Fortunately, neither the president nor Mrs. Kennedy was in residence at the time, but that didn't make it less frightening, just less of a national emergency.

I called the state police, but they said they didn't have a trooper to send out to me. So I called my supervisor, and he ordered us to proceed immediately to the house. We gathered up an arsenal of weapons and made preparations to charge the house. We set out in our jeep down the narrow, winding lane toward the house. There's something about fog swirling all around you that gives you the creeps anyway, and it certainly did nothing to calm our nerves that night. I had heard people use the expression "like something out of the Twilight Zone," and I gained firsthand knowledge that night what that meant. The house was dark, illuminated only by flashes of lightning, and I was absolutely terrified. I knew we had no choice but to check it out, and, just as surely, I expected to find an intruder. With each step we took through that deserted house, I expected to be confronted by one or more menacing KGB agents. My heart was thundering in my ears, and I had a death grip on my weapons. Fortunately the house wasn't that large, and we didn't have to search far. There were no foreign enemies to be found. Bendix's fail-proof system had demonstrated a flaw after all, and water had gotten into the "waterproof" system and shorted it out.

Because the president, who had a reputation as being frugal, was reportedly worried about the expense of the property, Mrs. Kennedy rented the house for the months of July and August, so we were released at the end of June to return to our regular assignments. I got through that assignment with little effect other than suffering an anxiety attack from time to time. And, as far as I know, the KGB didn't get through, even though we had serious attempts. Thirty-two years later, in 1995, when I happened to be in Washington, DC, I took some friends to see the Atoka property. I couldn't even find it; things had changed so in the ensuing years. I found an area Realtor and asked him about the property.

"Ironically enough," he said, "I sold that house." When I told him what my interest was in the property, he said, "Since you were a Secret Service agent out there at the time, you no doubt remember the KGB house."

"Yes, I remember it well," I told him.

"Well," he said "the Russians finally gave the house up about eighteen months ago." (This was in 1993.) "When the Realtors got in there," he continued, "the house was a mess. The Russians had so many antennas, phone lines, and electronic surveillance equipment that removing it caused extensive damage to the house." He laughed and said, "They even had antennas in the roof!"

We really laughed about that. By that time they were probably using it for some other reason, as a safe house or something else. The Kennedy house was finished only months prior to the assassination, so the president and Mrs. Kennedy spent very little time there before Dallas. As far as I knew, she never returned there, but in reading Ben Bradlee's book, he mentioned that he and his wife spent a couple of weekends with Jackie in Atoka in the month after the president's death (Bradlee, p. 262).

Chapter 4
On Assignment with the Secret Service

𝕬 FTER I COMPLETED MY VIRGINIA duties, I returned to Little Rock. I was scheduled for my final advanced course of training later that fall; then I expected to be transferred to the White House. During the summer of 1963, there was great political unrest in the South with all the civil rights problems, and Kennedy was a pro-civil rights president. Kennedy was planning a trip to Texas because the Texas Democratic Party was split as a result of a blazing feud between two of its leaders.

Ralph Yarborough, the senior senator from Texas, hero of the Democrats of Texas, led one faction of the Democratic Party. He was the only Texas liberal to hold statewide office. He had been at odds with the Texas Democratic Party and Vice President Lyndon Johnson, a Texan, since he threw his public backing to Kennedy instead of Johnson at the 1960 Democratic Convention. Add to the mix the fact that the conservative governor of Texas, John Connally, hoped to muscle Yarborough out of office in the '64 elections. Their bickering was ripping the party apart. In 1960, the Kennedy-Johnson ticket had carried Texas by just 46,233 votes, and Kennedy and Johnson both agreed that they had to shore up support in the Lone Star State if they hoped to win reelection in '64. The two planned to go down to Texas to mend some fences within the Democratic Party and make a big production of their trip by stopping in the three major metropolitan areas of the state—San Antonio, Houston, and Dallas—with a side trip to Johnson's ranch. The president was not exactly eager to go—he felt Johnson should be able to keep peace in his own backyard—but Jackie had agreed to accompany him on the trip, and he was anxious to show her off to the roughhouse Texans.

But before he undertook an arduous trip to Texas, Kennedy was advised to get his feet wet elsewhere first. Arkansas was Texas' neighbor to the northeast, and it was decided my home state would be a good place to test the waters. The president was considering Arkansas for another reason. Three of the most power-ful men in America at the time were from Arkansas: Congressman Wilbur Mills and Senators John McClellan and William Fulbright. Wilbur Mills was one of the most influential congressmen in America and had been for many years. I've heard it said since that Wilbur Mills didn't want to be president, because he'd lose his power if elected. He was chairman of the Ways and Means Committee and enjoyed the power that came with that post. John McClellan was the very powerful chairman of the Senate Appropriations Committee and one of the most mighty men in the Senate; his Senate colleague, Bill Fulbright, chairman of the Senate Foreign Relations Committee, was one of the brightest politicians in the capital. Veteran journalist Sander Vanocur, who covered the White House for NBC, has said that it was well known that "pound-for-pound the Arkansas delegation was the most powerful on the Hill."

Then, of course, Orval Faubus, against whom I had worked in several statewide elections, but whom I admired very much, was still governor of Arkansas. Faubus was a segregationist, although a moderate segregationist, and was very vocal in his opposition to Kennedy's pro-civil rights agenda. Any politician, if not a segregationist, would have had a difficult time holding office in the South during this time. There was concern that Faubus would present a problem for the pro-civil rights president and that Kennedy would find a less-than-welcoming atmosphere in Arkansas. However, Mills, McClellan, and Fulbright assured Kennedy they could control Faubus.

I knew Faubus not only from the local political campaigns on which I had worked but also through his son, Farrell, who had been in law school with me. Farrell, who completed law school after I dropped out to enter the Secret Service, was now in the Arkansas Attorney General's office. It was decided Kennedy would make the trip, and because of my relationship with Faubus, my boss, Roy Letteer, recommended that I be the liaison with the governor. So when the advance team came to Little Rock, I worked with Win Lawson, who was the White House agent in charge of preparing for the president's visit. The Secret Service was concerned that even though Mills and McClellan assured the president he would have the cooperation of the governor's office, they should talk to Faubus and get his personal assurance. Because of my long-standing relationship with the governor, I was asked to see him on behalf of the White House. Besides, the Secret Service had other concerns—such as security for the president.

I made an appointment with Faubus and went to see him. The governor could talk out both sides of his mouth, but I was aware of that going in. I was very honest with him. I told him that many people around the president were concerned about the reception he might receive if he came to Arkansas. He told me, "Bill, I guarantee you will have total cooperation from the Arkansas State Police. I'm not going to publicly endorse the president's visit here, but I can tell you not to pay attention to what you read in the press. I just don't want it known publicly what my position is. However, you have my personal assurance that the president will be secure while he is in this state." Well, Governor Faubus was as good as his word; we did have his complete cooperation. But from the speaker's platform at Greers Ferry Lake, where Kennedy was dedicating a dam, Faubus took a verbal pot shot at the president during his own speech.

Sharply critical of the Kennedy administration's stand on civil rights, which he considered to be the greatest threat to the southern states, Faubus said, "To take from the state without justification even more of the rights guaranteed to them under the Constitution; to abridge or destroy these basic rights, will constitute civil wrong even though the efforts to abridge or destroy may masquerade under the name civil rights."

In response, Kennedy did not mention any names, but blasted those he felt were trying to turn back the clock, referring to them as the "old South."

Years later a journalist from Arkansas called me just prior to Faubus' death, asking specifically about the former governor's lack of cooperation with Kennedy when he visited Arkansas. I told him that he was misinformed and that was absolutely not true. I assured him that while Faubus publicly criticized the president, privately we had the full cooperation of the state police. There was not a serious incident while Kennedy was in the state.

On September 26, 1963, Special Agent in Charge Letteer and I were on hand at the Little Rock Air Force Base to meet the advance team when they arrived. The agents on the advance team, Win Lawson, Ernie Olson, Dave Grant, and Ed Morey, arrived on a White House Jetstar to begin preparations for the president's October 3 visit. The plan for the Arkansas trip called for the president to visit Heber Springs, where he would dedicate the Greers Ferry Dam. Then he would fly down to Little Rock and make a speech at the Arkansas State Fair.

Jan and I were living in a duplex in Little Rock at the time of Kennedy's visit. While we were doing the advance, the team was staying at the Coachman's Inn, a hotel in Little Rock, and I spent most of my time there with them. *The Beverly Hillbillies* was the number one rated show on television at that time. The cast of that show—Buddy Ebsen, Irene Ryan, Donna Douglas, and Max Baer Jr.—were playing the State Fair at this same time and were staying at the Coachman. They were the hottest celebrities in the country that year. You couldn't help noticing Donna Douglas, who played Ellie May, so we became pals with her. When she found out the reason for our being there, she said she would like to meet the president. So Win Lawson, Ernie Olson, and Dave Grant decided to play a little trick on me. "If you want to meet the president," they said, "Bill Carter is the guy who can make that happen."

So she approached me. "I want to meet the president," she told me. "The other guys said you could arrange that." The heat was on me, not on them, to get her in to see the president, so if anybody got in trouble it would be me. I was so green I didn't realize that at the time, so I told her not to worry, I'd take care of her.

It was a beautiful, early fall day on October 3, 1963, when President Kennedy arrived at the Air Force base in Jacksonville. He was taken by helicopter to Heber Springs and traveled by a white Lincoln Continental convertible to the dam. Interestingly, the car had been specially flown down to Memphis and driven to Little Rock. Kennedy was in the car less than ten minutes that day. At the dam he was greeted by a crowd of 10,000 people, many more than were anticipated. He made a great speech, proving himself to be extraordinarily concerned with conservation and the environment. He opened the speech by acknowledging his strong relationship with Congressman Mills. "The *New York Times* reported this morning that if Wilbur Mills asked the president to sing 'Down by the Old Mill Stream,' he would do it. I'm happy to do so," he laughed. He had lunch in a tent with one hundred paying guests. Then he traveled to Little Rock.

The president arrived in Little Rock, at the State Fairgrounds, by helicopter, to the approving roar of the 35,000 people gathered to hear him speak. There was an area behind the stage where we had assembled all the VIPs from among the Arkansas Democratic Party. Well, I had Donna Douglas right up front in this area. She looked great—young, blonde, voluptuous, and very attractive. The first helicopter arrived. Out stepped Press Secretary Pierre Salinger, among others. Pierre spotted Donna right away, and it didn't take me a minute to know I was in trouble. Not a small man by any means, Pierre could look downright fierce when those great, winged black eyebrows drew toward his nose in a frown. "Who the hell got this woman in here?" he bellowed. Everybody pointed at me. "Damn it, Carter, you know better than this," he practically yelled at me. "This is nothing but a damn publicity stunt. Now get her out of here." I felt about the size of an ant because he said all this right in front of Donna. I was so embarrassed; I must have been twenty shades of red, but she handled it with a lot of class.

"Donna, I am so sorry," I groveled. "I honestly didn't know any better. I thought since Win and Dave told you to have me set it up, it would be fine."

Embarrassed herself, she graciously accepted my apology and said she would leave. Since I was already in deep with Pierre, I thought I'd push his buttons a little more, so I insisted she stay but suggested she just get back in the crowd so she wouldn't be quite so obvious. When the president got off the helicopter, he walked right to the speakers' platform, made his speech, and then went out and shook hands. After that he came back to greet all the VIPs. The president was heading back to the helicopter when he looked over to where Donna was standing. He shook a few more hands, and then looked back again.

"Bring that woman up here," I saw him mouth to one of his agents. He had picked her out way back in the crowd and brought her forward. Pierre looked right at me, and I just kind of smiled. We brought her up front, and the president had his picture made with her. It was kind of funny.

Other than that, it was pretty uneventful. Except for his little dig, Faubus behaved himself, and there were no other incidents. As always, when the president traveled to events around the country, there would be a local VIP list that would include prominent Democratic leaders from around the city, county, and state, all of whom wanted access to the president, but the Secret Service still had absolute authority. For example, Jack Pickens was a wealthy contractor and a powerful Democrat in the state of Arkansas, who later became a good friend of mine. In the VIP area, Jack was way down on the state VIP priority list. He came to me and told me he would like to be closer to the president and wanted to know if I could help him. I assured Jack I would move him up front, which I did, and he never forgot that. The Secret Service had complete authority when it came to a presidential visit, and it was within our right to overrule the local Democratic hierarchy if we felt it was necessary. They wouldn't question the advance man for the Secret Service, because the White House was the ultimate authority. The local political advance team made sure that the right people were there, but the ultimate decision about anything on-site was made by the Secret Service agents. We wouldn't bump somebody that the local political guys wanted up there, but we'd work it out. Of course, in this case I knew the local people because this was my home state; I knew practically everybody.

On that same Arkansas trip, I was able to get Jan in the VIP section at the Little Rock AFB, where the president's plane, Air Force One, landed, and Faubus himself introduced her to the president. She was wearing a little PT Boat pin that Kennedy had given me, and he spotted it immediately.

He stopped and talked at length to Jan, but when we asked her later what he had said to her, she couldn't remember any of it. She said she was totally mesmerized by his incredible eyes and his good looks. He was so dynamic and magnetic that he totally disarmed people when they met him.

He was that way with the press, too. I always said every candidate should study old Kennedy films and take lessons from how he dealt with the press. Pierre Salinger said that Kennedy had spoken with him of buying a newspaper in New England after he served his two terms in office (Salinger, p. 153). He also maintained that Kennedy had an insight into and an understanding of the press that was amazing (ibid., p. 76).

Ben Bradlee, who was an authority on the subject of Kennedy and the press, points out that "Kennedy and the press were made for each other, using each other comfortably, enjoying each other's company, squabbling from time to time the way real friends squabble, understanding the role each played in the other's life. Kennedy liked reporters because they shared a craving to know what was going on, and to know what people were like . . . . Kennedy liked to talk shop with reporters . . . . They shared a sense of excitement over current events. Reporters liked Kennedy for being instinctively graceful and natural, physically unable to be programmed or to be corny . . . everyone agreed that Kennedy enjoyed better relations with the press than any president ever" (Bradlee, pp. 236–237).

We had no way of knowing that six weeks after his visit to Arkansas, Kennedy would be dead, and my practical joker friend Win Lawson, who was in charge of the Dallas advance team, would find his life turned upside down.

Kennedy returned to Washington from Arkansas, and so did I. The trip was a complete success, both politically and from a security standpoint. He had been in the state only four hours, but it was his only stop of the day, so he paid a great honor to a small southern state by such a dedicated visit and proved once again the power of the congressional delegation.

I began my advanced course of training shortly after the trip, and during my stay in DC, when I'd be at the White House, I would often see Win Lawson—whom I had forgiven for the Donna Douglas incident and who had become a good friend—Ernie Olson, Ed Morey, and Dave Grant, the other agents from Little Rock. During one of my visits to the White House, Win advised me that he had been assigned to advance a presidential trip to Dallas. He was leaving on November 12 and wanted me to make the trip, but my course wouldn't be completed in time for me to accompany the advance team. On top of that, I had been away from home for six weeks or so, and I was anxious to see my family. I told Win I had a sister in Dallas, and he should go out and have dinner with her and her husband. He did call Doris about getting together, but there was so much pressure and stress on him during that trip that he didn't think he should take time off to socialize.

For the ten days before Air Force One touched down at Love Field, in Dallas, socializing was not a priority for Win Lawson. In addition to endless meetings with agents from the Dallas field office, members of the local host committee, and local law enforcement officials, he was visiting various venues being considered for the luncheon site, visiting Love Field to discuss "spotting" the three aircraft, and driving along the proposed motorcade routes, looking over security factors. He was involved in everything from the caterers, parking at the Trade Mart—where Kennedy was scheduled to deliver his remarks—the reception committee, head table guests, screening of luncheon guests, lessees of the Trade Mart and their customers, and the press area to police requirements for crowd control, underpass and overpass policing, railroad crossings, police control of heavily anticipated crowds, and details for escort participation. He would have outlined all this in his preliminary survey report, which had to be submitted to the White House for approval.

Win obviously had his hands full just fighting the locals in Dallas. Jerry Bruno, the chunky, saddle-nosed advance man for the Democratic National Committee, was encountering obstacles at every turn. He was having a hard time booking a venue for the president's speech because managers would not move other groups just because the president wanted the hall. Of the few buildings available to them, the Secret Service viewed the Women's Building as safer—there were sixteen hidden catwalks in the Trade Mart—but notice was sent to the White House that Kenny O'Donnell, special assistant to the president, had made the decision to go with the Trade Mart. Bruno could have insisted on the Women's Building, in which case the motorcade would not have passed the Texas School Book Depository, but he did not exercise that veto (Manchester, p. 24).

During my assignments to the White House, I got to know several of the staff members, some better than others. Malcom "Mac" Kilduff was Pierre Salinger's assistant in the White House Press Office, and Mac and I became great pals. As for the Secret Service, Jerry Behn was head of the White House detail, and Roy Kellerman (who accompanied the president to Arkansas) was his assistant. Kenny O'Donnell, the special assistant to the president, was one of the people closest to Kennedy. The president relied on him for everything. I really liked Kenny; he was a great, down-to-earth guy. O'Donnell is said to have had but one passion— President Kennedy—and his devotion was inflexible. Dave Powers, another old buddy of Kennedy's, was also close to the president. Kenny and Dave, as well as Larry O'Brien, were known as The Irish Mafia by Mrs. Kennedy. They had been with Kennedy for a long time and were among his most trusted advisors. Unlike O'Brien, Kenny wasn't one of the jolly Irish; he wasn't given to smiling a lot, but he still was a great guy.

Ted Sorensen, one of the president's few close advisors who was not a New Englander, had been with the president since 1953 and was so close to Kennedy that he had begun to adopt his mannerisms and even his speaking voice. Kennedy's brother, Bobby, was *the* guy. As well as being attorney general, Bobby was his closest advisor. In today's vernacular, he was the "go-to" guy.

Following the debacle of the Bay of Pigs, Kennedy became deeply distrustful of the CIA and eventually removed its head, Allen Dulles, as well as his second in command, Richard Bissell. From that day forward, the man whose loyalty and judgment he knew he could depend upon, his brother Bobby, would be present at all crucial meetings (Bradford, p. 192). The only man who spanned all aspects of the president's life was the attorney general. John Kennedy's true second self was Robert Kennedy (Manchester, p. 120). Ben Bradlee once asked President Kennedy why he thought his brother was so great. He answered, "First, his high moral standards, strict personal ethics. He's a puritan, absolutely incorruptible. Then he has terrific executive energy. We've got more guys around here with ideas. The problem is to get things done. Bobby's the best organizer I've ever seen . . . . His loyalty comes next" (Bradlee, p. 243).

Inside the White House at the time, unbeknownst to any of us, the president's staff was advising against his going to Dallas. They were very concerned. Some on Capitol Hill—including Bill Fulbright and Hubert Humphrey—were also concerned about the president's impending trip. The political atmosphere in Texas at that time was ultraconservative. The John Birch Society was big in Texas—that's where it started—and Dallas was a hotbed of political conservatives. I had been there when I went out to SMU, and I witnessed firsthand the conservative element there. When Adlai Stevenson, who was the U.S. Ambassador to the United Nations, had visited Dallas, they had thrown eggs at him and spit on him, and all of that was in the Secret Service report. It caused us great concern.

General Edwin Walker, who was a radical general and hero from the Korean War and World War II, was leading the conservative element in the John Birch Society. In the spring of 1961, Walker had been relieved of his division command in West Germany for spreading ultra-right-wing political material through the forces under him. He later retired to Dallas to promote the John Birch Society, an organization of isolationists, nationalists, and racists living, as Arthur Schlesinger put it, "in a dreamworld of no communism, no overseas entanglements, no United Nations, no federal government, no labor unions, no Negroes or foreigners . . ." (Bradford, p. 228). They were so conservative they were close to being militant. They were the far-right wing and were anti-everything.

As a result of the conservative atmosphere down there, there were ads—black-bordered and styled like death notices—taken out in newspapers and on billboards, making veiled threats aimed at Kennedy's liberalism, and the Secret Service was paying close attention to all these groups (Exhibit 1).

Every time I talked to Win Lawson, he had his hands full and was under a great deal of stress. The Secret Service details for both the president and the vice president were aware of how difficult things might be in Dallas, but they were mostly concerned about the possibility of demonstrations. To understand their concern, it is imperative to understand the prevailing climate in Dallas at the time.

A number of years ago, the city of Atlanta adopted the slogan "The City Too Busy to Hate." Dallas of the '60s might have adopted the slogan "The City *Never* Too Busy to Hate." People familiar only with the cosmopolitan and sophisticated city that Dallas is today may find it hard to reconcile the rabidly conservative Dallas of 1963. There was something in the city—something unrelated to conventional politics—a stridency, a disease of the spirit, a shrill, hysterical note suggestive of a deeply troubled society. In Dallas this was particularly dismaying because for some time the city's cherished image had been blemished by a dark streak of violence. The harlots and the grafters had gone, but the killers were multiplying. Texas led the United States in homicide, and Big D led Texas. There were more murders in Dallas each month than in all of England, and none of them could be traced to the underworld or to outsiders; they were the work of Dallas citizens. Furthermore, nearly three out of four slayings were by gunfire.

In that third year of the Kennedy presidency, a kind of fever lay over Dallas County. Mad things happened. Huge billboards screamed "Impeach [Chief Justice] Earl Warren." Jewish stores were smeared with crude swastikas. Fanatical young matrons swayed in public to the chant "Stevenson's going to die—his heart will stop, stop, stop, and he will burn, burn, burn!" Radical right polemics were distributed in public schools; Kennedy's name was booed in classrooms; junior executives were required to attend radical seminars. Dallas was the one American metropolis in which incitement to violence had become respectable (Manchester p. 44).

Senator Hubert Humphrey of Minnesota, speaking the night before the assassination to a meeting of the National Association of Mental Health in DC, offered uncanny insight into the sickness that hung like a pall over Dallas. Humphrey had been giving Dallas considerable thought and had concluded that communities as well as individuals "can be afflicted with emotional instability, frustrations, and irrational behavior." He cited, "That emotional instability that afflicts a significant but small minority in our midst that some call the extreme right, some of the Birchers, some the wild men of reaction . . . . They still see the world in total black and white. They are looking for immediate and final answers. They are still substituting dogma for creative thought. They are still angry, fearful, deeply and fundamentally disturbed by the world around them" (Manchester, p. 90). On that evening, Humphrey warned the behavioral scientists that "the act of an emotionally unstable person or irresponsible citizen can strike down a great leader" (ibid.).

Kennedy, the outsider from the liberal East who came from generations of old money and power, represented everything the conservative element hated. Everything about Kennedy fed the resentment of the right: He was young, rich, good-looking, Catholic, intelligent, Ivy League, Yankee, with a large, ambitious Irish Catholic family and a beautiful wife who wore foreign clothes and spoke foreign languages. In the two years after his visit to Texas in 1961, the Secret Service investigated thirty-four death threats against Kennedy from the state of Texas alone (Reeves, p. 337). Leading the charge against the vigorous young president was the *Dallas Morning News*, whose publisher, E.M. "Ted" Dealey, was already a thorn in Kennedy's side. In the fall of 1961, he was one of a group of Texas publishers who had been invited to a White House lunch. To the astonishment of his fellow guests, Dealey had produced and read aloud a savage indictment of his host. He had reached the conclusion that "we can annihilate Russia and should make that clear to the Soviet government." Unfortunately for America, he said, "You and your administration are weak sisters." What was needed was "a man on horseback to lead this nation, and many people in Texas and the Southwest think that you are riding Caroline's tricycle" (ibid.). The president flushed. He could ignore incivility, but—and this was what Dealey would never understand—he resented the allusion to his three-year-old daughter.

Frostily, Kennedy replied, "Wars are easier to talk about than they are to fight. I'm just as tough as you are, and I didn't get elected president by arriving at soft judgments" (ibid.).

None of this was a situation Kennedy had not faced before. His response was always the same: "The notion that an American president could not go into any American city was simply unacceptable" (Manchester, p. 14). When he made the decision to go to Dallas, regardless of the political climate, his fate was sealed.

Chapter 5
"Dallas, Nov. 22 (UPI)—Three Shots Were Fired . . ."

IN SPITE OF THE CHORUS OF alarm and doomsaying, the Texas visit was, by Friday morning, November 22, 1963, an unqualified success. Kicking off his Lone Star visit, Kennedy arrived in San Antonio on Thursday to wildly cheering crowds. A school holiday had been proclaimed, and more than 125,000 people lined the motorcade route. The next stop on the presidential itinerary was Houston, and it was a repetition of San Antonio, except that 175,000 people turned out.

On that November Friday, the rain in Fort Worth did not deter more than 5,000 faithful from waiting outside the Hotel Texas for hours to catch a glimpse of their president. After addressing the crowd, President Kennedy and his entourage walked down to the hotel ballroom for a well-attended breakfast. Buoyed by the response from Texans, the most pressing matter on the president's mind at the moment was the weather.

The presidential limousine, a midnight blue, specially built Lincoln Continental, had been flown by transport plane to Dallas. It was not armored, but it was equipped with a bubbletop that could be used in the event of inclement weather or upon the insistence of the Secret Service if they felt the president was in danger. The plastic bubbletop was not bulletproof; however, in the event of an assassination attempt, the top would have shattered or disrupted the trajectory of the bullet.

Many people, including Mrs. Kennedy and the Secret Service, had argued with the president about the necessity for a motorcade and also about not allowing the bubbletop to be raised on the car. Exposure, he reasoned, like patronage, was a source of political strength. You had to move through crowds. And you had to move slowly . . . . Pamela Turnure, his wife's press secretary, suggested putting up the bubbletop. No, he replied; that was out of the question. Barring rain, they had to be where the people would see them. Pam recommended a shorter route. Another veto; the motorcade had to last forty-five minutes (Manchester, p. 10).

When the president left Fort Worth, there was a light rain falling, but it had begun clearing over Dallas. If the rain had continued, it would have been necessary to use the bubbletop. However, just before leaving Love Field for the Trade

Mart, Kenny O'Donnell, acting on orders from the president, instructed the Secret Service to remove the top as the rain had stopped and the sky was clearing. Again, this was not an unusual request since the president frequently requested that the top be removed so he could be seen by the crowd. The president's car was driven by veteran Secret Service Agent William Greer, and sitting to his right was Agent Roy Kellerman, who was maintaining radio contact with the lead car, the vice president's limo, and both follow-up cars. Others in the car included President Kennedy, Mrs. Kennedy, Gov. John Connally, and Mrs. Connally.

Immediately in front of the presidential car was the lead car, carrying Agent Forrest Sorrels from the Dallas field office, Chief of Police Curry, Sheriff Decker, and Win Lawson. Immediately behind the president's car was the Secret Service follow-up car, which carried eight Secret Service agents. One of them—George Hickey—was armed with a high-powered rifle. Not all the agents in the follow-up car, however, were confined to the car. Four agents were riding on the running board of the follow-up car, which accounted for the fact that Clint Hill, who headed Mrs. Kennedy's detail, was able to react so quickly once he knew what had happened and climb over the trunk and into the limo with Mrs. Kennedy and the slain president.

This was all laid out according to recommended Secret Service procedure, which stated that two agents from the follow-up car would ride on running boards on each side and to the rear of the presidential limo. However, President Kennedy often complained about agents riding on his car and asked that they not take these positions; therefore, they remained in the follow-up car on this trip. The next car in the motorcade, after the follow-up car, was Vice President Johnson's limo. Behind them were the vice president's follow-up car and state and local officials, dignitaries, and press representatives, riding usually in buses.

Let me emphasize the stated Secret Service policy on special agents covering the presidential vehicle, which was issued by Jerry Behn, special agent in charge of the White House detail, at the request of the Warren Commission, two weeks following the assassination in Dallas.

It says, in part:

> The policy of special agents covering the presidential vehicle is flexible and is based on the speed of the motorcade; the amount or type of accompanying escort; the number, enthusiasm, and character of the people watching the motorcade and how well-controlled they are by the police; and finally, but certainly not least but perhaps the dominant factor, the desire or instructions of the president. There is always an experienced agent riding in the front seat of the presidential vehicle and there is an experienced agent either riding in the front seat of our follow-up car or standing on the front right running board. Either one or both of these agents have the authority, if it becomes necessary, to either motion or tell

the agents in the follow-up car to take their positions around the presidential car at any time . . . . On numerous occasions during motorcades where the pace was slow and crowds were fairly well-controlled by the police, but the agents were nonetheless in position around the presidential car, the president would either tell me to tell the agents, or he would attempt to tell the agents on his side of the car, to get back (Warren Commission, Exhibit 2).

Jerry relates incidents in Mexico City, West Berlin, and other places that illustrate why any of us were so reluctant to go against Kennedy's express wishes.

In Mexico City in June, 1962, an individual who had the appearance of a typical beatnik worked his way out into the middle of the street during the welcoming motorcade and attempted to stop the president's car. When he found out the driver would not stop, he came around the car on the president's side and I hit him and knocked him down. The president immediately told me I should not have done this. This individual was arrested by the Mexican police, questioned, and it was discovered he was an American citizen who had overstayed his visa and who had a police record in this country. In West Berlin last June the pace of the motorcade was, for most of the route, between 10 and 12 miles per hour, and the West Berlin police did a remarkable job of controlling the huge crowds. However, there were occasions when individuals would break away from the police lines, evade the motorcycle escort and stand out near the middle of the street waiting for the president's car to reach them. On these occasions, the agents on the running boards of the follow-up car would leap off, run forward and push the West Berliners away from the car. Practically every time this happened, the president would either tell me to tell the agents or would attempt to tell the agents himself not to do this. His feeling was that these people only wanted to shake his hand and should not be pushed away from him.

Shortly after I was promoted to Special Agent in Charge of the White House Detail . . . he told me that he did not want agents riding on the back of his car. As late as November 18 of this year, he told ASAIC Boring the same thing. He gave me no reason for this. The late President Kennedy believed he belonged to the people. As such, he wanted to meet the people and he wanted the people to see him . . . at times, the president himself was the major factor in determining whether the agents in the follow-up car took their positions around or on his car. It perhaps can be summed up by relating part of a brief conversation between Mr. Kenneth O'Donnell, appointments secretary, and Special Agent Clint Hill, in the Bethesda Naval Hospital. Mr. O'Donnell told Mr. Hill not to blame himself or the Secret Service for what had happened (in Dallas). Mr. O'Donnell went on to say that politicians and protection do not mix and that in order to reach a happy medium, both must suffer (ibid.).

Also according to Secret Service policy, there would have been a local policeman on every block down the motorcade route. So if one of the lead agents saw someone suspicious on the route, he'd radio the police and tell them there was a suspicious person in the block between First and Second streets, and the suspect was dressed in a manner inconsistent with the weather (for instance, he might be wearing an overcoat on a warm day) and had a box at his feet. It was that policeman's responsibility to check him out. There would have been forty to fifty agents with both the president and the vice president. Every shift was down there—there was no one left in Washington except the uniformed officers.

Air Force One arrived at Love Field in Dallas at about 11:40 a.m. After a lunch speech at the Dallas Trade Mart, the president was planning to fly down to Austin for a fund-raiser and then to LBJ's ranch near Austin. Win Lawson had approved the motorcade route from Love Field to the Trade Mart, a route that was recommended by the local political committee in order to guarantee that the president would be exposed to the greatest number of people along the way. The Dallas newspapers printed the president's travel route daily, beginning on November 19.

This is the way it worked, in the words of the White House agent in charge of advancing Dallas, Win Lawson:

> From the lead car, I was watching crowd conditions along the route, requesting Chief Curry to give specific instructions to escort vehicles, keeping Lead Car in proper position in front of President's car, depending on its speed and crowd conditions, watching for obstructions or other hazards, and in general performing normal duties of advance agent in the Lead Car. Chief Curry was giving instructions at my suggestion to escort vehicles for keeping crowd out of street, blocking traffic in certain areas, requesting pilot vehicle to speed or slow up, and giving orders needed for us to proceed unhampered. The President's car made one unscheduled stop, apparently at his direction, which was not uncommon. This lasted only a few minutes, which was not uncommon (Exhibit 3).

Just fifteen minutes prior to Kennedy's motorcade passing in front of the Texas School Book Depository, three employees in the building—Harold Norman, Bonnie Ray Williams, and James Jarman—had just finished their lunch and gone up to the fifth floor to watch the president pass by. When we interviewed Norman during our investigation, he told us, "We took a position in the southeast corner of the building on the fifth floor, and I was looking out the window which is closest to the east end of the building overlooking Elm Street." In the room directly above them, on the sixth floor, fellow TSBD employee, Lee Harvey Oswald, had positioned himself among a stack of boxes. In addition to his lunch and a bottle of Dr Pepper, he was armed with a high-powered rifle with a scope.

He, also, was preparing for the president to pass beneath his window.

Pipe fitter Howard Brennan had arrived in Dealy Plaza about twelve minutes before the presidential motorcade and had settled on a retaining wall on the edge of the plaza, directly across from the entrance to the Texas School Book Depository. He was forty yards beneath Oswald. He glanced up at the Hertz sign above the building, hoping to get a glimpse of the thermometer, and in so doing, his eyes dropped to the sixth floor window, where he observed the profile of Lee Harvey Oswald. He wondered why the man was standing so still (Manchester, p. 151). Oswald was also being observed by a young man named Arnold Rowland, who was familiar with guns. He too saw Oswald silhouetted in the window, holding what appeared to be a high-powered rifle mounted with a telescopic sight. One of Oswald's hands was on the stock and the other was on the barrel; he held the weapon diagonally across his body at port arms, like a Marine on a rifle range. A police officer stood twelve feet from Rowland, but it never occurred to Arnold to speak to him. He assumed that Oswald must be a Secret Service agent protecting the president (ibid., p. 150).

Abraham Zapruder, a clothing manufacturer, had left his office in the Dal-Tex Building, armed with a movie camera, which his secretary had urged him to return home for just an hour earlier. That trip home may have been one of the most providential trips in American history. He and a woman from his office were situated on a concrete abutment near the underpass. He began filming through his telephoto lens as the motorcade made the turn from Houston Street (ibid., p. 115).

The motorcade traveled through downtown Dallas, as planned, and turned on Houston Street, directly toward the Texas School Book Depository, before veering left on Elm Street, which provided entry to the Stemmons Freeway and led to the Trade Mart. As the president's car passed the Depository, Kennedy waved at a large cheering crowd, which had gathered in front of the building and along the street. The president's car had just turned by the Book Depository when, at exactly 12:30 p.m., shots rang out, fatally wounding President Kennedy and injuring Governor Connally. The first shot missed, and one bullet passed through the president's neck but did little damage before wounding Governor Connally. Another bullet entered the right rear of the president's skull and caused the right top side of his skull to explode, scattering parts of his brain throughout the car and onto the street. So intense was the internal explosion that pieces of Kennedy's skull were found on Elm Street.

Win Lawson recalled it this way:

> We were just approaching a railroad overpass, and I checked to see if a police officer was in position there and that no one was directly over our path. I noticed a police officer but also noticed a few persons on the bridge and made motions to have these persons removed from over our path. As the Lead Car was passing under this bridge I heard the first loud, sharp

report and in more rapid succession two more sounds like gunfire. I could see persons to the left of the motorcade vehicles running away. I noticed Agent Hickey standing up in the follow-up car with the automatic weapon and first thought he had fired at someone. Both the president's car and our lead car rapidly accelerated almost simultaneously. I heard a report over the two-way radio that we should proceed to the nearest hospital. I noticed Agent Hill hanging on to the rear of the president's vehicle. A motorcycle escort officer pulled alongside our lead car and said the president had been shot. Chief Curry gave a signal over his radio for police to converge on the area of the incident (Exhibit 3).

But it is Clint Hill's statement that is most chilling in its detail.

My instructions for Dallas were to work the left rear of the presidential automobile and remain in close proximity to Mrs. John F. Kennedy at all times. The agent assigned to work the left rear of the presidential automobile rides on the forward portion of the left hand running board of the Secret Service follow-up car and only moves forward to walk alongside the presidential automobile when it slows to such a pace that people can readily approach the auto on foot. If the crowd is very heavy, but the automobile is running at a rather rapid speed, the agent rides on the left rear of the presidential automobile on a step specifically designed for that purpose.

As the motorcade moved from Love Field through downtown Dallas toward the Trade Mart, there were four (4) occasions before we reached the end of Main Street where I moved from the forward portion of the left running board of the follow-up car to the rear step of the presidential automobile. I did this because the motorcycles that were along the left hand side of the follow-up car were unable to move up alongside the president's car due to the crowd surging into the street. The motorcycles were forced to drop back and so I jumped from the follow-up car and mounted the president's car. I remained in this position until the crowd thinned and was away from the president's automobile, allowing the motorcycles to once again move up alongside of the automobile. When we approached the end of Main Street the crowd was noticeably less dense than had been the case prior to that point. The motorcade made a right hand turn onto Elm Street. I was on the forward portion of the left running board of the follow-up car. The motorcade made a left turn from Elm Street toward an underpass. We were traveling about 12 to 15 miles per hour. On the left hand side was a grass area with a few people scattered along it observing the motorcade passing, and I was visually scanning these people when I heard a noise similar to a firecracker. The sound came from my right rear and I immediately moved my head in that direction. In so doing, my eyes had to cross the presidential automobile and I saw the president hunch forward and then slump to his left. I jumped from the follow-up car and ran toward the presidential automobile. I heard a second firecracker type noise, but it had a different sound—like the sound of shooting a revolver into something hard. I saw the president slump more forward toward his left.

I jumped onto the left rear step of the presidential automobile. Mrs. Kennedy shouted, "They've shot his head off"; then turned and raised out of her seat as if she were reaching to her right rear toward the back of the car for something that had blown out. I forced her back into her seat and placed my body above President and Mrs. Kennedy. SA Greer had, as I jumped onto the presidential automobile, accelerated the presidential automobile forward. I heard ASAIC Kellerman call SA Lawson on the two-way radio and say "To the nearest hospital, quick." I shouted as loud as I could at the lead car, "To the hospital, to the hospital." As I lay over the top of the back seat, I noticed a portion of the president's head on the right rear side was missing and he was bleeding profusely. Part of his brain was gone. I saw a part of his skull with hair on it lying in the seat. The time of the shooting was approximately 12:30 p.m., Dallas time. I looked forward to the jump seats and noticed Governor Connally's chest was covered with blood and he was slumped to his left and partially covered up by his wife. I had not realized until this point that the governor had been shot (Exhibit 4).

In a foreboding and ominous statement, just prior to leaving Fort Worth earlier in the day, President Kennedy remarked to Kenny O'Donnell that ". . . if anyone really wanted to shoot the President of the United States, it would not be a difficult job. All one would have to do would be to someday get a high building and a telescopic rifle, and there would be nothing anyone could do to defend against such an attempt." They say the Irish are a little fey, and John Kennedy was Irish through and through, so perhaps he did have a premonition of his impending fate. There were many instances, reported later by sources close to the president, which seemed to indicate that he sensed what lay in store for him. He apparently had a morbid fascination for assassination. As early as 1961, he had concocted the plot for a movie involving a Texas coup to remove him from the presidency. In a conversation with writer Gore Vidal, he talked, as he often did, of assassination. "If the assassin is willing to die, it couldn't be simpler . . ." (Bradford, pp. 212–213).

For myself, I believe it was his destiny to die that day in Dallas, for a number of reasons I'll outline further. But consider these factors: One of the most competent Secret Service agents, Win Lawson, had planned the trip; the exact route had not been announced until Tuesday as there were several possible; the president had wanted to drive rather than take a helicopter to the Trade Mart as the Service had wished; Oswald had been quarreling with his wife and, after the quarrel, had taken the gun from the home where it was kept; the skies had cleared after a morning rain, causing the president to direct that the bubbletop be left off his limo; and, finally, there were no agents on the running boards of the car to obstruct Oswald's shots.

Just thirty minutes after the first shots were fired in Dealy Plaza, the President of the United States was pronounced dead at Parkland Hospital, although by that time it was a matter of formality. The president had expired when Oswald's third bullet penetrated his thick chestnut hair and reached his brain. Mac Kilduff held his first-ever press conference from the road in an auditorium at Parkland Hospital. Red-eyed and tremulous, Kilduff was at first unable to speak. He started to announce the news, but paused and told the assembled media, "Excuse me, let me catch my breath." Then the dreaded words formed themselves and he made his brief announcement, "President John F. Kennedy died at approximately one o'clock Central Standard Time today here in Dallas" (Manchester, p. 220). The news of that death ricocheted throughout the world and became a defining moment in the life of a generation. "Life changed, forever, in the middle of a nice day, at the end of a good week, in a wonderful year of what looked like an extraordinary decade of promise. It would take months before we would begin to understand how, but the inevitability of wrenching change was plain as tears" (Bradlee, p. 258). Most people say they'll never forget where they were when they heard the news that President Kennedy had been shot. Well, it would be hard for me to forget where I was. My classmates and I were completing our advanced training course that Friday, November 22, in Washington, at the old Navy base. The chief of the Secret Service, James Rowley, had invited us to lunch that day at O'Donnell's Seafood Restaurant, which was next door to the Treasury Building and a block from the White House. We were eating lunch when the waiter came over and told Chief Rowley he had a phone call, although he didn't tell him it was an emergency of any kind, just a phone call. I have to stop and remind people every now and then that this was long before cell phones—phones were those big old black rotary-dial phones—so Rowley had to leave the table to take the call. I don't know for sure, but it's likely the call was from Jerry Behn, who was one of the few agents left behind in DC.

He returned to the table wearing a look that's impossible to describe—hurt, shock, stunned—and just quietly said, "The president has been shot. I'll try to get through to Dallas as quickly as possible and get a report." Because there were few agents on duty at the White House—everyone was traveling with the president and vice president—he assigned us various duties; I was to report to the Secret Service office at the White House and answer the telephones. There was a skeleton crew of White House Police—they're now called uniformed Secret Service—on duty around the perimeter of the property, but there were virtually no Secret Service agents and almost no staff to speak of. And the cabinet members, along with White House Press Secretary Pierre Salinger and members of Congress, were 35,000 feet above the Pacific on their way to Japan for meetings. At the time, we weren't certain exactly who was on the plane, but we later determined that the passengers included Secretary of State Dean Rusk, Secretary of Defense Robert S. McNamara, Secretary of the Treasury C. Douglas Dillon, Secretary of the Interior Stewart Udall, Secretary of Commerce Luther Hodges, Secretary of Agriculture Orville Freeman, and Secretary of Labor Willard Wirtz.

Pierre recalls being summoned into the cabin occupied by Dean Rusk, the senior cabinet member on board. "Rusk was seated, and looking for all the world as if someone had clubbed him into his chair. He held a yellow sheet of Teletype paper in his hand . . . sensing this was a grave matter, I looked over his shoulder. Whoever had sent the message had done so hurriedly, as there were misspellings—and one did not send misspelled messages to this aircraft. I read . . . LAST THREE SHOTS WERE FIRED AT PREXIENT KENNEDY'S MOTORCADE TODAY IN DOWNTOWN DALLAS . . . KENNEDY SERIOSTY WOUNDED. MAKE THAT PERHAPS PERHAPS SERIOUSLY WOUNDED . . . KENNEDY WOUNDED PERHAPS FATALLY BY VASSASSINS BULLET" (Salinger, p. 155).

They had to turn around in midair. There was a panicked call after we got to the White House—the FBI was looking for Speaker of the House John McCormack, who, after the vice president, was next in succession to assume the presidency. We were looking for him everywhere but the logical place; the House was in session at the Capitol, and he was presiding. It was total chaos. We didn't yet know who was on the plane to Japan, and we didn't know if this was a conspiracy, plus we couldn't get telephone lines to Dallas. Finally, Roy Kellerman, by then at Parkland Hospital, got a telephone line and called the Detail Office. He got the White House Signal Corps to hold that line open all the time, and that was the first link we had with Dallas. We didn't know anything at that point, except that the outlook wasn't good. Agents were out looking for government leaders to try to protect them, and I stayed at my post in the Secret Service office. In those days, the office was located in the West Wing, immediately inside the front door. I was getting calls from heads of state from around the world because they were calling the White House and there was no one else to take their calls. The phones were lit up, and we were grabbing one right after the other. Other agents were scrambling around all over the city. We were told of the president's death as soon as it happened. But there was no one around to get any counsel or advice from. Most people, especially those watching the popular CBS-TV soap *As the World Turns*, will never forget an emotionally overcome Walter Cronkite calling the president's death, while removing his thick, black-rimmed glasses and putting them back on repeatedly.

In referencing my activity log from those days, which I have kept all these years, I show I was officially assigned to the Detail Office from 2:00 p.m. until 6:00 p.m. At six, I was notified that President Johnson was arriving at the White House, and I was to meet the helicopter and accompany the presidential party to the Executive Office Building, next to the White House, where the former vice president had an office. There was to be a security briefing there. I know some of the senior senators had been located by then because when I got to the EOB with the former Vice President and now President Johnson, Senator Fulbright and several others were there for the briefing.

I show that I reported back to the Detail Office at 11:30 p.m. and was off duty at midnight. I walked the block back to the Willard Hotel, down Pennsylvania Avenue to 14th, and realized when I arrived that, because I had been planning to leave for home, I had no clean clothes to wear the next day. I had to wash out socks and underwear in the sink and let them dry on the radiator overnight. I'm sure I must have called home at that time, but for the life of me, I can't remember anything I would have said to Jan. I remember clearly on Sunday having a freshly pressed suit and a starched white shirt on, so I must have, at some point, sent my clothes to the Chinese laundry around the corner from the hotel.

President Kennedy's body arrived at the northwest gate of the White House at about four-thirty in the morning on Saturday, November 23. The hearse was greeted by a military honor guard. The corridors of the White House were lined with military honor guards as the casket was taken to the East Room. From that point on, highly decorated servicemen from each of the four branches of the armed services stood guard at the four corners of the flag-draped casket.

I had received a call from the White House at about four in the morning, and I was ordered, after only two hours of sleep, to report back to the White House for the arrival of the body. I was assigned to President Johnson's detail that morning; he was scheduled to attend a memorial service at St. John's Church at 16th and K streets. Mrs. Kennedy and the senior White House staff were also in attendance.

I went back to the White House and remained on standby duty for the rest of that day. Later that morning, the entire staff, including the Secret Service agents, assembled in the East Room to file past the casket and pay respect to their slain leader. I remember so clearly going through the line; a picture that stands out above all else is the four members of the honor guard keeping watch over their president's body, attired in full dress, the left side of their chests adorned by service medals, standing at attention with tears running down their faces. Mrs. Kennedy was the first person to view the casket, then the family, the senior staff, and the more junior staff. The atmosphere had gone from chaos to the most solemn mood imaginable; the people I knew on staff like Mac Kilduff wouldn't even talk. They were beyond words and in shock.

This remains the most solemn moment of my entire life. Over the years, I have been unable to recall these events without shedding tears. I actually had, for years, blocked these events from my memory because of the unbearable sorrow and pain. Ben Bradlee was among those present in the East Room, and his memories are parallel to mine. "Ted Sorensen was staring into space, present physically, but locked alone in an awful grief. Robert Kennedy seemed almost catatonic, glued to Jackie's side as he was to be for the next days. Everyone wept when the

'Navy Hymn' was played, the first of what was to seem like ten thousand times" (Bradlee, p. 261).

Sander Vanocur remembers watching a very visible sign of the passing of the reins of leadership. "It was raining on Saturday, and we were on vigil at the White House," he recalled in a television special produced by an Arkansas TV station marking the twenty-fifth anniversary of the assassination. "Suddenly my attention was diverted by a workman removing President Kennedy's rocking chair from the Oval Office. Not ten minutes later, two workmen appeared carrying a saddle with two six-guns attached. That was the most visible symbol of the order passing."

For me, also, it was so chaotic that it never really even hit me what had happened until after the ceremony at Arlington Cemetery. I was working eighteen-hour days and going to the hotel, falling into bed at midnight in total exhaustion, only to get up at five o'clock again the next morning. This was also a time of transition within the Secret Service, and because of that, all of us who were in Washington at the time, regardless of where we were assigned, had responsibilities surrounding the funeral and lying-in-state ceremonies. There had been specific agents assigned to President Kennedy, who was dead now, and specific agents assigned to the vice-presidential detail, and there was some degree of discomfort between the two details. Plus, most of the senior agents, both Kennedy's and Johnson's, had been in Dallas and were totally exhausted and emotionally overwrought. I have no recollection of seeing Win Lawson at all during that time. Again, there was no structure to the activities. The supervising agents would see someone in the office, and they used whomever that might be for whatever had come up where an agent was needed to fill in.

On Sunday, the twenty-fourth, the body was moved to the rotunda at the Capitol for public viewing, and I was assigned to the Capitol. In almost every photo I've seen since of Kennedy's coffin, draped in the Stars and Stripes, slowly ascending the capitol steps, borne by the military honor guard, I'm standing at the very top of the steps in my dark blue overcoat, staring out into the crowd. I stayed there all that day and night and was there when Mrs. Kennedy and President Johnson viewed the body. There were several things that stand out in my mind about that day.

I experienced mixed, unreasonable emotions about the hundreds of thousands of people filing past the funeral bier, mourning a president they didn't even know—I remember thinking that they didn't have the same right that we who had served with him did. I remember distinctly some college kids who drove in from Salt Lake City. There were so many of them in the same car that they kept rotating drivers so they wouldn't have to stop. I just recently related that story to my friend, Chet Flippo, and he said he and his friends from the University of Texas had done the very same thing. That Sunday had a profound impact on me—the thousands and thousands of people passing by that casket, hour after hour, never saying a word, very solemn in their grief. They stood in a chilly rain for as much as eight hours at a time, just to file silently past the casket. I couldn't believe there was such an outpouring of love for the president.

A bright light had been extinguished for an entire generation of young Americans.

Arthur Schlesinger maintains:

> Perhaps most important of all was the impact Kennedy had on a new generation of Americans. He liked to quote the Scottish author John Buchan: "Politics is still the greatest and most honorable adventure." At Kennedy's behest, bright, idealistic and capable young men and women, asking not what their country could do for them but what they could do for their country, flocked to Washington. They brought new ideas, hopes, vision, generosity and vitality to the national life . . . . JFK touched and remolded lives and gave young people the faith that individuals can make a difference to history. Inspired by his words, they dedicated themselves thereafter to public service, whether in government, in civil rights and human rights movements, in nonprofit sectors, in community organization, in their own hearts and souls (p. 179).

Through it all, we had to maintain our stoicism; we couldn't allow ourselves to become too emotional. But I do remember watching the president's body being borne into the capitol and not being able to stop the tears flowing down my face. Ashamed, I happened to glance at my colleague on the other side of the steps and saw that I was not alone; his face was wet with tears as well. I think many of us, however, had an emotional meltdown when it was all over. Once all the official ceremonies were over and we had no specific duties, we had too much idle time to reflect on what had happened. That's when the emotion of it all overtook us. The world came as close to stopping in its rotation as it ever had. I didn't think we would ever again experience such an impact on a nation and the world. Everybody was lifeless. It was a defining moment in all of our lives. The two men on President Kennedy's staff I knew best were Mac Kilduff and Kenny O'Donnell. When I'd see either of them, I'd want to say something to them, but I couldn't; we were all in total shock. There were no issues being discussed, although President Johnson was still relying on Kennedy's staff at this time. Bobby was around some, but I didn't see Jackie and the kids except at the official ceremonial events.

The other thing was, that Sunday, I was standing on the steps of the Capitol, but I had access to a television monitor and saw the tape-delayed clip of Jack Ruby shooting Lee Harvey Oswald. Oswald had been interrogated at City Hall in Dallas for more than thirty hours, and he was being transferred to the custody of the Dallas County Sheriff. At 11:25 a.m. (CST), Oswald emerged from the elevator that had brought him down from his fourth-floor cell to the basement. He was running about half an hour behind schedule because he had been detained for further questioning before being transferred to another jurisdiction. He was led out through the booking office to the open vestibule between two lines of detectives. Along with the rest of a grieving but transfixed nation, I watched as the slight, dark-haired Oswald, smiling slightly and dressed casually in a dark sweater, gray pants, and white, open-collared shirt, stepped out, handcuffed to a policeman, and surrounded by a phalanx of law enforcement personnel. As they turned right from the vestibule to walk up a ramp, Ruby jumped forward from against the railing. In disbelief, I watched this beefy man in a dark business suit and hat fight his way between a throng of law enforcement officers and newsmen, stick the .38 revolver he always carried into Oswald's midriff, and pull the trigger. Oswald immediately grabbed at his midsection with his manacled hands. Then the reporter's panicked voice kept repeating, "He's been shot. He's been shot. Lee Oswald has been shot."

I don't recall that there was any discussion among any of us agents during this time about what had happened or was happening. We didn't do our usual thirty minutes on and thirty minutes off; when we were assigned a post, we were there for the duration, so there wasn't much socializing. Dick Keiser and I met recently and talked about the president's shooting, and he remembered the duty he was assigned to. Monday, the twenty-fifth, I was slated for duty at eight a.m., but I seem to remember arriving sometime around five-thirty a.m. or so. I did not go to the National Cathedral where the ceremony was held. I had attended the memorial service on Saturday, and when the body was removed from the Capitol, I was then assigned to Arlington Cemetery, to the grave site. I remained there until they lowered his body into the grave. From my post at the head of the grave, I remember watching the processional make its way across Memorial Bridge and up the hill to the grave site. Most people have seen the picture hundreds of times, with Jackie leading the processional, a black veil shielding her face, holding onto Bobby's hand, and, following them, other members of the family and leaders from all over the world. I vividly remember when they got there thinking how tall French President Charles de Gaulle was; he rose head and shoulders above the rest of the party. I don't know what went into the selection process of which agent was assigned which post during this time, but I suspect the president's agents had been assigned to the church because most of us at the gravesite were field agents. President Johnson's normal detail would have been with him by that time. It was much easier to secure the church than it was Arlington National Cemetery; it's a wide-open place, and while we had it secured for miles around, it's almost impossible to have one hundred percent security at such a site. I was fortunate to be assigned to the immediate grave site, standing at the very head of the grave.

Chapter 6
Who Killed the President?

𝕴 STAYED IN WASHINGTON for the next couple of days, accompanying President Johnson when he addressed a joint session of Congress, among other duties. Each day, our duty assignment for the following day would be posted in the White House Detail Office. On Wednesday, when I checked the duty assignments for Thursday, my name was not posted to a specific assignment, so I called my boss in Little Rock, Roy Letteer. "What should I do? I don't have an assignment." Roy said, "I realize what you've been going through. Since it's Thanksgiving and you don't have an assignment, why don't you take a few days off? Get out of town and don't tell anyone, including me, where you're going."

So I went back to the hotel and checked out, retrieved my bags, and went immediately to Washington National Airport. Jan was driving my parents and our seven-month-old, Julia, down to Dallas to visit my sister, Doris King, for Thanksgiving, and I decided to join them there. However, I instructed Jan not to tell anyone where we were going. I called Doris' husband, Stan, from National Airport and told him to meet me at the Dallas airport at six a.m.

In the meantime, Inspector Thomas Kelley, who had been tapped to take charge of the Secret Service investigation into the assassination, was compiling his duty roster of hand-picked agents in Dallas. In looking over the list of agents from the twenty field offices, he saw my name listed in the Little Rock office, called Roy Letteer and told him I was needed in Dallas. Roy told him he'd given me a few days off and didn't know how to reach me. Kelley then called Howard Anderson, in the Secret Service personnel office, to find out the names of my relatives so he could begin tracking me down. When I arrived in Dallas, Stan met my flight with the word that Kelley had successfully tracked me down through him, and I was to report to the Secret Service office in Dallas that morning. I still had no clean clothes, but I reported for duty as ordered. I never made it out for Thanksgiving dinner.

I stayed there and worked for the Warren Commission, investigating the assassination for much of the rest of the year and eventually even got an apartment in Dallas. I went home for a few days but returned to Dallas and stayed until I accompanied Marina Oswald to Washington for her testimony before the Warren

53

Commission in early winter 1964. When I first got to Dallas, the primary concern was for the security of the key witnesses—the Oswald family.

One day in 1997, an assassination buff from a Nashville record label, Al Cooley, called me and told me he had discovered some new information on the assassination. He wanted me to go to lunch with him and talk about the alleged conspiracy. At lunch, he informed me that someone had been digging in the files, which by now had been released to the public, and had discovered that the government kidnapped the Oswald family and held them hostage somewhere and brainwashed them. I laughed and told him that not only did I know about the supposed brainwashing, but I was one of the people responsible for it. You hear about alleged conspiracy theories, and it's odd to realize you were a part of the conspiracy.

The first order of business when I arrived in Dallas was to report to a special investigation office that had been set up for the team of agents converging on Dallas from around the country. After I had arrived at the airport in Dallas early in the morning, having had no sleep, Stan took me to the office. I can still picture myself getting out of the car and reporting for duty, emotionally exhausted by the ordeal of the funeral, and not knowing what to expect from my new assignment. By this time, the Secret Service had obtained the raw footage of the film shot by Abraham Zapruder. Inspector Kelley assembled us in the conference room and showed that video over and over and over. That was almost more than I could handle—to watch that frame over and over again, in slow motion, where the bullet hits the president's head and it's blown all over the car, its occupants, and the street. It was emotionally devastating. To this day, it's hard for me to think back on that moment without cringing. In fact, when I visited the National Archives and attempted to read the autopsy report for the first time, I found I could not get through it. I kept seeing that film, and I broke down. When the film was eventually shown on television, years later, the portion that was so graphic had been cut out.

By this time, Kelley had assembled a long list of witnesses, so we were given interview assignments, and the process began of reconstructing the crime and getting inside the mind of the assassins. I say "assassins," because Lee Harvey Oswald had allegedly killed Kennedy and a Dallas policeman later that same day, and Jack Ruby had killed Oswald.

The Secret Service had been holding the entire Oswald family—Lee's wife, Marina, their two children, his mother Marguerite, and his brother, Robert—at the Inn of the Six Flags, a motel near Six Flags amusement park in Arlington, since Sunday the twenty-fourth. In a strange twist, Special Agents Charles Kunkel and Mike Howard had arrived at the Executive Inn Motel in Dallas and were waiting to meet the Oswalds when they heard over their radio about Lee Oswald being shot. Robert Oswald heard the same report over a radio and rushed immediately to Parkland Hospital, where Lee had been taken. The agents informed Marina, her two children, and Marguerite about the shooting when they were in the car, but the decision was made to proceed to Arlington. During the trip, the agents received the information on their two-way radio that Lee had died, and Marina and Marguerite insisted upon going to the hospital immediately.

On Monday the twenty-fifth, Agent Howard and Robert Oswald made funeral arrangements for Lee through Millers Funeral Home in Fort Worth. The funeral was to be at four that afternoon with interment in Rosehill Cemetery in Fort Worth. After several phone calls, Robert was able to get a Lutheran minister to officiate, although he apparently did not show, because Chief Hightower of the Fort Worth Police Department had to get a Disciple of Christ minister to replace the Lutheran minister at the last minute. There was some discussion between Robert and the cemetery officials about whether or not to even bury Oswald there. They had received numerous threats from the families of others who were buried there, even to the extent of threatened exhumation of Oswald's body. The family was strongly urged to either cremate the body or remove it from the cemetery. Agents Kunkel and Howard attended the funeral, which was secured by sixty-five uniformed officers from the Fort Worth Police Department. The family was then returned to Arlington and placed under twenty-four-hour protection.

During the next few days, Marina would be interviewed by the Secret Service, the FBI, and Immigration (she was Russian) on a number of occasions. On Thanksgiving morning, Marguerite, who had been complaining that no one seemed to care about her because she had received no sympathy mail, asked to be allowed to return to her home at 2220 Thomas Place in Fort Worth. She was allowed to go, although Special Agent Gary Seale was assigned to protect her. The manager of the Inn of the Six Flags Motel, Jim Martin, invited the family to his home for Thanksgiving dinner. The next day Mr. Martin advised the Secret Service that he would like for Marina and her children to live with him in his Dallas home, an idea to which Marina was apparently agreeable. She and the children, accompanied by Agents Kunkel, Art Blake, and Leon Gopadze, left soon after I arrived in Arlington.

On Friday, the twenty-ninth, my first day of field work on the Warren Commission team, I was sent out to join the protective detail for a couple of days. We were concerned about the secret location in Arlington leaking out through the hotel employees. As far as I know, however, no one ever found out, although there had to have been legions of press down in Dallas. That same day the Secret Service arranged to move Robert Oswald to join his wife, Vada, and his two small children at his in-laws' farm in Boyd, about forty miles outside Dallas.

This fairly ordinary white wood-frame farmhouse was set out in the middle of a farm of about 2,000 acres, with no houses anywhere near it, and it was an ideal place for us to keep the Oswald family for a few days. It was so flat in that part of the state that you could sit out in the yard of that house and see for miles. There were no trees to speak of. It was perfect for us because we had a small crew, and with the family inside the house, we could easily cover them and know well in advance if someone was approaching. We didn't have a lot of personnel, but we did employ a lot of weaponry. Even so, if there had been a serious conspiracy of another government, they'd have wiped us out in no time. If Lee had been involved in a conspiracy, and his co-conspirators had killed him, then what was to prevent them from killing his family? We were concerned about that.

None of us interviewed them; we were just there to protect them. I did spend some time talking to Robert, however, and remember liking him as a person. Robert was completely normal. He was sales coordinator with the Acme Brick Company in nearby Denton, and he was totally opposite from Lee. His boss, whom we interviewed, said Robert was a good employee and a loyal American. I got the impression that Robert was embarrassed by all of this, although I didn't specifically quiz him about it. At that time, I didn't have an agenda about trying to develop any evidence; I was on protective assignment and simply made friends with him. I'm not sure he wasn't still in shock; I doubt that it had hit him. We were all still operating in a state of shock. We soon accompanied Robert and his family back to Denton so they could resume a somewhat normal life. I returned to Dallas to begin interviewing witnesses, but Special Agents James Leckey, Anthony Sherman, and Lawrence Hess remained on the protective detail in Denton. On December 1, Agents Leckey and Talmadge Bailey accompanied Robert and his family to visit Marina in Dallas, and together with Marina's oldest daughter, June, they visited Lee's grave.

Our duties then shifted to sifting through the evidence in the case and determining exactly what had happened. Did Lee Harvey Oswald, in fact, kill President Kennedy? What happened before he was arrested, and what led Jack Ruby to pull the trigger that forever silenced our most valuable witness to the events of November 22? Lee Harvey Oswald had been interrogated after his arrest, but he did not confess. Why? I'm convinced that there were too many law enforcement officials around to conduct any type of effective interrogation. In fact, there were numerous law enforcement officials present at his interrogation from different agencies. Each interrogation session was attended by as many as eight law enforcement representatives, including detectives from the Dallas Homicide department, led by Capt. Will Fritz, several representatives of the U.S. Postal Service (because Oswald had obtained the gun through the mail), agents from the FBI, the Secret Service, and the U.S. Marshall's service.

In spite of the fact that the President of the United States had been killed, and it was imperative that we gather as much information from the key suspect as possible, this glut of law enforcement officials violated every basic rule of interrogation. I still wonder about the wisdom of that. I considered myself a pretty good interrogator, and we always held the belief that if you wanted information from a suspect, you'd send one good interrogator, at the most two, in to interrogate him. Too many investigators present would intimidate the suspect and probably cause him to clam up and resist. There was no way on earth Oswald was going to confess to a crowd of authorities he resented so much!

In this case, the city of Dallas had jurisdiction over the homicide, and the federal authorities' participation was as guests. It's my opinion that had one FBI and one Secret Service agent conducted the interview, it might have been successful. The first rule of interrogation is to be calm, take your time, and make the suspect feel comfortable. It is important that the suspect feel at ease with you and that you not represent an extreme authority figure. You must obtain his respect and confidence while making him relax and open up to you. It is best to talk at length about subjects unrelated to the crime. Sympathy to his feelings, however bizarre they may be, will encourage him to eventually release information to you.

The second rule is patience. Do the interview on his time—not yours. Rushing him will cause him to resist because you represent the ultimate authority for which he has developed a hatred. Thirdly, do not attempt to intimidate him. Appear as if he is in absolute control, and become nonthreatening to him so his guard remains at ease; otherwise, the interview should be terminated and resumed another time. The interview with Oswald was conducted with great urgency and with the utmost authority.

I'll always believe that at some point, when Oswald had the full attention of the media, he would have probably confessed. Instead, Jack Ruby's violent act, in taking the life of Lee Harvey Oswald, left the nation with an enduring mystery concerning the death of its beloved young president. However, during the time the police did have Oswald in custody, he denied over and over, even when threatened with death in the electric chair, that he had killed Kennedy or anyone else. Nonetheless, the majority of us who examined the evidence and those who interrogated Oswald have no doubt about his guilt.

At the conclusion of the investigation, I had formed an opinion about Oswald. Based on all the evidence, I felt that, if he had lived, at some point he would have beat his chest and said, "I did it! I did it! I'm proud I did it! I killed that SOB." I don't mean he was that mad at Kennedy; I think Lee Harvey Oswald killed Kennedy for recognition, for identity. His life had been one of total rejection, and he thought he'd finally stand up and say, "I'll show you; I'm somebody. I killed the President of the United States, and I'm an important guy."

In his studies of serial killers for the FBI's Behavioral Science Unit, Robert Ressler found that murderous behavior begins developing in early childhood. He wrote, "From birth to age six or seven, studies have shown the most important adult figure in a child's life is the mother, and it is in this time period that the child learns what love is. Relationships between our subjects and their mothers were uniformly cool, distant, unloving, neglectful. There was very little touching, emotional warmth, or training in the ways in which normal human beings cherish one another and demonstrate their affection and interdependence" (Ressler,

p. 74). In order to understand why I made these determinations about Oswald, it is important to examine his life, which gives new meaning to the word *dysfunctional*. Lee Oswald was born in New Orleans on October 18, 1939, two months after the death of his father. When Lee was three, his mother, Marguerite, placed him in an orphanage where his brother, Robert, and half-brother, John Pic, were already living. Her reasoning was that she had to work. In January, 1944, when Lee was four, he was taken out of the orphanage, and shortly thereafter, his mother moved with him to Dallas, where the two older boys joined them at the end of that school year. In May 1945 Marguerite Oswald married for the third time, but she and her husband separated after only a year. Marguerite then moved her family to Covington, Louisiana, where Lee reentered the first grade. They moved back to Texas—to Fort Worth—when Marguerite and her husband tried to reconcile. Two years later, the couple divorced.

In August 1952, after Lee finished sixth grade, Marguerite moved them to New York City to live with Marguerite's oldest son, John Pic, who was on active duty with the U.S. Coast Guard. The next eighteen months were marked by Lee's refusal to attend school and by his emotional and psychological problems, seemingly of a serious nature. According to John Pic, Lee slept with his mother until 1950, which would make him approximately eleven years old (Mailer, p. 360). Because he had become a chronic school truant, Lee underwent psychiatric study at Youth House, an institution in New York for juveniles who had bad truancy problems or difficulties with the law and who appeared to require psychiatric observation or other types of guidance.

The social worker assigned to his case described him as "seriously detached" and "withdrawn" and noticed "a rather pleasant, appealing quality about this emotionally starved, affectionless youngster." Lee expressed the feeling to this social worker that his mother did not care for him and regarded him as a burden. The chief psychiatrist of Youth House diagnosed Lee's problem as a "personality pattern disturbance with schizoid features and passive-aggressive tendencies." He concluded that the boy was "an emotionally, quite disturbed youngster" and recommended psychiatric treatment. His mother insisted that he did not need psychiatric assistance. Although there was apparently some improvement in Lee's behavior, the court recommended further treatment.

In January 1954, while Lee's case was still pending, Marguerite and Lee moved back to New Orleans. After starting the tenth grade, Lee forged a note, purportedly from his mother, saying she was withdrawing him from school to move to California. Lee worked odd jobs until he was finally accepted into the Marines six days after his seventeenth birthday. The date was October 24, 1956 (*Warren Commission*, p. 10). It's important to point this out: *Oswald had been a failure at everything he'd tried his entire life.* Throughout his school years, he was a loner who was easy prey for bullying classmates who picked on him and made fun of the youngster. He apparently joined the Marines to get away from his domineering mother in hopes that he might gain some sort of acceptance. Once in the Marines, he was constantly picked on by his macho colleagues, who thought he was gay. He failed to develop any friendships in the Marines, which is especially odd since the military operates on the team and buddy concept.

Some of my own closest relationships were developed in the four years I served in the Air Force. I spent eleven months in school at Keesler Air Force Base in Biloxi, Mississippi, where I was trained in maintaining and repairing radar systems used in air defense command. The barracks were the old open-bay style, which were just long wooden buildings. Forty or fifty of us shared a barrack, and each of us had a bunk. Only about three feet separated me from the guy on either side of me, and we shared an open latrine. There was no such thing as privacy. Still, I enjoyed the camaraderie of the living quarters. In the military, you rely on your buddies for moral and emotional support. Being away from family and childhood friends is an emotional shock that often results in isolation and loneliness. Since all your comrades are suffering the same emotional trauma, it is only natural that you rely on each other for friendship and support. I think one reason JFK was such a buddy to the Secret Service agents is because of his Navy experience, especially since he had little in common with the agents except that most had military backgrounds.

But Oswald remained a loner in the Marines, although it may not have been by choice. He had never relied on buddies, and the concept was foreign to him. Right away he was withdrawn and ostracized because he was thought to be homosexual, and being ostracized would have been traumatic for a Marine. He resisted authority, was disobedient, and always in trouble. Among the nicknames with which he was tagged were "Ozzie Rabbit," "Mrs. Oswald," and "Oswaldskovich" after he began to express his support of Communism. He was described as meek, frail, and shy—a demeanor totally at odds with the strong aggressive types in the Marine Corps, without doubt the most aggressive and macho of any of the branches of the armed services. In fact, his personality would typically isolate him from the group. But he was brazen enough to take up study of the Russian language and to receive Communist material through the mail delivered to the base. He was disobedient from the beginning and relegated to routine assignments, and his poor conduct led to courts-martial as well as his eventual undesirable discharge. His Marine career was short-lived.

Because Oswald never could adjust to life in the United States, and because of his growing interest in Communism, he thought he'd go to the Soviet Union after his discharge and they'd love him there. He thought he'd be someone important and special, so he defected. Instead, he was ultimately assigned to the industrial city of Minsk and given a job as a metalworker in a large factory. While he was considered somewhat of a celebrity at first because he was an American, the novelty soon wore off, and he fell into the boredom common among factory workers. According to Oswald's diary, he fell in love with a female co-worker and later proposed marriage, only to be summarily rejected. Rejection became as routine to his life as acceptance does in the life of most young Americans. He quickly became disillusioned with life in Russia and decided to return to the United States.

Only a short time before returning to America, he met Marina Prusakova at a dance and they began dating. Marina's mother was dead, and she apparently never knew who her father was. Alone at the age of nineteen, Marina married Lee just one month after they met. It can only be assumed that the young Oswald, barely out of his teens himself, hoped this marriage would be the meaningful and loving relationship he continued to seek and would bring some stability to his life.

The examination of Oswald's history clearly indicates that he was mentally unstable and had been since childhood. That is why it's hard to imagine him working in a sensitive position for any company or government agency, and even more difficult to imagine that Kennedy's assassination was part of an organized conspiracy by either the U.S. or the Soviet government. Agents for the U.S. government undergo a lengthy background investigation to ensure that someone like Oswald is never even considered. These agencies—both in the United States and in Russia—looked for young men who were physically and mentally strong, loyal, extremely obedient, well-disciplined, patriotic, and who possessed outgoing personalities, above-average intelligence, and good social skills. A candidate must have all these personal traits to qualify, and Lee Harvey Oswald had none of them. Lee had a history of resisting all authority, he had no social skills, and he was obviously emotionally unstable. The CIA and KGB would never have trusted any individual with a background such as Oswald's. Never in my wildest imagination would I have ever suspected Oswald was associated with any government agency.

To contrast this, let's do a profile on a government assassin. In doing so, I think of someone with a mindset like a G. Gordon Liddy. To my knowledge, he's not an assassin, but he was loyal to the extreme in the Watergate conspiracy trial and went to jail rather than reveal any information he possessed about his or anyone else's involvement. Qualifications for a secret, clandestine operator would read something like this: intelligent, totally dependable, loyal, secretive, disciplined, and patriotic. A person who would carry out his duties with the highest efficiency and would never discuss his assignment with any other person, including his wife.

In 1995 I met with just such a clandestine CIA operator in a suburb of Washington, DC. I was questioning him about ZRRifle, the CIA code name for President Kennedy's Executive Action Capability Committee. Kennedy conceived the idea to form a select, super-loyal, super-secretive group to carry out sensitive assignments at the direction of the president only. This was simply an assassination squad. However, from what we know from history, before they could carry out many assignments, President Kennedy lost confidence in the CIA and was apprehensive about trusting CIA individuals such as Richard Bissell and William Harvey, who were responsible for the ZRRifle operation. If the president didn't trust the most loyal and experienced personnel at the CIA to carry out his clandestine assignments, do you think he or anyone else would have chosen someone of Lee Harvey Oswald's character? I think not.

Vladimir Semichastny, once chairman of the KGB, was asked whether, when Oswald entered the Soviet Union, he thought Oswald worked for American intelligence. He commented, "Would the FBI or CIA really use such a pathetic person to work against their archenemy? I had always respected the CIA and FBI, and we knew their work and what they were capable of. It is clear Oswald was not an agent, couldn't be an agent for the U.S. secret services, either the CIA or the FBI" ("Inside the KGB," 1993).

The only good that came out of Oswald's Soviet experience was marrying Marina, but when they moved back to the States, it was the same story all over again. He couldn't hold a job, everything he did was a failure, and then the final insult came when the only thing in his life that had the possibility of being successful—his marriage—was ending, when Marina threw him out. So he decided to show her he could succeed in a big way—he'd kill the president. That's a typical pattern of behavior for someone like Oswald. Many criminals commit crimes for a psychological reason—consider the kids who commit school shootings—they're crying out for attention. They have often been teased about their appearance (overweight, underweight, thick glasses, physical handicap) or are the object of bullying, and they feel completely rejected by their peers. They want revenge by proving that they can be somebody. We would learn all this and more about Lee Harvey Oswald over the next few weeks.

After my protective detail was over, by December 1, I was heavily into the investigation every day. The first few days I worked with Special Agents Arthur Blake, Maurice Miller, Jerry Parr, Talmadge Bailey, Robert Jamison, Gary Seale, and Ed Moore, many of them very senior agents in the Secret Service. I was flattered they assigned me to this detail because everyone else involved was a polished, experienced investigator, and here I was, I'd been in the agency just over a year. One of my first assignments, on Monday, December 2, was to interview Jack Ruby, the man who shot Lee Harvey Oswald in front of a national television audience.

Jack Leon Rubenstein, aka Ruby, was fifty-two years old when he pulled the trigger, silencing the only person who could definitively answer the question for the ages, Who killed the president? He was a study in contrasts: On the one hand he was a tough guy—a small-time hoodlum with a string of arrests for carrying a concealed weapon and assault. But he was also a very emotional guy who, according to his sister, was "generous and warm, but hated anything done to this country." Press accounts from the day he killed Oswald, again quoting his sister on the president's death, described Ruby as an ardent admirer of the president who was ". . . sick inside about the shooting." Ruby had been in Dallas only about fifteen years and owned a strip club only four blocks from City Hall, as well as another club elsewhere in Dallas. His sister went so far as to say that she and Jack were more affected by Kennedy's death than they had been by their father's passing. By all accounts he was an unlikely character to be in the line of business he chose—he wasn't really interested in women, although he was considered a gentleman, and he neither smoked, drank, nor cursed. He did, however, work out regularly, often at the Y.

Jack Ruby was Jewish at a time when it wouldn't have been popular to be Jewish in Texas. His roommate was George Senator, and they lived upstairs above the burlesque club in a very small apartment. It was not the most livable or desirable accommodation. It has been alleged that Ruby was homosexual, but his sister and George Senator denied that. Nevertheless, I formed a definite opinion that there was more than just friendship between these two men. So he had two big strikes against him in conservative Dallas, Texas.

Senator stated that his roommate was a big-hearted man who had helped many people who were down on their luck. He characterized Ruby as very emotional and, although he did not appear to be very religious, took his faith very seriously, observing all the Orthodox Jewish holidays, particularly the memorial services for the dead. Senator also said that, while he had not been with Ruby on Saturday (the day after the assassination), he had heard that he sat around the Carousel Club and his sister's house for hours crying over the president's death. When Senator saw him early Sunday morning, Ruby seemed even more prostrated by grief, almost as if he was in shock. Senator confirmed the suspicion that Ruby had not planned to kill Oswald by relating that when he left the apartment to take money to one of his strippers, he took his dachshund, Sheba, with him. Senator did not see him again until after his arrest (*Warren Commission*).

Accompanied by Agent Moore, I interviewed Ruby for two hours in a small anteroom at the Dallas County Jail. Because Jack Ruby had obviously been interviewed previously, the lawyers on the Commission staff would give us an assignment sheet with a specific question they wanted answered, such as a question about Ruby's visit to Cuba. We would be assigned to ask him about this visit because we were trying to determine if he was part of a conspiracy and had been in Cuba receiving instructions. He was a gambler, and in those days the Mafia controlled the gambling in Cuba, so we were trying to find out if there was a Cuban connection. I vividly remember that interview because after we had our question answered, which would have been fairly quickly, we started talking. Ruby began talking about Kennedy and quickly became very emotional. He started out in a low tone of voice, then he began to sweat, and he worked himself up to a fever pitch of a speech. We just sat back and watched him. His killing Oswald was a classic example of what lawyers call *irresistible impulse*, the legal definition of which is: A criminal defendant is said to be relieved of criminal responsibility when his mental condition is such as to deprive him of his willpower to resist the impulse to commit the crime, despite his knowledge of whether the act is right or wrong.

Now, this is my opinion based on two interviews with Jack Ruby, but when somebody is emotionally ill to a degree that he loses control when something provokes him, it points to irresistible impulse. The more he talked, the more worked up and emotional he became, saying things like, "Oswald killed my idol; he ruined everything." By the time Ruby finished talking to me, he was wringing wet with sweat.

From my two interviews with him, I learned that Ruby didn't sleep at all after the assassination, he didn't eat, and he was totally devastated by Kennedy's death. And here they had the guy who killed his idol right in front of him, and he just snapped and pulled out a pistol and killed Oswald. Jack was known to all the police in Dallas, so they wouldn't have been at all suspicious of him. They wouldn't have checked him for weapons; it wasn't done in those days. The police departments were wide open; plus, Jack Ruby was well known and well liked by the police—they hung out at his club. Some people always questioned how Ruby could have gained access to the police department; in those days anyone could have been in there. There were no real security measures then. I can attest from experience because when I had been on numerous Secret Service investigations involving local police or sheriff departments, locals familiar with the departments would come in and sit down with the officials and just visit awhile. It was the accepted custom then. And everybody accompanying Oswald that day, when he was being moved, was either from the sheriff's office or the police department.

Special Agent in Charge of the Dallas Office, Forrest Sorrels, was with Inspector Kelley in the office of Assistant Chief of Police Charles Batchelor on the third floor of City Hall in Dallas at the time Oswald was shot, so they immediately went down to the basement to see what had happened. Because of that, they were able to interview Jack Ruby almost immediately. According to Sorrels, Ruby was in nothing but his shorts when they first saw him because his clothes had been taken from him. Sorrell's first question to Ruby was, "Jack, why?"

His answer indicated that it was a number of factors that tipped him over the edge. Ruby replied that on the morning that President Kennedy was assassinated, he had been to the office of the *Dallas Morning News* to place an ad for one of his clubs. When he heard the news about the president being shot, he canceled that ad and placed another announcing the closing of his clubs for the next three days. During this time he read that Mrs. Kennedy would have to come down to Dallas for the trial, and he thought, Why should she be brought down here and have to go through the ordeal on account of that no good $$##** Oswald? Then he had seen a letter to little Caroline Kennedy that moved him greatly. On Friday night, at his synagogue, a eulogy was read for the slain president, and, on top of that, his sister was in hysterics over the incident. "I guess I had worked myself up to a state of insanity where I had to show the world that a Jew had guts," Ruby explained. "I was afraid that Oswald might not get just punishment."

In addition to Ruby, we interviewed about a half-dozen witnesses at the Texas School Book Depository as well as a number of members of the Russian community in Dallas. Because Marina was Russian, the members of this large Russian community tried to help her learn English since Lee refused to teach her, and they often took food and milk by for the Oswalds' baby. We interviewed them to gain their impressions of Lee Harvey Oswald and how they had observed him in his treatment of Marina. We determined that he was physically abusive, often beating her and keeping her locked in their apartment. She couldn't drive, so she had no way of going anywhere, and he kept her a virtual prisoner. If she made too much contact with the outside world, he would beat her up. His refusal to teach her the English language was an example of how he controlled her. Without a command of the language, he could isolate her from all but the Russian-speaking community. We found the Russian community had been supportive of her, helping her get through difficult times. There was a lot of suspicion about the Russian community because in those Cold War days we were prone to see a Communist behind every tree. If you were Russian, you were automatically a Communist. When we interviewed them, there seemed to be nothing suspicious about them. They seemed pretty normal and grateful for the opportunities given them in America. I was impressed with their character and never felt there were any Communist spies in their group.

Two witnesses in particular from the Russian immigrants stand out in my mind. Ed Moore and I interviewed a woman by the name of Katherine "Kitty" Ford, a woman in her mid-thirties who had immigrated at the age of seventeen and was married to an American geologist. She had met the Oswalds the year before through some of her Russian friends. She had attempted to assist George Bouhe, who was especially close to Marina, in obtaining food, clothes, and a bed for the baby since Lee was without a job. Mrs. Ford said that Lee resented the help everyone gave Marina and the baby, and she said she always thought he was a "nut" because he seemed to blame others for his own problems. Mrs. Ford said she and her friends did not like Lee's preference of Russia over the United States and related that George Bouhe had seen several Communist pamphlets lying around the Oswald's apartment.

Lydia Dymitruk, also in her mid-thirties, who worked at Neiman Marcus in Fort Worth, not only gave us a clear picture of the relationship between Lee and Marina, but also explained why so many in the Russian community hated Lee, aside from his treatment of Marina and the baby. "We had each spent years struggling for our freedom, and we resented associating with an individual who had renounced his own freedom for Communism." She described Lee as hateful and cruel for neglecting the baby.

During the investigation, no reference to organized crime and Lee Harvey Oswald ever crossed *my* desk; all the focus was on the Russians and the Cubans. There were a lot of leads that we ran out, but we relied mostly on the FBI and CIA for those leads. One of the first things the KGB might do after the assassination was plant or create evidence that would point to someone—say, Castro—which would cause the United States to attack Cuba and give the Soviets the opportunity to defend the island. Conversely, if the prime minister of Israel was assassinated, the United States might try to make it look like Saddam Hussein did it. It was a game the intelligence communities played. On one occasion I did receive some clear evidence that was pointing to a country, and I immediately turned it over to the CIA, even though I had strong doubts about it. If a foreign government was going to assassinate someone, it would not leave evidence lying around, so if we found something, we automatically assumed it had been manufactured. The letter I intercepted was addressed to Lee Harvey Oswald, Mail Office, Dallas, Texas, USA. It was postmarked Havana, Cuba, on November 28, 1963, and was from a man named Pedro Charles. The body of the letter made it appear that Oswald was being paid by someone in Havana to "carry out their dream," for which he would be brought to Cuba, "the land of the free, of the beautiful women and the rich Habana tobacco." [See Exhibits 6-1—6-3.]

We turned the letter over to the CIA, who in turn sent it to the Warren Commission with several other "plants" other organizations had received. Obviously, none of us took these very seriously, but that's not to say we didn't pay attention to them.

Of the witnesses at the School Book Depository, the building where Lee Harvey Oswald worked and from where the shots were fired, Harold Norman became especially controversial. A twenty-five-year-old high school graduate, Norman finished his lunch at 12:15 p.m. and went to join his friends, Bonnie Ray Williams and James Jarman, on the fifth floor, looking out the window directly below the window from which Oswald fired the shots. I interviewed him, and my statement became the key piece of evidence in the Warren Commission investigation and was later subject to criticism by author Mark Lane in his book *Rush to Judgment*. He said I put words in Norman's mouth, and he alleged that I was part of the government conspiracy to cover up the real assassins. The implication was that I had created a statement for Mr. Norman to sign in which he pointed the finger at Lee Harvey Oswald, when the evidence might have been pointing somewhere else.

Not only would I never participate in a conspiracy, but if I were ever exposed to a government conspiracy, even if I was sworn to secrecy, I would probably call a press conference and announce the illegal activities that I refused to be a part of. I loved John Kennedy, and I certainly would not have been involved in covering up evidence about his death.

There is no evidence whatsoever indicating that anyone other than Lee Harvey Oswald killed John Kennedy. Many people have asked me over the years how I can be so sure that this is the truth, and I've always assured them that if any government had wanted to kill John Kennedy and done so, they could have covered it up better than using a weenie like Lee Harvey Oswald. They say, "Well, what about the Mafia?" Again, I say that the Mafia would not have used a small-time burlesque operator in Dallas, Texas, like Jack Ruby to knock off an assassin. I don't think the Mafia would have killed the President of the United States, no matter how much trouble Bobby Kennedy was giving them, because there was just too much risk involved. It would have meant the end of the Mafia.

In our training, we were aware of chemical assassination techniques such as ricin, which was so deadly that if you put a drop on the end of a pin and pricked the president's skin while shaking hands with him, he'd be dead in thirty seconds. In 1963, we didn't have the technology to be able to detect the presence of ricin; death would have appeared to be from a heart attack. Shellfish poison was another substance the CIA used frequently in those years, as was the poison from the Australian funnel-web spider. There are so many ways an assassination could have been done without it being detected. A few years after Kennedy's assassination, a Hungarian diplomat dropped dead on a London street corner for no apparent reason. His wife was suspicious and asked for an investigation, but nothing more than a minute pin hole on the man's skin was ever discovered. Then, after the fall of the Iron Curtain, evidence was uncovered in the KGB files that indicated one of their agents had killed this man, approaching him on the street and pricking him with the tip of an umbrella that had been coated with ricin, one of the undetectable poisons. That's the way you kill somebody.

Furthermore, if a foreign government had decided to take the president out, the assassin would likely have killed himself afterward rather than risk capture. Our own CIA agents were trained to use ricin or cyanide if they were captured. There was a huge controversy when Francis Gary Powers' U-2 plane was shot down over Russia in 1960 and he was captured without taking his own life with the cyanide-coated pin he wore. Countries were always afraid of their secrets being revealed if an agent was captured.

An interesting event occurred in 1990 or thereabouts. I had become acquainted with some former KGB agents through a friend in New York, and one of them was visiting in North America, presumably to attend the World Trade Conference in Canada. I received word that he wanted to get together with me and visit about the Kennedy days. I submitted his name to friends of mine in Washington, and they informed me he had been a senior KGB officer. We met at La Fontana restaurant, on 57th Street in Manhattan; he was accompanied by a friend, and I had a journalist friend with me. We drank a good amount of vodka, had dinner, and talked for about three hours. He related to me how curious the KGB was when Kennedy was killed and how suspicious they had been of Oswald. Astonishingly, he said they mourned Kennedy's death; that Kruschev had actually come to respect Kennedy, and they had no animosity toward him that would cause them to take his life. They were really surprised at his assassination and tried to find out who did it. They had never trusted Lee Oswald—they thought he was a nut and wondered why he was in Russia—and KGB files that were released in later years confirm how suspicious they were of Oswald.

Chapter 7
The Warren Commission Digs Deeper

EOPLE FREQUENTLY ASK ME about records and interviews from the assassination. Let me explain how the investigation was conducted. Inspector Kelly, who was heading the Secret Service investigation into the assassination, was communicating frequently, I assume, with the legal staff of the Warren Commission. Running concurrent with the Secret Service investigation was the investigation of the FBI, with both bureaus reporting directly to the Warren Commission. I assume that the staff in Washington was looking over the mountainous volume of paperwork that was being filed, and they would then flag items that needed clarifying or amplifying. There were many areas in which the two bureaus overlapped in the investigation. All of the agents working on the investigation had a mailbox at the temporary Secret Service office that we would check upon reporting for duty each morning. There would be slips of paper in the boxes with our assignment for the day detailed. Mine might say to go with Agent Art Blake and interview Jack Ruby or Harold Norman or Buell Frazier.

I would partner up with another agent, and we'd carry out our assignment. In those days, there were no portable tape recorders; they were reel-to-reel jobs that were as big as a suitcase. We didn't use them much except in the office, but it wasn't practical to round up 150 witnesses and bring them into our office in order to tape their statements. So we used notebooks. Standard procedure was to go to wherever the witness was, sit down with him in his home or office, and take notes. Afterward we would type out the statements on the portable manual typewriters we carried with us and have the witness read the typed statement and sign it, attesting to its accuracy. We didn't even have copiers, so for every statement I typed, I had to make five carbon copies—four for the Secret Service and one for me. As I reflect on that, I'm not sure any of us involved in the investigation was aware of the magnitude of the historical significance of the case. Speaking for myself, if I had it to do over again, I would keep better records; I would have spent a little more time with each witness. Unfortunately, we were under intense pressure to complete the investigation, so we may have rushed in some cases.

There was no video available to us, so we didn't get witnesses on videotape. Although it was a time of international crisis and we were rushed, in hindsight

I would have set up interview stations with sophisticated recording equipment, such as was available to us, and have the witnesses come in so that we would have their interviews on tape. No one did that, so these statements and reports were no better than the people preparing them. Because I'd been to law school, I knew a little bit about talking to witnesses, so I was very careful and cautious in taking these statements. I don't think there were any conspirators lurking out there, but I think we could have taken a little more time to disprove all the theories, which we did not do. Nevertheless, I think the Warren Commission investigators did as well as they could under the circumstances surrounding us in 1963.

There are many who were critical of the findings of the Warren Commission. I'm not one of those people; I have no doubt in my mind that Lee Harvey Oswald killed John Kennedy, for the reasons I've already outlined. I don't think anything else was involved. I spoke to more than 120 witnesses to the assassination, and not one of them—not one—ever said, "Gee, I think there were shots coming from the grassy knoll." Every witness I talked to *knew* exactly where the shots came from—they didn't hear any other shots. There's a great photo of the Secret Service follow-up car taken directly after the shots were fired. These trained, experienced agents on the left side of the follow-up car were looking up and to their right, directly at the upper floors of the Texas School Book Depository.

People get to believing something, and they let their imagination run away from them. I didn't hear anything about the grassy knoll until many, many years later. And it does make great press. I read one of the theories being put forth that said Kennedy was killed by a bullet accidentally discharged from the rifle of a Secret Service agent in the follow-up car. That's one of the most preposterous things I've ever heard.

I believe the Warren Commission reached the right conclusion, although in retrospect I think maybe a different approach should have been taken in how they reached it. They should have been a little more careful. And I'm saying that based on the criticism they received from the media and Congress. I don't have access to any of the evidence that was presented except that in which I participated. Speaking from my experience, every agent I knew who was working on the investigation was doing due diligence—was being very careful. Again, these were seasoned, experienced investigators and some of the best agents in the Secret Service.

Here's the way the investigation worked, at least from my perspective. I show that on Thursday, December 5, I was assigned to the Book Depository all day to take statements. At one o'clock, I was sent to interview Earline Roberts, who was the landlady at Oswald's boarding house. So rather than include that interview in my daily report, I would have to file the report of that interview separately, which would become part of the file. I kept copies of those interviews, but they were destroyed when my house in Little Rock was ravaged by fire ten years later, in 1973.

The residence where Oswald was living—alone, since he was separated from Marina—at the time of the assassination was at 1026 North Beckley in Oak Cliff; it was a rooming house owned by Mrs. A.C. Johnson, and Earline Roberts was the housekeeper. The house was a typical two-story structure built during the '40s; it had a porch across the front. It was a middle-class neighborhood, but typical of the times, when there weren't many apartment buildings, people who needed low-income housing lived in rooming houses. It was a reasonably well-kept neighborhood. Agent Art Blake (who's retired and lives in Albuquerque now) accompanied me to interview Mrs. Roberts, and when we went into the living room I noted that it was a clean, tidy house. Mrs. Roberts was probably in her late fifties, early sixties, rather matronly. She was very matter-of-fact when we interviewed her, and she seemed reasonably clear in her statements (although I found out later some of her statements were inconsistent). I had her sign a statement, which I wrote in longhand on a yellow legal pad because I was in her home and, for some reason, I was without my trusty typewriter. A clerk for the Warren Commission then typed my statement for clarity, and it was introduced into evidence as one of the Warren Commission's exhibits.

My copy of her statement reflects that she stated she was at home on Friday the twenty-second, in her living room, when a friend called her and told her the president had been shot, so she started watching it on television. At about one o'clock, Oswald entered the house in what she described as "unusual haste." She commented to him about his arrival, but he did not respond before entering his room. When he arrived, he was attired in just shirtsleeves, but when he left, three or four minutes later, he was zipping up a lightweight jacket that he had taken from his room. Mrs. Roberts said she looked out and saw him turn to the right and stand at the curb where there was a bus stop. She told me also that when Oswald came into the house and entered his room, a Dallas Police car pulled up to the curb in front of the house and honked two or three times. When she went to the door, she noticed that the car had the number 207 on it, but the car immediately pulled away without the officers saying anything. Mrs. Roberts resumed watching television. She gave this same statement to me, to FBI agents, and to others who interviewed her.

From her testimony to me, it was clear that Oswald did not get into a car when he left the house; he stood at the bus stop as if waiting for a bus. During the interview, I drew an outline of Oswald's room, which became an exhibit. I described it as being five feet by twelve feet, and to enter the room, you went through French doors. It was a very small room, with a twin bed, a little dresser, and a wardrobe cabinet.

In reconstructing Oswald's movements, we interviewed those in the School Book Depository who knew Oswald, as well as others with whom he came in contact that day. We determined that, after shooting the president, Oswald walked from the window, across the sixth floor area, hid the weapon, walked to the stairs, went down the stairs to the lunchroom on the second floor, spent approximately thirty seconds in the lunchroom, and continued down the stairs and out the front door. This took approximately five minutes. Dallas patrolman M.L. Baker was riding police escort for the motorcade when he heard the shots. He immediately decided they had come from the building on the northwest corner of Elm and Houston. He jumped off his motorcycle and ran inside the building, where he saw several people standing around. Roy Truly stepped forward and identified himself as the manager of the building and offered to accompany the patrolman upstairs. They took the stairway up to the second floor and were preparing to climb to the third floor when Truly realized the patrolman was not following him. He turned and found that the officer was standing near the entrance to the lunchroom with his weapon drawn. Just inside the lunchroom, Lee Oswald was standing with the officer facing him. The officer asked Truly if he knew the man, and he told him that Oswald worked in the building. With that, the officer let Oswald go and continued upward with Truly.

Oswald then walked several blocks from the Book Depository, boarded a bus, and traveled some six blocks to a taxi stand at Jackson and Lamar, where he left the bus. He hailed a taxi, which he instructed to drop him in the 500 block of North Beckley Street, less than a half-mile from his boarding house. He then walked the rest of the way to his rooming house. All this took about a half-hour. Apparently Oswald came to the rooming house for the purpose of recovering the firearm he kept concealed there. Then he stood for a short time at the bus stop out front before he left. We don't know why he left the bus stop and began walking, but at some point after he left the bus stop, a Dallas police officer, Officer J.D. Tippit, spotted him walking. He may have been acting suspiciously and he fit the description of the assassin, so Tippit probably decided to stop him and question him in the 400 block of East 10th Street.

It appears that Tippit stopped Oswald, who leaned in the officer's open passenger-side window and said something to him. Tippit got out of his car and started to walk around the left front side of the car, when Oswald backed up toward the sidewalk, pulled his pistol, shot three times, and killed the officer. When Tippit's body was found, it was lying at the left front of his patrol car, and a jacket found near the crime scene fit the description of the one Oswald was wearing when he left the boarding house. The Dallas police received a call from a citizen using a police radio at 1:17 p.m. that an officer had been shot.

Oswald then ran to the Texas Theatre on West Jefferson and entered the theatre in an attempt to hide and get away from the police. But there were several witnesses who saw him shoot the officer, cross the street, and go in a certain direction, and they were able to provide this information to the police who arrived at the scene of the Tippit shooting. The police surrounded and then entered the theatre, turned on the house lights, and identified Oswald sitting near a woman and two children. Oswald drew his pistol, saying, "I guess this is it." He attempted to shoot at the policemen, but one of the officers involved in the scuffle apparently got his thumb between the trigger and the firing mechanism and was able to jam Oswald's pistol before a shot was fired. Several other officers had arrived by this time, and they were able to wrestle the gun away from him, but he was still struggling and lashing out at the officers. The first officer who confronted him, I believe his name was McDonald, was hailed as something of a hero. In the photo taken when Ruby killed Oswald, there is an obvious cut above Oswald's left eye. He apparently received the cut during the scuffle at the theatre. The officers eventually subdued, arrested, and took Oswald to the jail at the Dallas City Hall.

My interviews with Harold Norman and Buell Wesley Frazier, both employees of the School Book Depository, were two of the most significant I conducted. Norman, along with his friends, was at the window of the room directly below Oswald's sixth-floor perch when the shots were fired. He testified that he clearly heard the spent shell casings hit the floor directly above him, he heard the bolt action on the rifle, and he saw dust particles fall from the ceiling above him, indicating that someone was firing from the room on the sixth floor. At that time, I had not been to the upper floor of the building, so I didn't know yet that there were cracks in the ceiling, which is why Norman saw dust particles falling.

In his book *Rush to Judgment*, Mark Lane implies that I put words in Harold Norman's mouth. However, in a later statement to CBS-TV, Norman said that *Lane* actually put words in *his* (Norman's) mouth. Norman confirmed the statement he gave me.

In taking his official statement, I asked him, "Do you remember making this exact statement: 'Just after the president passed by, I heard a shot and several seconds later, I heard two more shots.'?" Norman told me, "Yes. I heard three shots." I then asked, "Mr. Norman, can you tell me the order of the shots? Was it bang-bang-bang or was it bang—bang—bang?"

He answered, "I heard a shot, and then later I heard two more shots."

"How much later did you hear the other two shots?"

Art Blake and I continued interrogating him to get the conclusion that he heard a shot, then there was a pause and seconds went by, then he heard two more shots. We had to draw it out of him, but that was his description. In my report I show that Norman said, "I knew the shots came from directly above me, and I could hear the expended cartridges fall to the floor." Chances are he didn't say the words "expended cartridges," because that was not how he spoke. We were taught certain language in the military and law enforcement, and I probably substituted that phrase in typing my report. He probably said something more like, "I heard the empty shells hit the floor. I could also hear the bolt action of the rifle."

The hardest thing about taking a statement from a witness without using a tape recorder is to try to convert the statement into something meaningful while retaining the witness's own words. Harold Norman was a high school graduate; I had attended law school, so my vocabulary was probably somewhat broader than his, and I would have used some legalese that he would not have employed. We took the information he volunteered to us, put it down on paper, and the end result comprised his statement.

When we went in to talk with Harold Norman, Art Blake and I had no idea what he might have already said to others. We were going into the interview cold. The witnesses from the School Book Depository were eager to tell their stories. They had seen and heard things at the assassination that they wanted everyone to know. We hardly had to ask them anything because they were quick to volunteer what had taken place there. They all had a clear recollection of what happened, and they told their stories clearly and concisely. Harold Norman came into the interview, sat down, and we asked him, "Tell us what you observed."

Immediately he said, "We were down here. We heard the shots and we heard the shells hit the floor." I don't think he or any of the other witnesses realized how vital this information was; they just wanted to help. That's the kind of people they were. They were sincere witnesses, and they were not seeking publicity like some later witnesses. They were honest, humble guys. We took their statement on December 4, less than two weeks after the assassination, so the events were clear in their minds. It didn't take encouragement, and it didn't take classic interrogation techniques. It took me longer to prepare their statements than it did for them to tell their story. We would have spoken to each of the witnesses individually; we did not interview them in the presence of each other. I had absolutely no way of knowing at the time that these witnesses would be among the most important witnesses in the account of the president's assassination.

Buell Wesley Frazier was the young man who drove Oswald to work on the morning of November 22nd. He lived with his sister in a house near Ruth Paine in Irving. Ruth Paine was a friend of Marina's who had recommended to Oswald that he try for the job at the Book Depository. She was a sympathizer to the Russian community and helped the immigrants. Marina and the girls were staying at her house in Irving, between Dallas and Fort Worth, and Oswald usually caught a ride with Frazier, who also worked at the Book Depository, to Irving on Friday and returned with him on Monday morning.

I took a full written statement from Frazier on December 5. His statement also became an important part of the evidence in the investigation. Lee was learning to drive and, according to Frazier, had just taken his driver's test. It was very unusual, according to Frazier, when Oswald approached him on Thursday, the twenty-first, to ask if he could ride home with him that afternoon and return with him Friday morning. Since he had never gone to Irving during the week before, by way of explanation Oswald said he had to pick up some curtain rods for his apartment. Frazier said he was unaware at the time that Oswald's furnished room came complete with curtains already at the window. Oswald told Frazier he was not going back to Irving on Friday. To the best of Frazier's recollection, he said

Oswald approached him a few minutes after both had learned, from the map on the front page of the afternoon *Times Herald*, that Friday's parade would pass the warehouse. Frazier said that when Lee came over to his sister's house at 7:20 on Friday morning, he had a package under his arm. He described the package as being approximately two feet in length and was a brown paper sack, so the contents could not be seen. Lee told him it was curtain rods, but we know from later evidence that Lee had gone to Ruth Paine's to get his rifle. Ruth knew that Oswald was storing a gun in her garage, along with several other items, and she said he had gone out that morning and had been looking through his stuff. Oswald's palm print was found on the rifle that was found on the sixth floor, and later we were able to obtain a photo with him holding that very rifle.

I've spoken of Oswald's mental condition, but I think it's important to point out that Oswald was, among other things, paranoid. Experts say that in the end, the paranoiac loses all sense of reality. He is overpowered by a monstrous feeling of personal resentment and a blind craving for revenge. No one can predict what will trigger the catastrophe in any given case. But we now know that the firestorm in Lee Oswald's head ignited on the evening of Thursday, November 21, 1963 (Manchester, p. 93).

At some point during the assassination investigation, I concluded it was John Kennedy's destiny to die in Dallas that November day in 1963. Consider this:

1. Had the rain continued or even threatened to continue, the bubbletop would have remained on the car, and, in my opinion, though not bulletproof, it would have been sufficient to alter the course of the bullets.

2. Everyone in the Secret Service admired and respected President Kennedy and looked upon him as a friend. His friendship with the agents may have been his downfall. Why? What might have happened if two agents had been on the running board of the presidential limo? In reenacting the assassination later, it was demonstrated that the view through Oswald's rifle scope clearly shows that the agents would have created such an obstruction that his shot would be much more difficult. When he missed the first shot, the agents were close enough to the president that they would have sprung into the car and covered the president's body to protect him. However, while the relationship between the president and his agents *may* have contributed to his death, I am not critical of the agents. Had I been there that day, I would most certainly have followed the president's command. I remember a great illustration of how different the situation can be if you're not the president's friend. During Richard Nixon's presidency, the president was being driven to a meeting by the same William Greer who was at the wheel of Kennedy's limo in Dallas, and they were running late. Sitting in the jump seat directly in front of President Nixon was Richard Keiser, White House agent in charge. The president instructed Agent Greer to stop the car in order for him to greet some passersby on the street. Because it was a duty of the Secret Service to keep the president on schedule, Greer turned to

his supervisor, Agent Keiser, and asked him if he should stop. Keiser countered his commander's instructions and told Greer *not* to stop. That did not please Nixon, so he again told Keiser to stop the car. Agent Keiser told the president they were behind schedule and they were not stopping, and they didn't.

3. Lee Harvey Oswald just happened to have a job in a building by which the motorcade would pass. From the evidence I witnessed, which includes conversations with acquaintances of Oswald, his wife, Marina, his fellow workers, and his brother, Robert, *I do not believe Oswald had planned this assassination prior to the motorcade route being announced.* Oswald had resented authority throughout his life. He had failed at most things most people succeed at routinely. He was unsuccessful at school, had few if any friends (he was described by everyone as a loner), he could not hold a job, he failed in the Marines, and, finally, he failed at the only thing he might have made a success—his marriage. He isolated his wife and children and resented assistance Marina received from the Russian community in the Dallas area. He physically abused his wife on numerous occasions until she moved in with Ruth Paine. Lee kept a room in a Dallas boardinghouse and visited Marina on some weekends, but they continued to quarrel. Immediately prior to the assassination, they quarreled over the phone, and it was after their last quarrel that the president's motorcade route was announced. He surprised Marina and Ruth Paine by showing up at Ruth's house on Thursday night. Marina remained angry with Lee on this visit. He pleaded with her to return to Dallas with him; he was lonely and wanted her to move back in with him. However, Marina remained distant, often refusing to talk to him. Lee went to bed early—alone—and did not talk to Marina until the next morning. As he was leaving for work, he simply told her good-bye without giving her his usual good-bye kiss. It is my opinion that Oswald now realized that his marriage had also failed, he was now all alone in the world, and, in his anger and bitterness, he felt he must lash out and prove to the world that Lee Harvey Oswald was somebody and deserved to be respected and recognized. His actions weren't about politics or philosophy; they were to gain notoriety.

Let me emphasize again that I do not believe Oswald planned on killing Kennedy until just a day or two before November 22. Several indications led me to that conclusion. First, he did not go to visit Marina the weekend prior to the assassination, as was his usual routine, but instead stayed in Dallas to take the test for his drivers' license. If he had been planning to shoot the president, he would have taken the rifle that was stored in Ruth Paine's garage during his regularly scheduled weekend visit. As it was, he made a special, unscheduled trip to Ruth Paine's the very night before the assassination, just a couple of days after the motorcade route had been announced, in order to obtain the rifle to carry out his hastily conceived plan.

Secondly, he had made an attempt on a political figure before, but it was carefully planned months in advance. On April 10, 1963, just seven months prior to

Kennedy's assassination, Oswald, angered over being dismissed from his job at a photography business, attempted to assassinate Major Gen. Edwin Walker, the outspoken ultraconservative who frequently advocated his views in the Dallas media. But, unlike the Kennedy assassination, his attempt on Walker was something he had planned very carefully; however, his shot missed Walker. All through February and March, he carefully prepared his strike on Walker. According to Marina, he was in a surly mood through all of February and grew progressively more violent (Mailer, p. 492). In fact, his beatings of Marina had become more frequent and more fierce. His eyes were filled with hate . . . as if Marina were the author of every slight he had ever suffered and he was bent on wiping her out (ibid.).

Early in March, when he knew Walker was away on a five-week trip, Oswald began reconnaissance on Walker's home, photographing the backyard and rear of the house. Then he ordered a rifle from Klein's Sporting Goods in Chicago (the rifle that would become the most infamous weapon in American history). He kept a journal with the results of each reconnaissance of Walker's house, including bus routes near his target. He even buried the rifle near some railroad tracks close to Walker's Turtle Creek Boulevard residence a day or two before the General's return (ibid.).

Prior to leaving his residence to try to shoot General Walker, Oswald left Marina a note with instructions on what to do if he failed to return. Marina learned of his failed attempt on Walker's life upon Lee's return home. If he had thought to impress her, he was sadly mistaken. Two weeks later, he left for New Orleans to find a job, and Marina moved in with Ruth Paine (Manchester, p. 97).

On Friday morning, November 22, Oswald left the Paine home with his rifle before Marina awoke. But he left his wedding ring on the dresser in their room, and he placed his wallet containing $187 in the dresser drawer. Just as in the Walker case, Lee did not expect to return. I say that the assassination had nothing to do with political or philosophical convictions because President Kennedy was a Democrat who espoused liberal causes, and General Walker was a forceful voice for extreme conservative causes. The one thing they had in common was that they represented the authority that Oswald appeared to resent and had resented for most of his life. I also believe that had Oswald not died, he would have ultimately stood up proudly and proclaimed his guilt with defiance.

William Manchester makes an excellent point about Oswald: "Madness is not a virus. It does not strike all at once. Lee Oswald's disease had been in process all his life. Unquestionably his mother had been a far greater influence in his life than either Marina or Ruth. They were dealing with an abnormal man whose snarl of problems had existed long before either of them met him" (ibid., p. 104).

I did not render a judgment at all about Oswald, Jack Ruby, or any members of the Oswald family. In fact, I was very considerate of them, and I spent a great deal of time with Marina. At the end of her testimony before the Warren Commission, when we were separating for the last time, she asked if I would have my picture made with her. She made an extra one and wrote on the back before giving it to me. I placed so little significance on it that thirty years later I found the photo in a book, where I had been using it as a bookmark. I didn't get emotionally involved or judgmental, nor do I remember any of the other agents doing so—certainly none that I worked with. Our detachment may have been part of our training, and I should credit Roy Letteer, who was responsible for most of my training. He always instilled in me that when I was doing a job, it was not up to me to judge anyone, criminal or not; my job was simply to present the facts and keep my opinions to myself. And I pretty much did that. This is the first time in forty-two years that I have gone on record with my opinion on the assassination. During the investigation, there was such a challenge to gather the facts accurately that we simply didn't attach any emotion to it; we just did our job. While I may not have been aware at the time of the historical significance of what I was doing, I realized that this was a very important investigation. Although we've come under a lot of criticism for the way the investigation was handled, the Secret Service did a diligent job in trying to uncover any lead that might help prove who the assassin was. While I was involved in the investigation, I was open-minded. If I found anything in all the interviews I conducted, I jumped right on it. We all followed up every lead we received, no matter how far-fetched it may have been.

There was never any record that the Secret Service knew anything about Lee Harvey Oswald being a threat in Dallas. His name did not appear in any of our reports before the assassination. However, the FBI *did* have him under active surveillance. In fact, Marina testified that the FBI visited her husband on numerous occasions between the time they returned to the States from Russia and the day he shot the president. Author William Manchester had especially harsh criticism of the FBI:

> Inasmuch as the Bureau's handbook charged agents to be on the alert for information "indicating the possibility of an attempt against the person or safety of the president," one might have assumed that the seventy-five-man FBI office in Dallas would have relayed word of Oswald's presence to the five-man Secret Service office there. Nothing of the sort happened. His file was in the hands of FBI Agent James P. Hosty Jr., a husky, thirty-five-year-old Notre Dame graduate and an outspoken admirer of John F. Kennedy. Since November 4, 1963, Hosty had known that Oswald was employed as a laborer in the Texas School Book Depository at the corner of Houston and Elm streets. This warehouse provided the deadliest sniper's roost on the Presidential motorcade route, because the motorcade was scheduled to first zig and then zag directly beneath the windows. A gunman could size up the President's car as it approached the building from the front, wait while it pivoted sharply at his feet, and fire as it crept

slowly out of the turn to his right. Hosty, however, didn't make the connection. He had received no official notification of the route, and when local newspapers published a map of it, his sole concern was whether or not Jim Hosty could catch a glimpse of Kennedy (p. 32).

It is especially worth noting that in those days there was a great deal of tension between the FBI and the Secret Service, and both agencies later came under some criticism from the Warren Commission for their failure to share information. There was little to no cooperation between the two agencies, but the FBI didn't cooperate with anyone in those years. J. Edgar Hoover placed enormous restrictions on his agents to not cooperate with other agencies, even local police forces. Also, in 1963 it was not a federal crime to kill the president, so the FBI would not have been involved in any advance preparation for presidential visits. But I can assure you that if the Secret Service had known about Lee Harvey Oswald, we would have placed him under surveillance. And certainly if we had known about him working in a building that was on the parade route, we would have either had him under surveillance or we would have just picked him up and detained him until the president left Dallas. We would have interfered with his ability to carry out his intentions, even if we had to stand behind him if he were watching the motorcade from the sidewalk. Things were different in 1963; you could detain people without having a really good reason, other than they were considered a threat to the safety of the president. You'd pick up suspects, lock them up, and keep them out of harm's way until after the president had departed the city. You can't do that anymore. I can tell you that, back then, every person the Secret Service was aware of who might have posed a threat to the president would have been investigated and placed under surveillance.

We had just such an incident during the president's visit to Arkansas. There was a guy in a nearby town we considered to be a threat. We called the local sheriff and asked him to keep the man under surveillance twenty-four hours a day. This particular man never even left his house, but if he had, the sheriff's office would have notified the Secret Service, and the man would have been watched the entire time. If he had gone anywhere near Little Rock, he would have been detained.

The Warren Commission found "no evidence" of any connection between the crime of Lee Harvey Oswald and the city's "general atmosphere of hate." I do disagree with this finding. I think a radical extremist or mentally dysfunctional person looks for encouragement, support, or justification for his act. Around the time of the Oklahoma City bombing, in 1995, I hosted a dinner party at my home, and I noticed how much of the conversation was dominated by general disgruntlement with the government. Although most people love to rag on the IRS for imposing high taxes, most of my guests, who were successful business executives, were especially critical of the government's using their money to support wasteful practices. Many damned the FBI for employing excessive and arrogant force at Ruby Ridge and Waco. Perhaps the confessed bomber of the Murrah Federal Building in Oklahoma City, Timothy McVeigh, overheard conversations similar to these in my home and interpreted the comments to be anti-government, which justified his military action. It's simple human behavior in people who are about to undertake an act of wrongdoing to look for, in their perverted minds, anything that in some way justifies their illicit activities.

That evening made me reflect, not for the first time, about how much the attitude had changed toward authority since 1963. Even in Dallas at that time, FBI and Secret Service agents were respected and looked up to. As a Secret Service agent, I felt members of the community were respectful of my position and regarded me as someone whose position they admired. Oswald, the failure, had a fantasy of himself being a hero. For weeks, as his failed life was reaching a climax, the militant anti-Kennedy atmosphere in Dallas was feeding that fantasy by creating an environment in which it would appear that anyone killing Kennedy would be a hero in the eyes of the conservative Dallas anti-everything element. I'm not suggesting that if Dallas citizenry had conveyed a God-loving atmosphere, it would have prevented Kennedy's assassination; however, to say the totally negative press, with its anti-Kennedy campaign, didn't have some influence on a psychopath such as Lee Harvey Oswald is preposterous (Exhibit 1).

Another factor to consider is the competition that existed between the Secret Service and the FBI. There has been criticism of the FBI, especially Agent Hosty for mishandling the Oswald file. J. Edgar Hoover reportedly reprimanded as many as seventeen agents for their mishandling of the pre-assassination investigation of Oswald. The real FBI agent who should have been punished by removal from office was the pompous and arrogant J. Edgar Hoover. His jealousy of other agencies' jurisdiction, such as the Secret Service, resulted in his general policy not to cooperate with any of these competitors (as he saw them). If, as a Secret Service agent, I had wanted any information from the FBI, it would have been necessary for me to have a close, personal relationship with an FBI agent, and then anything he told me would have been in the strictest confidence. If Hoover had known an agent was talking, he would have been in deep trouble.

The Secret Service and the FBI generally got along well if we provided them with everything we knew, and we in turn received nothing from them. Robert K. Ressler, a retired FBI agent, in his book *Whoever Fights Monsters*, states, "There was what FBI insiders called a one-way street in operation; the FBI took from other law-enforcement agencies, but gave back nothing—ever" (p. 25). There was no real reason for the professional jealousy that existed between the two agencies; however, it was common knowledge that Hoover resented the Secret Service having jurisdiction over the president's security. We knew not to rely on Hoover's cooperation and that the FBI, under his orders, would do anything to make the Secret Service look bad. If Hoover had an ongoing FBI policy of cooperation between agencies, then Agent James Hosty would have provided Oswald's name to the Secret Service in Dallas. This is not hindsight—on other occasions, subjects with an emotional make-up similar to Oswald's were considered risks by the Secret Service. If Oswald's file had come across the desk of any Secret Service agent, that agent would have considered Oswald a threat and taken appropriate action. Hosty followed a Hoover rule, which was that the FBI had no responsibility to notify other law enforcement agencies about anything contained in their files. What if Hoover's obsession with autonomy and absolute power had not gotten the best of him and, in the interest of presidential security, he had instilled communication and cooperation with the Secret Service? A simple, unselfish policy by Hoover might have altered history.

A dedicated agent such as James Hosty, who was punished by Hoover to divert his own responsibility in the matter, should not have to shoulder any blame in this tragedy.

Late in December 1963, we were released; I returned to Arkansas for the Christmas holidays, and then returned to Dallas. The investigation was pretty much complete as far as the Secret Service was concerned, so I was assigned to accompany the witnesses to Washington to testify before the Warren Commission. I accompanied both Marina and Marguerite Oswald. We stayed at the Willard Hotel during these trips—the Oswalds in a suite with the agents posted outside the door. The suite consisted of a living room and a bedroom. The old Willard Hotel was heated by radiators, and the radiators in the corridors were all down by the elevators. So it was cold in the hallway outside the suite. Whenever I would come on duty—whatever shift I was on—Marina would come out and talk with me. She would invite me in, but I would not go into the suite.

My time with Marina was pleasant; she was very nice to me and we got along well. I never observed any long crying spells; she was unemotional about everything. Lee was violent to her; she didn't love this guy. She was trying to get away from him. We did have some conversation about the president's death—although not about whether Lee did it—but I remember her being remorseful about it. My opinion was that she deeply regretted the loss of Kennedy. She never offered any defense of Lee's conduct, but she did not express to me any hatred of him.

Marguerite, on the other hand, was defensive of Lee. She was a person of unsettled emotions. I think she may have been mentally disturbed because she was extreme about everything. I had a lot of conversations with her—I didn't have any choice—during which she was eager to talk. She rambled all the time and blamed others for everything. I did not like her, and although I treated her in a professional manner, I did not like being around her at all. I tried to avoid her whenever possible, which was not easy. She was very emotional, and always blaming others for mistreating her and Lee; she felt she had been abused all her life and blamed society for it. For years afterward, when anyone would ask me about Lee Oswald, my standard reply was, "Well, if you just knew his mother, you'd understand why Lee had been in psychiatric care during his childhood." I tried to figure out why

Robert was so different. It may have been that because his father was around during Robert's first five years, and he experienced a more stable home environment in those years, his character could have been set during that time; he never lived alone with Marguerite like Lee did. This could be the reason Robert was so normal. It was my opinion that Robert had accepted the fact that Lee had killed the president; he didn't offer any defense at all. He was a decent man, a good American, and he had a good family. I was very impressed with Robert Oswald.

In the forty-plus years since Dallas, I have never had even a one-sentence conversation about the Oswalds—this is the first time I've talked about them. Until now I've never been able to read any of the books about that time or watch any of the news shows dealing with the assassination. When I left the Secret Service, I blocked it out of my mind. I still can't talk about it without getting emotional. I suppose part of the reason is because that's just my make-up. I don't live beyond today—I don't go back and revisit things. I did go back on the twenty-fifth anniversary of the assassination to be interviewed by a TV station on the site where the president spoke in Little Rock, and I could hardly speak about it, I became so choked up.

It would probably be good for me to talk about it now. But as you get older you get more sentimental, so the memory of those events becomes even more painful as time passes. A friend asked me to take him to the Texas School Book Depository about five years ago. It was one of the most difficult things I've ever done. I couldn't watch the videos of the motorcade; I had to step outside. Several years ago, an agent I knew was retiring and he came by and talked with me. He had served under Nixon, and although he wasn't particularly fond of him, he said he became very emotional when Nixon died—he mourned him like he had lost a member of his family. I told him I had felt the same way when Jackie died.

There's an unusual bond an agent has with his protectee. I was in Washington, at the Madison Hotel, when President Johnson died, and I remember sitting in the hotel while his funeral was being conducted half a block away, and it really affected me. I was at home by myself when John Jr. was killed. I suffered so much through that, that I didn't leave the house for several days. I had been in New York the December prior to his death with my daughters, Joanna and Julia, and son-in-law Stuart, and we saw John at the theatre. The girls tried to get me to go up and say something to him, but I didn't want to intrude, so I didn't. I wish now I had gone up and said, "Hey, I served with your dad, and was proud to have done so. I loved him and just wanted to tell you so."

The only two people I've met on this planet that I feel God has given such an incredible gift of magnetism are John Kennedy and Billy Graham. If you were in a room that was totally dark and there was no one else in the room except John Kennedy—or Billy Graham—you would feel him in that room. Their magnetism was that strong. I've never seen anything like the way Kennedy could charm his way out of a situation or attract adversaries to him. He could go into a hostile crowd and have them eating out of his hand by the time he left. He had a magic about him that no one else in the family had.

When the investigation was finished and when all the evidence was put to rest, I felt I understood Lee Harvey Oswald. His home life was one of men coming and going all the time, no stability with parents, and a child pretty much being shoved aside. The things that I've taken for granted all my life—good home, good parents, good schools, good friends—were not there for him. He did not have a solid foundation. He was only twenty-four when he killed the president.

When I think back on what we might have done differently, I can find no real criticism about my conduct or that of the other agents in Dallas. No one sat us down and briefed us and said, "Now, we've got to get Lee Oswald." We were independent thinkers, and we were given assignments with no specific instructions other than to go out and get the facts. These agents were the best guys the Secret Service had: Ed Moore, from Miami; Maurice Miller, from Memphis, who was an old friend and is now deceased, but became agent-in-charge in San Antonio; Elmer Moore, from the West Coast; Art Blake, a wonderful investigator who was even-tempered and intelligent. These guys were the best, and I was in awe of their talents. None of them would ever have done anything improper. We were all patriotic, flag-waving, regular guys. And our president—the man we worked for and loved—had been killed. I look at it now and realize I have never had enough appreciation for participating in such a historical event.

After the investigation was over and the Secret Service and FBI had come under intense scrutiny for their actions surrounding the assassination, I had the opportunity to put down on paper my observations and recommendations about some of the ways the Secret Service might amend their procedures. That report read, in part:

> After the assassin fired into the motorcade killing the President, the automobiles all sped in the direction of the hospital. As the President's car sped away, the follow-up car naturally followed, leaving the scene of the crime completely unattended by Secret Service agents. Immediately after the shots were fired, one Dallas motorcycle patrolman entered the Texas School Book Depository building, from which the shots were fired, and attempted to locate and apprehend the assassin. As he entered the building alone, he was unable to secure and search it successfully, and as a result, the assassin subsequently walked out.

> In this particular case, I think the Secret Service should have had agents on the scene directing and coordinating the search and capture of the assassin. The result may very well have been that two or three of our agents would have secured the building and called for help from the city police as they arrived; therefore, Lee Harvey Oswald would have been trapped in the building. Another result of such action would be having

our own agents involved in the investigation from the very beginning until the finish. These agents that remain at the scene of the crime would stay with the local authorities until the investigation was completed. I realize we would technically be outside our jurisdiction, but, in my opinion, regardless of whether or not his bullet struck, the escaped assassin is a threat to our security, and it would be to our advantage for some of our agents to remain at the scene and insure his capture. I personally feel that it is our responsibility to take charge and assist and coordinate such an investigation instantaneous to the assassination or attempt.

In order to carry out such a plan, our motorcade would have to include a second follow-up car, which would respond to the Dallas situation by stopping, and [agents] immediately proceeding on foot to the building, surrounding and securing it. They would take command of the situation and use local forces as they arrived. The immediate plan at Dallas would have been to close off the Depository Building to conduct their search and investigation. The agents in this second follow-up car could also direct the remainder of the motorcade to an alternate route. This car should contain at least two agents and two local detectives.

From my insight in the circumstances immediately following the assassination of President Kennedy, we would have had much greater success in catching Oswald, interviewing eye witnesses at the scene, and in gathering the evidence of the crime had we had agents remain.

I also prepared a document I titled "Suggested Amendment to Presidential Protection in Motorcades." It read, in part:

In reflection on events that transpired at Dallas on November 22, 1963, and subsequent inquiries, no doubt many suggestions and evaluations have been made to help prevent a recurrence of such events and to take proper counteraction should such events be duplicated. In this vein, I offer this suggestion:

Place a ranking SS agent and a field agent in the first car of the motorcade behind the press party that can stop the remainder of the motorcade, if by reason of an emergency such as in Dallas it becomes necessary to evacuate the President and party.

The advance SA, during advance, would identify the Agent or Agents so assigned to the cooperating local law enforcement people. The assignment of this Agent or Agents would be to halt the remainder of the motorcade when an emergency developed. He/they would dismount and take charge of the scene jointly with local authority on an emergency basis leaving the presidential party with follow-up car free to depart.

The purpose of this suggestion is to have SS personnel on the scene from the inception of an incident and to remain there throughout subsequent events that may occur to provide leadership, assistance, direction and procure whatever facts may be available for later evaluation . . . . It is not always possible on the scene and at that point to form a clear-cut dividing line of where Presidential protection duties end, and in such a case it cannot be doubted that overreaction in emergency is better than too little or incomplete action. In retrospect, it appears that if such a plan as here suggested had been available in Dallas, the accused assassin may have been captured in the Book Depository before fleeing the scene. In such an event, he would have been under joint custody and control from the virtual inception of the crime.

For thirty-eight years, I never watched anything about Kennedy on television, nor did I read most of the huge volume of books written about Kennedy, in spite of the fact that I own many of them. Just recently, I've tried to watch a couple of programs and have not been able to get through them without being overcome emotionally. I think part of the reason we didn't break down during all the ceremonies and the investigation was a result of our military training. Also, the Secret Service trains its agents to be professional at all times. After the movie *Saving Private Ryan* was released, I saw interview after interview with World War II veterans and survivors of the Normandy invasion who said they had never talked about D-Day, even to their families. I understand that. You don't want to talk about it. When soldiers hit the beach at Normandy, and their best buddy got his brains blown out beside them, that's not something they want to talk about and remember.

I know Clint Hill suffered enormously, as I know Win Lawson did. Win is one of the nicest human beings in the world, but he happened to be on duty at the wrong time. He was greatly loved within the Secret Service, and he has maintained a strong Christian faith. I think that helped get him through it. I truly can't think of a better agent. I remember that after we had returned to Washington from the Little Rock trip, President Kennedy called Win into his office and thanked him and congratulated him on the success of that trip. I think the fact that he was chosen to advance the Dallas trip was a clear indication of the confidence the Service had in him. We knew about the problems in Dallas. The fact that he drew that assignment spoke volumes about the esteem in which Jerry Behn held Win.

Then it was over. All the testimony had been given; all the facts laid out for history. The judgment was rendered. Lee Harvey Oswald, acting alone, killed John F. Kennedy. I returned to Little Rock and to my regular duties, but I would never be the same again. I stayed in the Secret Service another year, spending much of that time traveling around the country with Lyndon Johnson as he ran for election. But the events of November 22, 1963, were indelibly stamped on my heart—and mind—forever.

Chapter 8
Why Kennedy's Death Was a Tragedy

T HERE ARE SO MANY REASONS President Kennedy's death was a tragedy; however, we will never know for sure how history would have been different if he had not been killed. I do know from personal experience and observation that his youthful vigor and vision were such an enlightenment compared to the elder statesmen such as Eisenhower, Truman, and Roosevelt. The youth of America had a new spirit. While standing by Kennedy's casket at the Capitol rotunda, I listened to young America pass by with tears streaming down their cheeks as they talked of the fact that their hopes for a new America had been crushed. I shared that same hope and excitement prior to Kennedy's death and mourned his loss, fearful that a bright and progressive future was now lost forever.

One of the most significant changes in history could possibly have come in America's policy in Vietnam. Kennedy had inherited the Bay of Pigs and Vietnam from Eisenhower, and his experience with the Bay of Pigs disaster had created a distrust for the military and, especially, the CIA. We know the CIA was perhaps even more involved in influencing U.S. policy on Vietnam than was the military. Secret Service agents were not privy to White House policy discussions, but senior agents were frequently in a position to know what was being discussed. The behind-the-scenes whispers at the time indicated that Kennedy was, at best, discouraged by the situation in Vietnam and had already ordered a thousand military advisors to return from South Vietnam and planned future reductions. After his death, it was, in fact, revealed that he planned a complete withdrawal from South Vietnam by 1965. President Kennedy approached Vietnam as a political problem. Many of the White House staffers were buzzing with excitement and admiration for Kennedy's courage in resisting the CIA and the military in his plans to pull out of Vietnam.

On numerous occasions over the years since his assassination, I have been asked what I consider to be the greatest loss from Kennedy's death. My answer has always been the same—that thousands of young American lives would most likely not have been sacrificed for such a hopeless political cause if Kennedy had lived.

Special advisor to President Kennedy Arthur Schlesinger Jr. wrote:

This was a problem Kennedy approached with well-ingrained doubts.
As a young Congressman in 1951, he had visited Indochina and watched

a crack French army fail to subdue Vietnamese nationalists. He left with the conviction that the dispatch of non-Asian troops to decide the future of Vietnam would only rouse nationalist emotions against the intruder and would, as he said in a radio address on his return to the United States, mean "foredoomed failure." By the time, a decade later, that Kennedy came to the White House, a commitment to save South Vietnam from communism had crystallized in the Eisenhower years. Kennedy thought it an overcommitment. But the commitment having been made, it could not be abandoned except at a price; and he was prepared to give the government in Saigon a run for its money. He offered Saigon economic assistance and increased the number of American military advisers attached to the South Vietnamese army (though at his death there were far fewer American troops in Vietnam than Soviet troops in Cuba during the missile crisis or American troops in the Dominican Republic in 1965).

But he rejected every proposal to send American combat units to Vietnam and, in effect, Americanize the war. If the United States converted the Vietnam fighting into an American war, he believed, we would lose—as the French had lost a decade before. "The last thing he wanted," Gen. Maxwell Taylor, chairman of the Joint Chiefs and later Lyndon Johnson's ambassador to Vietnam, later said, "was to put in ground forces." Kennedy was reinforced in this view by a talk with Gen. Douglas MacArthur, who told him it would be foolish to fight in Southeast Asia; the future of Vietnam should be decided at the diplomatic table. Thereafter, when the Pentagon called for the commitment of American ground forces, Kennedy would say, "Well, now, you gentlemen, you go back and convince General MacArthur, then I'll be convinced." In 1962, he directed the Pentagon to draw up plans for the withdrawal of the American military advisers in 1965. The plan was approved in May 1963, with the first 1,000 men to return at the end of the year . . . . It is difficult to suppose that Kennedy would ever have reversed himself and sent ground forces into Vietnam (Schlesinger, pp. 170, 175).

Chapter 9
Life After Kennedy

$\mathfrak{I}$ WAS STILL WORKING ON the Warren Commission investigation in early 1964, but there were times when I would return to Little Rock, then go back to Dallas after a couple of weeks. It was during these times in Little Rock that I got the assignments that I truly loved.

On one of my return trips, Letteer had a counterfeiting case going. The Secret Service had suppliers we called upon on a regular basis. If a counterfeiter is going to print money, he needs a quantity of quality paper, ink, and printing equipment, so we used the suppliers as informants. In this case, we were working on a tip we had from a supplier in Memphis. This was a joint case between the two offices since the suspect lived in a small town in northeast Arkansas. Letteer decided to set up surveillance on this guy. The two of us were up there watching the suspect when he got in his truck and headed to Memphis, where he'd been buying his supplies.

When we crossed the bridge and got into downtown Memphis, we met Bob Taylor, the agent in charge in Memphis, and Maurice Miller, the other agent in that office. Letteer and Taylor got into one car while Miller and I got in another. Miller and I were tailing the suspect to the supply house. Letteer and Taylor decided they would go back out to the bridge and wait because that was the only way the suspect could reenter Arkansas. Miller and I were afraid we were going to lose him; we'd have been really easy to spot because we were in our 1962 four-door Ford with no chrome, black tires—typical government issue. Sometimes when we were on serious surveillance, we'd go to a used car lot and get the owner to lend us cars on a rotating basis so that we could go in every few days and trade cars. But not this time.

Letteer and Taylor figured that if, for some reason, we lost our tail on him, they could always pick him up at the Mississippi River bridge. The two cars had no means of keeping in touch with each other because they weren't radio-equipped. However, we had borrowed these great big old walkie-talkies from the local police department, but you had to be outside to talk on them. I manned one of the walkie-talkies, while Miller was driving because he knew Memphis. I had to hang out the car window in order to talk to Letteer and Taylor on the walkie-talkie so I could get a clear signal. We were like Keystone Cops.

So Maurice Miller and I were trailing this guy in his truck, and we're right in the heart of downtown Memphis, which in those days was a happening place. Everybody worked and shopped downtown—there were no suburban office buildings or malls. Downtown was the hub. This was midday and the streets were packed with shoppers and office workers on their lunch breaks.

It's important to point out here that the fashion trend of the day was the miniskirt. The suspect's truck had just turned left ahead of us, when we were stopped by a red light. People were crossing the street in front of us, including a miniskirted girl with the most incredible legs we'd ever seen. Naturally, Miller and I shifted our attention to this girl's legs. When we looked up, the truck was nowhere in sight. Miller and I looked at each other, and I said, "Oh, my God, what do we do?"

About that time, Letteer and Taylor come over the walkie-talkie. "You got 'im in sight?"

I hung out the window and said, "Yeah. We've got 'im. Don't worry."

Miller ripped the car around the corner and we tore up the street trying to find that damn truck. We were frantic, and Letteer and Taylor keep radioing, asking us our location and if we still had the suspect in sight. We were sweating it out when Miller ripped around another side street and we spotted the truck. I never did tell Letteer how close we came to losing that suspect. We ended up arresting him and charging him with counterfeiting.

That's just the way it was in those days. This was still very soon after Kennedy's death; shortly after, Congress enacted legislation that got the Secret Service better law enforcement equipment. Still, the White House agents did not carry any kind of radios; certainly nothing like you see today, when agents talk into their sleeves through their tiny microphones and receivers. The cars used by the White House agents had radios, and they also had some big hand-held radios, but they couldn't carry them. I never had a radio when I was in the Secret Service.

Another case came our way in March 1964. The Timothy Jackson (not his real name) gang was a group of notorious government-check thieves and burglars operating out of East Little Rock. Timothy Jackson Jr. himself was a six-foot-six black man who led six or eight guys in all kinds of theft. All they did was sit around and plan how they could steal from other folks, and they were pretty good at it. The Little Rock police had not been able to nail Jackson. But since he'd been stealing government checks, we were able to pursue him.

He had been going to little towns within a fifty- to sixty-mile radius of Little Rock and burglarizing them, but none of the local law had been able to apprehend him. He'd then use some kid to sell the stuff for him so he wouldn't get caught with the goods. We never could get anyone to testify against him, so we could never make anything stick; but we knew what he was doing. We were dogging him constantly, but he was so sly we couldn't nail him. This went on for over a year.

We finally got an indictment against him and then couldn't catch him. One day we got a tip that he was at a house in the East End. Little Rock Detective John Terry, the postal inspector, and I went out to apprehend him. They sent me behind the house by myself while the two of them planned to go in the front door. They felt confident the two of them could capture him, but they wanted me out back, just in case. But when they entered the front door, Timothy Jackson Jr. immediately ran out the back door at full speed. I had my gun drawn, and Jackson had a gun in his hand. The house backed onto an alley, and I was in the alley just south of the house, maybe twenty-five yards away. I hadn't even gotten completely into place when Jackson bolted out the back door. I was off after him. I yelled, "Halt. We're federal agents, and we've got you surrounded." He never even checked his speed, he just kept trucking. I could have shot him because he ran in my direction with a gun in hand, but instead I holstered my gun and gave chase.

He was six inches taller than I, scaling walls and fences, and I was chasing him in my federal agent suit and tie. In those days agents weren't allowed to wear jeans and running shoes. After several blocks, I lost him. I went up to a house on the corner and knocked on the door to see if any of the occupants had seen anything. A young woman came to the door—she might have been twenty-eight or thirty—and she was naked from the waist up. Obviously this was nothing unusual for her, because she said, "Can I help you?" and I couldn't do anything but sputter.

Finally, I just laughed and said, "No. I don't even know what I came here for." I turned around and left. He may have been in that house, and if he was, he did the right thing in sending a half-naked woman to the door. It turned me upside down.

When I got back, Terry chewed me out big time for not shooting Jackson when I had the chance. Well, time went on and we still hadn't caught Timothy Jackson Jr., and his notoriety was growing. About nine o'clock one hot summer Sunday night, I was at home when I got a call from an informant telling me that Timothy Jackson Jr. and his girlfriend were riding around the East End in his old Desoto that was all chromed up. I called the Little Rock detective bureau, but it was Sunday night and no one was there. Then I called Letteer, but he was gone. I called the postal inspector next, but I didn't get him, either. I had no recourse but to get in my car and drive over to the East End—alone.

Finally, I saw the car coming toward me. There was an intersection between us, and I knew I had to get to that intersection before he did so I could block it and keep him from turning. I got there, turned my car across the intersection sideways, and blocked his escape. I jumped out of my car, drew my pistol, and ordered him to get out of the car. As Jackson got out of his car, a whole bunch of guys standing on the street corner become vocal in their support of him. I put Jackson up against the car and searched him. Finding that he did not have a gun, I handcuffed him and put him in my car to transport him to jail. His supporters kept mouthing off and began moving toward me. I turned my pistol toward them and announced, "I've got six bullets in this gun, and if one of you sumbitches wants one of them, just step forward. I'm gonna kill the first six men that step toward Timothy Jackson Jr. It's your choice." There wasn't another word said.

Now, if that incident occurred today, they'd have pulled out an Uzi and blown me away, but in the '60s there was still a lot of respect for law enforcement officers—especially federal officers. The criminals I knew respected me, and I never mistreated those I arrested. Timothy Jackson Jr. was just a challenge. It was like playing ball; we had a game going, and right then I won. We tried him on federal charges, and we had a great case because we had so much on him. The judge sentenced him to ten years.

Ten years later, on Christmas Eve, I got a call at my law office just as we were closing for the holiday. We'd had a little office party that day, but only Kathy Woods, my legal assistant, and my receptionist were still there with me. The man on the phone said, "Lawyer Carter, this is Timothy Jackson Jr., and I want to come out and see you." I told him to come on out. I warned Kathy and Carla, the receptionist, that this might mean trouble since I had been responsible for sending Jackson to the penitentiary ten years before. I kept a .45 in my desk, but I told them to go into another office and be prepared to call the police at the first sign of trouble.

When Jackson arrived, he had a woman and child with him. He came into my office and shook my hand. He told me that he had served his time in a federal penitentiary in Wisconsin, and his wife—the woman with him—was the girlfriend who had been with him when I arrested him. She'd stood by him all those years and had followed him to Wisconsin, where she attended college and had become a teacher. They got married and had a child. Then what he said really stunned me. He offered me his thanks for not shooting him when I had the drop on him all those years ago. He said he had a good job in Milwaukee, where his wife was teaching, and he had served his time and had learned his lesson and didn't plan on getting so much as a speeding ticket from then on. Probably the best Christmas present I ever got.

In early '65, I had a case concerning a man who had written a threatening letter and had also made phone calls to the president. The family of this individual lived in Little Rock, and Washington called us to investigate. They had not been able to locate the man in Dallas, where he had been living. He was a well-educated man, holding a PhD from SMU. They sent me out to interview his parents, who were very well-respected citizens of Little Rock. They had not heard from him but agreed to cooperate, and we had an all-points bulletin out for him. He rode a motorcycle, and I'd get memos from all over the country saying that he'd been spotted in various places. One of those memos was from Panama City, Florida, and it stated that the subject in question had been spotted at a shopping center in Panama City riding his motorcycle—naked. I started looking, and other reports said the same thing. This man was riding all over on his motorcycle, unencumbered by clothes. This was a little before the hippie craze, so most people were still conservative in their dress and haircuts, but this guy had long, flowing hair. We later did locate him, and I worked with his family to have him committed because of his mental problems.

Back then, there were three categories of threats against the president: (1) Those who were angry. Someone might be getting his hair cut in the barbershop, and the men get to talking, saying things like "That s.o.b. raised my taxes. He ought to be killed." We investigated those threats, but people are always getting mad at politicians and making idle threats. (2) The mentally disturbed. The bulk of the threats are from the mentally deranged. The ones you really had to worry about were the paranoid schizophrenics who were talking to a "voice," which was telling them to kill the president. That's fairly common. Lee Harvey Oswald was obviously mentally unstable, but he was fueled by a number of outside influences and was in a different category of mentally deranged. (3) Those who develop a hatred for the president. In Kennedy's case, I think religion played a part in the hatred for him, as did his stand on civil rights.

Letteer and I also worked on a huge counterfeiting case in Abilene, Texas. In February 1965, we had to travel there to testify in the case along with agents from the Dallas field office. It was an interesting case because drugs were involved, too. This was a hardened gang, and there were a lot of defendants and a lot of defense attorneys. The Texas Rangers were also involved in this case, and it was my first experience with them. The government had a key witness, and right in the middle of this trial, we got a call that this witness—who had been scheduled to testify the next day—had disappeared. The prosecutor asked for a delay, but the judge wasn't going to delay the case very long. The U.S. attorney called a conference with all the investigators and told us we had to find the witness or he was going to lose the case. Since Letteer and I were just there as witnesses, they could use us to try to track down the missing man, and they also called in every other law enforcement official that was available. We figured the witness had either been kidnapped or killed.

I was assigned to this wiry little Hispanic Texas Ranger. He wasn't a big guy— maybe five foot nine or so—but he carried a big gun. We had to get out on the street and try to draw information from the informants. If we had been in Little Rock, I'd have known what to do, but this was Abilene. One of the Ranger's informants turned him on to a guy who knew something about our witness, so we had to go into a really bad part of the city to talk to him. We arrived at the place where this guy was, and the Ranger kicked down the door, grabbed the guy by the front of the shirt, put a gun to his head, and started roughing him up a little. This guy told us that the gang had kidnapped and drugged the witness and were holding him at a farmhouse. We located the farmhouse and took charge of the witness, who was pretty drugged up, but we got the drugs out of his system and got him in shape to testify. I had never encountered anything like the justice dispensed by the Texas Rangers. Their methods may have been crude, but they worked. One day Letteer got a call from another field office about a counterfeiting case at Mammoth

Springs, Arkansas, a town on the state line across from Thayer, Missouri. They thought the suspect's parents lived in Arkansas, but it turned out the house was actually just across the Missouri line. Letteer and I went up to investigate the case, but Letteer left me up there, and I had to blend in with the community to maintain spot surveillance on the house. I obtained a truck and a sign from the Corps of Engineers and settled into the very rural area of Mammoth Springs. It was a little bitty town, with one side of the street being Arkansas while the other side was Missouri. Because I was a stranger, I'd go into a restaurant and stick out like a sore thumb. But my posing as a surveyor was a good ruse because they didn't suspect me of being anything else. I was there for quite a while, so I made friends with the locals.

I finally determined that the suspect was indeed staying at the farmhouse. After I made the initial assessment, I went to Kansas City to meet with the special agent in charge of that office. The Kansas City office sent some agents back with me to help me maintain surveillance. Now, I grew up in the country, so I was very familiar with being in the woods. This was in April, and this was a very woody, hilly area. When Letteer and I first went up there, I bought up all the insect repellent I could find. The only way you could watch the house was to be in front of it, in the woods. I had to be dropped off a ways from there and walk through the woods. Then I had to stand there behind the trees and watch the house. I didn't have any problems, but I forgot to tell my friends from the north about chiggers. One of the agents was from Philadelphia, and he was kind of a know-it-all guy anyway, so I let him find out about chiggers all by himself.

Chapter 10
The Future Is Now

Æ‌FTER KENNEDY'S ASSASSINATION, things changed in the Secret Service. Whereas before, you might be assigned to the White House detail temporarily if somebody was on vacation or to fill a slot, the new policy was that when the president moved, agents from the field office would supplement the White House detail. When President Johnson moved, I—fortunately or unfortunately, I couldn't decide—frequently moved with him. Letteer had me keep a bag packed and ready to go at a moment's notice.

I was painting my house one Saturday when I got a call that I had to be at the airport in two hours to join the White House detail. I had to stop what I was doing, shower, jump into a suit, and get to the airport. Another time I had to fly to Nashville, Letteer having told me I didn't even need to take a bag, because I wouldn't need to stay overnight. I arrived and met the presidential party, and the shift leader singled me out and informed me I was to continue with the president to his next stop. Here I was with only the suit on my back, and I was on the road with the president for the next three or four days. I had to scrape up and buy underwear, a toothbrush, and a razor. The suit I had on was a lightweight olive-khaki suit, and after a few days in the summer sun, perspiration had stained the suit under my arms. I wore another light suit one time on an airplane. I turned on the faucet in the lavatory to wash my hands, and the pressure that had built up caused the water to splatter all over my suit. After that trip, I never owned another suit that wasn't navy or dark gray or black when I traveled with the president. I learned.

I had just returned to Little Rock from a trip to Washington, where the Warren Commission was sitting, when I got a call to go to Homestead Air Force Base in Miami to await the president's arrival and participate in the advance. The president arrived three days later. From that time forward, until I resigned, I spent most of my time supplementing the White House detail when the president moved. I wasn't restricted to my part of the country—I went with him to California and Idaho, among other places. It was obvious that the Secret Service needed more agents to protect the president, but they didn't have a lot of time to go out and hire new agents for the White House detail, so they used field agents.

93

In 1964, Lyndon Johnson was running for re-election, so I was off somewhere every month. During this time, I was also on temporary assignment in Washington. In reviewing my daily reports for this book, I discovered that I had interviewed a Mary Jo Kopechne at 2912 Olive Street, in DC, in June 1964, regarding a background check on someone who had applied for a job. It was just a few years later when she would die in the back seat of Teddy Kennedy's car at Chappaquiddick.

I worked on a variety of things during this time. I advanced the president's visit to Texarkana, where there were some potential threats against Johnson. I was sent in for six days to investigate as well as advance the date. We made an arrest in that case of someone in the crowd carrying a handgun. He was held a few days, but I don't think we could ever link him to a serious threat against Johnson. Then, in October, I went on a western swing with Johnson—Kansas, Wyoming, Idaho, Montana, Colorado. I hadn't been back for long before I went out with Ladybird Johnson and was gone for a good while. I traveled with President Johnson right up until the election in November. I remember voting by absentee ballot—for Barry Goldwater—from the road.

I was doing well in the Secret Service. Jan and I had bought our first house in Little Rock, for $19,200. It was a three-bedroom brick house in Cardinal Heights. We were expecting our second child, a daughter, Joanna Lynn, who would be born on June 10, 1965. I was being paid a $14 per diem when I was on the road, and my salary was just over $10,000.

Chief Rowley retired about this time, and Johnson named Stu Knight to succeed Rowley. Bob Taylor, the agent in charge in Memphis had previously been on the White House detail for years, and Stu brought him back to head it up again. Bob had been telling me I was slated for the White House detail, but I never wanted that assignment. I wanted to be a criminal investigator. I loved the challenge of chasing criminals; I loved the heat of the chase. That's what I wanted to do, and I told them that. But I don't think either Taylor or Letteer took me seriously, so immediately when Taylor was transferred to Washington, I got the call. With Taylor back in the White House, I became one of a number of field agents he would call on whenever President Johnson traveled.

In June 1965, Harry Truman, the elder statesman of the Democratic Party and a former president, had taken a fall and was hospitalized at Research Hospital in Kansas City. President Johnson decided to visit Truman, and I was assigned, along with a White House agent, to advance the visit, an assignment I relished.

I idolized Truman—he was kind of the hero of the common man. Plus, the veteran SS agents had told me stories about Truman—about how he drank beer and played poker with them. I was in awe of him. I was really excited to get to meet him. The agent I was with on that first visit had worked with Truman. We went into his hospital room. He was laid up in bed from his fall, although he wasn't in traction, but he'd hurt his back. Right away he recognized the agent and said hello to him. Mrs. Truman was in the room, but no one else. The agent introduced me, and President Truman shook my hand and introduced me to Bess. The agent got to talking to the president, "What's going on; how're you doing?"

And the president asked the same questions of the agent. "What have you been doing since I saw you?" He was everything I'd ever heard that he was. It was just like going to see your grandfather in the hospital. He was in great spirits and was very alert, although he was getting up in years by that time. Very quick-witted. We talked to him about the upcoming visit and what would be required.

A few days later the president came in and visited Truman in his hospital room. It was a very brief visit. Later in 1965 President Johnson went back to Kansas City to visit with Truman because he was about to sign the Medicare Bill into law. Truman always advocated national health insurance, which was one of the first reasons I had admired him so much. The bill was to be signed at the Truman Library, in Independence, Missouri, and President Truman was to be at the signing.

I got there about three days before Johnson, since I was serving on the advance team—I arrived on July 22, and Johnson didn't arrive until July 25. It had been eight months since I saw Truman in the hospital, but he remembered me and sought me out and shook hands with me. He even remembered where I was from. If there had ever been a president I had really wanted to meet, it was Truman. He was the nicest guy—you'd have never thought he had been president by the way he dealt with people. After I got back home from that trip, I received an autographed picture in the mail from him. I think he also sent me a note, but, unfortunately, most of my presidential mementos were lost when my house burned in 1973. It was just a stroke of luck that I had the photo hanging on the wall in my office; so I have that, but notes from Truman and Lady Bird and others were lost.

I stayed in the Secret Service until the end of the summer, and then I resigned. I didn't want to spend years on the White House detail and in Washington, because I really preferred the field work. But if you're going to advance and succeed in a job, you have to accept the assignments that are given to you and not complain about them. I learned that when I was in the Air Force.

When I graduated from radar school, the Air Force sent me to Wadena, Minnesota, a small town in north central Minnesota. I was assigned to a radar site, which was part of the North American Air Defense Command. Wadena was probably no larger than 5,000 to 6,000 people, and the airmen were treated like heroes around there. The locals would welcome us into their homes, we dated many of the local girls, and we were invited to all the town activities.

The first girl I met after I arrived in Wadena who really showed any interest in me was a German girl named Alice. I felt like she was the one. She was my first real love, and we were convinced we should get married. Then, just as I was about to make what could have been a serious mistake—getting married—I learned I was to be transferred to Iceland. The Bendix Corporation made the equipment we had at the site in Wadena, and they always had a civilian representative on site to aid in the maintenance of this equipment. I got along so well with their engineer,

Mr. Shaw, that I asked him to intervene on my behalf. I wasn't transferred at that time, but then Bendix transferred Mr. Shaw. I think my commanding officers, who must have resented Mr. Shaw's interference, transferred me to Iceland at their first opportunity. I still thought the Air Force was the coolest thing, but if I was going to end up being stationed in out-of-the-way posts like Iceland, then it wasn't the life for me.

So in that fall of 1965, while weighing the decision about my career with the Secret Service, I went to see my friend Orval Faubus to seek his counsel. He provided me with valuable advice I follow to this day. He said, "When you face a major decision in your life, you must look within for the answer. I could tell you what I think you should do, Bill, but only your inner self knows what you should do." He went on to say that while our friends, professors, siblings, and parents may each have opinions, not one of these advisors really has the answers. He talked of his own experience with important decisions and said he always returned to his home in Madison County. He would walk into the woods, sit down on a log, and pray, asking for guidance from within. While giving consideration to all his advisors, he really just listened to his inner guidance.

When I left Faubus, I went to my hometown of Rector and sat in a lawn chair under the big pecan tree in my backyard, and I prayed. I weighed my options: If I was going to stay in the Secret Service, I had to accept the White House assignment, go up there, do the job and do it well—just as I did in the Air Force—or I needed to resign and go back to law school. Frankly, I was tired of the Secret Service. Before I had gotten into the Secret Service, I had been active politically, and through my years with the Agency, I had gotten acquainted with some of the most influential politicians in the country, and it just seemed the natural thing for me to do was to go back and finish law school in preparation for whatever was to come next.

I had always been encouraged to get into politics, and I'm sure that entered into my thinking. Or I could see myself as a United States attorney or a prosecuting attorney. I had a number of friends from when I had been in law school the first time who were now practicing law—Lindsey Fairley was an assistant U.S. attorney, Jim Gallman was the chief deputy U.S. attorney, Jeff Davis was an assistant U.S. attorney. As an agent, I worked closely with these guys, and I thought a lot of them. Gallman, particularly, encouraged me to go back to law school.

After a few hours of meditation, I decided to leave the Secret Service and return to law school. For my entire life, God has blessed me with divine guidance.

1-1. Bill Carter (highlighted, behind Kennedy), on assignment with President John F. Kennedy, Jacksonville, Arkansas, October, 1963

1-2. Governor Orval Faubus, center, introduces Bill's wife, Jan, to President Kennedy during his Arkansas visit, 1963

1-3.Bill standing sentry (right, beside pillar) as the body of President Kennedy ascends the Capitol steps followed by Mrs. Kennedy, Caroline, John, Jr. and members of the Kennedy family

1-4. The Texas School Book Depository from which the fatal shots were fired on November 22, 1963. Photographer positioned on Houston Street. The picture shows the front side of the building on Elm Street. The position of the windows are the same as at the time of the assassination.

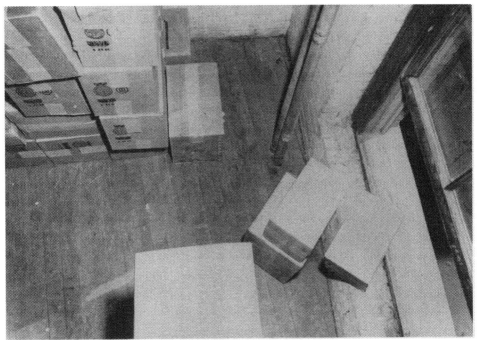

1-5. The sixth floor room used as a sniper's perch by Lee Harvey Oswald. The boxes have been re-constructed. The boxes at the window were apparently used for support and bracing of the weapon and also as cover from exterior viewers. The single box to the left of the vertical pipes was apparently used as a seat by the assassin. A latent palm print of Lee Harvey Oswald was found on the single box.

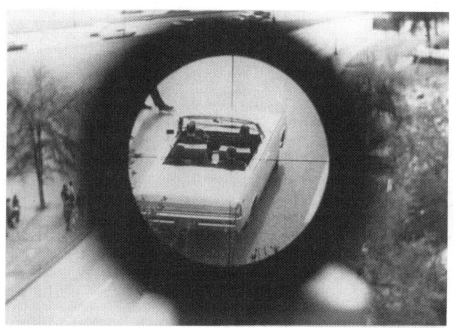

1-6. View Oswald had from his position in the Texas School Book Depository and in the scope of the rifle he used. Demonstration by FBI and Secret Service agents.

1-7. Secret Service agents on the running board of the follow-up car look upward towards the sixth floor room of the Texas School Book Depository, indicating the direction from where the shots were fired.

From Marina Oswald
to Bill Carter

Washington. D.C
feb. 6. 1964.

1-8. Marina Oswald insisted that Bill pose with her at the end of his assignment escorting her to testify before the Warren Commission, 1964.

1-9. Campaigning with First Lady Lady Byrd Johnson, 1964.

1-10. On the campaign trail with President Lyndon B. Johnson, 1964.

Part II

Chapter 11
Lawyer Carter

WHEN I FINISHED LAW SCHOOL in 1967, the offers I received from law firms were low, as was typical for young lawyers in those days, and there were no opportunities I could afford to take. Plus, the U.S. Attorney's office had no openings at the time—those were much sought-after positions. I had scouted everywhere for a job but there was nothing available to me. When I passed the bar, I went back to Rector to try to decide what to do. Lindsey Fairley, a classmate from my first time in law school, was in West Memphis and was going through a divorce at the time. I had thought about practicing with him, but that seemed impractical due to his situation.

I didn't know anything about practicing law, but while I was living in Rector, people in Clay County would still come to me when they had a legal problem. They had confidence in me, so I'd take the case. Then I'd call Lindsey or one of my other friends and tell them I had accepted a case I knew nothing about, and they would help me with it. I'd go to Lindsey's office in West Memphis, and his staff would do the paperwork for me. I was practically practicing law out of my car.

Another of my friends from my first stint in law school, Paul Henson, called me one day and said he was practicing law in Little Rock with Farrell Faubus, the governor's son, and another former classmate. They wanted me to come join them, but I told him I didn't have the money to move the 180 miles. At the time, our furniture—what little there was of it—was still in Fayetteville.

Being the generous man he is, Paul offered to let me move into his house—he'd move into the basement—and live rent-free; plus, I could move into his office also rent-free. He told me when I started making some money I could pay him. Bob Evers, in Rector, had an old International pick-up truck with a cattle rack on it, and he and I went to Fayetteville and loaded everything Jan and I had and moved it to Little Rock. It broke down twice between Fayetteville and Little Rock, but we finally made it. Paul's place was a big house in Leawood. Our furniture didn't begin to fill it, but it was more than we could ever have dreamed of at that point in our lives.

The first thing I did was to make the rounds of prominent lawyers in Little Rock to tell them I needed help. Because of my high-profile job with the Secret Service, most everyone in Little Rock knew me. I went to Max Howell, who was a state senator and, with Dale Price, had a very successful law practice; they assured me they'd send me business. I made more money the first month than the annual salary any of the law firms had offered me, and I was able to pay Paul rent from the very first month.

I should add that during my final year in law school, I had been hired by Commissioner Harvey G. Combs, of the Arkansas Insurance Commission, to investigate corruption that was rampant in the state's insurance industry. Shortly after my graduation, the *Arkansas Gazette* got wind of my employment and broke the story that a full-time law student and friend of Gov. Faubus had been on the state payroll as a full-time employee. It had all the appearances of a full-blown scandal, although Commissioner Combs defended me as one of the best investigators in the department.

The legislature called for an investigation into the law-student scandal, and Commissioner Harkey was asked to explain. He had just taken office and knew nothing of my employment, so Harkey called me in to meet with him. The insurance department in Arkansas had a well-deserved reputation as being corrupt. I'd been working on investigating the agents, but the companies themselves were corrupt at the highest level. When Rockefeller appointed Harkey to head the department, that sent a signal to everyone.

Before our meeting I did not know John Norman Harkey except by reputation—and it was quite a reputation. He was famous as a prosecuting attorney in Batesville—an ex-Marine and combative sort of guy. Naturally, I was a little apprehensive about our meeting.

When I entered the commissioner's office, he had a stack of files on his desk, but before he could say anything, I told him I was sorry for any embarrassment I had caused and offered to resign. He laughed and said there were five full-time investigators in the department, and I had handled more cases that resulted in successful prosecutions than all of the other investigators. Then he said, "I've been looking through your files, and I'm gonna keep you, but you don't need to be doing this. I'm gonna recommend you for a job with the Arkansas Commerce Commission; there's an opening for a lawyer over there." It was not a full-time job, but I would have an office at the ACC—in the transportation department—and could practice law on the side. I could spend whatever time was required in the state office, then go down to my law office. That provided me with a base income right away. It paid $1,000 or so a month; plus, I was making $500 to $600 a month practicing law, and that was good money for 1967. I was in tall cotton.

Not long after he took office, Rockefeller nominated several people to political appointments on the Arkansas Law Enforcement Training Commission to supervise the training of all law enforcement officers in the state. Usually a sheriff served on that commission; one of the better and more prominent ones, Robert Moore, was serving, as was the chief of police from Fayetteville, but there was an opening. The Senate would not agree on anybody Rockefeller nominated, so Harkey suggested to Rockefeller that he nominate me since I was a Democrat and well-liked by all the legislators. Governor Rockefeller called me out to the governor's mansion to meet with him. He asked me if I'd accept the appointment, and I thought, why not? I later regretted having done so because there were continual meetings, and it was an unpaid position—more of a prestige thing—and I didn't need the prestige.

It sailed right through and I was confirmed.

I accepted the appointment and served for a couple of years, until Dale Bumpers was elected governor. At that time, Sen. Max Howell came to see me and said, "You can be reappointed to this post, but I need a thousand dollars for Bumpers' election."

I looked at him and said, "Hell, Max, if you're telling me I've gotta contribute to get reappointed to a position that's costing me several thousand a year to serve in, I believe I'll pass." The only thing it was good for was to keep me from getting speeding tickets from state troopers. I wasn't in a financial position then to continue serving on the commission; it just got in my way.

Harkey called me one day, while Rockefeller was still governor, and asked me to meet him at Governor Rockefeller's office. Rockefeller had his top advisers there. He said they'd been investigating the State Game and Fish Commission, trying to get evidence on Raymond Farris from Brisco, near Brinkley. Supposedly he'd been buying surplus Game and Fish equipment at auction for his own use but using other people's names to make the purchases. He was a commissioner, and it was improper for him to buy it, so he'd have somebody who worked on his farm buy it. The state had lots of allegations against him, but they couldn't prove it. The governor asked if I had any suggestions. I said, "Well, have you asked him?"

Everybody looked at each other, then at me, and said, "Naw, of course we haven't asked him."

"Why not?"

They shot back, "He's not gonna admit it." One of the lawyers chided, "Do you think you're just gonna walk up to Raymond Farris and get him to admit it?"

I came right back, "I don't know, but that's where I'd start." With that, the meeting broke up.

It wasn't long until Rockefeller called me again, but this time he asked me to come out to the mansion. "I think I'm gonna let you take a stab at this," he said when we were seated. "You'll probably need some help with this, so get another lawyer to help you."

I got a friend of mine, Frank Watson, who later became my law partner, to help me. The first thing I did was drive out to Raymond Farris' farm, in Brisco. It was during farming season, and Farris was out in the field. Parked out in plain sight were the jeep and some of the other equipment he was accused of buying. I walked up to him, showed him my credentials from the governor's office, and said, "Mr. Farris, does this jeep belong to you?"

He swelled up and answered, "You're damned right it does."

He admitted everything I asked him. Sometimes the direct way is the best way. There were other commissioners involved and other allegations that needed further investigation, and we spent several months on the case.

The interesting thing about this case was that Rockefeller paid me a retainer out of his own personal funds. In fact, the whole investigation of the Game and Fish Commission was paid for at Winthrop Rockefeller's personal expense. Nothing was charged to the state. When he hired me, he asked what I charged an hour. At that time, I was charging whatever I could get, but he wanted to know if $135 an hour sounded reasonable. I don't remember exactly how much I billed the governor, but it was a thorough investigation, so it was a large amount.

I learned something from the governor that I'd never run across before. I sent in an expense report for some of my travel, and he had an aide look over the report for him. She sent me back a note saying, "In the future, the governor wishes you would tip chambermaids when you stay in a hotel and put that on your expense account." I'd never heard of anyone tipping a chambermaid, but I've done that ever since when I stay in a hotel for several days.

I was beginning to develop a nice little law practice in addition to my work for the governor. In my early law practice, it was natural that I develop a criminal practice since I had been a federal agent and knew all the police officers, the criminal procedures, and the prosecutors and judges. In 1969 the courts appointed members of the bar to defend indigents. Most of the time the lawyers simply had to devote their time, and the maximum they could receive was $250. It was deemed our contribution to the judicial system.

I built a reputation for myself as a trial lawyer who would take on just about anyone. One of the very first cases I tried, right after I got out of law school, was given to me by Judge William Kirby. The case was that of an uneducated black man, Booker McDonald, fifty-five years old, who had killed a Little Rock police officer, also black. I argued with the judge that I was a former federal agent—a law enforcement officer—and my heart was with law enforcement. He said, "That's why I'm appointing you. I need a strong representation." So I took the Booker McDonald murder case—the most controversial murder case in Little Rock in years. I think it would be fair to say that I had never faced such a difficult challenge as an attorney.

Booker McDonald, even though he was black, hated all African Americans, and he had just been released from the County Farm for having severely beaten up another black. He broke into the house of another black man he knew, stealing a fully loaded pistol. He then proceeded to get drunk and was walking east on Roosevelt Road in Little Rock—in the middle of the street—just as the first black police officer the city had ever hired drove by in a squad car. The officer, Lloyd Worthy, stopped his vehicle, got out, and tried to apprehend Booker, who ran into a ditch, then up an embankment. Just as the officer was about to overtake him, Booker pulled the stolen gun from his pocket and shot the officer four times, killing him instantly.

Dozens of police officers hunted Booker for over three weeks before he was captured. The news of the manhunt was front-page headlines every day. Story after story was written about the very fine person who was killed, and the criminal record of the suspect was repeated like a mantra. Booker looked mean and vicious, and his looks accurately depicted his personality; Booker *was* mean. In fact, ten years before he shot the Little Rock policeman, he was sentenced to Tucker prison for shooting another policeman. He'd also done time in the same prison for stealing and was a frequent resident of the County Farm in Pulaski County. The prosecutors were trying to give him the electric chair, and there really was no defense I could offer. He had killed this policeman right in front of numerous witnesses.

I talked Lindsey Fairley and Paul Henson into trying the case with me. Our chief goal was to keep him from being electrocuted, and that's all Booker really wanted. This was a major undertaking, and being appointed like I was, it was pro bono work. I didn't get paid anything, and these kinds of cases were time-consuming. Booker pleaded not guilty to begin with; then, in an effort to get a life sentence instead of death, he changed his plea to guilty. If I'd been the prosecutor, I'd have sought the death penalty; I don't know how we talked the prosecutor into a life sentence. Life in the penitentiary would have been pleasant for Booker; he didn't have a home, and he could neither read nor write.

The press had already convicted him a hundred times over, and every police officer, prosecutor, and judge was ready to fry Booker in the electric chair and exile all three of his defense lawyers to someplace like Texas. We took tremendous heat from the law enforcement community and others in Little Rock for defending Booker McDonald. But that came to be the norm—I began to expect criticism for the cases I took, the scum I represented. I'd be at a cocktail party and a prominent doctor would say to me, "How could you represent the scum of the earth?" I'd tell him that a lawyer is nothing but an advocate—whatever side you may be representing, you're supposed to mount your strongest case. A lawyer can't get caught up philosophically in a case. If the prosecutor is an aggressive, competent prosecutor, and the defense attorney is equally competent and strong, then justice will be served. If either side breaks down, then justice will not be served. That's just the way the legal system works.

I also had another murder case for which I took a lot of heat—the Baggett murder case. This young man was accused of murdering a well-known Little Rock pharmacist, a man named Schillcut, whose family had owned a drugstore in the city for decades. This was another sensational Little Rock headline case on the front page of the paper every day. Kirby appointed me on this case, too. I said to him, "Judge, I'm trying to make a living, and you keep appointing me on these murder cases that take weeks and months of intense preparation. I'll starve to death." Hell, Kirby didn't care. He'd always say he'd take care of me down the line. He'd always appoint more than one attorney to a case since it was too much of a burden for any one person to bear. On the Baggett case, he also appointed Jim Howard, a former deputy prosecuting attorney. We tried the case and got a hung jury. Then we got a mistrial because the prosecuting attorney made some prejudicial remarks. We tried it either two or three times and got a mistrial in each case. Then I hurt my back, so my partner, Frank Watson Jr., went in and tried it with Jim Howard. Baggett was finally convicted to a life sentence that time, which, again, was a victory.

As bad as the Booker McDonald and Baggett cases were, it was the Thomas Simmons case that really haunted me. I was appointed to a case in 1971 in which Thomas W. Simmons was the defendant. This was a horrible, horrible case.

Simmons was a common thief with a long rap sheet in Oklahoma. He was driving through Little Rock and stopped for gas at a service station on West Third Street. He didn't have any money, so he intended to rob the station. The attendant was a seventeen-year-old high school student, Gary Wyllia, who, by all accounts, was a great student and a fine young man. Simmons had the kid fill his tank up with gas; then, while the kid was vacuuming out the car, Simmons placed a knife to his side and ordered him to scoot over and put his head between his legs. Simmons drove him to a wooded area out in Saline County, tied him up, choked him with a leather strap, and stabbed him in the back. Then he buried him under some leaves. Well, guess what? The kid didn't die. He crawled out of the leaves to a country road, where he was found by a couple who had heard his cries for help. Not only was the kid able to identify his abductor, but the prosecution had all kinds of physical evidence against Thomas Simmons. They had him cold. Of all cases for me to catch! I had to go to trial against a model seventeen-year-old kid who'd been kidnapped, his throat slit, and left for dead!

The judge was Charles Light, from Paragould, near my hometown of Rector, who was sitting while Judge Kirby was on vacation. He had appointed a young kid just out of law school, John Harmon, to defend Simmons. Harmon asked the judge for help, and because the judge knew me, I got the nod.

Simmons was charged with kidnapping, which called for a mandatory sentence of life, or death if the victim was injured or killed. I remembered that the legislature had passed a new law just that year, making kidnapping a first-degree offense unless the person committing the crime "voluntarily releases the victim alive and in a safe place prior to trial, [in which case] it is a second-degree offense." The punishment for second-degree was one to three years compared to one to twenty for first-degree under the old law. I challenged the old law. The prosecutor was going for the maximum—which he should have—because this guy had a long history of crime. I was certain the new law applied in this case, so I had them on a technicality.

Judge Light was known for being one of the straightest and best judges, and he ruled against me, deciding that they could try him under the old statute.

From the time John and I had spent in the county jail interviewing Thomas Simmons, we sensed he was a serial killer who had killed lots of people. He didn't confess any of his crimes to us; we just had a feeling about him. As his attorneys, there was nothing we could do but defend him. John and I mounted a vigorous defense, but the prosecution's case was too strong.

Six months after Judge Light's ruling, we were readying to go to trial, and we felt we had the judge on a reversible error; we really felt the new law applied in this case. The prosecutor was obviously concerned that our interpretation would hold up on appeal. I suggested that we negotiate a plea, and the prosecutor was willing to talk. The state waived the death penalty, but they were seeking ninety-nine years under the old law. We knew if we went to trial, Simmons would get the maximum because this was one of the most horrendous cases in Little Rock history. As I said, we mounted a vigorous defense, but it was a horrible crime, and the defendant had a chilling personality. He had decided to kill the teenager for a tank of gas. Simmons had no remorse whatsoever.

The Simmons case was on the front page of the Little Rock papers during the trial, and one day an old friend of mine, W.A. Tudor, of the state police criminal investigation division, called me to say he had an outstanding warrant against a man who allegedly committed a crime in Hot Springs. He'd been reading about Simmons in the papers and believed our client was the perpetrator in his open investigation. Tudor thought it was likely Simmons that had committed a crime in Hot Springs five days after the Little Rock kidnapping.

It seems on September 11, 1970, just five days after the Wyllia kidnapping, an FBI agent had stopped Simmons and his wife outside Hot Springs as they were leaving a local tavern. Simmons pulled his own gun, overpowered the FBI agent, and took his pistol and government car and left the agent unharmed. They located Simmons in a nearby motel where he was staying with his wife and three children. I don't know why they had not apprehended Simmons at the time. So, the state came in and filed charges against Simmons while our case was pending. He was charged with assaulting a federal officer and theft of government property. In the meantime, Tudor was looking into even more possible crimes.

During talks with Simmons, he told me he knew he was going to get some federal time, and he wanted to serve everything concurrently, whatever sentence he received. I knew Judge Light pretty well, and I think I convinced him that we had a good shot at getting his ruling reversed.

We finally got everybody to agree to a forty-five-year sentence. That looked pretty good when it hit the papers, but Simmons only had to serve fifteen years of that. He felt great about that, and why shouldn't he?

In 1981, I was preparing to move to Nashville when I got a call that Thomas Simmons had been paroled after serving only eight years. The next thing I knew, the headlines in the newspapers were screaming MURDER SUSPECT HAS LONG

HISTORY OF CRIME, VIOLENCE. It seems that Simmons had gone on a killing spree after his release, leaving four people dead in Fort Smith. Two of his victims had been stuffed into a huge tractor tire and covered with five-gallon cans in a field near Fort Smith. He got the death sentence in that case and ended up committing suicide in prison. Does this kind of thing bother a lawyer? No. If I'd been the prosecutor, I don't think I'd have accepted that negotiated plea. I didn't parole him—the State Parole Board did. That's where the system breaks down.

I was involved in another horrendous case that involved a young man from my home county. His wife had left him, and in retribution, he beat their baby girl with a broomstick and stuck the broomstick up her vagina. He was prosecuted and went to the penitentiary. His family came to see me in Little Rock and asked me to represent him before the parole board. I took the case, and I got the parole board to agree to his release. Governor Rockefeller called me soon after and requested that I come out to his office. The request from the state parole board had crossed his desk for his approval, and one of his aides had flagged this request as one that might need more careful attention. He started right in.

"Bill, I've got to tell you I'm dumbfounded by this case that just came across my desk. You got the parole board to agree to parole this guy, but, my God, I can't do this. This is unconscionable. I'm not going to recommend that this guy be released." I couldn't say much, because I didn't really disagree with him.

I was up in Clay County later on another matter, and I ran into the man's dad on the street. When he saw me, he confronted me with, "You're that crooked s.o.b of a lawyer, and I'm gonna get my gun to you." He started walking toward his pick-up truck nearby.

Well, I always carried a gun—a hold-over from my Secret Service days—and I reached into my own car for my gun and threatened with deadly calm, "Don't reach for that rifle or I'll blow you away." He got in the truck and sped away. Then his son escaped from the penitentiary and threatened me. I remember it was very tense, and I had to warn Jan about answering the door or letting the girls out in the yard. The FBI was looking for him. They had a tip that he had been spotted at a motel in Georgia. When they confronted him, he came out firing, and he killed an FBI agent before they could kill him. Shortly after that, his dad had threatened somebody and the sheriff went out to arrest him, and he shot the sheriff and two deputies. He went to the penitentiary for life.

That case and the Simmons case were the two worst ones I had.

I had begun representing a group known as the Dixie Mafia, who operated the gambling establishments in Hot Springs, among other things. My first case for them was as defense counsel for one of their runners, who had been arrested for something, and I got him a suspended sentence. I guess he was a pretty important Mafia runner, so his bosses started sending me cases involving prostitutes, burglars, drug rings, whatever, because they knew I could get them resolved pretty quickly.

There was a madam in Dallas who ran a prostitution ring throughout the Southwest. One of her top girls got arrested in Little Rock on a hot check charge, and the madam called me. I went to see the young lady, who was quite beautiful and very well-endowed, a fact made even more obvious because she was still dressed in her "working" clothes. She was scheduled to appear in court. I'd already told the judge that we'd make restitution on the check, but I needed to get her out of Little Rock and out of the state, and he'd agreed to all that. I brought her into the courtroom, and the judge was sitting on the bench with his reading glasses down on his nose. There were several cases before us, but he looked up and said, "Lawyer Carter, approach the bench." I went forward. "Bring your defendant up here," he ordered. I complied. He looked her over real good, and I can't repeat what he had to say, but he gave her a suspended sentence and she was on her way.

I later made a serious mistake in judgment with the Dixie Mafia. A runner I'd gotten off came through Little Rock some years after his trial and called me to meet him down at the Sheraton for a drink. Now, I had a policy never to meet clients outside my office—never meet them in public because there's no telling what they might have in their possession. Against my better judgment I went, but I took Kathy Woods, my legal assistant, with me as insurance. The runner told me he'd just picked up a delivery in Chicago and was taking it to Houston. He had a satchel with him, and he reached down inside it, pulled out a little bag, and took something out that was wrapped in white paper. He carefully unwrapped the paper, and inside was the largest emerald I'd ever seen in my life. It had to have been fifty carats. He was taking it to Houston to be cut. I told him to put it back in his bag and I didn't want to hear another word about it. That really scared me. People always wanted to pay me in diamonds or guns—usually hot—but I never accepted anything like that.

I gradually began to drift away from criminal law, although I was good at it and had begun charging a lot of money. I just got tired of it as well as dealing with the scum of the earth.

Bill Wilson, who had his own law firm in Little Rock, and I used to handle cases together. Especially after Kathy Woods passed the bar and we started practicing together, he'd enlist us to help him try cases on occasion. He was an outstanding trial lawyer; in fact, I don't think there was a better trial lawyer in the state of Arkansas. He went to law school at Vanderbilt, and he was much smarter than the average lawyer—a lot smarter than I was, that's for sure. We frequently associated with each other. In criminal cases, Wilson and I were both notorious for challenging judges we considered to be incorrect or who failed to follow the law.

Most judges were former prosecutors, and Wilson and I felt they tended to interpret the law in favor of the prosecution. On occasion if state court judges in Arkansas felt a defendant was a criminal and deserved to be incarcerated, they would disregard the law as it applied to that case and sentence the defendant to the penitentiary. Bill and I kind of resented that, and we would frequently challenge the judge in such cases. Wilson always had me on standby to go to the Supreme Court and get him out of jail. He used to go up to East Arkansas and every time, he'd call me. "I'm going up to so-and-so's court, so get your writ ready, 'cause I'm likely to get locked up for contempt." He never did, nor did I, but we both came very close on many occasions. When you stand up in court and read a Supreme Court case directly on point, and ask the trial judge to rule for you because that's the law of the Supreme Court by which he's bound, and he rules against you and disregards the case, it tends to get one a little upset.

One day I was in the office when Wilson called. "I'm up in Fayetteville," he started. "I'm trying this malpractice case against a lawyer up here." Because Wilson had gone to law school at Vanderbilt, then gone into JAG in the Navy, he was at a distinct disadvantage from those of us who had gone to school in-state and had classmates scattered throughout the state. He didn't know that many other lawyers. I had even more of an advantage because I'd gone to law school at two different times, so I had two sets of classmates. I knew practically every lawyer in the state—especially those in Fayetteville. And there he was up in Fayetteville, and he had sued another lawyer for malpractice. So every day all these lawyers would come and sit in the courtroom in an attempt to intimidate him. There had even been threats against him. He wanted me to come up and help him, and I couldn't get there fast enough! I called E.J. Ball and Jim Gallman and told them I was coming up, although they weren't very encouraging about my participation in this particular case. There was nothing more unpopular back then than one lawyer suing another.

But this was a case I resented more than usual because it involved the wife of another lawyer who had come to the attorney we were suing seeking a divorce. She was vulnerable and distraught, and this lawyer had taken advantage of her sexually. That was despicable. I had encountered many women in the same position, and it would have been quite easy to take advantage of them if I'd been so inclined. To do so, however, is totally unethical and the worst sin of all. I just can't imagine doing this to a helpless person. I rejoiced at the opportunity to get in and wage war against this unscrupulous lawyer.

All the lawyers in Fayetteville hung out in a particular watering hole every afternoon after work, and they all congregated at one communal table. I told Gallman and Ball to meet me at this bar, and I instructed them not to sit at the communal table but to take a table across the room. After Kathy and I came in and joined them, I got up and went over to the large table, where there were ten or twelve lawyers drinking. They all said, "How you doing, Carter? Good to see you. What are you doing up here?"

That was my cue. "I've come up to associate with Bill Wilson on the malpractice case," I drawled. "I understand there've been a lot of statements made around here about that case and about Bill Wilson, and by God, I'm here to challenge anyone who wants to step forward and take us on about that case. We're gonna try that case, and we're gonna win that case." There wasn't a word said as I turned and went back to our table across the room.

What was really bizarre was what happened when we were in the courtroom. In through the back door bolts John Norman Harkey from Batesville, Arkansas—lawyer and former insurance commissioner and kind of a distant cousin of Wilson. He'd heard about the problems, and he came in and announced to the court: "Your Honor, I'm John Norman Harkey, and I'm here to associate with Mr. Carter and Mr. Wilson on this case." We had already picked the jury when the other side decided to settle the case.

Without doubt one of the most colorful cases in which I was involved was that of Maxine Harris, an infamous madam in Hot Springs in the days before Governor Rockefeller cleaned up the illegal gambling industry in that resort. That was the main plank in his platform when he ran for governor—doing away with illegal gambling. In the early part of the century, gangsters used to go to Hot Springs to hide out and take the mineral baths. There was a horse track there, and at some point, gambling was established, too. Oney Madden, owner of the Cotton Club in Manhattan, moved his base of operation to Hot Springs, and he controlled illegal gambling there. There were big-time casinos in Hot Springs, and it was a booming gambling town. As a result, the Vapors Club, a very plush nightclub where all the biggest acts in show business played, was mob-owned. Madden would bring mobsters down to enjoy the baths.

Along with gambling comes prostitution, and Maxine Harris ran all the prostitution in Hot Springs. I don't know how old Maxine was when she entered my life, but probably in her fifties.

She was a huge, tall, stout woman and tough as nails. I'd known about her for years—she was always in the press for one thing or another. Then one day, in 1968, I got a call from Governor Rockefeller's office saying that Maxine Harris had called them because she'd been arrested in Hot Springs. She called the governor's office, told them she was in trouble, and asked them to recommend a good lawyer to represent her. They referred her to me.

She came to see me, and I quoted her a retainer fee, which she promptly paid. She had shot at a deputy sheriff as he approached her house to serve a warrant. She was charged with disorderly conduct and resisting arrest, and she wanted to go to trial. The judge was Judge Henry Britt, a circuit court judge in Hot Springs. He had a wandering eye, so his right eye looked in the opposite direction from his left eye. It made him look a bit strange. Being the loud, boisterous woman she was, Maxine was always looking for a forum from which to speak. She'd talked about Judge Britt just like she had all the other public officials, so it was a delicate situation, to say the least.

Paul Henson, with whom I shared office space in the Rector Building, was helping me try the case.

We were arguing some motions, and the judge was overruling us on everything. Paul and I had a stack of law books we'd brought into the courtroom with us, anticipating that the judge would overrule us on particular issues. Because he was ruling against us, I wanted to read into the record the Supreme Court law to protect the record to appeal the case, which wasn't necessary. All I really had to do was note my exception and the judge's ruling and later appeal the decision. But it made for a good show. I was standing up, reading out of a law book, when Judge Britt unloaded on me.

"Sit down and shut up; I've heard enough," he roared. "Move on with the case." I continued arguing with him, and the exchange became rather heated and tense. Finally, the judge rapped his gavel and ordered me to sit down.

That flew all over Maxine, so she shouted at him, "Why, you old gauche-eyed son of a bitch!"

He rapped his gavel and shouted above her, "Contempt of court! Eighteen months in the county jail. Sheriff, take her away."

They hauled Maxine off and locked her up in the county jail, and the judge wouldn't set a bond or release her. Paul and I went to the Supreme Court and finally got her released on bail. She was due to appear in court later, but she skipped out on her bond. She became a fugitive.

Then one day she just showed up at the office. My office suite was very small, and you could see into my private office from the reception area. She walked right past the receptionist and sat down in front of my desk and started cussing me. She said, "I want my money back, every cent I paid you, and I want it right now." She started to reach down into her purse, and I could see there was a .38 snubbed-nosed revolver there. Before she could get it out, I eased open my desk drawer and drew out my .45 automatic. I didn't have a bullet in the chamber, but there's nothing like the sound of pulling that slide back and letting it go forward to pull the bullet into the chamber.

I looked her square in the eye, and I said, "Maxine, you drop that gun back in your purse, and you get your ass out of my office, and I don't want to see or hear from you again or I'll blow your brains out." She dropped the gun back into her purse, stood up and exited the office. That was the last time I saw her. I don't know how the case was finally settled, but they caught her later in Blytheville, Arkansas, and she was brought back to justice.

I had moved to Nashville in the early eighties when I got a call from Maxine one day. She was writing an exposé, and she wanted my help in getting her book published. I didn't want anything to do with her, because she supposedly was going to expose the secrets of several politicians. That was just Maxine. Once we had our little showdown, it all blew over. I referred her to a literary agent and didn't hear from her again. I heard recently that a friend of a friend purchased her now-out-of-print book for $50 on eBay.

Governor Rockefeller also referred the defendants in the Alcoholic Beverage Control Department scandal to me. The case involved four former agents of the state ABC who had been charged with drug possession. One of the defendants was related to one of the governor's staff members. The governor asked me to represent them, and I did. It's funny, but I always seemed to get cases that ended up in the newspaper. Most folks knew I wouldn't hesitate to blast anyone I felt needed blasting. If I was trying a criminal case, I'd try it in the press because I usually had somewhat hopeless situations. But the press also liked to tear me up because I often tried to have them barred from the courtroom. I'd even have friends of mine who were journalists call my hand on it. They'd say, "You're unbelievable. You want to exclude the press, but every time you need publicity for one of your clients, you don't hesitate to call a journalist. You'll talk to us outside the courtroom to get the print that's favorable to you, but you keep us from observing the proceedings inside. You use us at your convenience." That's true; I did.

I was never an academic kind of lawyer. My friend Jim Gallman, a former assistant U.S. attorney who taught law at the University of Arkansas, was a scholarly lawyer. I'd be telling Gallman about a case I was trying, and I'd come up against a particular issue. Gallman would go over to the bookcase, pull out a book and say, "Here—here's your authority." I was never any good at research, either, but I had a sense for the law; law is what's reasonable. A law is established on what's fair and reasonable. I had an uncanny ability to predict not always what the law was but what it ought to be, and I'd have to find some precedents to back up my theory. If someone came to me with a problem, I pretty much knew if it was against the law or against the authority, and then I'd have to go and find the authority to back it up.

The reason Kathy Woods and I were so good together was that Kathy was a very smart book lawyer; she knew how to prepare the law in a case, and I didn't care about that. Kathy started working for me as a secretary while she was still in college. She completed law school and passed the bar during the time she worked in my office, but she learned so much law by practical application that she laughs today, telling me I credit her with practicing law long before she was board certified. She was invaluable to me in my practice and enabled me to take on a lot of the clients I did because of her knowledge of the law. I'm happy to say she lives in Nashville today and is senior vice president of legal and business affairs at the RCA Label Group. My wife and I get together with Kathy and her husband fairly often, and I still rely on her for practical advice.

I liked being in a position to help people, but for the most part the people I was dealing with were criminals. One of the girls I had working for me—I never had more than a couple—told me that the people I had waiting to see me made her nervous. I represented murderers, rapists, thieves, kidnappers, cutthroats, the lowest forms of human life, and after a while I got tired of dealing with that element. Many lawyers suffer burnout in their careers for that reason. A lawyer deals in someone else's misery; it's a human problem you're dealing with constantly, and it takes its toll on you. When you take on someone's case, you live that case for however long it takes to try it. If you don't win or don't achieve your desired result, then you're disappointed and the client is distraught.

I remember one time Bill Wilson asked me to help him with a death case over in East Arkansas—it involved the death of a truck driver—and we tried that case in federal court. I can still see the truck driver's wife and little kids. It's hard to become calloused to that kind of thing. People put their trust in you—they depend on you, and you've got to deliver the goods for them. If you're trying a personal injury case in which, for example, a man's been crippled and is going to spend the rest of his life disabled, you have to get enough compensation to take care of him for as long as he lives, and oftentimes that doesn't happen.

I was the same kind of lawyer as I was Secret Service agent. I was talking to a former Secret Service agent the other day—a longtime buddy—about some of the guys we had worked with through the years. I like to think that if another agent had been going into a gun battle, he would have wanted me by his side. I'm proud that people could depend on me—they could trust me—and they relied on me to get the job done. I've always said, "My strength is my weakness." I'm single-minded. When I'm on something, I'm totally focused; I'm going to get the job done. A single-minded person tends to overlook the things going on around him. I used to be critical of lawyers who took so many cases that they couldn't finish any of them very well. I tried to keep a smaller caseload, and I was completely focused.

Chapter 12
Mr. Smith Sends Me to Washington

HILE I WAS PRACTICING law in Little Rock in late 1969, a lawyer friend of mine, Frank Watson Jr., called me one Sunday morning. "Bill," he said, "I have someone I want you to meet. I think you'll be very interested in what he has to show you." I agreed to meet with them that very afternoon. That was my first introduction to Fred Smith, who, at twenty-seven, had recently been discharged from the Marines after serving two tours of combat duty in Vietnam. A much-decorated veteran, Fred had received the Silver Star, Bronze Star, two Purple Hearts, the Navy Commendation Medal and the Vietnamese Cross of Gallantry. While in the Marines, Fred had invested in a Little Rock-based company, Arkansas Aviation, which was a fixed-base operator. In late 1969, after being discharged from the Marines, Fred took over the company and converted it into a sales company specializing in used corporate jets.

"I have an idea," were his understated words to me, and on Frank's living room floor, the young man laid out an air cargo concept he wanted to develop. The problem was that he wanted to use Falcon 20 aircraft and operate as an air taxi carrier under the Civil Aeronautics Board regulations. The weight of the Falcon 20 exceeded the maximum weight requirements for air taxi operators. Part 298 of the CAB regulations provided air taxi operators could fly whenever and anywhere they liked in the United States. The restriction was that the aircraft could not have a take-off weight exceeding 12,500 pounds, and the Falcon weight exceeded this limitation.

I had resigned from the Secret Service only three years before, so I knew my way around Washington. In particular, I had developed a close personal friendship with Congressman Wilbur Mills, from Arkansas, who was at that time the powerful chairman of the House Ways and Means Committee. Mills was often described as the most powerful man in Washington outside of the president. I also had a similar relationship with Senator John McClellan, who was the powerful chairman of the Senate Appropriations Committee, and Senator William Fulbright and young Congressman Bill Alexander, all of whom were from Arkansas. Frank must have explained all this to Fred because he asked if he could retain me to proceed to Washington and investigate how to change the CAB regulations so that his company (later to be called Federal Express) could operate with the Falcon 20.

I went to Washington in 1969 and discussed our problem with Chairman Mills. Mills advised that the proper strategy would be to develop personal relationships with key people on the board so that when the issue came before them, they would be more likely to rule in our favor than if we were complete strangers. In addition, I would have to overcome the personal relationships the major airlines had developed over many years with the CAB. Mills' advice was simple: He would introduce me to friends of the decision makers, but I would be on my own to develop the personal relationships that might help me later on. He specifically advised me there could be nothing improper about my conduct, and I would have to rely solely on my friendships. He explained that often evidence in a case is equal on both sides, and the ruling authority may, within their discretion, rule either way, and many times would rule for the party they believed to have the most credibility.

Chairman Mills introduced me into social circles that offered me the opportunity to develop these relationships, and from 1969 through 1972, that was my main responsibility. I represented Federal Express; however, I never appeared before the CAB on their behalf. Fred later retained CAB counsel in Washington to file the necessary applications that preceded the CAB hearings in 1972. Fred was asking the board to eliminate the weight limitations and issue new regulations permitting air taxi operators to fly aircraft with a thirty-passenger configuration and a payload capacity of 7,500 pounds. The CAB was notorious for taking forever to hand down decisions; however, Fred's legal staff had done a superb job. Still, it was a shock to many in the industry when the board handed down its decision on July 18, 1972, adopting Fred's proposed change, fewer than six months after Fred's petition was filed. There was strong opposition to the petition, and the opponents appealed the board's decision, which was later upheld by the court of appeals.

Part of the strategy was to proceed quietly throughout the whole process and represent Fred as a small-town operator who was no threat to anyone. I think we all succeeded with that image. I know firsthand the significance of our friendship with Mills and McClellan. They were both so powerful at that time that just the association with such power often made the difference without saying anything. Sometimes, if I was meeting with a government agency on behalf of FedEx, I would have Mills or McClellan make the appointment for me since I was a constituent of both. Once inside the agency, meeting with the proper authority, it also really helped that I was a former Secret Service agent and, of course, the conversation always began with my service with President Kennedy and the assassination investigation. After that, we were old pals, and the bureaucrat usually started with "How can I help you?" I don't mind admitting that I used my association with Congress and my service with Kennedy and Johnson to my advantage. Having the opportunity to help Fred Smith, and later in my career, the Rolling Stones, was mainly due to my personal relationships.

Frank Watson Jr. and I became law partners in Little Rock and, in 1973, Fred moved FedEx to Memphis and asked Frank and me to move with him. Frank moved, but I chose to keep my law practice in Little Rock. I did some things for Fred afterward but drifted away to other things. Before Fred made the decision to move to Memphis, we went to Little Rock officials, including the Airport Authority, and asked that they expand their facilities to meet FedEx's requirements. This included adding another runway and property for a sorting center. I also enlisted the aid of Chairman Mills, in whose district Little Rock was located. He intervened and agreed to provide the necessary federal support that might be required. Months of negotiations took place, and the Airport Authority subsequently rejected Fred's request for the required support. Mr. Mills requested additional time to try to work things out; however, Little Rock was out of time. FedEx had to begin operations on a larger scale than the city could possibly support.

At the same time, Fred's hometown, Memphis, agreed to provide hangar facilities and to float a bond issue to build more hangar space, office buildings, and a cargo-sorting center and improve and expand runways at the Memphis airport. It is my opinion that city officials in Little Rock did not take Fred Smith seriously. After all, he was a brash young man of thirty with big ideas. The city simply had no vision for the future and little confidence in Fred. Chairman Mills, on the other hand, had complete confidence in Fred, and I think he also recognized the potential of Fred's air cargo system. When Fred made the final decision to move to Memphis, it was up to me to inform Mr. Mills. When I told him, he said he was, of course, disappointed, but he did not blame Fred. He understood Fred's decision was based on receiving the support he needed from the much more aggressive city of Memphis.

Through the years, people have asked me about Fred Smith and what kind of person he is. I still maintain contact with Fred and consider him a friend. I have the highest respect for him. He is a man committed to both his family and his country. His commitment to FedEx made that company a success, and if his complete story is ever told, the reader will be absolutely amazed at his drive. Fred is the only person on this planet who could have held that company together in its early development, and he made it the phenomenal success it is today. I always encouraged Fred to run for president because I thought he would provide the strong leadership this country needs that would result in a brighter future for all of us.

Chapter 13
On the Road with the Rolling Stones

HEN I WAS GROWING UP, in Rector, Arkansas, entertainment was simple. The Cotton Belt Railroad ran through Rector, and I remember as a little boy going down to the station to see the trains as they came through town, especially because they brought the mail. Everything centered around the train station in that small town, mainly because that's where the telegraph was. Other than radio, the telegraph was our only form of communication with the outside world. The radio, however, was our main source of entertainment. We used to sit at home, especially at night, and listen to the radio—the news broadcasts, *Gangbusters*, and all of the old radio serials.

The Rolling Stones, however, produced a different kind of entertainment, one that I could scarcely have imagined during my childhood.

Much of my history with the Rolling Stones was detailed by a journalist from *Rolling Stone* magazine, Chet Flippo, who was granted extraordinary access to the Stones for a number of years. The Rolling Stones—Mick Jagger, Keith Richards, Charlie Watts, Bill Wyman, and Ron Wood—is the most important group to come out of rock and roll's first thirty years and the one with the most enduring following and track record. As Chet points out in his book, *On the Road with the Rolling Stones: 20 Years of Lipstick, Handcuffs and Chemicals*, the reason their influence was greater than that of even the Beatles was that the Beatles were together for a relatively short time, and their influence was mostly musical. The Stones' impact was more far-reaching, and the reason for that was their touring. They continue to tour today, when all the guys are well into their fifties and sixties.

My story with the Stones began in 1973.

I was practicing criminal law in Little Rock when I got a call from my old friend Wilbur Mills, in Washington. It seemed that certain people in government were afraid there was going to be a revolution, and Congressman Mills, who was still chairman of the House Ways and Means Committee, and therefore one of the most powerful people in the United States, wanted my help.

Trying to anticipate what Mills wanted of me, I did a mental rundown of the current state of affairs in Washington. The last of the Watergate burglars, G. Gordon Liddy and James McCord, had been convicted and sent to jail; Senate hearings to investigate the possible involvement of the Nixon administration in the scandal were gearing up; and a bribery scandal had ensnared Nixon's vice president, Spiro T. Agnew. Nixon himself would be on the ropes by the end of the year.

The Chairman of the House Ways and Means Committee hadn't called about any of that.

"The problem," Mills explained, "has to do with the Rolling Stones, or as they're known around Washington, the most dangerous rock-and-roll band in the world."

Incredulous, I asked, "And how can I possibly help you with a rock band?"

I listened as Mills filled me in on the background.

"Earlier this year," he said, "the State Department and Immigration and Naturalization denied entry visas to the Rolling Stones that would allow them to tour in the United States."

Mills explained that the government was also trying to deport ex-Beatle John Lennon and his wife, Yoko Ono, who were living in New York City. On paper, the reason was that Lennon had been arrested for possession of hashish residue in London and was therefore an undesirable drug addict. In reality, certain elements in the U.S. Government—among them Nixon himself and Attorney General John Mitchell—feared that Lennon's influence on the youth of America made him too powerful.

"These guys were afraid that with a few concerts and public appearances, Lennon could have easily incited young people into open rebellion against the government," Mills said. "Now they're worried about the Rolling Stones."

The Stones ban started in late February 1973, when lead singer Mick Jagger was flying back to London from Australia and was denied permission to set foot on U.S. soil. After Jagger was flagged away from U.S. airports, the Stones were informed that their plans for another tour of the United States were unthinkable. To the Stones, being banned from the United States was a personal affront. But it was also an overwhelming economic disaster, coming at a time when their future depended on a successful U.S. tour. So they decided to buy some muscle. Someone in the Stones organization knew Elliott Janeway, who was a respected economist and financial writer. Janeway knew Congressman Mills and agreed to call him and ask for his help in solving the band's problems with the State Department.

Mills knew yours truly.

"Where do I fit into this?" I asked Mills. And thus the journey began.

Janeway said he would set up a meeting between the Rolling Stones' manager, Peter Rudge, and me. Before the meeting, I tried to gather as much information as I could, discussing the matter briefly with officials at the State Department. They were adamant about their position. According to State, the Stones' 1972 tour of the United States had incited riots, civil disobedience, arrests, and drug use. Therefore, when the group had asked to come back for a benefit concert, the

State Department had refused to issue them visas, stating that they were a negative influence on the youth of America.

Department officials had no shortage of reasons for their decision. Uncontrolled crowds had sparked riots at their concerts; Keith Richards, Mick Jagger, and Rolling Stones Records president Marshall Chess were arrested for assaulting a police officer in Warwick, Rhode Island, and the Stones allegedly used drugs openly. The official I spoke with told me the band had already had "pinstripes" (Harvard- and Yale-educated lawyers) from New York and Washington make formal appearances before the State Department to demand that visa rights be restored. State's reply was that the Stones had no rights since they were not U.S. citizens, and they would never be allowed in this country again.

I wasn't optimistic going into my meeting with the band. I was, however, sympathetic. I hadn't been an angel when I was a child; I had developed into quite a mischievous kid. In the seventh and eighth grades I was always in trouble of some kind, and by high school I became more rebellious and mischievous and began skipping school. I found that the secret to getting attention was to misbehave. Back then what that meant was cutting up in class, talking, and pulling pranks. I probably held the record in the Rector school system for the most suspensions. I think it was eleven times I was suspended from school. So even though the Stones were no longer kids, I could still empathize with their antics.

But arranging a meeting with the group was proving to be problematic.

Being granted an audience with the chairman of the House Ways and Means Committee and with the U.S. State Department was easy compared to setting up a meeting with the Stones themselves. First, I had to meet several times with Peter Rudge, the band's youngish and elegant, chain-smoking and fast-talking British manager, in New York. Rudge, a Cambridge University graduate, came to prominence while still in his twenties as the manager of The Who and was the operations manager for the Stones' 1972 tour, when he was only twenty-five. His Sir Productions offices, at 130 W. 57th in Manhattan, became Stones headquarters.

The next step was to meet Prince Rupert Ludwig Ferdinand von Loewenstein-Wertheim-Freudenberg, the band's London financial advisor. Prince Rupert (a real prince, by the way, whose family is from Bavaria) was probably the first international jet-set money advisor. He had been introduced to Mick in 1968 by Mick's future wife, Bianca Rosa Perez-Mora, and he had supervised and advised on the Stones' severing from former manager Allen Klein.

Finally, after all the pre-meetings and screenings, I was summoned to Mick's suite in the Plaza Hotel in New York for a meeting with Jagger, Prince Rupert, Rudge, and Allan Arrow and Peter Parcher, two of the Stones' New York lawyers. My eyes were drawn to Mick Jagger immediately, sitting silently in an armchair with his legs crossed, staring at me intently. Foregoing any social niceties, Arrow took the lead in questioning me, and he got straight to the point.

127 — *Get Carter*

"How do you plan to accomplish what I, Parcher, and the best Washington lawyers have been unable to do?"

I had no strategy worked out, so I simply said, "I'll look into the matter and do my very best to succeed." But then I added, "However, I can make no promises."

Arrow clearly didn't appreciate the vagueness of my non-plan, and the tone of the meeting quickly became adversarial.

"I know what you'll do," he said. "You'll do something illegal or improper, and you must know that we will have no part of such a thing."

I was furious. I didn't care who was in the room, I wasn't about to have anyone question my ethics or my character.

"I am highly insulted that you would suggest I'd do anything illegal for the Stones or anyone else. May I remind you, I am a former federal agent and a practicing lawyer. I understand the oaths I have taken, but I don't even need an oath to make me honest."

At this point, I knew my life would not suffer if I didn't represent the Stones, so I rose to walk out. "Get someone else," I fired over my shoulder as I began to leave.

"Shut up!" screamed Mick Jagger. The room instantly went silent, and I stopped in my tracks. He jumped up from his seat and yelled again at his lawyers. "Shut up! You're attacking his character just because you're afraid a lawyer from Little Rock might be able to do what you can't." Jagger turned to me, looked me straight in the eye, and said, "I'm going to give you a chance."

Just like that, I was hired. I would report to Peter Rudge and Mick. It took but one short meeting for me to realize that Mick Jagger was definitely in charge.

My mission was to untangle the web of bureaucracy that the State Department and the INS had cast over the band after the end of the 1972 STP, or Stones Touring Party, tour. In order to reenter the United States as a touring band, the Stones needed to obtain admission under a so-called H-1 petition—a work permit that allows a person of creative talent to perform at an event. Since State and INS were refusing to grant the H-1 petition, I had to get Mick into the country under a B-1 visa, which allowed him to enter the United States only for a specific business meeting—in this case to attend meetings with me and his other lawyers and his record company. This required us to submit a specific itinerary for each visit; Mick's travel could not vary from that. He had to stay at a specific hotel. If his meetings were in LA, he could not leave LA except to fly directly back to London. Keith Richards had to travel in the same way.

Each time a visa application was filed, Mick or Keith had to appear in person at the U.S. Embassy in London for interrogation that was often demeaning. Once, they were summoned before Ambassador Walter H. Annenberg himself. Jagger and Richards were supposed to have been at the embassy on a Friday, but they didn't arrive until after it closed for the day. When they returned on Saturday to pick up their visas, they were ushered into the ambassador's office. Keith Richards described the look on Annenberg's face as one of contempt. Richards and Jagger were not invited to sit, and Annenberg was curt with them, saying, "The Rolling Stones will require divine intervention to enter the United States in the future." Paddy Grafton-Green, Mick and Keith's London attorney, tried to defend them. Annenberg cut Green short, waved a handful of documents at him, and said, "It's a pity you can't read the State Department file on the Rolling Stones, but these files are not open to everyone to read."

The campaign to exclude the Rolling Stones from the United States was partly a response to the Nixon administration's paranoia about anti-Vietnam War protesters and urban rioters, and partly a response to the negative press that had surrounded their 1972 tour. The '72 tour had been the band's first return trip to the country since Altamont, the notorious 1969 California concert where Hell's Angels security guards had killed one concert-goer and several others were killed or injured in other ways. When the band announced the two-month, thirty-city, fifty-concert tour for the summer of '72, a scandal-hungry press came out in droves.

Tommy Thompson's observations in *Life* magazine were typical:

The Rolling Stones! Are *they* still among us? How can they be? . . . . In a decade—ten years!—of performing, they have earned some of the worst press clippings since Mussolini. To read them is to scan the underside of a rock . . . . Their official trademark—on record labels, posters, jeweled pins—is a taunting, devil's-red tongue stuck out at the world. Their spoor is scandal, dark rumor, divorce, adultery, illegitimate children, drugs (when Jagger wears the trademark "Coke" sewn onto his jacket, he is not endorsing cola), even blood and violent death. But here it is, the summer of '72, and once again, the Rolling Stones are sweeping across America. Eight weeks, 30 cities, 50 concerts, 750,000 customers ecstatically pulling between $3 and $4 million from their jeans pockets and shoving it through the ticket windows after waiting in line for sometimes 48 hours . . . . With the Beatles disintegrated and Bob Dylan not appearing in public anymore, the Stones are the only deities visible on Olympus (Thompson, p. 30).

The band and its promoters were not prepared for that kind of response in 1972. The Stones had never toured the United States in large arenas before, and it seemed that virtually every stop was the occasion for rioting, arrests, and physical injuries. Vancouver's Pacific Coliseum was sold out on June 3, the opening day of the tour, and two thousand fans tried to crash the concert, resulting in injuries to thirty policemen, who arrested eight people. Ten days later, on June 13, at the Sports Arena in San Diego, riots resulted in sixty arrests and fifteen injuries. The next night, at the sold-out Civic Arena in Tucson, three hundred kids tried to crash the concert, and police had to use tear gas to disperse the crowd. The same thing happened in Albuquerque the next day, when a disturbance at the University of New Mexico broke out after two hundred counterfeit tickets were presented. On

July 4, there were sixty-one arrests at RFK Stadium, in Washington, DC, with 45,000 in attendance. On July 17, in Montreal, there was a riot outside the Forum, and the Rolling Stones' equipment truck was bombed. Policemen were injured and replacement equipment had to be brought in, causing the show to be delayed. The three days at Madison Square Garden in New York City, July 24–26, featured riots that led to ten arrests and injuries to policemen.

Part of the problem was that arenas sold out immediately, and there were not nearly enough tickets to meet the demand. People outside who couldn't get tickets rioted, and those inside were unruly and rebellious in reaction to Jagger and the Stones' taunting, sex, drugs, and defiance. Several governments would later brand Jagger a revolutionary and concurred with the U.S. government in expressing fear that if the Rolling Stones came to their countries, they might incite youth to rebellion.

The most famous incident of the '72 tour came late in the summer, when the band was en route to a concert in Boston. Their plane, unable to land in Boston because of fog, was diverted to Warwick, Rhode Island, where a local newspaper photographer had been tipped off that celebrities were arriving. The touring party disembarked and milled around on the tarmac while Rudge and his staff tried to find alternate transportation to Boston. Meanwhile, the newspaper photographer insisted that he be allowed to photograph the stars. Keith objected. The reporter refused to desist, citing freedom of the press. Keith scuffled with him, and the Warwick police arrested him on an assault charge. They arrested Mick and Rolling Stones Records president Marshall Chess for good measure. Mick allegedly resisted arrest, so he was charged with "obstructing a police officer while he was in the performance of his duty." Then everyone went to jail.

Meanwhile, Boston Garden was full of Stones fans. The arrest had made immediate headlines on radio, television, and later in the print press, and as word spread, the Boston crowd made ready to go to the aid of the incarcerated Stones. At the same time, a race riot was brewing in South Boston, and Mayor Kevin White didn't have enough police to control both scenes. Opening act Stevie Wonder played two hours. Still no Stones. Stage manager Chip Monck read aloud from *Jonathan Livingston Seagull*. Still no Stones. The atmosphere became so explosive that Mayor White, who had been negotiating with the Rhode Island authorities to release the Stones, went to the Garden and begged the crowd to be patient. The whole thing was broadcast later on television.

"I've got some good news and some bad news," the mayor told the jeering crowd. "The bad news is Mick Jagger has been arrested in Warwick, Rhode Island." There was a deafening chorus of boos.

"I got them out," the mayor continued. A huge cheer went up.

"Now the other end of my city is in flames tonight," said the mayor. "I'm leaving and you can tear the place apart . . . but I am asking you to do me a favor. I'm taking all the police out, and when the concert is over, I hope you will go home."

Later that night, the Stones, with full police escort, finally arrived and played a full set. The crowd went home without incident. Mayor White had acted on good instinct—I would learn later in Toronto that the rabid Stones fans can get out of control quickly.

Meanwhile, this was the atmosphere in which I set out to persuade the U.S. government that Mick Jagger, Keith Richards, et al. were the victims of a bum rap. My first official act was to visit the State Department and size up the problem. Congressman Mills arranged a meeting with the Office of Congressional Relations, which in turn set up a meeting with the officer in the visa office who was handling the case.

This was 1973, and everyone had long hair and wide neckties. The case officer I went to meet had a crew haircut and a tie no more than two inches wide; he was a career government employee who resisted change to the last minute. This officer told me that the Stones were guilty of such gross misconduct and contempt for our laws that they would never be allowed back into this country if he had anything to do with making the decision. And he had *everything* to do with it. Anyone whose name was on State's list of questionable characters was referred to Washington's visa office for a decision any time they applied for a visa through an American embassy anywhere in the world. I became pretty sure I would never change this guy's mind when he told me that—in addition to the civil disobedience, drug use, illicit sex, and violence—it was unforgivable that Mick Jagger would mock the U.S. government by wearing an Uncle Sam costume, including the top hat, on stage.

I immediately changed the subject from the Rolling Stones to my government service and probably agreed with him, that day, that the Rolling Stones represented the devil himself. After visiting with him about my days in the Secret Service, I excused myself. I returned to Gene Krizek, my contact in Congressional Relations, and discussed my problem. He was one of the senior guys in the Office of Congressional Relations, which is the State Department's lobby with Congress, and he had the best contacts on the Hill. When Mills had anyone call the State Department to grease things for me, they'd call Krizek, who would go to the department head and set it up.

I had several meetings with the director in the visa office, Julio Arias, and other meetings as well over the next several weeks, and I finally worked my way up to Loren Lawrence, the administrator for the Bureau of Security and Consular Affairs, which supervised the visa office. After explaining my initial contacts, I told him of my impression of Mick Jagger and the Rolling Stones. Since Jagger was the leader and the one who got most of the press, he was the primary subject of attack, but my problem was simple: I had to convince the State Department that all of the Stones were really choir boys and would be an asset to any community.

I began carefully. "I understand that the Stones have no rights, since they're not American citizens. But I hope you can understand that the Rolling Stones—particularly Mick Jagger—are entertainers; that's their job—to entertain—and the things that are being said about him personally are just not true." So far, so good. "Far from being the devil most people see him, Mick Jagger is highly intelligent, well read, and a very good businessman." I encouraged Loren Lawrence and his associates to meet the man who was more than a file number.

Lawrence could not have been more receptive. "None of us have any idea who your Mr. Jagger is," he said to me. One major hurdle cleared.

I told Peter Rudge that I thought it unrealistic to believe we would get approval soon enough for a tour in the spring of 1974. However, I had laid the groundwork for an H-1 petition, which was required for a tour. In the meantime, Mick and Keith were still being hassled by State every time they applied for a visa to visit the United States for meetings with Rudge or their record company or me.

Keith had a drug conviction in Europe, and even if I got that through State, I still had to get an exclusion waiver from the INS before he could be approved to enter the United States. Basically, if an applicant has ever been convicted of a crime, he or she cannot be granted a visa without a waiver excluding the conviction. I had been working INS at the same time I was working State and had developed a personal relationship with Neal Leary, the assistant commissioner of Immigration. Neal was a lawyer, and for a career government bureaucrat, he was very reasonable.

Rudge was now planning a full-scale U.S. tour for the summer of 1975, which meant that I would have to get everything processed so the band could enter the country in early 1975 to rehearse and plan the tour. I had met with Frederick Smith Jr. (not of FedEx fame), Loren Lawrence's deputy, and then with Neal Leary on May 29. I had everything in order by June 1974 and requested the U.S. visas in London. Once we had processed Keith through INS and obtained his waiver (the hard part), we would file an H-1 petition in the United States, asking for a change of status for Mick and Keith from their B-1 visas to an H-1 work visa. At the time, Mick was in the United States doing promotional visits for the Stones' new album, *It's Only Rock and Roll*, and trying to set up the tour. He could do this under a B-1, but I had to submit a specific itinerary of his whereabouts, including city, hotel, and appointments. If we varied his travels, I would have to advise State and INS.

June 12, 1974, was a milestone. Fred Smith called to tell me that State had approved Mick's H-1 and that the ambassador would notify Jagger, which he did the following day in London. The Stones' London lawyer went to the embassy to pick up Mick's visa and reported that he was greeted warmly and everything went as planned. The change of attitude at the London Embassy meant progress.

Keith's application had been filed on June 10, 1974, along with all the supporting information about his arrest and medical documents stating that he was of sound mind and not using illegal drugs. Basically, these reports were nothing more than a scam because all you had to do was get a doctor friendly to your cause to certify what we wanted to say, and he'd do it. Then a bomb fell on June 18.

I had gone to INS to meet Paul Murphy, the officer who would grant Keith's waiver. He told me that Dorothy Gilcrest, at State, had notified him that she would not grant the waiver. I immediately went to see Fred Smith and told him I was shocked that Ms. Gilcrest had made such a determination. He said he would call a staff meeting at three o'clock that day and that I should call him after that. When I phoned him at four-thirty, he reported that State was reconsidering its decision, and a recommendation would be forthcoming. I called Fred Smith on June 20, 22, and 24. Each time, I was told there was no decision. Finally, when I called Smith on June 25, he said State had made a favorable recommendation to INS that Keith's waiver be granted. I called Neal Leary that same day, but he still hadn't heard from State. He still had no word on June 27 or 28. On July 2, Neal Leary told me State had advised INS of its recommendation, but he had still not received any written communication.

I figured Ms. Gilcrest was slow-walking me because she had been overruled. Sure enough, I talked with Fred Smith on July 3, and he told me there was disagreement among his staff. He said State would need further justification—to wit, a current medical exam—before it could approve Keith's application. This was a huge dilemma for me, which was why I had wanted to facilitate a personal meeting between Mick and State. My challenge wasn't with the hierarchy at the State Department, it was with lower-level staff who resented Mick and the Stones and kept erecting roadblocks in our way, with one nitpicking item after another. Their supervisors felt that rather than overriding their staff and rubber-stamping the petitions, they had to make us comply with one demand after another. This really slowed the process for us.

While Mick's image had been an obstacle for us, it was Keith's drug addiction that posed a different set of problems. Both Mick and Keith had records in England, but Mick's were very minor violations, like being busted at a party with a small amount of pot. Mick Jagger was not a drug addict nor was he known as one. Keith was another story entirely. He was widely known to be addicted to heroin, although I wasn't aware of just how severe his addiction was. So we had to get Keith certified by a doctor before his petition could be granted.

Herman Dunbar, an American doctor living in London, had already examined Keith once, and his report was attached to our original visa application. When I learned we'd need another medical report, I called Paddy Grafton-Green, the London lawyer, and we tracked down Dr. Dunbar in Paris. Since he'd seen Keith several times over the preceding two years, we sent Keith to Paris.

Meanwhile, I met Mick and Peter at the Plaza Hotel in New York on July 17 and brought them up to date. We decided I should try to expedite the H-1 in the hope that we could still tour in early 1975. My experience as a bureaucrat now became a tremendous help. In my earlier conversations with State about Mick or Keith, officials had simply referred to them by file number. I knew their image of Mick Jagger was that of an entertainer who disrespected America by dressing in the

Uncle Sam costume, but the Mick I was coming to know was extremely intelligent, well read, and articulate. I had to get State and INS to see this other side of him. I knew Fred Smith would not arbitrarily order his staff to reverse its decision; I must at least make a favorable case from the London Embassy to the director of the visa office. If I could not convince them, then I could appeal to Smith or Loren Lawrence. So we decided to take Mick to the State Department. Loren Lawrence was surprised that I was willing to expose my client to department scrutiny, but we set up an appointment, and Mick and Peter came to Washington.

To avoid fans, we checked into the exclusive Madison Hotel, known for housing high-level lobbyists, foreign heads of state, wealthy bankers, and businessmen. But when we appeared in the lobby, all the businessmen and gray-haired ladies immediately swarmed Jagger, seeking autographs, supposedly for their children. Mick was one of the most recognizable personalities in the world, and the nation's capital was no exception. We arrived at the State Department for a morning meeting on September 26. Word had gotten around that Mick Jagger was going to be in the building, and when he arrived, every woman who worked there, young or old, came out of her office to greet him. His presence completely disrupted the entire building. Mick signed autographs and had photos made as we made our way to the meeting. Fred Smith told me that not even visiting heads of state generated that kind of response from the staff.

The meeting with Smith was quite warm and cordial. Jagger was dressed in a conservative business suit and he was very businesslike and charming, handling the meeting just as I had instructed him to. I didn't have to do more than urge him to conduct himself in a civil manner; essentially, I told him just to be himself and apply some of his charm to the employees of the State Department. I couldn't have had a better client, and Smith later told me that the meeting with Jagger had changed his opinion about a man they knew only as a file number.

I took Mick and Peter to meet Neal Leary at INS the same day. My problem was actually at State, but INS issued waivers, and in the case of questionable characters who had criminal records, INS acted solely on the recommendations of State. The meeting lasted about an hour, and then Mick signed autographs and was introduced to all the appropriate officials.

To seal the deal, I had invited Loren Lawrence to have dinner with Jagger. With the help of Congressman Mills' staff, I arranged for a room in an exclusive private club in Georgetown; the guest list included Lawrence and his wife; Mick and his wife, Bianca; Rudge; my legal assistant, Kathy Woods; and me. I had already briefed Jagger on Lawrence's expertise on Chinese and Filipino affairs, and he'd read extensively on these subjects. At dinner most of us were quiet, enjoying the great meal and fine wines while Mick had a lengthy, intelligent, and spirited discussion on the history of the Philippines and the politics of China with Lawrence. Mick made quite an impression on Loren Lawrence, and I've always believed that these meetings solidified our relations with the State Department.

Dr. Dunbar said he was ready to file his report on October 14. He sent the report directly to me four days later, giving Keith a clean bill of health. I filed it with the State Department on October 23. On November 14, Peter Rudge was in my office in Little Rock when Fred Smith called.

"I have some good news for you," he said. "Everything has been approved—but there are some conditions."

Peter and I could barely contain our elation, but I still was surprised to learn what my role would be in the conditions. The approval was conditioned upon my submitting a plan that would guarantee the safety of concert-goers and property at the venues. In addition, I would be required to tour with the Stones and personally assure the government of security and prevent any illegal activities during the tour.

It looked like Bill Carter would be going on the road with the Rolling Stones.

Chapter 14
U.S. Tour—1975

I WORKED OFTEN WITH Peter Rudge in his office in New York City in the fall of 1974 and the early months of 1975, making plans for the Tour of Americas, the grand title we used in the beginning. The tour was to begin in North America on June 1 and continue in South America from August 6 to 25. A second phase later in the year would include the Far East. That meant we had to finalize the arrangements for the U.S. leg with promoters and local authorities, look for venues in South America, and deal with the governments of several countries all at once. We spent much of the first part of the year cutting deals with promoters throughout the United States and visiting venues where the Stones would appear. Rudge made the financial deals, while I advanced the date with mayors' offices and local chiefs of police, outlining our security plans and describing our requirements for them.

Since I would be the locals' direct liaison with the Rolling Stones organization, I requested police departments in each city to assign a senior officer with a police radio to accompany me at all times during concerts. That way I would be alerted immediately if any incidents took place inside or outside the hall and could get right to the scene and perhaps defuse it before major damage occurred. Coordinating concerts with local authorities was not usual practice in the rock-and-roll world at that time. Our procedure came directly from my experience with Secret Service protocol for presidential visits, and it would pay off repeatedly during the tour.

My job was political as well. The U.S. State Department wasn't the only government agency that was leery of the notorious Rolling Stones. Local boards and commissions all over America had anxiety attacks as soon as they heard that the Stones were coming to their town.

The first serious challenge to the tour (and a subsequent tour by Pink Floyd) came in April 1975 via a seemingly obscure park commission resolution presented before the city government in Milwaukee, Wisconsin.

> Resolution by Supervisor Ament, requesting that the decision of the Park Commission, leasing the County Stadium to Daydream Productions on June 8, 1975, and June 22, 1975, for the presentation of rock concerts

and musical shows be reversed; and that the Park Commission, the General Manager of the Parks and the Stadium Director be directed not to execute any contract or lease for use of the stadium on the aforesaid dates to Daydream Productions for rock concerts or musical shows.

Daydream Productions was promoting the Stones' appearance in Milwaukee, and the permit to present the concert on June 8 at Milwaukee County Stadium had already been granted when County Commissioner F. Thomas Ament asked the county board to override the park commission, which had granted the original permit, and prohibit the concert. He argued that disturbances and violence at past Stones concerts meant that the safety of Milwaukee concert-goers would be at risk. Daydream's Randy McElrath asked me to appear formally before the board and speak on behalf of the Rolling Stones and Daydream.

So I was there on Wednesday, April 22, listening to a Milwaukee police lieutenant testify that he had called San Francisco police for information about crime surrounding a Rolling Stones appearance in their city in 1972. San Francisco's department told Milwaukee's that a girl had been gang raped on the night of the Stones concert, implying that the Rolling Stones appearance somehow caused the rape. Tipped beforehand that the lieutenant would bring this information to the board, I had found an article about the crime from the *San Francisco Examiner*, which did indeed imply that the mere presence of the Rolling Stones in the community caused the crime rate to increase. I had also called an old friend who was an inspector with the San Francisco Police Department, and after reviewing the file, he told me that the rape was committed miles from the concert and that there was no evidence the crime was in any way connected to the event.

When I was allowed to cross-examine the lieutenant, I got him to admit the crime was committed more than eleven blocks from the concert, and he could not testify there was a connection. I argued that much of the blame-it-on-the-Stones mentality was undeserved and that the band presented no more of a threat to the community than any other concert or sporting event. I also noted that violent drunken brawls resulting in injuries and arrests frequently occurred at Milwaukee Brewers baseball games. I then made a commitment to meet with local law enforcement officers to coordinate arrangements for the concert, and I explained that I had helped draft Daydream's security plan, which had been submitted to the board.

On April 24, the *Milwaukee Sentinel* reported that "The committee, several of its members argued, had no more right to ban the Stones from the Stadium than to keep out Henry Aaron." The show would go on in Milwaukee.

South America, however, was out. In April, just prior to my mission to Milwaukee, I went to South America with Rudge; Mike Crowley from the Stones' team; Tom Collins, a U. S. promoter with South American experience; and Patrick Stansfield, the Stones' production coordinator, to investigate the feasibility of a tour there. We landed in Rio de Janeiro on April 8 and spent the next day looking at a 16,000-seat arena and a 250,000-seat soccer stadium. The stadium manager told us that Billy

Graham held the attendance record (250,000, plus thousands outside). Two days later, we visited two venues and met with promoters in Sao Paolo.

On April 12, we flew on to Caracas, Venezuela, where we had meetings at El Poliedro, a beautiful 13,000-seat glass-fronted venue operated by the Venezuelan government. The building manager, Felipe Poleo, had two security staffers at the meeting—both were in military uniform and had guns slung over their shoulders. Rudge and I asked them how we would protect the glass exterior of the building if the crowd got out of control and began throwing rocks. Before our interpreter, Fernando Castenedo, could speak, one of the security officers pointed his gun at an imaginary crowd and pretended to shoot. Apparently, Venezuelan crowd control meant shooting into the crowd. They assured us that young Venezuelans were well disciplined and would not get out of control. I guess not, if they valued their lives! We visited Mexico City the next day and then I went home to Little Rock.

South America had been experiencing some political unrest at the time, and the economy was so weak that we concluded we would have had to keep ticket prices fairly low. Even then, there were problems with getting the money out of the country. When Rudge met with the Stones on his return, they decided it would not be economically or politically feasible for them to tour South America in 1975. Japan didn't pan out, either. I had known a Japan tour was a possibility since the fall of '74, and at that time several of my Secret Service buddies were still on active duty. When Rudge asked me to file a visa request for the Stones to tour Japan, I went to these friends, as well as to Loren Lawrence, for information. Wilbur Mills made introductions to the Japanese cultural attaché in Washington and to the Consulate General of Japan in New Orleans, where it was recommended that I file the visa application.

I asked the consul general to inquire about visas for the Rolling Stones and named each one. I felt they might reject Keith or Mick or both. Jagger had been denied entry to Japan in 1973 because of his drug conviction. Sure enough, my inside intelligence reported that the Japanese government was nervous about having the rebellious Stones tour their country. It was said that the decadent Rolling Stones, with their crude behavior, including openly advocating sex, illicit drug use, defiance of authority, and revolution, were a threat to the Japanese culture.

It seemed that everywhere I went, the response was the same—everyone loved to hate the Stones. This would become even more of a reality later. But for now, with South America and Japan out, at least for 1975, the attention was focused entirely on the United States. The U.S. tour schedule was final.

June 1	Baton Rouge, Louisiana
June 3–4	San Antonio, Texas
June 6	Kansas City, Missouri
June 8	Milwaukee, Wisconsin
June 9	St. Paul, Minnesota

June 11–12	Boston, Massachusetts
June 14	Cleveland, Ohio
June 15	Buffalo, New York
June 17–18	Toronto, Canada
June 22–27	New York City, New York
June 29–30	Philadelphia, Pennsylvania
July 1–2	Washington, DC
July 4	Memphis, Tennessee
July 6	Dallas, Texas
July 9–13	Los Angeles, California
July 15–16	San Francisco, California
July 18	Seattle, Washington
July 20	Denver, Colorado
July 23–24	Chicago, Illinois
July 26	Indianapolis, Indiana
July 27–28	Detroit, Michigan
July 30	Atlanta, Georgia
July 31	Greensboro, North Carolina
August 2	Jacksonville, Florida
August 4	Louisville, Kentucky
August 6	Hampton Roads, Virginia

We were ready to hit the road.

I would become friends with *Rolling Stone* magazine writer Chet Flippo on this tour, and his description of what it's like to be on the road with the band is dead on:

Being on the road with the Stones is an existence quite unlike any other. If you take a bit of a traveling circus and a dark hint of a carnival geek sideshow and some of the blatant hype and horn blowing of a political campaign and a whiff of the musky lures of the flesh peddlers and some of the mindless frenzy of a bikers' run and the giddy hysteria of young and rich and coked-up socialites determined to be hip at any cost and the pied piper effect on a tattered teenaged Stones army too young and perhaps too cough-syruped out to perceive of the Stones as anything but middle-aged roues and then you throw in some local pols who are strictly from the blow-dry generation and are eager-beaver to glad-hand it with Mick and then you stir in some tough cops from the old school who wouldn't mind putting the bracelets on these mincing foreign fairy rock stars—and you put all that together over a couple of decades, and, brother, you have got yourself one hell of a rock show. (Flippo, p. 7)

The first date was in Baton Rouge on June 1, and the Stones rehearsed for several days at the venue, Louisiana State University's Assembly Center, going back and forth from New Orleans, where the band and the staff were staying in the ritzy Royal Orleans, in the French Quarter. New Orleans was a very nice place to kick off the tour. I arrived about ten days prior to the opening date and spent most of that time eating at the best restaurants in the city. One day, two of the tour members, Paul Wasserman and Bill Zysblat, along with several more people from the tour, went with me at eleven to lunch at Tortorici's, an Italian restaurant across from the hotel, on Royal and St. Louis, and we finished our eight-course meal and a little wine about three-thirty. There was little else to do, other than trying to isolate the Stones from the worldwide press that had gathered. Press relations fell mostly to Wasserman, a highly regarded Los Angeles press agent, whose main duties with such prestigious clients as Linda Ronstadt, Bob Dylan, Dennis Hopper, and Jack Nicholson seemed to be keeping them out of the press much more than they were in it. Wasserman was a large man of somber mien who appeared every morning at the hotel coffee shop—in whatever city we were in—at daybreak, with an armload of newspapers from around the country and around the world.

This was my first real experience with the rock-and-roll media, and the first team was present: Flippo of *Rolling Stone*, Robert Hilburn of the *Los Angeles Times*, and John Rockwell of the *New York Times*. These were all music biz veterans. They were excited and revved up and aggressive, but they were nothing like the non-music media. There were reporters from all over the world; the aggressive British and Australian tabloid newspaper staffers were like hyperactive dog packs, circling and sniffing at rumors in hotel lobbies; television crews appeared from all the networks, including such ferret-like reporters as Geraldo Rivera, and local TV crews in every city lay in waiting. It was as if good and evil were about to clash—good being the authorities, and evil, of course, the Rolling Stones. Everyone seemed to be waiting for the Stones to live up to their demonic images. Temptation would surely arise from their appearance—sex, drugs, riots, and every evil known to society would erupt! The media were hoping to experience a catastrophic opening by the band that the authorities would love to hate.

"Where have we failed that this pimply-faced disciple of dirt is a hero, a rootin', tootin' hero to our teenage kids?" transplanted conservative Australian columnist Steve Dunleavy wrote in the *National Star*, the new sensationalist weekly tabloid started by Australian media mogul Rupert Murdoch to compete with the *National Enquirer*. "It's time we exorcised this demonic influence over our children!" exhorted Dunleavy.

While Wasserman fought off the slavering media, the tour staff was concerned only about how local police would feel about the giant inflatable phallus, which rose twenty feet above the stage during Jagger's performance of "Starfucker." They needn't have worried. Both the Sunday afternoon opener at LSU and the second show that night went off without a hitch.

Flippo described the afternoon opening:

The rule exploded with cheers at 5:20 when the house lights went down and the first keening notes of Aaron Copland's "Fanfare for the Common Man" flooded the hall, and the crowd surged forward and strobe lights winked like angry flying insects around the hall. A surging Super Trooper spotlight pinioned Jagger as he lay on his back at the tip of the star point out front. Keith ground into the down-and-dirty opening chords of "Honky Tonk Woman" and we were off to the races. Later in the set, Jagger started "Star, Star" (better known as "Starf...er"), and as he did so, the trap door in front of him, that houses the giant dick and the inflatable dragon as well as other special effects, opened. A moment later, the same trap door rises to release the gradually hardening, large, white phallus. It slowly billowed forth, to much front laughter (. . . as Mick sings "Starf...er" he starts to play with the huge condom and then, inexplicably, it de-tumesces and disappears back through its little door . . . . After speeding through "Rip This Joint," the band finally—after almost two hours—hits its groove and "Street Fighting Man" is a textbook lesson in how to rock and roll. Now that these collegians have warmed to the Stones so much that they're going apeshit here at LSU's Assembly Center, stomping enough to raise Huey Long from the dead, how is Mick gonna work an encore that will empty the joint so that it will be refilled half an hour later by ticket holders for the second show, and what if the first show fans decide to stay the hell there? Mick leaps out of a sudden darkness into a hot red spotlight and caresses his way through a steamy version of "Midnight Rambler." He's howling and kneeling on the stage as he fingers his silver-studded belt and starts lashing out with it. Not bad for a Baton Rouge encore. Outside, Baton Rouge has suddenly been Stoned: as in when angelic-faced, teenaged girls who had not even been born when these Stones yahoos first raised a ruckus start acting moon-eyed over these old farts and when the scalpers suddenly wake up and raise their ticket prices by a sudden few dollars and when those incredibly beautiful women (the ones in the stiletto heels and the black net stockings and the slit skirts and the push-up bras . . . enough, already) appear out of nowhere and announce that they are guests of the Rolling Stones. Well, why not? What is rock and roll for if not for fun? (p. 23)

The second show was another huge success, and by the time we got back to New Orleans, it was two-thirty in the morning, but it didn't matter because we had Monday off and wouldn't depart for San Antonio until 2:00 p.m. Tuesday. Everything in New Orleans had gone smoothly from my perspective. Jagger's post-show meetings had to do with technical problems and press matters. Rudge was especially pleased that the giant phallus hadn't seemed to create that much of a stir. At this point, the tour seemed pretty normal to me, and I was preparing for a mundane trip, wondering what there might be for me to do. Rudge and Wasserman may have been stressed out over problems with the mass of media that accompanied the tour and how to control its every move, but security and crowd control went without incident. I recall thinking how well-controlled were the youth of Baton Rouge.

On to San Antone! A high school mariachi band and a large crowd of teenaged fans greeted our plane. What a welcome, I thought, as I stepped off the plane. Then Rudge and Terry Bassett, the Dallas promoter who was promoting the San Antonio show, greeted me with the front page headline of the *San Antonio News*: STONES ROLL INTO SAN ANTONIO. It was not good publicity. The article covered every negative aspect of the Stones' bad-boy image. The paper was one of three that Australia's Rupert Murdoch had just acquired, and the *News* became known right away for sensational headlines—particularly their (inaccurate) screamer, KILLER BEES MOVE NORTH. Bassett said the Stones story was typical and we should be prepared for the worst. A freaked-out Rudge called a meeting as soon as we got to the hotel so we could prepare for trouble in Texas.

In an effort to keep fans from mobbing the Stones, we brought them to the venue in the back of a beer truck!

Many—too many—on-duty uniformed police officers wearing sidearms attended the first night's show. They stationed themselves near the stage, out front, and backstage; their mere presence came close to causing a riot. I was with the local police officer assigned to me when we heard that an officer had stopped and pushed a young teen, who had responded by spitting on the lawman. The kid was about to be handcuffed when we came upon the scene. A large crowd of teenagers was shouting obscenities at the police. We were able to resolve the matter without an arrest, and a full-scale riot was barely averted. The next day, I held a security meeting with the promoter's staff, our security staff, and the San Antonio police officers in charge. I had to explain the basic premise that police uniforms and teens do not mix well at a rock concert. I told the promoter that if he had to use off-duty police officers on-site, they would be required to dress in T-shirts and jeans and leave their sidearms in their cruisers. Young, rebellious, and backed up by 10,000 other kids shouting encouragement, most teens will feel obligated to challenge authority. Confronting them with tough, stern-looking uniformed officers is simply foolish when security could be provided in an alternative manner. The next night, security personnel showed up in T-shirts and jeans, and the crowd was well behaved.

We were also just able to avert another near explosion that first night when the police officer assigned to me heard on his radio that 5,000 kids had formed a mob outside the hall. Angry because they couldn't get tickets, they were loud and threatening violence. San Antonio police officers had tried to disperse the crowd without success, and the small security force at the venue had radioed headquarters for assistance—they'd asked for the riot squad, complete with attack dogs and buses to haul the violators to jail. My police advisor and I hurried outside to where the standoff was occurring. Although the kids didn't look violent to me—they were sitting around, drinking beer, and throwing Frisbees—I took the bullhorn and spoke to the crowd before the goon squad got there. I told them I was the Stones' lawyer and that Mick had asked me to plead with them to disperse in order to avoid any bloodshed and arrests. The crowd listened quietly and simply broke up, scattering in all directions. When the storm troopers arrived with the buses and eager dogs on chains, ready to bite, they were disappointed that the opportunity to smash heads had eluded them.

Meanwhile, inside the hall, there was a tense atmosphere at the first show because some local vice squad officers had gotten inside, while others without the proper ID were turned away. After the show, Wasserman alerted me that he had received a tip that the next morning's edition of Murdoch's rag would call for the arrest of the Stones for exhibiting pornographic material (the giant penis). Sure enough, early the next morning, the bold headline across the top of the *San Antonio News'* front page read, STONES VICE RAID URGED. The article quoted Judge Michael O'Quinn as ordering the vice squad to go to the show to arrest Mick Jagger for displaying the obscene phallus and for allowing drug use at the concert. When Rudge and I discussed the matter with Jagger, he suggested I look into the situation and report back to him before the show that evening.

I went to see Judge O'Quinn, and he assured me that his quote was grossly exaggerated. He said he had told the reporter that his office had received several calls about the phallus and the dope smoking, and he had simply reported the information to the vice officers and asked that they investigate. I told the judge that I was working closely with Police Chief Peters and his staff, and we intended to cooperate fully. However, I also advised him that in my legal opinion, the giant unit was not obscene and that if Mick Jagger were arrested, we would litigate the matter all the way to the U.S. Supreme Court. That, I pointed out, would come only after local kids left the city of San Antonio in ruins when they saw Jagger being taken off stage in handcuffs. The judge told me he would leave it to Chief Peters.

Back at the arena, I prepared for a showdown. As the hall began to fill, three San Antonio detectives sought me out and advised me that the mayor had sent them with specific instructions to haul the Stones to jail if the penis rose that night. I stood toe-to-toe with the officer in charge and warned him that they would be held responsible when the kids burned the building down—which they most assuredly would. The detectives backed down from threatening to arrest the Stones on stage but said they had already determined that the show was pornographic, and if we raised the penis, they would go immediately to the judge and obtain an arrest warrant that would be served after the show. My response was: "If you file charges, I'll beat your ass in court and make fools of you all."

I was in a Mexican standoff with the police, I explained to Rudge and the Stones. They got more laughs out of this than they would have from watching a *Three Stooges* episode. However, since I'd seen the mature, diplomatic side of Jagger in Washington, his response didn't surprise me.

"While guests of San Antonio," he said, "we will honor their request that we not display the phallus on stage." Jagger couldn't understand why San Antonio would take this so seriously when just down the road in Baton Rouge officials hadn't found it offensive. The peace at Baton Rouge had lulled me into a false sense of security, but now the honeymoon with the police was over. From now on, confrontations with local police—sometimes fierce, sometimes funny—would become the routine, rather than the exception, for the tour.

A funny one happened on June 8 in Milwaukee. The stadium was sold out, and the only snag was being alerted by one of our security people that some of Milwaukee's finest—motorcycle officers dressed in leather boots and helmets—were standing on boxes outside the Stones' dressing room windows, hoping to smell marijuana smoke. I confronted the officers and told them I had free meal tickets for them if they wanted to eat; they all climbed down from their perches and headed for the food.

I couldn't help thinking back to my early days in Rector. I used to chop cotton with Jackie Parrish, a job that paid three dollars a day for ten hours of work. One day we were out on the south side of town, working in a field, when Jackie threw his hoe down and said "The hell with this; I'm hitchhiking to Detroit, and getting me a job on the Detroit police force." And that's exactly what he did. He went out and hitched a ride to Detroit and became a policeman, a job he held until he retired. When he came back to Rector to visit, Jackie was riding a motorcycle and he was a cop. I thought that would be a great thing to do—go to Detroit and get on the police force. After seeing a few local police forces in action, I was glad I hadn't followed up on that idea.

The tour continued with sell-out, enthusiastic crowds of 53,231 in Arrowhead Stadium, in Kansas City—which was a record—54,000 in Milwaukee County Stadium, and in Cleveland, where 82,000 fans jammed the stadium. Both local newspapers in each city carried front-page headlines and stories about the Stones concert. By now I was beginning to realize just how newsworthy the Stones had become.

Onward through the United States we rolled, and the members of the Stones were feeling as confident and arrogant as General Patton when he rolled through Italy and Germany in World War II. This attitude prevailed in spite of the constant confrontational atmosphere in absolutely every city. Flippo wrote of cops versus Rolling Stones when he said:

> Cops dearly wanted to be known as the cops who finally busted the law-flaunting Rolling Stones. It was as if there was a bounty on their heads. Police departments knew that Mick and Keith's visas were on

waiver because of their history of drug arrests, and the cops were just eagerly sniffing the air in anticipation of a historic bust. It would be the final payday of the whole sixties radical business; chickens finally coming home to roost for these arrogant, long-haired, short, doped-up, sick foreigners who only want to get high school football players onto hard drugs and then gang-f... all the high school cheerleaders. Some cops were serious about all this stuff (pp. 51-52).

I have always felt the Stones were victims of the times and that rock's bad boys were not nearly as evil as they were portrayed. Granted, they pushed the envelope at times, but that was just brashness; they were, after all, entertainers. Their fans expected a certain amount of naughtiness. But with the exception of Keith, I never saw a flagrant abuse of drugs. Were there recreational drugs? Sure, but nothing flagrant. This was still the dope-smoking, hippie generation, and the Stones mirrored the culture. The drug use was more than I had ever been exposed to, but probably less than in the financial circles of any middle-America city at the time. In my youth, drinking was the big thing. Clay County, where I grew up, was a dry county, so everyone went just over the state line to Missouri to drink. If you went to Kennett, Missouri, to a beer joint, it didn't matter how old you were, they'd serve you. You could go into Leroy French's West End Café, which was nothing more than a bar, and buy ten-cent beer with no questions asked. But the Stones were part of a new generation, and drug use was just as common as drinking was in my day.

Mick was calling the shots on the tour, so he stayed in control of himself, to my knowledge, but Keith was a different story.

Keith used to say he could corrupt anyone, and sometimes it appeared that way. One of Keith's doctors had become friends with him outside his medical practice, and he ended up on drugs, abandoning his practice and family to run off with a Rolling Stones groupie. I explained to Keith that some people are basically unhappy with themselves and are just waiting for someone to corrupt them. Keith used to say he could corrupt me, but to this day, I haven't used drugs, and I drank very little on the Rolling Stones tour. I have plenty of fun just like I am—I enjoy my life very much and prefer my pleasures to be the result of a realistic lifestyle rather than a false euphoria based on the short-lived ecstasy one might receive from drugs. If your problems go away when you're on drugs, then they must loom even larger when you return from fantasyland.

Other than routine Keystone Cops matters, the ugly police didn't rear their heads again until Memphis. The concert was set for July 4, and there are few places on this Earth where it is hotter or more humid than Memphis, Tennessee, in the summer. Our outdoor stage was pretty standard for normal concert use, but as it was being constructed, Jagger decided he would enter the stage riding on the back of an elephant. Hurriedly and at considerable cost, Rudge located some elephants in Wisconsin. The elephant trainer didn't have to be a Rhodes scholar to know he had us over a barrel. How many places have elephants on standby waiting for the Stones to call? Once we had the expensive elephant, we had to figure out how to get Mick's beast from the ground to the stage. Well, we had to first reinforce the stage to support Mick and his carrier, who weighed in at 12,000 pounds. This required bracing the stage to support the weight as well as laying down an additional floor of one-inch plywood on top of the existing floor. We were setting up the stage on Thursday, July 3, and everyone was trying to get off early to get out of town for the long holiday weekend. It was a nightmare just trying to secure the materials necessary to rebuild the stage, but somehow the crew performed a miracle and eventually completed it. Next we had to construct an elevator by building a floor on a heavy-duty forklift and then building a cage on three sides. The pachyderm would be lifted by our homemade elevator to the rear of the stage, where Jagger would mount the beast and ride out to the much-anticipated roar of the crowd.

After everything was finally completed and all the elaborate arrangements were made, Jagger announced he had changed his mind. There would be no grand pooh-bah entrance on the back of an elephant. Now, did Mick ever really plan to ride that elephant? It's only rock and roll!

On July 4, the day of the show, after we had resolved the elephant's entry challenge and before Mick changed his mind, I was anxiously awaiting Jagger's arrival on the elephant's back—what could possibly happen next? Enter the Memphis vice squad. In the blistering midafternoon heat of Independence Day, I was summoned to meet an officer of the Memphis vice squad who announced to me that they had been informed by other city police departments that Jagger performed the song, "Star, Star"—better known by its nickname "Starf...er"—in the show, and if he did so in their city they intended to arrest Mick when he finished the song. Memphis had a censor board at that time, and the lyrics of this song were in violation of the city's obscenity code.

Rudge was nearby and overheard the confrontation and went ballistic—he screamed at the officers, and I had to have him led away to avoid arrest. I personally had absolutely had it. I can't remember what I said, but I can tell you it may have been the strongest language I ever directed at a police officer. I think I secretly hoped they would arrest me because my able legal assistant, Kathy Woods, was always quietly waiting in the wings to take over and to get me out of jail if necessary. The publicity from such an arrest would only have enhanced the reputation I was gaining for standing up for my clients' rights, even when threatened by incarceration.

This confrontation was more serious by far than the one in San Antonio. We had now played twenty-three shows to sold-out crowds in twelve cities without major incident, but we were never without the presence of representatives of the local gestapo (my new label for the local police). As an attorney and former federal agent, I was appalled by and ashamed of the law enforcement I witnessed. They always arrived with the clear intention of arresting the Rolling Stones for something. By now they had been informed that the group itself was not vulnerable—they were kept isolated from the police and the public. Their hotel was so secure that friends and associates had a difficult time gaining access to the band when they were not on stage. The hotels and backstage areas at the venues were totally secured from everyone. When the show was over, limos were waiting backstage for the band, who, dripping with sweat, left the stage and stepped into the cars to be swept away. Before the police or fans knew what had happened, they were at their hotel, safely secreted behind a wall of security. The only access to the Stones was when they were on stage.

As the tour wore on, the challenge to arrest the Stones grew with each date. I have stood against police abuses both as a Secret Service agent and as a lawyer. I have to say that in 1975, I found the police attitude toward the Stones to be universally consistent: London, Buffalo, Milwaukee, Memphis, San Antonio, or Seattle—it made little difference. Where the Stones were concerned, they should be arrested because they corrupted our society.

Blame it on the Stones seemed to be the motto of every police shift commander in every city we visited.

I had asked the Memphis vice squad to leave the area; at that point they had not observed a violation of the law, and they had no legal right to be there since the Stones had rented the venue. The patrol officer who was assigned to work with me on crowd and traffic control was told by the vice officer to inform me that he was pulling all officers off the date unless the vice squad officers were allowed to stay. I called Rudge and Wasserman over. "If you pull your troops out," I threatened, "we'll call a press conference and we'll tell the good people of Memphis exactly why a major rock concert was left without police presence." I called his bluff and made it unequivocally clear who would receive the blame for traffic jams and injuries to fans. By now Wasserman had gathered local as well as national press backstage. This was no longer about the Rolling Stones; it was a white-beans-and-cornbread lawyer against both the Shelby County Censor Board and a bunch of redneck cops who were attempting to enforce a code that was clearly contrary to rulings of the U.S. Supreme Court. The patrol captain backed down, but I was not able to remove the vice squad from backstage. The line in the sand had been drawn.

Jagger had also had enough—he announced he would sing "Starf...er," and if he was arrested on stage as threatened by the local police, then the safety of the city of Memphis was beyond his responsibility and control.

Throughout the tour, when these confrontations arose, I would immediately brief the State Department and INS. This was something the local police didn't count on. The U.S. government, which in the past had relied on press coverage of the tours, now had one of its own, a former U.S. Secret Service agent, on hand to deliver blow-by-blow news of the police atrocities that were all an abuse of the powers granted them by their legislatures and the U.S. Supreme Court. There was an INS office in Memphis where I had filed the original H-1 Petition for the

1975 tour and where I also had friends. I was confident the Stones were in no trouble with the U.S. government, but the Memphis police were about to provide me with a national soapbox from which to lash out at police abuses throughout the United States.

The '60s were over, and I was sick of seeing kids whacked over the head with police billy clubs just for being kids. In every city we played, I had ticket requests from cabinet members, congressmen and endless federal and state bureaucrats (for their children). I personally provided more than 5,000 tickets to public officials on the 1975 tour on behalf of the Rolling Stones. I was essentially saying, "So, there, you local bullies. You damn well better be right if you take on the Stones and Bill Carter."

In Memphis, Mick stood firm on my advice, and I was prepared for a fight. The atmosphere backstage was tense, and the adrenaline was flowing on both sides. The press was standing by, waiting for the bell to ring to start this championship bout. Suddenly the general manager of a Memphis radio station rushed up to me. He told me his station had been airing "Starf...er" since 1973 without a complaint from the censor board or the Memphis police. He'd brought written playlists, which the station prepared weekly as proof of the songs it played. I immediately waved the playlists in the vice squad's faces, and then I threatened them with personal lawsuits and promised to litigate them into bankruptcy. I had now won and showed little mercy in my treatment of these goons. The Memphis police department and the Mayor's office, as in all cities on the tour, had cooperated fully with our tour; however, in every city, there was a police contingency that wished to gain publicity and notoriety. The gloves were now off, as far as I was concerned.

The Memphis vice squad called someone of higher authority and reported the information from the radio station. They were called off the case and told me they would not be staying for the concert. I invited them to remain for the show as guests of the Rolling Stones, but they declined and disappeared into the sweltering heat of the early evening. The show was wildly received by a dedicated 50,000 fans, and when I arrived at my hotel, I enjoyed a cocktail and retired for the evening.

We were off the next day, so I decided to visit my law school classmate, Lindsey Fairley, who was now a judge in West Memphis. He had planned an early cookout in honor of my visit and the holiday weekend. Later that night Rudge called to report that Keith and Ron Wood planned to rent a car and drive to Dallas so they could see the Arkansas countryside. I immediately talked to Keith and advised against the trip. There was too much risk involved in having two band members out of pocket, and Arkansas was the state where the legislature had tried unsuccessfully to outlaw rock and roll. I knew the terrain all too well and knew that the least slip by Keith and Ron in my home state would result in their being jailed. Keith assured me he would give up the idea.

Saturday, I slept late and then prepared to go to West Memphis, knowing that Keith and Ronnie would sleep until five or six that evening. I arrived at Judge

Fairley's home and was enjoying a nice visit with Lindsey and his wife, Ella Lea. While they were smoking meat on the grill at about four o'clock, I got a frantic call from Peter Rudge. Keith, Ronnie, Jim Callaghan of the Stones' security staff, and a well-known Rolling Stones camp follower, Fred Sessler, had not only defied my advice and driven through Arkansas, but they were in a Fordyce, Arkansas, jail on drug charges. If there was a place in Arkansas where a Limey rock musician could be arrested for just driving through, it was Fordyce, the birthplace of Alabama football god Bear Bryant and a town that had adopted the chigger as its high school mascot. We had only one thing in our favor—I had campaigned in Fordyce and knew all the officials, including the sheriff, who was a friend from my Secret Service days and from my service on the Arkansas Law Enforcement Academy Commission.

I asked Judge Fairley to secure a private plane to fly us to Fordyce and to accompany me on the trip. My trusted aide, Kathy, had returned to Little Rock for the weekend, and I was afraid of what I would be confronted with in Fordyce. Lindsey and I had a good laugh recently recalling the events of this trip.

Lindsey was still in a pair of shorts and looked like anything but the respected judge he was. For insurance, we stopped by and picked up a friend of his who was a bail bondsman. This guy was terrified of flying, and we were in just a small twin-engine plane. His butt didn't touch the seat the entire trip. To access the Fordyce strip, you came in over the pine trees and set down immediately. Apparently the experience was too much for Lindsey's friend because he ended up driving back to West Memphis.

We had hoped to keep all this a big secret, thinking we would just fly into Fordyce, spring Keith and Ron, send them off to Dallas on a plane Kathy was chartering for that purpose, and be back in West Memphis in time to enjoy a little barbecue. In our dreams! By the time Lindsey secured the plane and we were off, the arrests had hit the wire services, and it was all over radio and television throughout the United States. When we arrived, the state police escort that met us at the airport informed us that the small town of Fordyce was growing by leaps and bounds as kids from all over the South converged there after learning of Keith and Ron's arrest. It wouldn't be long before the new fans in Fordyce would outnumber the town's population.

It was five-thirty when we arrived at the police station. A Dallas TV crew was already there, as were several radio reporters. Television crews from Jackson, Mississippi; Memphis; and Little Rock were due to arrive any moment, as were newspaper and wire service reporters from all those same cities. In addition, the *New York Times* had called. I immediately met with Keith and Ron, and after surveying the situation, I met with the chief of police, the city attorney, and the judge.

It seems that the boys had stopped for lunch at the Red Bug (named for the school mascot) drive-in restaurant in Fordyce, and by the time they'd finished, word had spread around that the Rolling Stones were in town. Fans began to show up, as did two over-zealous Fordyce policemen, who sat waiting for the car with Ron and Keith to depart. As soon as it did, with Keith driving, the police pulled it over. The arresting officers said the state police had received a call saying that the driver of the car carrying Keith, Ron, and entourage had been observed driving erratically; that's why they had been stopped. The police also said they smelled marijuana smoke as they approached the car, so they placed the occupants under arrest. The state police investigator they'd called to search the car, Charlie Bowles, was a guy who used to be stationed in West Memphis, and Lindsey knew him. We called him before we left, and he agreed to hold up searching the car until we got down there. When they finally did search the car, we almost burst out laughing. Keith and Ron had apparently stopped at the first liquor store when they crossed the river into Arkansas and bought a half-pint of everything they had in there—all this wild and crazy stuff. Fortunately they waited until they got to Arkansas, so the cops couldn't get them for un-tax-paid liquor. They were just standing around shaking their heads when they opened up the trunk and saw all that liquor.

Although they found no illegal substances in the car on the scene, cocaine was discovered in a briefcase belonging to passenger Fred Sessler when the luggage in the trunk was searched—without consent—at the police station. A hunting knife that belonged to Keith was also found in the car.

This smacked of a trumped-up charge if I ever heard of one. The guys had just left the restaurant and pulled from the parking lot onto the highway—there wasn't even enough time to light a cigarette—when they were pulled over. If the officers did indeed have a citizen's complaint, which they allegedly had from the state police, then why hadn't they confronted the subjects with the complaint? Supposedly, this was their probable cause to stop the car. Hell, these guys must have thought I just fell off the watermelon truck. I supervised and sometimes lectured at the Arkansas Law Enforcement Training Academy and had coauthored a criminal procedural manual for the University of Arkansas Law School. I had also received an award from the Criminal Procedure Institute in recognition of lectures given throughout the state of Arkansas in seminars for law enforcement officers. These officers had no legal cause to search the luggage in the trunk, and Judge Fairley and I knew it. But it was not to be so simple.

The presiding judge in Fordyce, Tom Wynn, was known to take a drink, plus he'd been out on the golf course all day, so by the time we located him, he was pretty well inebriated. His brother, Frank, was the prosecuting attorney, and he was at a wedding reception while all this was going on.

I had already discussed the matter with Chief of Police Bill Gober when Judge Wynn arrived from the golf course. Chief Gober knew all too well that he had him a catch. By now, newspapers from New York, LA, Dallas, London, and Paris were calling. News cameras from all over the South were outside the courtroom, and thousands of young people had arrived. If there was ever a chance in Chief Gober's life to be a hero, it was now. He had two of the Rolling Stones in jail, and he was in front of the microphones and cameras. He had two major obstacles—Bill Carter and Judge Lindsey Fairley. The city attorney, a young kid just out of law school named Tommy Mayes, had arrived, and after he was briefed suggested I bring the matter before Judge Wynn, saying he expected the judge would follow the law. But by now the judge too was enjoying the press a bit too much. In one of the funniest moments, Judge Wynn got a call from the BBC wanting information on their famous citizens. All the judge wanted to talk about was the fine golf courses he'd played in England when he was stationed there during World War II.

Seeing the shape the judge was in, Chief Gober accused him of being drunk and threatened to arrest him on the spot and take him to jail. A shoving match erupted, and Judge Fairley and I had to separate the two. During a brief recess, I sent for Frank Wynn at the wedding reception in an effort to negotiate peace and keep the chief under control. Frank came by and had a private conversation with both parties. If he hadn't arrived when he did, we'd probably still be in Fordyce.

In the meantime, a full-scale riot threatened to develop outside the courtroom. Thousands of kids were massed outside, chanting "Release Keith, Release Keith!" The state police were calling in reinforcements. Kathy Woods was flying to our rescue from Little Rock with a chartered King Air plane to airlift us out if I could secure the release. I instructed her to stock the plane with bottles of Jack Daniel's Black Label and stand by. I had also called Memphis and asked Mike Crowley, a Stones staff member, to obtain $50,000 cash, charter a plane, and come immediately to Fordyce. The rest of the band and entourage had already departed for Dallas for the next day's concert. Bill Graham, the promoter for the Dallas show, was calling every thirty minutes for an update. The Cotton Bowl in Dallas was sold out, and there would be hell to pay if we didn't get there.

I had a riot building outside the Fordyce courthouse and the threat of a riot in Dallas. The pressure was definitely on!

Inside, Judge Wynn suddenly looked at his watch, and jumped straight up and said, "Ya'll have to excuse me a minute." With that, he rushed out of the courthouse while we were left looking at each other in bewilderment. Suddenly it dawned on us that the liquor stores closed at ten o'clock, and the judge needed to get there before they locked the doors. When he came back, he had a little pint concealed in his sock, and he'd reach down every few minutes and take a nip. We'd be arguing a point, and someone would come in and say, "Judge, you've got a call from New York" (or Paris). The judge would excuse himself and go out and do an interview, then come back to the courtroom. It was just one hilarious moment after another. Hollywood couldn't have scripted a sitcom any better.

Before we resumed the hearing, Judge Fairley had a private conversation with Judge Wynn. In fact, Lindsey had to have several little conferences with the judge before the evening was over. At the hearing, Judge Wynn reduced the charge for Keith to reckless driving and possession of a concealed weapon (the knife) and set bond at $162.50. No charges were filed against Ron Wood and Jim Callahan, and cocaine charges were bound over against Fred Sessler with bond set at $5,000. Both Frank Wynn and Judge Wynn agreed that the law against concealed weapons—I maintained that a hunting knife did not fall under the category of a concealed weapon in the statutes—would not hold up for the knife, but Chief Gober refused to agree to dismiss his charge. Privately we agreed that I would make bond and get out of town. I could later file a motion to dismiss on the weapons charge and forfeit bond on the reckless driving charge. It was now eleven o'clock, and Kathy was at the airport with the King Air, its engines idling as it waited on us.

Before we could depart the fair city of Fordyce, however, we had two more items of rather bizarre business to attend to. As part of our agreement for Ron and Keith's release, the judge insisted on staging a press conference. Finally, he wanted to have his picture taken with Keith and Ron! Leaving behind a bitter Chief of Police Gober, we departed the building to a roaring cheer from thousands of fans as the state police escorted us to the airport. Although the state police had sealed off incoming roads to Fordyce as the crowd of young people had grown beyond anything they could control, we could never have made the airport without the help of my state police buddies.

As we got on the plane, Kathy greeted each of us with a glass of Jack-on-the-rocks. Wheels up—what a feeling of relief! We arrived in Dallas at 3:00 a.m. to a hero's welcome from Peter Rudge and Bill Graham. Lindsey told me recently he heard they still have Keith's hunting knife hanging on the wall in the Fordyce courthouse along with the photo of the judge with Keith and Ron.

On August 2, the Stones were scheduled to play the Gator Bowl, in Jacksonville, Florida. The promoter for the show had not signed the contract nor sent in the required $250,000 deposit by July, in spite of the fact that I was sending him telegrams advising him of the urgency of the situation. We had spent weeks making changes to the contract to suit the promoter, and we had finally agreed to everything, but we had still not received the deposit or signed contract. He was now disputing the proposed budget for production costs and refused to approve these costs. We arrived in Jacksonville on Thursday, July 31, to find there was still no contract or deposit. Rudge was frantic over the promoter's irresponsible attitude regarding the contract, and we were now in Jacksonville with the Gator Bowl sold out, but we would not play the date if the contract wasn't executed. On August 1, Rudge and I met with the promoter and his attorney, Harold Horowitz, hoping to get an executed contract and check, but it was not to be. The promoter complained that he could lose money if he couldn't control the expenses. The contract provided the Stones with a deposit, plus a percent of the gross receipts, and expenses, and the promoter's fee came out of the remainder. Rudge had agreed that expenses would not exceed a certain amount, but the guy still held out.

It appeared clear to me that there was an unknown agenda here, but I still don't know what was behind the promoter's holdout. I could speculate he may have thought at this late date, with 75,000 tickets sold, the Stones would have to play the date, and he would be in control of the money and could dictate his own terms. Rudge was a volatile personality to start with, and his frustration with the promoter was about to push him over the edge. On the day of the show, August 2, we still had not resolved the deal. Rudge, the Stones' business manager; Bill Zysblat; and I were trying to resolve the deal, but Rudge and the promoter spent most of the time threatening each other. The show was scheduled to begin at two o'clock, and according to the stadium rental contract executed with the city, the show had to be over by six-thirty. By late morning, with nothing resolved, Rudge called the hotel and told the Stones to remain there until the dispute was resolved. He then informed the promoter that the Stones would not leave their hotel until he had executed the contract. In other words, the Stones would not take the stage.

This was a serious standoff. The consequences of the Stones not playing the show would be catastrophic. Seventy-five thousand fans had paid to see the Stones, and if the band refused to go on—would they understand or care who was responsible? Rudge and the promoter were playing poker, and the possible losers were the Rolling Stones fans.

During the negotiations taking place in the production trailer around noon, the promoter's mother came by and wanted her son to take her for—of all things—a walk. The guy simply departed for a walk in one-hundred-degree weather with his mother while the fans were screaming for the show to begin. Rudge refused to budge, and we all stood by his decision. Upon the promoter's casual return, Rudge, Zysblat and I proposed that a sum of $25,000 be put in escrow to cover the disputed expenses, and the promoter, acting under pressure from the mayor's office and the chief of police, finally agreed. The city extended the curfew on the condition that the Rolling Stones be on stage by 6:00 p.m. After a delay of six hours, with fans enduring hundred-degree heat and a powerful thunderstorm, the Stones finally took the stage and swung into "Honky Tonk Woman." It was exactly 5:58 p.m., and the fans had obviously forgiven everyone as Jagger threw aside his purple cape and commenced to rock.

Earlier, when the Stones finally arrived at the stadium, the promoter asked me to take him, his mother, and some VIPs to meet Jagger, who was in his trailer. I knocked on the door, and Mick responded by cracking the door open and talking to me. As this guy and his party stood a few feet behind me, I relayed his request to Mick. Jagger was well aware of this jerk's holdout, so he turned to the party, gave them the middle-finger salute, and told them to "bleep off" before slamming his trailer door. Stunned, the promoter and his party walked away as I laughed and applauded Jagger. Mick had the courage to do what all the rest of us wanted to do.

Jagger, in his red-and-white suit, jumped, ran from side to side on the stage, and clung to the struts supporting a yellow-and-white canopy while 75,000 fans screamed and cheered his every move.

During the tour, it was decided to add three dates after Jacksonville, the first being Louisville, Kentucky, on August 14. Ironically, the date was to be played at Freedom Hall; however, if the Louisville storm troopers had their way, there would be no freedom for the Rolling Stones. I had advanced the date and met with William "Trigg" Black from radio station WAKY, who was working with Sunshine Productions to present the concert. Trigg called me August 1 and told me that he'd gotten some inside information from a source in the Louisville Police Department that indicated that the police were committed to arresting the Stones when they arrived in town. In fact, they had already obtained a search warrant for the airplane, which would be searched as soon as it arrived. They'd arrest the Stones if they found contraband on board.

Rudge and I discussed the situation in Louisville, and after briefing the Stones, we devised a plan. I would leave for Louisville immediately after the Jacksonville show, while everyone else remained in Florida. I would scope out the situation, and the band would arrive just prior to the show. In Louisville, I conferred with Trigg Black and his informant. It was obvious that any search warrant issued would be erroneous unless someone had actually observed contraband on the plane. However, it didn't take me long to realize that Louisville's finest had little regard for the law, and they fully intended to bust the Stones by whatever means available. The informant was very credible, and I was convinced we were facing our most serious confrontation yet. I was able to identify by name the officers on the detail assigned to arrest the Stones. So I devised a plan. Although I had no intention of allowing the authorities to search the plane, I explained to Rudge that he should be absolutely certain that no member of the crew or staff had any illegal drugs on that plane. I asked him to have the plane arrive in Louisville just in time for them to get to the show and to tell the pilot to taxi to a holding area at the far end of the airport to unload his passengers. Vans would be there to pick up the band and entourage and speed them away to the venue.

Trigg Black and I escorted a delegation to meet the plane at the announced arrival time. The police were there in full force—we all stood around at the fixed-based operator terminal talking and laughing. I had been very friendly with the officers and had given them absolutely no indication that I knew of their plan. Kathy Woods was on the airplane to ensure the police did not board the aircraft, at least until I arrived. Once the passengers had disembarked at the end of the runway, the door to the plane would be closed, and if the police approached the plane, the captain was to taxi to the end of the runway and take off for Cincinnati. He would return after the show and pick us up. If the police did not approach, the captain would taxi forward and park the plane at the holding area until we returned.

So the plane landed and taxied to the end of the runway and stopped. The officers asked what was happening, but we assured them the pilot was just awaiting clearance to taxi to the terminal. The plane was so far away that you couldn't actually see what was going on, and Rudge advised me via radio that all had departed and were on their way to the venue. As we turned to get in our car, I announced to the police that the band was on their way to the venue, and the plane was taking off for Cincinnati. The police were absolutely furious as they watched the empty plane prepare to take off again. Trigg and I sped away while the cops discovered they had been had and changed their game plan.

They decided their best chance of an arrest was with the Rolling Stones themselves, so they followed us to the venue. We had gotten the Stones to safety behind a locked dressing room door—the most secure, large area available—and stocked it with food and drink so the guys would not have to leave the room until they went on stage. I had also had the lock changed on the door, and the Stones' staff controlled the only keys. Our biggest and toughest security man, Bob Bender, was stationed in front of the door with instructions that no one was to enter except the band and staff. When I arrived at Freedom Hall, the place was crawling with cops. From our informant, we had also learned that the narcotics squad planned to enter the dressing room and arrest the Stones if they observed the presence of drugs. Now, surely these Louisville goons wouldn't stoop to enter the dressing room and conveniently plant some drugs, would they? I was absolutely certain they would resort to any tactics necessary to accomplish their mission. The tour was almost over, and Louisville had to protect the image of all U.S. policemen by arresting these devils! They were the last line of defense against the British invaders who were spreading evil to our nation.

I had previously met with the local district attorney and briefed him on my situation, and while he would not permit any violation of the law, he also would not tolerate any abuses by the police. He had no plans to attend the concert, but he indicated he would be at home if we needed him and gave me his home phone number. The Stones' security men reported to me that there were forty plainclothes narcs backstage (they had an accurate count since they were not in uniform and did not have a ticket or pass, so the only way they were admitted was by showing their badge). In addition, there was a large contingent of uniformed officers. We had never experienced this kind of show of force before, even on the stadium dates. Bender reported that a large group of about fifteen narcs was huddled not far from the dressing room, as if planning to attack. I joined Bender at the door, and sure enough, moments later they swooped down like a bunch of vultures about to attack their prey.

"Stand aside. We are here," they announced with badges displayed, "to search the dressing rooms." I stood in front of Bender, who was square in front of the door, and said, "Show me your warrant." "We don't need a warrant," was their response. "I am the Stones' lawyer," I said, "and you will have to remove me in handcuffs before you will be allowed to enter that room. I also am a former federal agent as well as a lawyer, and I have been in touch with the mayor's office as well as the district attorney. I have no intention of allowing you to enter without a court-executed warrant." They acted as if they didn't know what to do—they sure didn't seem eager to remove me by arresting me, and I'm sure by now they knew exactly who I was from their contacts in other cities as well as from Sunshine Promotions. They advised me that they fully intended to enter the dressing room but would confer with their superiors first, and with that, they withdrew in a group, several feet from the door.

I immediately called the district attorney and told him of my plight. I said I felt sure the narcs would make another push to enter, which would probably result in my arrest. He agreed to come to the venue immediately since he lived only a short distance away. We agreed that upon his arrival, he would enter the dressing room alone, and the premises would be completely open to his examination. I then told the bloodthirsty narcs that their DA was on the way to lead them, and I suggested they wait for him. I assured them I would abide by the DA's decision. Shortly thereafter, the DA arrived, and he told the police to remain outside while he went in and examined the dressing room. They were furious with his decision, which resulted in a violent argument. He issued a firm order for them to remain outside and take no action unless they received specific instructions from him. Anger and discontent were apparent in the stares and body language of the men.

I escorted the DA into the dressing room and introduced him to all the Stones as well as to Rudge, Wasserman, Zysblat and anyone else important who was present. The DA ate with the Stones and swapped stories as well as having his photo made with Jagger. He went out only long enough to tell the narcs that everything was clean in the dressing room, and they should take the rest of the night off. The cops had been betrayed and they couldn't believe it. They were cussing, shaking their heads in total disbelief. They had missed their one opportunity to gain international notoriety by cleansing society from the scourge of the devilish Limey group.

This was really a victory for law and order because the conduct of the Louisville officers and others like them was appalling, and the officers themselves showed no respect whatsoever for the law or proper police procedures. Some police in the United States were so convinced the Stones were evil, whether or not they had violated any laws and because they didn't like their music or images, they would use any methods to bust the Stones. They couldn't let the law get in their way.

Hail, Hail, Rock and Roll!

Chapter 15
The Reports of the Premature Death of the Rolling Stones Are Not Exaggerated

𝕴N 1977 THE ROLLING STONES were beginning to feel pressure from a number of areas. They had released an album in 1976, *Black and Blue*, but it had sold only 600,000 copies—a good showing, but the Fleetwood Mac album had sold four million copies during the same period. They were also nearing the end of their contract with Atlantic Records, and because they were being courted by both CBS and MCA, they hoped to spur a bidding war to drive their price up. But most importantly, the Stones were an aging rock-and-roll band who felt enormous stress to live up to their reputation. For that reason it was vital that their next record be really hot. That something hot was to be a live double album representing the 1975 U.S. tour and the 1976 European tour.

The tapes from the U.S. tour of 1975 were spotty and erratic, but they had a hot show from June 1976, in Paris. That was enough material for three sides of a four-sided double album. For the rest, the band decided to pull a surprise show in a small club or bar someplace, where the sound would be good, the audience excitement would be feverish, and where everything would be on a small enough scale as to not get out of hand. And someplace out of the way, so it would not turn into a freakish, full-blown, Stones-crazy media event. And someplace close enough to New York City for the band to carry on negotiations with the major record companies for a new contract. The El Macambo just across the Canadian border in Toronto was the ideal spot.

Mick, who was by then effectively running the band (primarily because Keith had become addicted to heroin), was the one who made that decision. It looked pretty easy and comfortable: Fly into Toronto, rehearse for a few days, dine well, play a couple of nights at a small club, sign a great new contract, and then get the hell out. How tough could that be? (Flippo, pp. 63–64).

When Rudge told me about the Toronto dates, I asked him if I should plan on being there. Whether he really thought anything involving the Stones could be without a certain amount of peril or if he was just squeezing the pennies, I don't know, but he told me I wasn't needed. Fine by me; that left me free to devote my energies to my law practice. Which is exactly what I was doing on February

24—concluding meetings about country singer Tanya Tucker in Los Angeles—about the time that Keith (fresh from an English trial for possession of cocaine and LSD), his common-law wife, Anita Pallenberg, and their son Marlon, flew into the Toronto airport and failed to clear customs. That single incident came very close to spelling the end to not only the dreams of a fat new recording contract but also the Rolling Stones as a band.

It was far from a funny incident; in fact, the potential fallout was downright terrifying, but the way Flippo describes how Keith and Anita came to the attention of the customs officials is pretty hilarious. As he relates it, "Keith was apparently not holding any drugs when they landed, but he failed to vet Anita's luggage. And Anita had twenty-eight pieces of luggage. Maybe that's what prompted the search. Maybe it was the fact that Anita acts and dresses rather flamboyantly—gold boots and dresses that resemble taffeta bedspreads. At any rate, the Richards party drew considerable attention from customs officials at the airport" (p. 64).

An excerpt from the secret report filed to the Royal Canadian Mounted Police by RCMP Constable A.J. Hachinski, of the RCMP's Drug Enforcement Section, reads as follows:

> On Thursday, February 24, 1977, I was on duty at the Toronto International Airport Drug Section. At approximately 7:25 p.m., arrived at Terminal #2. Upon arrival I was advised by Canada Customs they had in custody a lady with a small quantity of hashish and other drug-related paraphernalia, namely spoon [and] hypodermic needle. The lady identified herself as Anita PALLENBERG, common-law wife of Rolling Stones guitarist Keith RICHARDS. She was subsequently arrested and taken to the office of Terminal #1 and charged with Possession of Hashish (10 grams) and released on a[n] appearance notice. The spoon and hypodermic needle was taken to the Dominion Analyst and the hypodermic needle was found to contain traces of heroin. Subsequently a warrant was obtained for the arrest of Anita PALLENBERG and a warrant to search her residence was obtained.

Anita was arrested and taken to Brampton (which has jurisdiction over the Toronto airport, but not Toronto), while Keith and seven-year-old Marlon were driven to the Harbour Castle Hilton, the Stones' Toronto headquarters. At this point they were fairly nonchalant about the whole matter; after all, arrest on drug charges was nothing new to this band of rock and rollers. But someone—either Mick or Rudge—was concerned enough to have Kathy Woods, in my Little Rock office, attempt to locate me, which prompted her to put in an emergency call to American Airlines, who then notified the captain of my flight home. Meanwhile, I was blissfully unaware of the tumultuous events taking place half a continent away. The flight attendant's announcement of our impending approach into the Dallas/Fort Worth Airport had awakened me from a fitful sleep, and I was still a little disoriented when the captain stopped beside my seat and touched me lightly on the shoulder.

"Mr. Carter," he said, as I looked at him in some puzzlement. It would not have been unusual in my old Secret Service days for the captain to be aware of who I was, mostly because we always let them know that, as government agents, we were carrying weapons. But there was no good reason that I could think of why the captain was seeking me out when he should have been getting ready to land the plane. Then he really rocked my world. "Mr. Carter, we've been contacted by the ground crew in Dallas," he continued. "As soon as we're on the ground, you have been asked to call your home in Little Rock. This is an emergency, but they asked me to assure you that it's not a family emergency." That did little to reassure me, and my phone call to my wife did even less. "There's an emergency with the Stones," Jan told me. "Kathy Woods wants you to call her before you board the flight to Little Rock." Since it was close to seven, I dialed Kathy's home phone.

She informed me of Anita's arrest and the implications for Keith and the entire future of the Rolling Stones. They were scared, she said, and wanted me on the next plane to Toronto. I, in turn, told Kathy to get on the next plane to Toronto to meet me. It just so happened that there was an American flight from Dallas to Toronto that left within the hour, and I was able to get a seat on that flight.

Before I boarded the plane, I called an entertainment lawyer in Toronto, William Hinkson, and said I needed a good criminal attorney there. Of the ones recommended, I chose a former federal prosecutor, Clay Powell; I wanted someone who had been a prosecutor and therefore knew the courts and the judges. I told Clay to get to Keith immediately since I couldn't be there. Powell then called the RCMP, arranging for the release of Anita Pallenburg at Brampton. In the meantime, Mick and other members of the Stones were gathering in Canada, and the Stones' faithful were closing ranks in a belated attempt at damage control.

Even the solidarity of the Stones' well-oiled machine couldn't stop what happened three days later, an event that changed the entire complexion of the incident and earned the Royal Canadian Mounted Police a place in the annals of rock and roll. Another excerpt from RCMP Hachinski's report reads:

> Accompanied by four members of the RCMP . . . I attended at the temporary residence of Anita PALLENBERG at the Harbour Castle Hotel and after approximately two hours of attempting to locate her room, a search warrant was executed at room 3223-24-25, which was registered under the name of K. Redbland, which is an alias used by Keith RICH- ARDS. The following exhibits were seized:
> - One passport in the name of Keith Richards
> - Minister's Permit to enter Canada
> - Hypodermic needle cover
> - Plastic bag with traces of white powder

- Plastic bag with traces of white powder (*sic*)
- Three red-coloured pills
- Harbour Castle sugar bag containing 2 grams of resin material (believed to be hashish)
- Gold foil paper with traces of white powder
- Plastic bag containing 5 grams of cocaine
- Razor blade with white traces of white powder
- Switchblade knife with traces of white powder
- Hypodermic needle with liquid in the base
- Brass lighter with traces of white powder
- Silver bowl with traces of white powder
- Teaspoon with traces of white powder
- Purple pouch with traces of white powder
- Plastic bag containing 22 grams of Heroin.

These exhibits were turned over to Constable SEWARD, RCMP, who acted as exhibit officer. RICHARDS admitted ownership of the exhibits and was arrested on the charge of "Possession for the Purpose of Trafficking." Mr. RICHARDS was released later the same evening after a mini-bail hearing before a Justice of the Peace in the presence of Mr. Clay POWELL, who was Mr. RICHARDS' attorney at the time.

As I recall, they surprised everyone with the search on Sunday, and we didn't know about it until after it happened. They took Keith to jail, charging him not only with heroin possession, but with drug trafficking. They kept secret the cocaine charges. That was not mentioned in the Constable's report, and even Keith and I didn't know until later that cocaine was listed as evidence. The RCMP document excerpt is as remarkable for what it did not say as for what it indeed did spell out. Almost everything in it was never made public (until Flippo's book came out), and none of it was ever introduced in court hearings or at Keith's trial or anywhere else. That extraordinary shopping list of goods the Mounties seized from Keith's rooms was never made known at the time. Chet laughingly points out that it's amazing that the Mounties would admit to having spent two hours trying to locate Keith and Anita's rooms when all it took him was ten minutes and a well-placed $10 bill to a chambermaid to learn the location of their suite. Another humorous aside to the Mounties' search of the suite was that for the majority of the search, Keith was asleep, and until he was arrested he thought his visitors were executives from his record company.

There were a couple of things about the arrest that would later cause problems in the courts. First, Keith's name was not on the search warrant. They were there to search *Anita's* residence. Secondly, the Mounties took Keith back to Brampton because that's where they had taken Anita, but he was arrested in Toronto's jurisdiction. I called Clay Powell and had him meet us at Brampton to secure Keith's release. The justice of the peace at Brampton did not seem concerned that possession of heroin can carry a maximum sentence of life imprisonment, because he released Keith on a $1,000 no-deposit bond. He walked out of there without dropping a cent.

As Chet so aptly points out, "He [Keith] immediately became a hot political issue in Canada. The RCMP, particularly, were furious that he seemed to be getting preferential treatment just because he was a rock and roll star and they were angry that this case seemed to be portraying the Mounties as ineffectual goofs who couldn't quite nail a drugged-up, scruffy, rich hippie who was giving the finger to the Dominion" (p. 68).

However, the international press was beginning to get wind of the heroin possession arrest, and it was becoming great fodder for them. The bad boys of rock and roll were up to their usual tricks. The newspapers screamed: "Keith Richards, lead guitarist with the Rolling Stones, has been charged here with possession of heroin for the purpose of trafficking. An ounce of heroin with an estimated street value of $4,000 was seized in a downtown hotel after a week-long investigation at Toronto International Airport . . . ." (Flippo, p. 67). Like sharks on a feeding frenzy, reporters and photographers from throughout the Western world wanted to be present when the nails were driven in the coffin of the world's greatest rock-and-roll band.

Keith had to agree to appear at another hearing on March 7, at which point his bail could very well be revoked and he could be jailed on the spot. The state's prosecutor had decided that nailing Keith Richards was very high on the Canadian government's list of priorities.

The rest of the Stones, who had begun arriving at the hotel, were furious at Keith and Anita and were outraged at their blatant disregard for the rules of the road and what it might mean to their future, or lack thereof. *Keith was in very serious trouble.* He almost certainly was facing a minimum of seven years in a Canadian prison, but he literally could have found himself incarcerated for the rest of his life. We were staring into the unpleasant face of the premature end to the Rolling Stones as we knew them, and that was unthinkable to all of us. Mick may have assumed the mantle of leader of the band, but Keith was the musical heart. Here the Stones thought they were coming to Toronto to celebrate a milestone of sorts in their recording career—the making of a cool live project, not to mention a possible new record deal—and instead, Keith had lofted that career a possible life-ending grenade. In the planning stages of this live record, the Stones actually thought this might be their career swan song anyway because they felt they were aging and doubted that their career had many legs left. But they wanted that to be *their* choice—not the Canadian government's. So they were naturally depressed and in despair.

On top of all this turmoil, there were a number of things puzzling us. No one could understand how Keith could have flown in the face of common sense to the point of almost flaunting his arrival in Canada with the outlandish style of Anita's dress and her attention-demanding demeanor. She wasn't even on the official Stones' list and therefore was not expected in Toronto. Plus, if artists wanted to transport drugs, they usually employed a "handler" who assumed the load and the risk for the more well-known celebrity.

We also were in the dark about how Keith could have scored five grams of coke and twenty-two grams of heroin when he had been clean when he cleared customs. Was Keith so clueless that he didn't think Anita's arrest—not to mention his own drug arrest history—would make him the target of every Mountie in the vicinity? At one point Clay Powell even discovered a bug that the RCMP had planted in Keith's suite, so they meant business.

Surprisingly, until the date of the hearing, still almost ten days away, life went on as usual, but suddenly my role in dealing with security—which had been unnecessary in the planning stages—became crucial in Toronto. With the usual assortment of Stones' faithful gathering in hordes in the hotel lobby, it was becoming impossible to maintain any semblance of normalcy. Amazingly, the performances at the El Macambo club, in Toronto, proceeded as planned on Friday and Saturday, March 4 and 5. Keith was confined to the hotel, except for these two nights, and it was just a matter of protecting the other guys since people were showing up from all over the world thinking this might be the last performance *ever* for the Stones. That little club didn't seat but three hundred people, and there was a furious demand for tickets.

Because of the El Macambo dates, the Stones would make international headlines again, due to the appearance of Margaret Trudeau, the party-loving young wife of Canadian Prime Minister Pierre Trudeau. Because the Canadian press was not allowed to report on unsettled court cases and was thereby barred from reporting the Keith Richards drug bust, they were primed for a great news story, and Maggie was their target. Rudge called me before the Saturday show and alerted me that we were going to be having a visitor. He wanted me to meet this unnamed VIP and guests, and he wanted them to sit at my table. At the club, a man in a suit and tie asked for me, and when I met him he identified himself as a member of the Royal Canadian Mounted Police, escorting the prime minister's wife.

With all the hoopla going on over Keith's arrest, Maggie had been able to slip unnoticed into a suite of rooms at the Harbour Castle, registering under her maiden name of Margaret Sinclair. But her anonymity went up in flashbulbs as soon as she stepped foot from Mick Jagger's black limousine in the alley behind El Macambo. She accompanied Mick, whom she had met the month before at a New York photo exhibit, and Ronnie Wood down to the beer cellar/dressing room and hung around, pouring beer for the Stones and their crew. Only when the Stones prepared to take the stage did she join our table. Mrs. Trudeau was accompanied by Judy Welch, the owner of a Toronto modeling agency; Ms. Welch's attorney; and two of the agency's models. The RCMPs declined to sit at the table with us and remained somewhere in the background. However, a plainclothes Toronto policeman did sit at the table with us, a noticeable irritant to the fun-loving First Lady.

What had started out to be a quiet little recording session had become one of the biggest fiascos in the much-ballyhooed career of the Rolling Stones. But at least the speculation about Maggie was keeping a little heat off us about Keith's arrest. However, it was just one more thing for us to deal with, and we already had plenty of problems.

Leading up to the bond hearing on the seventh, we were concerned that the prosecutor was going to try to get Keith held without bond. Wasserman, Rudge, and I all conferred about it, and Rudge felt he should put intense pressure on the local authorities to release Keith. He and Wasso got on the phone and called radio stations all across the northeastern part of the United States—Detroit, Buffalo, wherever. It had already been all over the wire services and the international press that Keith Richards had been busted in Canada, and this was the end of the Rolling Stones. The United States government had already said, "One more incident with Mr. Richards, and it's over as far as we're concerned." I knew from the minute I got Kathy's phone call that I needed to take quick action with our own government, so I had been on the phone with my contacts in Washington even before I got to Toronto. There was nothing I could do except admit that Keith was a heroin addict. It was a little late to come up with excuses.

But first I had to get the bail made. I had to put intense pressure on the courts to make that bail; $25,000 was a figure I had deemed appropriate. So the technique we employed was to get the rabidly loyal Stones fans to come to Toronto to "free" Keith. I mean, these were rabid fans. There was one guy who wore the same Stones T-shirt for ten years—the same shirt! There was a blind girl who traveled all over the United States on a bus, following the Stones tour. When we became aware of this, we collected money for her and I got her into every show. So I was aware of just how far fans would go for the Stones. And we didn't underestimate them. By the time we went to court, there were thousands of Stones fans in front of Old City Hall.

I told the court there were two reasons to allow Keith bail: (1) to save Keith's life, and I would absolutely guarantee medical treatment, and (2) there would be a riot if he was not released. Well, the police were very civil to deal with in Toronto, and the police chief began calling around to the local rock station and to some of the American border cities' stations, and they confirmed that it had been all over the news and that kids were coming in from everywhere.

Keith was slated to appear for his bond hearing at Old City Hall at two o'clock on the seventh, and the local rock station, CHUM, began announcing that fact at noon that day. Our strategy was for Keith to arrive by the front door, in a full show of bravado, and that's exactly what he did—although he was running just a bit late. Because the band had rehearsed into the night, Keith had overslept, a fact I was apprised of when Anita knocked on my door at one-thirty to borrow a razor for

Keith. We took Keith to the courthouse in a station wagon from which he emerged in fine fashion, wearing a black velvet suit and white silk scarf. Vintage Keith!

Our hearing was scheduled for Courtroom 26, which was closed to the public, although a few members of the press were present. Judge Vincent McEwan was the presiding judge. Clay and the prosecutor, David Scott, agreed to remand Keith's hearing on the heroin charges to the following Monday, the fourteenth. With that decided, the local reporters departed the courtroom. But the judge requested a meeting with Clay, Scott, and me in his chambers. While we met, Keith was put in a holding cell. It was at this meeting that Scott informed us of the second charge against Keith—cocaine possession. The judge ordered us to produce Keith for a hearing on that charge the following day, and Scott made no secret of the fact that he planned to ask for revocation of bail and to move that Keith be jailed immediately. However, since the reporters had already departed, they planned to keep the hearing under wraps. But they hadn't counted on one thing—if they jailed Keith, the rabid Stones fans would go apes and cause a riot. They released Keith to return to the hotel, with the stipulation that he return to face additional charges the next day.

The Keith who appeared at the hearing on the eighth was a far cry from the Keith of the day before. The last twenty-four hours had obviously taken their toll on him because Flippo described him as looking extremely nervous, appearing slightly hangdog in the witness box.

What was not known, nor even reported by Flippo in his book, was the maneuvering I was doing behind the scenes. I went to the judge and admitted that Keith was a heroin addict. But I also said, "Your honor, I've already acknowledged that you're dealing with a man seriously addicted to heroin, but if you lock him up, he'll die. There is no way he can withdraw from heroin cold turkey." That was my main argument for getting him released and on such a low bond at that. He was essentially released into our custody. There was a good deal of arguing in those chambers. They were holding him on trafficking, and I made the argument that Keith never sold any drugs in his life. If he had any he would give them away, but he wouldn't sell them. I pointed out rather persuasively that he was not a drug trafficker but rather a drug user. The large amount of drugs he had in his possession was for his own use; at that time he was using 50 percent-pure heroin. That would have killed an ordinary person, but Keith's system had become almost immune to it. The quantity indicated to the authorities that it was being sold, when it was in fact for the personal use of a heavy user.

The judge was incredulous. "Are you saying that he'll have to continue to use heroin to stay alive?" he postured.

"That's exactly what I'm saying," I confessed, but I did agree to begin immediately to obtain medical help to aid Keith with his addiction. I said I would attempt to obtain a drug substitute, but the fact was that we had to keep supplying Keith with heroin. That task fell to someone on the staff; I didn't participate in that.

I made a passionate argument against locking Keith up, and they bought it. They agreed to the $25,000, but we had to surrender Keith's passport to guarantee that he did not leave the country. He was to appear again on the fourteenth.

I had been consulting with Mick and the rest of the band, and we had a couple of immediate problems to deal with: Keith Richards was in trouble and facing jail time in Toronto, and the United States was never going to allow him back into the country, and we were already planning the '78 tour. So after all my problems in '75, now I had Keith in Canada busted on drug trafficking.

I had promised the court to get help for Keith, so I started calling all over trying to get Keith medical help. I contacted the Drug Research Foundation in Toronto; then I called the Menninger Clinic in Topeka, Kansas, and spoke with one of the Menningers. He was stunned that Keith was shooting heroin with such a high concentration of purity. He said that eventually Keith would go, what he called, "over the hump"—he'd become immune to it and wouldn't even get a high from it. We had to do something with Keith. He couldn't come into the United States with another drug conviction, and at this point it was unknown whether he would ever be allowed to return. But it was crucial that we move him to the United States to treat him. I don't remember now why we felt that the only place we could effectively treat him was in the United States, but we all came to that decision. Keith in all likelihood was going to jail, but if I could convince the court that I had cured him, then his possession of drugs would be deemed an illness rather than a crime. Jane Rose, Keith's manager, told us that Eric Clapton had been cured of his addiction by a female British physician, Dr. Meg Patterson, who had studied acupuncture. She lived in Hong Kong and had perfected a frequency impulse technique in which she had designed a transmitter to feed frequency impulse into the earlobe, and it would stop the craving for heroin.

I located her in Hong Kong and asked her if she could come to the States to treat Keith. Dr. Patterson agreed to come to the States to treat Keith. But there was another obstacle: She could not practice in the United States and therefore would not be able to administer her treatment, which was not FDA-approved in the States. In order to overcome that challenge, I had to travel to Washington to get government approval as well as a waiver from the American Medical Association. We also had to have an American board-certified physician sponsor her.

At some point, after things were secure, I left Kathy in charge of things in Toronto and returned to the States. Jimmy Carter was president then, and I had contacts at the White House; I got them to agree with what I was proposing and to smooth the way with the AMA. We selected a doctor—Dr. Corbett—in Camden, New Jersey, who specialized in drug treatment and counseling, and he sponsored Dr. Patterson. Jane arranged to rent an estate outside Philadelphia, and we had it all set up. Now I had to get Immigration and the State Department to agree to let Keith enter the United States. After this hearing, I was also conferring with the Canadian ambassador, laying the groundwork for getting Keith admitted to the United States.

Every element was contingent upon another—the White House wouldn't agree to let Keith come into the United States unless State and Immigration gave their approval, and it was kind of like using one against the other. I'd say to State and Immigration, "The White House has endorsed this treatment." What the White House had actually said to the AMA was, "We'll consent to this doctor coming in and administering this treatment on a one-time basis if an American doctor will sponsor and administer the treatment jointly with this British doctor." It was really up to Dr. Corbett in Camden. Everybody was attempting to pass the buck on down the line, but I had been dealing with the people in those bureaus for so long that they just took what I said at face value. Plus, the Canadians were still holding Keith's passport, and they would not return it until they had been assured that he was leaving *only* to seek treatment for his illness. His travel would be restricted.

On the ninth, Flippo, Wasserman, and I flew back to the States, and what happened on that flight from Toronto to New York was one of the funniest things I've ever witnessed. We had given Flippo the ticket purchased for Charlie Watts, so all three of us were sitting in first class. But what happened next really needs to be told in Chet's words:

> As soon as the plane took off, Wasserman, who surely hadn't slept in days, nodded right off . . . . The gunboat wing-tip crowd could only look on sullenly as the stewardesses brought Carter and me fresh drinks and perched prettily on the arms of our chairs and begged us to tell them how we had just managed to outfox the entire government of Canada and who was the large, suspicious-looking man whom we were guarding (and who was now twitching in his sleep). All of a sudden, without any warning, Wasserman rose up out of his seat like a massive avenging angel, threw back his head, and uttered a long, howling blood-curdling scream. Just as abruptly, he slumped back down into his seat and went into a peaceful sleep. The plane seemed to suddenly drop a hundred feet. The ensuing silence was as absolute as a silence can be on a jetliner (p. 108).

Wasso was a big, jovial guy. He was probably forty at that time. He was a gentle, big bear kind of guy. He wanted to be liked by everyone. He was always playing jokes on people, but I was very fond of him. One night, during Keith's troubles in Toronto, I was having dinner with Wasserman and a friend of his at an exclusive restaurant in Toronto. Right in the middle of a very expensive dinner, Wasso got in a spat with his friend, stood up and called his friend a filthy name at the top of his voice. He then reached across the table, slapped him, and turned and walked out of the restaurant. This kid and I were left with nothing but the stares of every patron in the upscale restaurant. I laughed that Wasso would do anything to get out of paying the check. That's just Wasserman. I'm not sure he had a temper; I think he just liked to shock people. He was a fun guy, and I loved him. At that time, he had a lot of high-powered clients—Gregory Peck, Bob Dylan, and George C. Scott.

Mahoney-Wasserman was probably the number one PR agency in Beverly Hills. He was a great publicist and did a wonderful job for the Stones. But he was a wild man.

Keith was scheduled to appear in court on Monday, and we were doing damage control in the meantime. Margaret Trudeau's association with the Stones was threatening to become an international incident, and rumors were flying all through the streets of New York (where the lovely Mrs. Trudeau had flown after El Macambo) and Toronto. Because most of the rumors centered around a possible romantic liaison between Mick and Maggie, Rudge had to get Mick to go public with a denial through the near-tabloid pages of the *New York Post*. On Friday the eleventh, the *Toronto Sun* ran a damning editorial about Keith's treatment in the Canadian courts, entitled ROLLING STONED. It said:

> Perhaps the most scandalous thing about the whole Rolling Stones caper in Toronto was not Maggie Trudeau's bizarre antics, but the treatment Keith Richards of the Stones got from our court. Richards was charged with possession of heroin for the purpose of trafficking and later with possession of cocaine. That's pretty serious stuff. Especially for a guy with his record—make it the group's record, which is long and awful. For the first offense Richards was released on $1,000 bail, which some call "disposable bottle bail"—no deposit, no return. And $25,000 bail on the second charge is ridiculously low considering his millionaire status. Police say that normally bail for a foreign national, involving possession of heroin or cocaine, would be denied—or set at a very high figure. One can only conclude that there is indeed one law for the rich or renowned and another for the people—contrary to all our principles of justice . . . (Flippo, p. 113).

The night before the third hearing on March 14, photographer Annie Liebovitz had kept Keith up all night posing for *Rolling Stone*, and he had passed out with a needle in his arm. I literally had to carry him to court for his hearing and prop him up; in fact, there is a picture of me holding him up. Anita was also in court that day, and Clay was able to get her released with only a $400 fine, although she had to surrender her passport. Keith could barely keep his eyes open during the proceedings against him, but that was of little consequence since the hearing took less than a minute. Keith was ordered to return on June 27, at which time a plea could be entered and an actual trial date set.

I was successful in my attempt to get a limited visa issued to Keith to enter the United States for drug treatment. I presented that to the Canadian court, and they released Keith's passport to him. We had a Learjet standing by to take Keith, Anita, and Marlon to Philadelphia. I had guaranteed the Canadian and U.S. governments that security would be present at all times—which it was—and Jane Rose, Keith's manager, remained with them the entire time. I returned to Little Rock but flew back every few days. In a very short time—three weeks—Keith was cured of his heroin addiction. I went back up there a couple of weeks later and played tennis with him. It was a revolutionary treatment, and it worked. Dr. Patterson completed the rehabilitation on May 9.

A month later, Clay Powell was successful in getting the Supreme Court of Ontario to declare invalid the RCMP's search warrant under which Keith Richards had been busted. Why? No specific officer had been listed on the warrant. Now successfully cured of heroin addiction, Keith was scheduled to appear in court in Toronto on June 27. He was a no-show, as he was for his next three court dates. He finally appeared on October 23, 1978, and when he arrived he was accompanied by, among others, Lorne Michaels and Dan Akroyd of *Saturday Night Live* fame, both of them big stars in their native Canada. Keith came off looking almost like a Boy Scout to the court, with a new attorney, Austin Cooper, extolling the success of his rehabilitation. As a result, the cocaine charges were dropped and Keith pleaded to a lesser charge of heroin possession. Finally, on October 24, the judge handed down the following sentence for Keith:

> Maybe the Rolling Stones have encouraged drug use in their songs. Still, his efforts have been to move himself away from the drug culture and can only encourage those who emulate him. No jail or fine is appropriate. The long-term benefit to the community, a large community, entails the continuing treatment for your addiction . . . . Judgment is suspended for one year.

The terms of his probation were to keep the peace, to report to his probation officer within twenty-four hours, to continue treatment at the Stevens Center in New York City, to return to Toronto on May 7 and September 24 to report to his probation officer, and to give a benefit performance within the next six months for the Canadian National Institute for the Blind. Keith walked out of the courtroom a free man! And the Rolling Stones lived to play another day.

Chapter 16
Life As Usual—The 1978 Tour

WE HAD BEEN PLANNING for the '78 tour of the United States for some time; in fact, the release of the live record was planned to coincide with the tour. And when it came time for us to plan the '78 tour, we had no problems with the government. When we applied for their H-1 petitions, we submitted the documents from Dr. Patterson that proved Keith was cured. They still had to grant a waiver, but it didn't cause any more problems than it always had. The whole time the Canadian thing was going on, I was back and forth to Washington, meeting with the U.S. government agencies, keeping them informed of what was happening with Keith, and playing it down. I was very honest in telling them that Keith had a drug abuse problem, like many others, and we were curing him of it; it was a blessing that he got busted in Canada.

The tour started June 10 at the Civic Center in Lakeland, Florida. Ordinarily, three or four months before the tour, Peter Rudge would call me, I'd go to New York, and we'd start planning the tour. If Keith had not been arrested in Canada, I'm not sure they would have thought there was any need for me to be out on this tour. The government didn't really demand it as they had in '75. I think my presence was just a comfort for both the Stones and the U.S. government. However, no one in the Stones organization—neither Prince Rupert nor Peter Rudge—was feeling any sense of ease about the Stones' position with local authorities on this tour, so there was never any question about my coming along. The climate was still not favorable toward the Stones three years after the last tour; plus, we were just a year removed from Keith's much-publicized Canadian arrest. By 1981 it became obvious that society was changing, as were the Stones, and there was less need for me, although we did have a few incidents on that tour. But by the end of it, I think we all understood that there was not really any need for me to be out with them on tour in any capacity—attorney, problem solver, whatever. The band was older and more mature.

But when we began the '78 tour, I had again assured the government that the Stones were clean and, to the extent that it was within our control, there would be no drug use on the tour. While they never intimated that if one of our truck drivers got caught with marijuana we'd be held responsible, we clearly understood that any of the Stones or their hierarchy would be accountable for their behavior.

We were in Lakeland, getting ready for the commencement of the tour, and that afternoon Bill Zysblat rushed up to me at the hotel to say that two of the tour publicists had been arrested for drugs and were being held in a dressing room backstage. I immediately set out for the venue. When I arrived, there were a uniformed captain and a couple of officers in the room, and they had the two publicists facing the wall with their hands on the wall and their legs spread-eagled. They had all this drug stuff laid out on the table in the room. I asked what was going on, and they told me they had arrested a couple of "my people" on charges of possession of cocaine. I'm not naïve, but at the time I guess I just didn't want to know that they were using drugs. The publicists' drug use was not apparent to me until that point, so I was shocked. After all I had been through with the Stones' drug use, here were their tour publicists splayed against the wall with a pocketful of cocaine! I was disappointed and very irritated—it was only the first day of the tour. If this hit the press, we were dead.

This was, in my mind, one of our most serious incidents yet. My only option was to plead with the police, and they were not in the mood to negotiate. They had them cold, with a substantial amount of cocaine. I finally convinced them that these guys were off the tour and that the Stones knew nothing about it and would not tolerate such behavior. They were pretty adamant that they didn't want these two in the state of Florida. I asked them to release them in my custody, and I'd make sure they were off the Stones tour and on the next flight out of Florida to New York. They finally agreed to release them, and I had the police take them out. They exited the tour at that moment—as far as the police knew. I think what we did was send them as far as Atlanta, where they caught up with us the next day. I asked Zysblat about this recently, and he didn't think the band was ever aware that the guys had been busted. We'd kept it that quiet.

This tour was very different from the '75 tour in that we played smaller venues—theatres rather than stadiums. In Lakeland we played the civic center, in Atlanta it was the Fox Theatre, and so forth. Apparently this was something Keith had insisted on because he wanted to take the Stones music into places they didn't usually tour. After the '75 tour, at a wrap-up meeting in New York, Prince Rupert, Rudge, Joe Rascoff, Bill Zysblat, and I analyzed the expenses of the tour, especially because the band made so little from that tour. We had 102 people, as I recall, on the '75 Stones payroll. When we went back out three years later, we were looking for ways to cut expenses. One way was to contract out most of the services. The tour lasted only six and a half weeks, rather than ten, and we cut the number of crew members way back. The gross on the tour wasn't great, but it was better than in '75.

About midway through the tour, in Myrtle Beach, Mick asked if I would assume the additional responsibility of signing checks that were over $2,500, just as a double-check on all expenses. I was happy to comply. Rudge was a genius, but he was liable to tell me to charter Mick a plane, while also telling his assistant, Mary Beth Medley, to do the same. We might need just one plane; instead we would charter—and unnecessarily pay for—two planes. It was chaotic out there sometimes, which resulted in a great deal of waste. We put a stop to that in '78, and it was a better financial arrangement for the band.

The Fox show in Atlanta was incredible. The Stones are never any better than they are in a 4,500-seat theatre, with the crowd right on the stage. We went to the Capital Theatre, in Passaic, New Jersey, which had fewer than 5,000 seats. Then, on June 15, we played the Warner Theatre, in Washington, DC, which seated 2,000 people: I gave away 1,500 VIP tickets, and we had to bring in 200 chairs. For dates like that, we never announced that the Stones were going to play. The marquee would read The Cockroaches or some such name that Mick or Keith had dreamed up. We had all kinds of politicians and dignitaries. I still have in my files a letter from Rosalyn Carter's assistant thanking me for the tickets for her kids. Loren Lawrence from the State Department and his kids were there. I had to bring Kathy Woods up just to coordinate the VIP tickets. I had so many other things to do that I had to put her in charge of nothing but the ticket requests. It was another incredible show—absolutely awesome.

From there, we went to JFK Stadium in Philadelphia and played to 100,000 people. We had to do something to make money. On the Warner Theatre date, the production costs were around $40,000, so we probably lost $75,000 playing that date. Then we went to New York, and what do we do? We play the Palladium, which is another small theatre. Then on to the Orpheum Theatre, in Boston. Again, no money. Then Hampton Roads, Virginia; and Greensboro, North Carolina, where we played regular venues, as we did at the Mid-South Coliseum in Memphis. Now we were back making money.

On June 29, we played Rupp Arena, in Lexington, Kentucky. We were still having some police problems. They weren't so much out to arrest the Stones this time, but they were still abusive to the kids. In Rupp, the sections are divided by a pipe railing. If a kid had tickets in Section C and he wanted to go over and visit with his buddy in Section D, these Nazi cops would toss the kid out of the arena. I got irritated at this behavior, and I tried to stop them, until they threatened to arrest me. Finally, I went around backstage and collected all the unused comp tickets from the crew. I gave them to one of our guys and stationed him outside the arena. When the cops would throw a kid out, our guy would walk up and hand him a better seat than the one he had been tossed from. They caught me doing that, and we had a big stand-off. We finally resolved it and they quit throwing the kids out, but not until we had exchanged some serious words.

My brother-in-law, Stan King, was plant manager of the Ford Plant in Louisville, so his son, Brian, who was a teenager at the time, came over for the concert, and he was hanging with me. Before we reached a resolution to our problems, we were standing backstage as they were dragging this young guy out. There was a policeman on one arm, a policeman on the other arm, and one on each of his legs, and they were physically throwing him out of the arena. This guy was screaming, "Dammit, you don't know what you're doing. You don't know how much trouble you're gonna be in. You don't know who you're dealing with—you're gonna hear from Stan King! I work for Stan King."

I said, "Hold it. Wait a minute." They stopped, and I asked this kid to tell me again who he worked for.

"I work for Stan King," he shouted. "They don't seem to know who Stan King is, but he has more power in this state than the governor, and by God, they're gonna hear about this."

I told the officers that the kid was right, and they should release him and let him take his seat. The officers wanted to know, "Who the hell's Stan King?"

I said, "He's my brother-in-law, and this guy goes back in." I laughed and later told Stan I bet that guy had been thrown in jail ten times, and every time he caused trouble he'd evoke Stan King's name. Stan knew exactly who I was talking about. The young man thought Stan knew everybody, and even if Stan *didn't* know everyone, at least he knew the right people that night.

July 1 we played Municipal Stadium, in Cleveland, again. All these dates were sold out. Then for the Fourth, we played Bills Stadium, in Buffalo. Then to Masonic Hall, in Detroit, and on to Soldier Field, in Chicago—sold out. In Chicago there was a young female reporter for one of the local television affiliates, and she was interviewing people coming into the stadium. Interestingly, one of the groups she stopped was a mother, her daughter, and her granddaughter, coming together to the Stones concert. The granddaughter was preteen, but both the mother and daughter were Stones fans. By now there could be four or five generations of Stones fans out there.

We went from there to St. Paul and then to the Keil Opera House, in St. Louis. I remember that show specifically because that had to be one of the best concerts I've ever seen. To see the Stones in that beautiful facility was incredible. They had no production. They just stood up there and played music and totally rocked the Keil Opera House. Everyone there that night was aware of what a special event it was. But then, all these small theatres were special.

Chapter 17
Mick and the China Trip

IN LATE 1979, THE STONES started talking about going to the People's Republic of China, and Rudge asked me to explore the possibilities of such a trip. Although Nixon had reopened diplomatic channels years before, outsiders still were not free to travel in China. This would have been a very unusual move, for a rock-and-roll band to tour in Communist China. The Stones would be the first, and I thought it would be a big coup.

This was the '70s, and travel in a Communist country was far from an easy task to arrange, but there is nothing I like better than a challenge. I began my exploration of the idea by going to the Chinese desk at the State Department, where officials briefed me on the climate and tutored me in what steps I needed to take to open dialogue with the Chinese. Then I went to the CIA and, again, they briefed me. I still had some buddies in the White House at that time—some of them were still working with the Secret Service—so I had all the intelligence on China I needed. The new Chinese ambassador to Washington, Chai Zemin, was the first progressive Chinese official in years, and the Chinese Premier at the time, Hua Guofeng, was also more progressive than his predecessors. Zemin was sent to strengthen relations with the West. I was told that this ambassador would be receptive.

Bill Alexander, who was a congressman from Arkansas, was a friend of mine. Alexander had made two trips to China and established ties with the Chinese Embassy in Washington in an attempt to export Arkansas farm products. He also chaired the House task force on exports, which seeks to expand U.S. foreign trade, and as such he knew the ambassador quite well. I had made a couple of visits to the Chinese Embassy already, and even though they were more progressive, the only person who wore a Western suit was the ambassador. All the rest wore those little Chinese military uniforms, so once you entered the embassy, it was a bit cold. The atmosphere was formal—very sterile. After my courtesy visits to their embassy, Alexander thought it would be appropriate to bring the ambassador to the capitol, so he set up a lunch in one of the committee rooms for the ambassador and his interpreter, some of Alexander's staff, Mick, and me.

John Bennett, who was in the Washington bureau of the *Memphis Commercial Appeal* at the time, wrote about the lunch:

At an improbable meeting arranged by Rep. Bill Alexander (D-Ark) this week, Chai Zemin, the Washington ambassador for the People's Republic of China, sat down with Mick Jagger, lead singer for the Rolling Stones, to talk a little rock and roll . . . . Jagger, dressed in a suit and tie, brought Bill Carter of Little Rock, the British band's lawyer and chief security officer, to open the Washington parley in the same room where former House Speaker Sam Rayburn once made deals with House lieutenants . . . . The idea was to brief the Chinese official on the nature of rock and the essence of the sensual Rolling Stones' style and to prepare him to carry to Peking the idea of holding a concert in that city and possibly another city. The ambassador reportedly laughed and smiled a lot as the six men dined and discussed what a Rolling Stones concert might mean in China and how Chinese youth might react.

The lunch went very well, and Mick was as impressive as I expected him to be. I had to submit a proposal to the Chinese, and Mick chose Chet Flippo to write a background piece on the Rolling Stones. He wanted Chet to write it philosophically but slanted toward the Chinese political philosophy. It was a brilliant piece. Chet wrote:

On April 28, 1963, the day that the rock and roll band called the Rolling Stones were signed to a management contract in Richmond, England (thus setting into motion a musical force that endures to this day), Cuban Prime Minister Fidel Castro Ruz was in Moscow, being bugged by Soviet Premier Kruschchev. The United States of America was wracked with civil rights demonstrations. England's power was in its final ascendancy. Clearly, new forces, new alignments were at work in the world, and "sleepy London town" would never be the same again; nor would the United States, which was being thrust pell-mell from the cold-war complacency of the Eisenhower era into crisis at home and abroad.

Nothing was the same. Both the U.S. and England faced a seemingly insurmountable problem at home: both countries were experiencing the results of the "baby boom" of World War II—an enormous population of young people—so many young people that there were no jobs for them, and little chances of higher education for most of them. They literally faced no future and the governments of both the U.S. and Britain had no idea what to do about it. Their solution was to do nothing, which only worsened the problem. There were millions of working-class young people with no leadership, no destiny. Even so, they were not looking so much for leaders as they were searching for a voice, a collective voice, one that could focus their aimlessness, that would give a definition.

Rock and roll, born of African roots, was virtually a spontaneous movement, the collective voice of an entire generation bursting loose. It was a genuine folk upheaval in the U.S. and England, a throwing-off of the notion that the giant corporations and institutions would determine what music young people could hear. It was literally peer-group music: written by and performed by young people for other young people. It was both a reaction to and a substitute for the hypocrisy that young people sensed in their elders. Even though it was in some ways an angry music, a music of rebellion, it was mostly music of affirmation, almost a joyous communal rite; just as the African music it came from was a music of a tribal nature, of a sharing experience.

Leading the way was the Rolling Stones, a group of young Britons who had assimilated American black music; so much so, in fact, that they actually re-introduced black rhythm and blues music to America, which had ignored it. The Stones were the leading edge of what has come to be called the "mod" (an abbreviation for "modernists") movement—a reaction to the anonymity of the technological era and the initial feeling of uselessness and frustration of being reduced to a cipher. Unlike their popular contemporaries, the Beatles, who composed and performed a more romantic, escapist form of music, the Stones practiced musical realism. Apart from the American rhythm and blues songs they performed, the Stones' own compositions dealt with the realities and problems and joys of everyday life. They wrote songs that were, leading music critics agreed, as immediate as tomorrow's newspaper. They generated considerable controversy along the way, as was to be expected, but they were and continue to be the leaders of a new art form and they literally created a revolution in popular culture. They created mass culture that was, in fact, relevant to the masses and the response was overwhelming. The public—the young people and many who were a little older—welcomed the Rolling Stones' freshness and admired their refusal to compromise, their willingness to take musical risks, their attacks on upper-class hypocrisy, and, above all, their own self-determinism. They were the first rock and roll band to be true individuals, to decide what songs they would perform, where they would perform them, and just when and how they would perform them. The public was ready for them: since 1963, the Rolling Stones have performed before millions of people in England, America, Austria, France, Holland, Germany, Italy, Canada, Australia, New Zealand, South America, Sweden, Belgium, Denmark, Poland. They were the first rock band to refuse to go to South Africa, because of that country's apartheid policies.

Leading music critics call them "The World's Greatest Rock and Roll Band" and, as of yet, no one has challenged the title. Their worldwide record sales total in the hundreds of millions. They have been criticized for becoming successful, but it's apparent from their actions that profits alone are not their incentive for continuing to make music. They raised three-quarters of a million dollars in a concert to benefit earthquake victims in Nicaragua. One of their most memorable appearances was a free concert played from a flat-bed truck on Fifth Avenue in New York City in 1975. Another was a money-losing concert in 1977 before 400 persons in a small Toronto club. The show was every bit as dedicated as their 1978 appearance before 100,000 rock fans at the John F. Kennedy Stadium in Philadelphia.

Many of their shows have been not as profitable as they could have been because the group insist on providing state-of-the-art staging and lighting for their shows. Their monumental 1975 Tour of the Americas, which spanned three months and was witnessed by about two million concert-goers, is a prime example. For that tour, they had Broadway designers build for them two enormous five-petal lotus flower stages, one of which weighed ten tons and the other twenty-five tons. The result, however, was spectacular: as the concert opened, the stage resembled a closed lotus flower and the petals were lowered hydraulically as the show began. That same tour had a sound system that weighed eight tons, entailing thirty-two speakers; as well as an elaborate lighting system that weighed six tons and contained seven hundred different lights and forty miles of copper cables to supply the lights.

No other rock band has paid such detail to the entertainment of the concert-goer, whether it be to a 400-seat intimate gathering or to an outdoor crowd of 100,000.

Musically, the Stones devote the same attention to their work. Their music defies categorization: it is truly international and knows no national boundaries, no class lines, no racial or ethnic bounds.

Their music has drawn praise from leading figures in other fields of music. Leonard Bernstein, the prominent American classical conductor, attended a Stones concert in New York City and went backstage to congratulate the members of the band for their music. The German classical composer Hans Werner Henze went to a Stones concert in Rome and came away transfixed. "They made an enormous impression on me, and for weeks after I attempted to reproduce this impression in my music," Henze later told the *Washington Post*. As a result, he composed the cantate "Muses of Sicily," which was performed as a resounding success at the Kennedy Center in Washington, D.C., with the Choral Arts Society Chamber Chorus and the National Symphony Orchestra. The London Symphony Orchestra recently recorded a Stones' composition.

The Stones' own music—stingingly original lyrics and music with a blues flavor—has become the hallmark against which other rock bands are measured. Their own compositions range widely afield—one oft-quoted line that delineates their working-class background in England reads,

"What can a poor boy do, except sing for a rock and roll band?"—and they deal with common human emotions, the problem of violence, poetic wanderings: anything any gifted songwriter would address himself to.

On the one hand, the Rolling Stones have written what are vital anthems for young people.

On the other hand, the Stones have composed lyrical paeans to everyman, as in "Salt of the Earth."

And still again, they have composed what might be called love songs but are poetically lyrical, as with "Child of the Moon."

There is no disputing the fact that the Rolling Stones are the most controversial rock and roll band that has come along; at the same time, however, there is no disputing that they are the *best* rock and roll band to yet appear. The Beatles, their only real rivals, long ago went into retirement. No group has yet to appear to challenge their credentials as the best. They are also the only true international band: British-born, weaned on Afro-American music, they have roamed the world for sixteen years, proving on several continents that they are the best available at what they do. Nine years ago, the eminent American music critic Lester Bangs said of the Stones, "The Stones, alone among their generation of groups, are not about to fall by the wayside. And as long as they continue to thrive this way, the era of true rock and roll music will remain alive and kicking with them." Another critic, Greil Marcus, said of them: "The Stones are not only rhythmic historians but aesthetic politicians, and their [music], while hardly political, is a kind of political event in our vague and aimless political community."

The Rolling Stones themselves, when asked about their motives for wanting to visit China, said that they wanted to, said Stones leader Mick Jagger, because "We want an exchange with the Chinese people, on all possible levels, on mass culture levels—our appeal is to mass culture. We seek a fuller understanding between our two peoples. This transcends ideology and we want to share our ideas and music with the people of China." Since the Rolling Stones have long since moved from Britain to America, the Stones feel that in many ways they represent America and they seemed eager to do so. "We welcome an interchange with the people of China," Jagger said, "and we trust they feel the same."

I submitted all this to the Chinese. Some time passed, and then I received a phone call from a woman—whose name I don't recall—in New York who identified herself as a representative of the Chinese government. She requested that I come to New York at my earliest convenience to meet with her, which I did, at a hotel in Manhattan. What a surprise! She was an extremely good-looking Chinese woman, but totally Westernized. She was dressed in designer Western clothes and dripped with diamonds. She was a fashion queen, spoke excellent English, yet her address, when she gave me her card, was listed as Hong Kong. She certainly didn't fit any of my preconceived images of a Chinese Communist. She said she had been sent by the Chinese government to further explore the feasibility of a Rolling Stones visit to China. That threw me a bit of a curve. I didn't expect the Chinese to send a Westernized *woman* to do business for them.

After our meeting, I flew to Washington and began immediately to investigate this woman. My sources came back and assured me that she was indeed a Communist, but she specialized in dealings with Westerners. Because the Communist Chinese government wasn't going to do business with Westerners, they set up fronts in Hong Kong who were token Westerners. Those people dealt with the West. This woman, for instance, had been buying Caterpillar bulldozers for China. They were purchased by and shipped to her company in Hong Kong and were in turn sold to the mainland Chinese. It was merely a front so that the Chinese didn't have to buy from Americans or other Westerners; they could buy from the Chinese in Hong Kong. So if we were going to go to China, we would have to go through a Hong Kong company. The Chinese government was not going to deal directly with us.

Our next step was to facilitate a meeting between this lady and Mick Jagger, so I reserved a suite at the Park Lane Hotel, in New York, and arranged a meeting. Madame X and I were already in the suite when Mr. Jagger arrived, accompanied by Charlie Watts. He was dressed very casually in jeans, T-shirt, and tennis shoes, and he was anything but well mannered and polite. Suffice it to say, he did not come to impress anyone. I won't recount the meeting in its entirety, because I still cringe when I think about it. When it was over, I was a bit embarrassed by Mick and Charlie's performance, and I apologized to the Chinese delegation. Their response: "No need to apologize. That's just what we expected from everything we'd heard about the Rolling Stones."

Some time later, I laughingly quizzed Mick about his behavior that day. "After all those months and months of effort we put into this trip," I asked, "why would you do such a thing?" He never responded, and that was the end of the China trip. To this day I don't know the reason Mick killed the trip. Rudge and I speculated that maybe Mick decided he didn't want to go, and that was his way of getting out of it. Just one of the fourteen faces of Mick Jagger.

Chapter 18
Stand-Off in Jamaica

N A 1986 TABLOID STORY, Mary Beth Medley, who had been a member of the Stones' staff for the '75 and '78 tours, talked of a party fling every night—the drugs, the drink, the fun, and the fights. From my perspective, I was the straight guy on tour, and my role was to keep everyone out of trouble. I disagree with Mary Beth's assessment, unless she was involved in something I was unaware of. My perspective of the Stones tour was that it was all business. I'm not saying there wasn't a little Jack Daniels, and I'm sure there were some drugs and some parties, but I can tell you there was not a party every night. More typically, after a Stones concert, Mr. Jagger would call a staff meeting. He may not have liked the sound, and he wanted to deal with that. He may not have liked the publicity, so he wanted to talk to Wasso and Rudge and see what was going on. He'd call me in if we had any kind of a problem with the police or security. *That's* the Rolling Stones tour I remember. But everybody has a different perspective of things. I see from the more narrow viewpoint of a former federal agent and lawyer, and I didn't think anything was out of hand. Mick ran that tour very much like a business. And when things began to get a little bit out of hand on the '78 tour, he took immediate steps and worked out a deal with Prince Rupert for me to begin signing checks.

Mick was aware of everything. There was one incident on tour when Mick came to me and said he understood there was drug use going on by one of the staff, and he wanted it stopped; he wanted me to get control of it. A lot of people wouldn't believe it, but Jagger wasn't sitting around snorting cocaine and partying; he was concerned about the tour. He was concerned about the bottom line—the business—and he didn't intend to have somebody interfere with it. Not too long ago someone said to me, "Well, I guess Mick Jagger must be every bit the devil he portrays."

I countered, "Quite the contrary. Mick Jagger is nothing like the character he portrays on stage. He's a very bright and a very smart individual." That's not to say he doesn't go out and drink and have a good time—hell, lawyers and doctors do that. Mick has his own way of having fun—I've seen him have a good time. But he's not an irresponsible drunk, drug-abuser, or woman-chaser. It's obvious he has a lot of problems with women—he has a lot of children by several different women—but so have a lot of executives and movie stars and sports figures. From my observation, he is a responsible businessman. I don't know how much he's worth today, but it must be in the hundreds of millions. I have a lot of respect for him and his uncanny ability to make the right decision at the right time. He has great intuition about when to push and shove and when to pull back. His timing is great; he knows when to say yes and when to say no.

Do I know Mick? No, I wouldn't say that. Keith once told me Mick had fourteen different personalities. He's pretty unpredictable. Maybe in a particular situation I might have been able to predict his decision, but just when I thought I had him figured out, he'd throw me a curve.

Now, do I know Keith? Absolutely. Keith is a straight-ahead guy 24/7/365. He's the same, solid personality. Keith's Keith and he's never pretended to be anything else. Do I consider Mick and Keith friends? Yeah, I consider them to be friends of mine. I say that not because I hung out with them a lot, but because I liked them, and I was never unhappy to be with them. I spent a good deal of time with them, and I've sat and talked with Mick a lot at times in his hotel room. I've dined with him and traveled with him. I like Mick.

What kept them from being prisoners of their success, like Elvis? I read that Mick once said that Elvis started believing his own press. I was in Hawaii doing a television taping, and Bob Peterson, the lighting designer, and I were having dinner at some restaurant, when one of his former superstar clients came into the restaurant with an entourage of about twelve people. I thought that was ridiculous, and I made the comment that I had gone to dinner in New York and Washington when it was just Mick and me. Jagger doesn't go out with an entourage of ten to twelve goons. If he's not on tour, he might take a security person with him, but I've never seen Mick Jagger or Keith Richards go anywhere with an entourage to look after them and protect them. You'll meet Mick Jagger bopping down the street in New York with just blue jeans, tennis shoes, and a T-shirt on. Keith and Ronnie Wood also go out by themselves. I've sat in the bar at the Parker Meridien Hotel, in New York, with Ronnie Wood and had a quiet drink. No big deal. They're just not caught up in their own thing, and I think that's the difference. Their egos are not that out of control.

Most of the dealings I had with the Stones were with Mick and Keith. When I first got involved with the group, they were the ones having waiver problems. Then the Canadian trouble was Keith's alone. And later I helped Keith with his property in Jamaica and spent time with him there.

I had heard about this house in Jamaica for a long time, and after the '81 tour Keith told me he had a problem with it. The prime minister of Jamaica, Michael N. Manley, was a Socialist and had pretty much allowed locals to overrun the property of foreigners. Law and order was almost nonexistent. Tourism had diminished. I knew an International Creative Management agent who went there on vacation and was robbed at gunpoint. Keith's house had been taken over by the locals, and he had about given up on it because he didn't think he had any recourse as long as Manley was in office. Finally, in 1980, Jamaica had an election, and Edward Seaga, a Harvard graduate, defeated Manley. He was an advocate of democracy and set about trying to restore law and order and develop tourism again. Jane Rose was the first person to sound me out about going to Jamaica. Jane worked in Rudge's office in New York but more and more had moved into the role of Keith's manager. As soon as the '81 tour was over, she asked if I would accompany her and Patty Hanson, Keith's wife, to Jamaica to see about the house. The property had originally been handled by the lawyers in London, so I began communicating with British lawyer Paddy Grafton-Green. I guess I was selected because no other lawyer wanted to go there, and when I went, I found out why.

Patty, Jane, and I flew to Jamaica and checked into the Hilton Hotel. The next day we drove up to Keith's house, at Point of View, a high point in Ocho Rios, which overlooks the bay. It's in a gorgeous location, probably 800 feet above the bay. You can see the whole town of Ocho Rios and the ships coming into port. It's incredibly picturesque, and the house has a big veranda and a pool from which you can see the ocean clearly. A hurricane in '79 had damaged the house, but that was minor compared to the damage inflicted upon it by the thirteen Jamaicans and three goats that were inhabiting it when we drove up that day. It was a disaster; the goats were actually living in the house, and their droppings were everywhere. I would have recommended bulldozing it down, except that its thick stucco walls were probably eighteen inches thick. There was virtually nothing that could be saved. Amazingly, Keith still had a housekeeper who came every week but did nothing. We told the inhabitants who we were, but it made no difference to them—this was their house and they weren't leaving.

Now a little background. These squatters were friends of Peter Tosh, a reggae artist from Jamaica whom Keith had befriended and signed to Rolling Stones Records. He toured with the Stones until they had a falling out. Peter alleged that the Stones owed him a million dollars, and he was taking Keith's house as payment. We surveyed the situation and then went back to New York and reported to Keith. He wanted to reclaim the house, get the squatters cleared out of there, and remodel it. He wanted to get it fixed so he and Patty could go down there and live. I then went back by myself. Keith wanted me to try asking them to leave; he didn't want to have to resort to force. Well, that kind of handicapped me, but I went back down there, and I met with them again; they were not going anywhere. I don't know how many more times I returned, but Keith was insistent that I try to negotiate with them. Then Peter Tosh entered the picture, and he affirmed that he had taken possession of the house and I was to inform Keith of that fact. Our conversation was not polite.

When I went back to New York after that trip, I told Keith I had had a serious confrontation, with violence against me implied. I told him I had also met with the police commissioner who had taken over, and he assured me that law and order was present in Jamaica and they would put these people out of Keith's house at my direction. I just needed Keith's authority. He told me to try again to negotiate with them, but he did authorize me to take a security person along because he didn't want me to get hurt. I told him I wasn't worried about getting hurt, but I was worried about getting in trouble. So I suggested I take my partner, Kathy Woods, with me because it might be me who ended up in jail. I needed someone who could get the American ambassador or someone in Washington to get me out. So Kathy and I set off back to Jamaica, but this time I went straight to the police commissioner and told him the time had come. I informed him that I was going out there once more to try to negotiate with the squatters, but I might need him to back me up. I told the police commissioner that I needed to hire a security person to go with me to improve my odds a little. He recommended a guy named Ashley, who, he told me, was absolutely fearless and carried a machete with which he could cut off a man's head without hesitation. I knew that was just the man I needed.

I hired Ashley. He was a slim man, about six foot one, kind of wiry, maybe in his forties, and quiet—he didn't say much; he let the machete do his talking. Now, Peter Tosh was about six foot six, and he had a big afro that made him look even taller. Kathy, Ashley, and I went up to the house, and I told the squatters they were going to have to get out that day. While I was there negotiating, Peter Tosh drove up in his old Mercedes. Since Keith's house sat up on a hill above Ocho Rios and there was a winding road approaching it from town, you could see cars coming up the road from quite a distance. Then when a car drives through the gates and on up to the house, you could stand on his veranda and watch the car all the way. I saw Tosh coming, and when he arrived he stormed out onto the veranda, flaming angry. I said, "If everyone isn't out of the house by noon, I will have them removed." I added, "The police commissioner said there could well be some blood spilled." Tosh looked me right in the eye and said, "If there's going to be any bleeping blood spilled, it'll be yours." It was about eleven in the morning, and we still had an hour until my deadline. Tosh said, "I'll tell you what, if you want to bring the police, that's fine with me, but they'll find your blood rolling down the hill when they arrive." With that, he turned to leave but warned that he'd be back, and he roared off. I told Kathy she'd better go get the police, so she took our rental car and drove back into town to get the police.

Was I frightened? No, I don't think I was frightened. I had a license to carry my gun in Jamaica, and I had all kinds of political clout in Washington, so I wasn't frightened. I didn't get frightened back then. If it meant a showdown, then Ashley and I would take them on. I had a couple of custom-made billy clubs with me that I'd had made out of the hardest wood imaginable, and I welcomed the confrontation. I wasn't one bit concerned about taking on any or all of those thirteen Jamaicans in the house; I was confident we could handle them. But after a while I began to look at my watch, wondering where Kathy and the police could be. Thirty minutes passed, and still no police. Where the hell could they be? Then I heard a car way down the road, and I was watching for it to come into view. Then I heard more than one car, so I figured it was the police. But when the cars came into view, it was Tosh's Mercedes, loaded with his goons, and a Volkswagen bus behind it, loaded with more of his goons, with their clubs hanging out the windows. There must have been fifteen goons with him, plus the thirteen already in the house, and *no Kathy*!

Now I was getting very nervous. The odds definitely were not in our favor. Ashley and I stood on the veranda, watching our fate drive up that long driveway, and I was cussing Kathy with every breath. They roared into the driveway and were getting out of the car when I saw the blue lights coming up the hill. The police flew into the driveway with sirens screaming, just as Tosh was getting his goons unloaded. The cops came out in full riot gear with machine guns drawn. An officer ordered them back into their vehicles, took them into custody, and ordered the squatters in the house to load their possessions into the Volkswagen bus and vacate the property immediately. Kathy had ridden up in one of the police cars, and I lit into her, wanting to know what the hell had taken her so long. She'd had a flat tire going into town and had to walk part of the way to get the police. We came very close to getting murdered because of a flat tire!

With Tosh and all his people gone, I surveyed the damage and hired a contractor to come out and begin to remodel the house. It took us about eighteen months to completely rebuild that house, and I was supervising the progress for Keith. But Peter Tosh was still a presence in Jamaica, and he had threatened to get me. Then one day I received a welcome phone call. Jane Rose called and said she had some news for me that I would probably consider *good* news—Peter Tosh had been murdered in Kingston just that day. It was said to be a home invasion, but more than likely it was a drug deal gone south, and somebody killed him. I didn't realize until that moment how tense I had been every time I set foot on that island. I continued to look after the house for the next ten years, going down there several times a year, occasionally with Keith.

I took my daughter Joanna with me once to Barbados with Keith and Patty, but other than that I didn't have the girls around the Stones much. They were just little girls when I started with the group, and I would take them to other places, like Myrtle Beach, when they got older and could appreciate where they were. Paul Wasserman used to tell me that God was going to get me for what I had done to the youth of America by having one of my daughters marry a Rolling Stone. Julia was sixteen and Joanna was fourteen during the '81 tour, so I arranged for them to come out on the road, but Joanna had had her wisdom teeth extracted and wasn't able to make the trip. Julia came out with me and left Joanna to recuperate back in Little Rock. All their lives my daughters have tried to figure out which of the two of them I give favored treatment, but the truth is, it's whichever one happens to be with me at the time. Well, I knew I would have to do something to make it up to Joanna. Her birthday was coming up, and I told her I'd take her to New York to compensate for her missing the Stones trip.

Keith and Patty were in Barbados, and after the New York trip I was going to have to meet him there to get him to sign some papers. I thought as a special birthday present, I would surprise Joanna and take her on to Barbados with me. But I wanted it to be a total surprise, so I told her I would take her to New York first, take her out on the town to have some fun, then I'd put her on a plane back to Little Rock and I'd go on to Barbados. That was cool with her. When I talked to Keith I told him I thought I was going to bring my daughter to Barbados with me as a surprise, but I didn't ask him to do anything, and I certainly didn't expect any favors. Jane Rose was going with me to Barbados, and when I got to New York I told Jane the whole story. We spent a couple of days having fun in New York, and when we got ready to leave, I told Joanna we were going to pick up Jane Rose; then Jane and I would drop her off at LaGuardia on our way to JFK. When we got to Queens, we made only one stop—at JFK—and when we pulled up out front, Joanna was concerned that we'd forgotten to drop her at LaGuardia. I just looked at her and grinned. "Surprise," I said. "You're going on to Barbados with us." She just flipped, and we all flew off to Barbados to stay at the Sandy Lane Hotel.

The next morning I called Keith about nine at the villa he and Patty had rented. I told Keith I needed to come over and see him, and he said, "Why don't you bring Joanna with you?" I asked him if he was sure, and he insisted, so we went over there about an hour later. When we arrived, Keith was sitting out by the pool in his bathing suit. We sat there with him for a while, just enjoying the beauty of the surroundings; then Keith asked Joanna if she wanted to play Chinese Checkers with him. They played for a while; then he talked her into going into the pool. But then it was time for the adults to play. Keith and Patty and I started drinking, and they insisted that Joanna and I stay for lunch.

The whole time we were there, Keith was just so kind and gracious to Joanna. I didn't expect him to do that, and it kind of surprised me. He was always like that around his inner circle, but I'd never seen him reach out like that, and he truly made Joanna feel comfortable and at home. Through lunch and into the afternoon, we kept on drinking and were getting wasted. Then we stayed for dinner and kept on drinking. Finally, when Patty started running and jumping up into my arms, Joanna had taken as much of the adult fun as she could handle. She took me aside and said, "Daddy, I think it's time to go," and we did. But it was a wonderful day and one I don't think Joanna ever forgot, although I don't think any of her friends believed her when she told them what had happened.

Chapter 19
Lynyrd Skynyrd Plane Crash

ETER RUDGE REPRESENTED a number of other rock-and-roll bands in addition to the Rolling Stones, including the southern rock band Lynyrd Skynyrd ("Free Bird" and "Sweet Home Alabama"). They had come to Rudge's attention when one of his clients, The Who, persuaded him to sign the Florida natives to open their tour in 1972. About halfway through that tour, Rudge became the band's manager.

On October 17, 1977, I received a phone call at my home in Little Rock. It was Peter, and he was calling me because Lynyrd Skynyrd's chartered 1947 Convair 240 airplane had not arrived at its destination in Baton Rouge. There was some concern that the plane might have crashed. He'd called the FAA and several other places, but he'd been unable to find out anything. He was aware that I knew people at the Civil Aeronautics Board and FAA, as well as other Washington bureaus, and he needed me to see if I could find out what he had been unable to. I made some phone calls and determined that the plane had indeed crashed. It was first reported missing; then there was a report from witnesses on the ground of a plane crashing in a forest near McComb, Mississippi. They had confirmed that it was Lynyrd Skynyrd's airplane, so I called Rudge, who by that time had already heard from AP or some other news source. Band members Steve Gaines, Cassie Gaines, and Ronnie Van Zant were killed upon impact.

McComb was only about a thirty-minute flight from Little Rock, so Rudge asked if I would go over there immediately and take control of the situation. I called Central Arkansas Aviation, arranged for a charter flight, and rushed out to the airport and flew directly to McComb.

When I arrived in McComb, I went right over to the hospital where the remaining members of the band—Artimus Pyle, Allen Collins, Gary Rossington, Billy Powell, and Leon Wilkison—had been taken. Most had suffered serious injuries that, in some cases, caused permanent physical damage. When our immediate concern for the health of the survivors had passed, Rudge turned his attention to the cause of the crash, which was officially described as, "The plane ran out of gas due to an engine malfunction of undetermined nature." He asked me to find an aviation law expert and retain him to represent the band. I checked and found that one of the top aviation attorneys in America was Jerry Sterns, in San Francisco. So I retained him, and he went on to successfully resolve the case, although it took a few years. The plane that crashed was one the band had chartered, and looking into the crash with Sterns caused me to question the maintenance practices of the charter airline industry.

In '75 the Stones had flown in a chartered 707 that they had gotten from an air charter service, one of the few that would have had a plane big enough for their needs. These companies used retired planes from airlines, which basically meant they were airliners that were worn out and had been sold by the airlines. Now, the Convair that Lynyrd Skynyrd was on was not in itself an unsafe aircraft. But it was the circumstances under which it was chartered that made the difference—this company didn't have any pilots on staff and retained off-duty Allegheny Airlines pilots to fly the plane on this trip. It was just too much of a makeshift organization. The aircraft was thirty years old at the time of the crash.

I knew from being involved with Fred Smith of FedEx that charter companies aren't under the same regulations and requirements by the FAA as the airlines are. They're not inspected as frequently, so they tend to sweep maintenance under the rug. One needs to be very cautious about going out and chartering just any old Learjet. Since Rudge was also managing the Stones when the '78 tour rolled around, I went to them and said, "You know, guys, we ought to look into this whole business of chartering planes. Let me call Jerry Sterns and see if there's someone we can retain to take care of this for us." I had met many experts through Sterns because he was bringing in expert witnesses in the Lynyrd Skynyrd case. I thought maybe we could ask some of these people to investigate possible charter services to ensure the safety of the Stones in the future. They readily agreed.

Every time after that, when we had a plane suggested as a charter, I would send in a team of experts, and they'd send a retired American A&E mechanic to break down the engines and check all the maintenance records. An air frame guy would do the same with the structure. The pilots would be interviewed, and we'd do psychologicals on them. Some planes didn't pass. I remember that we sent the team somewhere in Arizona to examine either a 707 or 727, and in that specific instance the engines were not up to par. The mechanics would keep checking planes until they found one that passed the tests, and then they'd recommend that plane. And that's the procedure we followed on both the '78 and '81 tours. To my knowledge, we were the first entertainers to do this; I'm not aware of anybody doing that before, and the Stones still follow this regimen. I would hope it would become the standard of the entertainment industry. It should.

Sterns came to Little Rock once when we were going to McComb, and we went out to charter a plane—a Beechcraft Baron, a little twin-engine plane. When we went into the office and they told us what we'd be flying, Sterns asked them for the serial number of the plane. When they told him, he informed them that we didn't want that plane—we wanted a later model of that plane—so we were given a different plane. He explained that he had sued Beech over that plane because the first planes didn't have baffles in the wing tanks. Under storm conditions and without baffles, a plane would be thrown from side to side. If the plane was low on fuel, it would throw the fuel away from the fuel pump and cause the engine to lose power. It would crash in a thunderstorm. The problem had been corrected in later models by adding baffles to the wing tanks. It pays to pay attention.

Chapter 20
Little Miss TNT

URING MY VERY EARLY days of hobnobbing with Peter Rudge on Stones business in New York, which was in January of '73, I met Jonathon Caffino and Don DeVito of CBS Records. Jonathan was product manager and Don was in the A&R department at the label. They kept telling me they had this young artist on the label—Tanya Tucker— who needed some help.

Tanya was managed by a guy named John Kelly at the time, but her dad, Beau, was instrumental in her career. She was only about fourteen at this time, but she'd already had hit singles with "Delta Dawn" and "Blood Red and Goin' Down." The family was living in Las Vegas. CBS didn't think much of Kelly as a manager, and subsequently there were all sorts of problems with Tanya's career. Caffino told me they'd love for me to be involved since I was in Little Rock and "spoke their language." The joke ended up being on CBS for thinking I was an Arkansas hick. Jonathon referred them to me, and Beau called; he wanted to get together and talk. I agreed, and we set up a meeting in Little Rock.

But instead of just Beau showing up for the meeting, the entire family—Tanya; her dad, Beau; mother, Juanita; sister, LaCosta; brother, Donald; and LaCosta's husband, Darrell—drove from Las Vegas to Little Rock in a Chrysler station wagon, with all their belongings inside, and showed up at my office. They came in and hired me to represent them and announced they were moving to Little Rock. Now they needed a place to live.

There were some apartments right across from my office—the Watergate Apartments—and I knew the owners were having a hard time renting them. I called the manager, and they agreed to rent an apartment to the Tuckers for a while. We rented furniture as well, and they moved in. The first thing we had to do was to get rid of Tanya's manager, so I negotiated his release. Beau was left in charge, but Peter Rudge and I were giving them management advice. I worked with Tanya for the next four years, until late 1977, during some of her best years, and she actually lived in an apartment near my house for a couple of those years, treating Julia and Joanna like they were her little sisters.

One of the reasons Beau wanted to get rid of John Kelly was that Kelly had renegotiated a new contract with CBS Records for a $50,000 advance and a moderate increase—a standard CBS contract. But Tanya was really hot then and Beau felt they were being shortchanged. Beau asked me to scout around and find out the real value for Tanya Tucker. I began by calling several labels in Nashville. Elektra had a division headed by Jim Malloy, and I called him. Playboy had a hot label in Nashville then, and I called them. MCA was really hot at the time, but they didn't have an office in Nashville then. So I called Wilbur Mills because on one of the occasions when I had been hobnobbing with him around the country, I had been his guest at a fund-raiser at Lew Wasserman's house in LA. Wasserman was CEO of Universal, the parent company of MCA, but I didn't know him well enough to just pick up the phone and call him.

I asked Mr. Mills to make a call on my behalf. He called Lew Wasserman, who in turn called me. Lew told me he wanted to set up a meeting between Mike Maitland, president of MCA in LA, and me, so I went out to see Mike. They definitely knew who Tanya Tucker was, and they were very much interested in signing her. They made a multimillion dollar offer, compared to the $250,000 five-year contract offer from CBS, which was just a token even for that time. Although CBS's offer was almost an insult, John Kelly had already verbally accepted it.

When we paid Kelly off and dismissed him, I notified CBS it was a new ballgame. The guy from business affairs was really irritated and insisted that they had a deal. I told him in no uncertain terms that he had a deal with the former manager, but he didn't have a deal with the artist. They contended that it was a firm offer and they didn't intend to change it. Billy Sherrill was producing Tanya then, and Billy and Tanya were close, but he was in-house at CBS. Beau kept saying to me, "Hey, this is about money . . . about getting what Tanya is worth. But if CBS's offer is anywhere close, we'll stay with CBS."

So I went back to CBS and let them know that I had a multimillion dollar offer on the table from MCA. I urged them to make a better offer. I was practically on my knees, begging CBS to make an offer that was reasonable, but they refused to do so—they were arrogant about it. I kept telling them I didn't want to leave CBS, but they were leaving us no alternative. There was another year on the existing contract, so we actually had to litigate the matter. It seems that when CBS signed her initially, they never got her minorities removed. She was barely in her teens when she was signed, well below legal age. I filed suit in Arkansas Chancery court and petitioned to have a guardian appointed for Tanya. The court then had jurisdiction over her so she couldn't enter into a contract without it being court-approved. The judge was Judge Darrell Hickman, and I went to him and told him we were being rube-a-doobed by these slick New Yorkers, and the court ruled that Tanya was a minor and any business concerning her would have to be court-approved. The CBS contract was then ruled invalid. I next asked the court for the authority to enter into a new contract, which they granted, but it still had to be court-approved.

Bruce Lundvall was head of CBS, and he was a very nice man. He called me and I explained that I had been begging for a new contract with CBS but hadn't gotten one. He said he was flying to Little Rock immediately, which he did. He upped the offer by $500,000 total, but that still wasn't anywhere close to the MCA offer. I think they always assumed that Billy Sherrill's production relationship with Tanya would be their ace in the hole. They either underestimated or misjudged Beau, who was much more interested in the money than in a relationship with a producer. But it wasn't just Beau—I was giving Beau and Tanya the advice that, if possible, they should stay with CBS. But I asked them to think about just how much loyalty they owed CBS. Do you stay there and accept pennies, or do you go across the street for gold dollars? My advice was to change. There was a lot of controversy about changing, and Beau took most of the heat. But the ultimate decision was made by Beau and the court. Beau was Tanya's legal guardian, and the court mandated that he accept the MCA contract. It wasn't like it was a $100,000 difference; the difference was millions. We ultimately accepted the MCA deal, and that made me very unpopular for a while at CBS.

After we signed with MCA, to celebrate Tanya's sixteenth birthday, the label threw her a birthday/signing party at an amusement park in Little Rock. All the MCA staff in LA flew in for it. Mike Maitland, MCA's president, came, and we had rides, food, and everything else you'd associate with an amusement park. The highlight was when Harry Reasoner came to do a piece for *The Harry Reasoner Show*, a *Dateline*-like show on ABC. He did a twenty-minute segment on national television all about Tanya's sixteenth birthday party. I've seen footage from that show on A&E's *Biography*.

I worked with Tanya until she turned eighteen and her guardianship was up and until Beau got mad at me when I was in Toronto with Keith Richards. Beau wanted me to go to LA and negotiate a management contract with Steve Gold, a notorious LA manager at that time. I told him I couldn't leave at that moment, but I would send Kathy Woods. He didn't want Kathy and he didn't want me to go later. He complained that every time he called me I was involved with the Rolling Stones. I explained to him that Keith was in serious trouble in Toronto and we were at a crucial negotiating point, so I couldn't walk away right then. I told him we could do the contract with Gold any time—it wasn't a big deal. He was furious and threatened to get another lawyer. I told him I thought the time had come for him to do just that and we should go ahead and part company. When I finally returned to the States, the guardianship was up and they could move anywhere they wanted to, so they were moving to Nashville. Beau took control of her career then.

But before all this, we got Tanya on the cover of *Rolling Stone* magazine—the very first Nashville artist to grace the cover. Ron Overman was head of publicity for CBS in New York at that point, and Peter Rudge and the Stones influenced the people at both CBS and *Rolling Stone* then. Chet Flippo was assigned to write the story; then it turned into a cover, which was just unheard of then. Only the hottest rock acts were chosen for the cover of *Rolling Stone*. That was quite a coup.

Chapter 21
Do You Know How to Skin a Catfish?

OR WHATEVER REASON, I've been blessed to know some great men, and Wilbur Mills definitely tops the list. As I've said so often already, Mr. Mills was, at one time, probably the most powerful person in Washington, next to the president. Some felt he even wielded more power than the occupant of the White House. Because we were both Arkansans, there was a bond between us, and because of Mr. Mills I was given both a front-row seat and a backstage pass to many of the great historical events of the twentieth century. Mr. Mills may have commanded more power in his little finger than most people will ever enjoy, but you'd never know it from his humble demeanor. He was my friend and mentor as well as my congressman. So I thought nothing of him calling me one day in mid-January 1974.

I was already spending more time in Washington, DC, than in Little Rock, what with trying to deal with the State Department almost daily on getting the maverick Rolling Stones readmitted to the United States so they could tour. So it was not out of the ordinary for Mr. Mills to call and ask me to stop by his office. What did surprise me, though, was that he wanted my help on an entirely different maverick—Jimmy Hoffa, one of the most controversial figures of the late twentieth century. Hoffa had been the very powerful head of the International Brotherhood of Teamsters, probably the most influential and corrupt labor union in the country, before being sentenced to prison in the mid–'60s for jury tampering, among other things. He had gained an early release, thanks to a presidential commutation of his sentence, but there had been some funny business with his pardon.

Mr. Mills explained that when Hoffa's sentence had been commuted by President Richard Nixon a couple of years before, someone at the White House counsel's office involved with the pardon had inserted a clause that barred Hoffa from resuming his union leadership until 1980, and he wanted to mount a challenge, charging that it was unconstitutional. The congressman wanted me to meet with Hoffa and see if I could help him in his efforts. Mr. Mills felt I needed to put pressure on the president by threatening to go to the media with the story. You have to remember that this was at the height of Nixon's Watergate mess, and I'm not sure the president was even aware that the clause had been inserted into the pardon. He had problems enough just dealing with the daily fallout from the break-in at

190

Democratic National Headquarters in the Watergate Hotel, what with most of his campaign and White House staff being under indictment for criminal charges.

What the government had done to Hoffa was clearly illegal because both sides had agreed to the terms of the pardon and, afterward, unbeknownst to Hoffa, someone had inserted a clause into the pardon, which was essentially stacking another sentence on Hoffa after he was pardoned. There was no provision under the law for anyone to have done that.

Hoffa had turned to Congressman Mills to help with his problem, and Mr. Mills in turn requested that I see what I could do to assist Mr. Hoffa in obtaining justice. When I agreed, he then sent me to see Jimmy Hoffa himself. Joe Johnson, from Mills' congressional staff, accompanied me when I met with Hoffa in his suite at the Barkley Hotel, in New York. There were two big, burly bodyguards in the hallway outside his suite, obviously armed, and another couple of them inside the suite. They sat off to the side, outside of hearing, but never took their eyes off Hoffa and his guests.

When we entered the suite and Hoffa shook my hand, he asked me rather cryptically, "Do you know how to skin a catfish?" I looked down at Hoffa, a good seven inches shorter than I, and told him I did. That seemed to please him because he said, "Okay, I can trust a man who knows how to skin a catfish." To this day I have no idea why he asked me that question or what it meant. I can't even speculate what the outcome would have been if I had said I didn't know how to skin a catfish.

We met for a couple of hours initially, talking about strategy. He matter-of-factly laid out the case: The White House had basically screwed him by inserting a clause in his pardon of which he had no knowledge beforehand, and consequently he was unable to return to the only work he had ever known. I believed him—if he had known there was a clause in that pardon that barred him from running for his old office in the Teamsters for six years, he would have fought it. I didn't know Hoffa, but I knew of him and I had observed his relatively modest lifestyle. So I knew it wasn't so much money as power, and I felt his power was everything to him. He wanted me to try to get the president to strike that clause from his pardon by threatening to expose his double-dealing in the media.

I outlined what my retainer and total fee would be, and he agreed to my terms. He was on his way back to Florida, so Joe and I flew back to Washington after the meeting but not before Hoffa invited me to his condo at Blair House in Miami Beach to collect my retainer.

Back in Washington, I talked to Hoffa's son, James, an attorney in Detroit, who had drafted a letter to the pardons attorney in DC. He sent me a copy of that letter to my hotel in DC.

I then flew down to Miami a couple of days later, again with Joe Johnson. There were no bodyguards evident in the secure building, but this time Hoffa's wife, Jo, was present. "I'm gonna pay your ten grand retainer in cash," Hoffa told me. "That's the way I do business. I don't want any paper on this."

Having already agreed to that amount as a retainer, and anticipating what he would do, I countered with, "I have to report the money to the IRS, and I have a letter with me confirming the receipt of your retainer." Hoffa took the letter and tore it in pieces before us. I had to assume Hoffa was under constant surveillance by the FBI, and I wasn't about to take money from him without reporting it to the IRS. Joe and I flew right back to DC so that I could hand carry the letter Hoffa's son had drafted to Lawrence Traylor, a pardon attorney at the Justice Department, on January 22.

I delivered the letter and went right back up to the Hill, where I found myself seated across the desk from Mr. Mills in his office. He picked up the phone and called President Nixon. "Mr. President," he said, in his soft Arkansas drawl, "I have someone here you need to see on a very important matter." He was told to send me right over, and within minutes I was in the presence of Richard Nixon and Alexander Haig, his Chief of Staff. Much of Nixon's staff was already depleted by resignations caused by Watergate, so Haldeman and Ehrlichmann were both gone, and Alexander Haig was serving in their stead. Nixon was cordial, but I told him in no uncertain terms that what he had done to Jimmy Hoffa was wrong, and I had been retained to get to the bottom of the situation and find out who at the White House had changed the original pardon. He handed me off immediately to General Haig. I was firm with Haig. I told him that Mr. Hoffa's constitutional rights had been abused, and we intended to file a lawsuit if they did not remove the offending restriction from the pardon. Haig was unresponsive except to say that he would look into the matter. He was so new to his job I'm not sure he was even aware of the pardon.

I reported back to Mr. Mills after that meeting, and I remember quite clearly telling him I thought our threat to the president would be a veiled threat at best because we really had no bargaining power. President Nixon had already fallen just about as low as it was possible to go because of his Watergate activities, and his presidency was on life support as it was. Why would our threat of exposure mean anything compared to what he was already experiencing? It was a nonthreat. If he had been squeaky clean and wanting to avoid scandal at any cost, our threat of exposure might have worked.

As I saw it, I had two problems: (1) To get media sympathy for Jimmy Hoffa would not be an easy task, and (2) the president didn't need to curry political favor with Hoffa. If the president had believed that Hoffa could have come out of prison and gained control of the Teamsters Union again, thereby making him a political ally, it's possible he might have been more interested. But Nixon's presidency was in tatters, and even if it had not been, he was in his second term and would most likely never run for national office of any kind again, so he didn't need Hoffa politically. Mr. Mills and I both agreed that we had no political leverage, so Hoffa's only recourse was to challenge Nixon in court.

Following my meeting with Mr. Mills, I called Hoffa. He was flying back through DC a day or two later, and we agreed to meet in a conference room at National Airport. Just as in New York, he was accompanied by the four powerful bodyguards. I told him I felt I had exhausted my options because what we were threatening Nixon with was a misdemeanor compared to what he was facing with Watergate. I also told Hoffa it would be hard to gain sympathy in the press for him. He pretty much agreed but asked me to speak to his son, James, again, which I did.

I conferred with Hoffa's son and with Morris Shenker, a labor attorney employed by Hoffa in St. Louis. They too agreed that we had exhausted our political means, so their only recourse was to file a lawsuit. There was no further need for my legal services since Hoffa already had an army of experienced attorneys of every specialty, although I continued to confer with them for a couple of months after that. The lawsuit was filed on March 13 of that year by a renowned civil rights attorney, Leonard Boudin. It was felt that Shenker was too closely identified with organized labor and they should choose someone totally without those ties.

The lawsuit claimed that the restriction did not originate from a proper source, such as the attorney general, but had "originated and derived from no regular clemency procedure but was caused to be added to said commutation by Charles Colson, Special Counsel to the President, pursuant to an agreement and conspiracy" (Brandt, p. 230). Hoffa contended that Colson took such action to ingratiate himself with Frank Fitzsimmons (who was then president of the Teamsters Union) because, when he left the White House and before he went to prison after his Watergate indictment, Colson was given a $100,000 retainer by the Teamsters Union to represent them.

We all felt confident that Hoffa would ultimately prevail and the courts would find for him. However, he lost the first round in July 1974, when the district court in DC ruled against him. We were all shocked, but the attorneys filed an appeal, and we felt the appellate court would find in his favor. We will never know whether or not that's true, because shortly after losing the first round, Jimmy Hoffa disappeared and has never been seen again. There have been jokes, accusations, and speculations for thirty years, and it was only recently that a close associate of Hoffa's has taken credit for killing Hoffa. Maybe we weren't the only ones who thought he might prevail in his lawsuit.

In an era when few people are even aware of who is in power in the labor unions, I probably should back up and explain why all this was such a big deal to Hoffa and to Fitzsimmons, who was trying to hold onto his power with the Teamsters. I can't pretend to do justice to detailing who Jimmy Hoffa was, because most people over the age of thirty today know his name only as the butt of a joke about where his body is buried. A fellow attorney and author, Charles Brandt, comes very close to nailing Hoffa's persona in his book *I Heard You Paint Houses* (which, by the way, is a euphemism for a hit man):

It is no doubt difficult for some people today to appreciate the degree of fame or infamy Jimmy Hoffa enjoyed in his heyday and before his death, a span of roughly two decades from the mid-fifties to the mid-seventies. While in his heyday he was the most powerful labor leader in the nation, how can that mean anything in these times when labor leaders are virtually unknown to the general public? . . . Today Jimmy Hoffa is famous mostly because he was the victim of the most infamous disappearance in American history. Yet during a twenty-year period there wasn't an American alive who wouldn't have recognized Jimmy Hoffa immediately, the way Tony Soprano is recognized today. The vast majority of Americans would have known him by the sound of his voice alone. From 1955 until 1965, Jimmy Hoffa was as famous as Elvis. From 1965 until 1975 Jimmy Hoffa was as famous as the Beatles (p. 86).

I don't know all the historical facts, but for years organized labor's prime bargaining weapon was the strike. As of this writing, an entire season of the National Hockey League has been wiped out by a players' strike, but strikes by professional sports teams are about as close as the last two generations have come to an organized strike. Not so in the mid-twentieth century, when there were thousands of strikes in labor—truck drivers, grocery workers, auto workers, etc.—each year. Brandt relates that in the two years after World War II (1946–47), there were 8,000 strikes in the forty-eight states, or 160 separate strikes per year per state (p. 86). Jimmy Hoffa, a man short in stature (five foot five) but big on muscle, came to power as an organizer in the powerful Teamsters Union in Detroit, home of the nation's auto industry and fertile ground for union organizing. Again, in Brandt's words, ". . . unions like the Teamsters often employed their own muscle, their own reigns of terror, including bombings, arsons, beatings and murders. The warfare and violence were not just between labor and management. It was often between rival unions vying for the same membership . . . . The alliances Hoffa made with mobsters around the country as he and his union rose together are now a matter of historical record . . . . Bobby Kennedy called Jimmy Hoffa 'the most powerful man in the country next to the president' " (pp. 88–90).

I think it's important for me to paint this picture of Jimmy Hoffa for a number of reasons, some of which I've already mentioned. It is only by knowing about Hoffa that one can understand why my own very small role was important to him. Hoffa was elected president of the International Brotherhood of Teamsters in 1957, and perhaps his greatest contribution to the union also proved, in the end, to be his undoing. Two years before his ascendancy to the presidency of the Teamsters, Hoffa created a pension fund—the Central States Pension Fund—for management to make contributions toward retirement benefits for their employees. This pension fund not only came to be worth more than a billion dollars, but it also provided Hoffa his greatest power. "The Teamsters pension fund organized by Hoffa almost immediately became a source of loans to the national crime syndicate known to the public as La Costa Nostra. With its own private bank, this crime monopoly grew and flourished . . . . Teamsters-funded ventures, especially the construction of casinos in Havana and Las Vegas, were dreams come true for the godfather entrepreneurs . . . . Jimmy's cut was to get a finder's fee off the books. He took points under the table for approving the loans . . . . The pension fund was the goose that laid the golden eggs" (Brandt, p. 105).

For many years Hoffa was the sworn enemy of Bobby Kennedy and Senator John McClelland (also from Arkansas) because of his ties to organized crime. The FBI was aware of his every move and phone call, and he was the target of just about every federal prosecutor in the country for one offense or another. There was even a "Get Hoffa Squad" that Bobby Kennedy, in his role as attorney general, had put together. In 1962 they had enough evidence on Hoffa for violating the Taft-Hartley labor racketeering law to try him in federal court in Nashville, of all places. The charges against Hoffa amounted to a misdemeanor, but Hoffa's actions as a result of that trial began his downfall. The Get Hoffa Squad had planted a mole in Hoffa's army camped out in Nashville; Hoffa was caught blatantly tampering with the jury and was sentenced to eight years in prison. While his trial was still underway in Tennessee, Hoffa was again indicted, this time by a grand jury in Chicago, for fraudulent misuse of the Central States Pension Fund for personal profit. He had pledged $400,000 out of that fund to a real estate development company in Florida in which he was alleged to hold an undisclosed 22 percent interest. The noose was tightening around Jimmy Hoffa's neck.

In March 1964 Hoffa was sentenced to eight years in prison for the jury-tampering incident. In August he had five years tacked onto that sentence when a jury in Chicago found him guilty of pension-fund fraud. Hoffa may have been facing years in prison, but he had no intention of giving up his hard-earned position as powerful head of the Teamsters Union, so he had to handpick someone who would hand "his" union back to him upon his release from jail. "Jimmy Hoffa didn't care anything about money," writes Brandt. "He gave it away. But he did like the power. And jail or no jail, he wasn't about to give that power away . . . . Once he got out of jail, he was going to take back control of everything" (p. 182). The logical person to step in would have been his loyal associate, Harold Gibbons, but he had gotten mad at Gibbons for lowering the flag on his union headquarters to half-staff when President Kennedy was assassinated. That apparently infuriated Hoffa, who violently hated the Kennedys.

So he created a special title in 1966 that would transfer the power of running the union while he was in jail, without bestowing the presidency. He thought the man he installed, Frank Fitzsimmons, would be nothing more than a puppet whose strings he could pull from his jail cell. With all the pieces in place, Hoffa reported to Lewisburg Prison, in Pennsylvania, in March 1967. The next year, Richard Nixon was elected president, and John Mitchell was confirmed as his attorney general. From that point on, according to Brandt's book, which, by the way, is a first-person account of hit man Frank "The Irishman" Sheeran's role as Hoffa's close friend and eventual killer, money was going down to Mitchell in an attempt to buy Hoffa a presidential pardon. The Irishman himself recounts meeting Mitchell in the lobby of the Washington Hilton and handing him a briefcase supposedly containing a half-million dollars for the pardon (p. 204). In the meantime, Fitzsimmons announced his intention to run for the presidency of the Teamsters Union in 1972, and unbeknownst to Hoffa, mob friends of Fitzsimmons were paying Mitchell the same amount to put a restriction in the pardon that would prevent Hoffa from running for Teamsters president until the 1980 election. Fitzsimmons loyalists thought that by that time, all of Hoffa's cronies would be out of power in the union.

Hoffa's pardon, or executive grant of clemency, was signed by Nixon just before Christmas 1971. It was not until after he was released from prison that Hoffa learned of the new language inserted into his pardon: ". . . the said James R. Hoffa not engage in direct or indirect management of any labor organization prior to March 6, 1980, and if the aforesaid condition is not fulfilled this commutation will be null and void in its entirety." Hoffa immediately began planning a constitutional challenge to the condition in his pardon, but he was powerless to do anything openly until his full parole was up in March 1973. The argument was that Nixon had exceeded his authority by adding a condition to the pardon.

There was a good deal of finger-pointing about whose fault this was, but Hoffa, according to Brandt, always suspected that White House Special Counsel to the President Charles Colson had been responsible for inserting that language. Here's what Brandt says:

> A lot of allegations and finger-pointing were to come out of the Nixon White House on the topic of how the restriction ended up in the pardon. John Dean, White House counsel and Watergate witness against his confederates, testified that it had been his idea to stick the restriction language in at the last minute. He testified that he was merely being a good lawyer, because when Mitchell asked him to prepare the papers Mitchell casually mentioned that Hoffa had orally agreed to stay out of union activity until 1980 . . . . The other White House counsel and future Watergate jailbird to be suspected of complicity in the restriction language caper was attorney Charles Colson . . . . Jimmy Hoffa testified in a deposition, "I blame one man [for the restriction on my pardon] . . . Charles Colson." Colson took the Fifth on the topic during the Watergate hearings, although he did admit discussing the pardon with Fitzsimmons before it was granted (pp. 211–212).

Hoffa was naturally incensed, and had his son, James, draft the letter that I hand-delivered to the pardons attorney. It was a "formal request that the restrictions placed upon his activities in the labor movement be removed immediately . . . . Mr. Hoffa has never recognized these restrictions as he feels that they constitute a denial of his constitutional rights under the 1st and 14th Amendments to the U.S. Constitution."

In the midst of all this, Hoffa had, according to associates, been making enemies within the mob and the union by making threats and accusations. His prison experience had apparently changed him, and he was making his former allies nervous. He was even accusing Fitzsimmons of "selling out to mobsters and letting known racketeers into the Teamsters" (Brandt, p. 236). There were even rumors floating around by mid-1975 that Hoffa was cooperating with the FBI, although these were apparently coming from the Fitzsimmons camp.

While the appeals process was going on, Jimmy Hoffa got into a car in the parking lot of a Detroit restaurant with his longtime friend, Frank Sheeran, hit man for crime family leader Russell Bufalino, and was never seen again. Sheeran maintains in Brandt's book that he and Hoffa (along with two other associates Hoffa would have trusted) drove to a nearby house, where he shot Hoffa twice in the back of the head inside the front door of the house. Waiting in the rear were two "cleanup" men who picked up the body, took it to a nearby meat-packing plant where it was disposed of, and cleaned up any evidence of the crime in the house. The pieces of Hoffa's body were then fed into a crematorium at a mob-friendly funeral home (pp. 256–257). I accept The Irishman's deathbed confession as fact. Because Hoffa was surrounded by armed bodyguards whenever I met with him, I always felt he could only have been killed by someone close to him. That's just the way the mob did business.

As to how I felt about Hoffa, I liked what I knew of him. I judge people not by the things I read about them but how they are with me. I was well aware of his reputation, and I knew him to be a thug and a gangster, but with me he was very pleasant. Make no mistake, he was all business, and I was very careful not to cross any lines, but I matched him tit for tat. It would seem, however, that Mr. Hoffa was a victim of Watergate that no one even knew about.

Chapter 22
The Release of Steve McQueen's Body
The Reality and the Myth

ETWEEN MY TIMES on the road with the Rolling Stones, I was practicing law in Little Rock, Arkansas. It was through my law practice that I came to manage Tanya Tucker, barely in her teens and setting the music world on fire in the mid-1970s. During my negotiations to sign Tanya to the powerhouse talent agency, International Creative Management, E.O. Stacey, an agent at ICM, who was considered the dean of the state fair booking agents, became a friend and mentor to me and taught me a lot about the entertainment business. He was actually responsible for signing Tanya to ICM.

During this time I also met a remarkable man—Bill Maher—who would become a lifelong, treasured friend. Bill was a senior corporate officer in the LA office of ICM—one of the top men—and was actor Steve McQueen's closest advisor. A few years before, he had untangled and straightened out Steve's financial life and career and went on to become one of Steve's few real friends. At that time Steve was one of the biggest box-office draws in Hollywood, known for playing hard-living, hard-fighting characters like Lt. Frank Bullitt in the movie *Bullitt*.

Through Maher I came to be around Steve on a number of occasions. Steve kept an apartment at the Beverly Wilshire Hotel in Beverly Hills, and because of its proximity to the ICM office, I often stayed there when I was in LA doing business for Tanya. Bill and I were meeting at Hernando's Hideaway in the Beverly Wilshire one time, and he told me Steve was coming down to join us. I knew from what Bill had told me that this was fairly unusual because Steve was not a very sociable person and didn't like making small talk, especially with strangers. But apparently Bill had told him about my Secret Service background and the fact that I was working with the Stones. Steve was a big Stones fan. I had formed an impression of him before I met him as someone much like the characters he played so well—maybe because he was essentially playing himself. And he was just about what I expected.

He was a two-fisted beer-drinking (Old Milwaukee) hell-raiser who pushed with full force the throttle of life. He was definitely on a fast track, but I liked him a lot. We didn't talk about anything earth-shattering on that first evening, and certainly nothing about business. I remember he had a good sense of humor. I was amazed that he ordered his Old Milwaukee served over ice. That kind of blew my image of him. He didn't say much, but talking to him was like talking to any old buddy. He asked me questions about Kennedy and about the Stones, but little else. Another time Bill and I went up to Steve's apartment in the hotel, which overlooked the pool. The apartment was a one-bedroom unit with great furnishings that Steve's decorator had chosen. One interesting feature was that the closet in the bedroom had been turned into a sauna that Steve—and his lady friends—used to relax.

Bill told me years later that after that initial meeting, when Bill would mention in passing to Steve that I was in LA, Steve would ask if we could all get together again. Maybe because he could be himself around me or that I wasn't impressed with his celebrity, he wanted to hang out with us. There were few people in Hollywood Steve really wanted to be with. On another occasion we all three met in the bar at the Beverly Wilshire and then decided to go to a private club, PIPS, which had a big backgammon room, a dining room, bar, and disco. Steve was a member, although he made it clear that his wife was unaware of that fact. He was married to actress Ali McGraw at that time.

Steve had a big black 6.3 model Mercedes, which he drove like the race car driver he was, and he drove us to the club, which was on Robertson Boulevard, close to Beverly Hills. It was the Hollywood establishment club and attracted lots of pretty girls. We'd all had a few drinks, and the girls started to approach McQueen. He was a well-known ladies man, so he knew most of them and had even been with a few. It was amazing to see how the ladies, young and not so young, tried to get close to him in the club. Some succeeded, as he would tell them to meet him at the hotel later.

After he had gotten to know me a little better, we were having drinks one night at the hotel, and he kind of opened up about what life was like as a movie star. He talked about everyone wanting a piece of him and that there were few in life he could trust. "In America, movie stars are like the royals are in England," he said. "People think movie stars shit crushed pineapple." One of the things he liked so much about Bill Maher was that he hadn't "gone Hollywood," as Steve put it. Steve had been screwed around royally by his prior advisors, which is what Maher had untangled a few years before. Maher was not like the usual Hollywood suck-ups who would pat you on the back with one hand and stab you with the other, cheating you and lying to you. Maher says that's what Steve liked about me as well. I was honest—and straightforward.

Because he was such a big Stones fan, Steve requested tickets for the Stones' LA show at the Forum in 1975 and again in Anaheim in 1978, and I was happy to arrange them. In Anaheim, he brought along his girlfriend, Barbara Minty, whom he would later marry (he was divorced from Ali McGraw by this time), his son Chad, and Maher. They arrived in the backstage area about midafternoon on the day of the show. They sat at picnic tables we had outside the trailers in the backstage area, drinking beer and talking to Ronnie Wood. For the show we put them in a VIP suite with Prince Rupert. So we all hung out for the better part of the day, just drinking and shooting the breeze. But in spite of the fact that I had been around Steve on numerous occasions, I would never presume to say that we were friends—friendly, yes—but not friends in the truest sense of the word. We enjoyed each other's company and had a good time together like most friends do. Maher frequently said that Steve was always happy to see me, thought highly of me, and that I was as close to Steve as all but a few.

One of the last times I went out drinking with Steve was at the Palomino Club, in North Hollywood. He had gained a lot of weight and grown a full, bushy beard, and he reminded me of the old Western character actor Gabby Hayes. I remember that occasion because there were some fans trying to get Steve's autograph, and that really pissed him off. He actually thought people would not recognize him—one of the world's most recognizable actors—with the beard. He couldn't understand why people hounded him when he was out in public.

A year later, when McQueen was diagnosed with a rare and virulent form of lung cancer, mesothelioma, his every move became fodder for the international press. At that time there were only twenty-four known cases of the rare cancer, and each of those twenty-four had died. The profession and the hobby Steve loved most—acting and racing—may have contributed to his disease since mesothelioma is directly related to exposure to asbestos, found on sound stages, in the brake linings of race cars, and in the protective helmets and fire-retardant sweaters worn by race car drivers that were pulled up over the lower face. When he was initially diagnosed, he was given only a couple of months to live, but he wouldn't accept that diagnosis and set about exploring every option. Especially controversial was his decision to abandon conventional treatment in the United States in favor of experimental therapies, which at that time were banned in the United States.

When told that his condition was inoperable, Steve checked into a Mexican clinic—really a trailer park used as a clinic—the Plaza Santa Maria, run by Dr. William Donald Kelley, where he underwent a torturous three-month regimen of animal cell injections, the drug laetrile, coffee enemas, and over one hundred vitamin pills each day. Dr. Kelley was a former dentist who believed in treating the immune system and metabolism; he claimed to have successfully cured himself from pancreatic and liver cancer. Maher suspected that Kelley was only after Steve's money—especially when Steve asked Bill to cut him a check for $375,000 to pay Kelley—and publicity, hoping to fill up the so-called clinic with cancer victims.

Steve's condition only worsened, and when it was discovered that he had a huge tumor in his stomach, he flew to Juarez, directly across the border from El Paso, Texas, for surgery at the Santa Rosa Clinic. From what Maher told me, Steve went to Mexico to prevent the U.S. press from getting to him.

Interestingly, one of the last people he saw before departing for Mexico from his home in Santa Paula, California, was Dr. Billy Graham. Steve had become a devout Christian, and the last words he said to Dr. Graham were "I'll see you in Heaven" (Sandford, p. 397). The last time Maher saw Steve at the trailer park/clinic in Mexico, Steve told him, "I have my head in the lion's mouth," meaning he knew he was not going to make it. Steve asked Maher to handle his death—to keep it private in all ways and to handle the estate and protect the kids. Maher told me later they both cried during that last meeting, knowing full well it would be the last job Maher would handle for Steve.

The Juarez surgical clinic was an old red brick building that resembled a warehouse or garage (Sandford, p. 398). On November 6, 1980, Steve was operated on to remove the tumor. He came through the surgery successfully, but lived only twelve hours. Surprisingly, it was confirmed that he died of a heart attack—not the cancer.

About midafternoon the next day, Bill called me at my office in Little Rock. I could tell immediately he was distraught about something, but the tale he related shocked and angered me. "I need your help, Bill," he plead. "Steve died in Mexico last night, and the Mexican government is refusing to release the body. As you can imagine, the family is beside themselves with grief over the situation. Steve's attorneys out here have been trying everything since we got the word, but they can't move the federales. I don't care what it takes, but I want that body out, and I know you can do it."

I laughed and told him, "I am well acquainted with the tactics of the Mexican government when it comes to Americans." The authorities across the border had made a tidy living for years preying on unsuspecting Ivy League college kids and their wealthy parents. This was the end of the drug-crazed '70s, and college kids would often go into Mexico, buy a toke of marijuana, and before they knew it they would be busted flat and a guest of the Mexican authorities. Because of my work with the Rolling Stones, I had received numerous phone calls from distraught parents who were being held up for $50,000 bail money. Those were cases I would not touch with a ten-foot pole—I considered it unethical—so I always referred them to an attorney in Tucson, a "fixer" who made a tidy fortune taking such cases and going down to Mexico to pay off the authorities and get the kids released from jail.

I assured Bill that he had definitely called the right person, and I would check into the situation.

I hung up the phone and launched into full attack mode, which anyone who has ever worked with me can tell you is an awesome—and not very pretty—sight to behold. I was bellowing orders right and left to Kathy Woods and my receptionist and being my most belligerent self. I guess I can best be called The Intimidator when I engage this mode.

Maher had told me the attorneys in LA didn't have any idea why Mexico wouldn't release the body, but the official word was they were holding it for "investigation." Investigation into what? I knew immediately why they wouldn't release the body;

they were holding it for ransom. My weapon of choice in dealing with the matter was the telephone, and my first phone call was to the funeral home in Juarez. The funeral director gave me some double-talk, confirming what they had told the LA attorneys, that the authorities were holding the body for investigation.

"Look," I said to him, in my most terse voice, "I want to know what it will take to get the authorities to release that body *right now*. How much will it take?"

I don't think he expected to be confronted so baldly, so he started justifying his position, saying something about for all the trouble this one and that one had gone to . . . . Finally he cut to the chase and threw out a figure of $160,000. Kathy and Maher disagree about the amount—Kathy thinks it was just $60,000, but Maher is confident they demanded $160,000. I suspect the truth falls somewhere in between.

"Is that what it will take to get the body released—$160,000 cash?" He said it was. I told him I'd call him back.

My next call was to a high-ranking customs official in Washington with whom I had dealt on a regular basis with the Stones. Then I called my old friend, Neal Leary, in Immigration. Neither offered much encouragement; they didn't know what they could do to help. I explained to them what I needed. "I'm going to get that body out of Mexico," I said. "But I don't want to have to stop at the border, because that's where the Mexican authorities will be. I want to be able to leave the funeral home and drive straight across the border without being detained by the Mexicans." They were quick to say they didn't know how that would be possible, and they thought I was a bit crazy. I thought so, too, because I had visions of the Mexican border patrol shooting at us as we attempted to barrel through their checkpoint. I'll be honest, I didn't think I could do it, but I wanted to give it a try before I chartered a Learjet to get me to Juarez where I knew I would stand toe-to-toe with the Mexicans. The words *Mexican stand-off* entered my mind at that point.

I got the officials in Washington to call the U.S. Border Patrol, alert them that I would be calling, and to obtain their cooperation. Because I did not plan to stop at the border, I asked them to send an inspector to the airport in El Paso where Bill Maher had a Learjet standing by to transport the body back to Los Angeles. I wanted them to check the casket at the airport rather than at the border.

When I called the Immigration and Customs officials at the border, they had already received their instructions from Washington, and they were fine with the arrangement. I cautioned them not to say anything to their Mexican counterparts. They too doubted that I would be successful in my attempt, but I told them I would worry about that. I then called a funeral home in El Paso and asked them to send a hearse to the funeral home in Juarez. But I strongly urged them to hire some security to accompany the hearse, and they hired an off-duty El Paso policeman to ride along with the driver.

By this time it was late afternoon on the East Coast, and I knew the Washington offices were closing. I instructed my ambulance driver to enter the Juarez funeral home precisely at 4:00 p.m. Mountain Standard Time because that's when I planned to make my next call, and it was crucial that they be in place at that time. The funeral home was only a short distance from the border. I told them to walk into that funeral home, go directly to Steve McQueen's casket, and take charge of it. They were to immediately roll it out of there and load it into the hearse. I assured them the funeral director in Juarez would not interfere with them. How did I know that? Because at that moment he would be deep in conversation with me and would be unable to concentrate on anything else but the sound of my voice.

This was a preposterous scheme—totally unworkable—but it all came down just the way I planned it. You could have written this script and rehearsed it and it wouldn't have worked, but luck and timing were on our side. At four o'clock, while Kathy was calling the funeral director in Juarez on one phone for me, I was getting the Mexican police major who was in charge of the case on the other phone. When he answered, I spoke in my most intimidating voice, "This is Bill Carter in the United States. I have spoken to the State Department, the Bureau of Customs, and the Immigration and Naturalization Service, and there is about to be a major international incident if you detain Steve McQueen's body any longer. *I want that body released.*"

I talked to this man like I'd never talked to anybody before. I told him he was going to be answering to Mexico City about this if he didn't release the body, and I intimated that I had the State Department on the phone with Mexico City at that very moment. Jimmy Carter was still president at this point, and he had a brother named Billy Carter, so I think all that the Mexican official heard was "Bill Carter" and the pure authority in my voice. He spoke a little English, but believe me, he wasn't saying much because I never paused. I had to catch him completely by surprise. This tactic went back to my Secret Service days, training with Charlie Newton, who taught me that you get control of a situation from the beginning through intimidation. He instilled in me that if you speak with authority, you can immediately wrest control of any situation and succeed, but you must maintain control of the situation at all costs.

Well, I had control of this guy from the time he picked up the phone. In the meantime, the funeral director was on hold on the other phone. I said, "Hold on just a second; I have to talk to the State Department on the other phone." At that point, I hadn't even talked to the State Department; that was pure bluff. But I made him think I was talking to the State Department, who in turn was talking to the counsel general in Mexico City. Then I came back to the police major and said that the counsel general had ordered the release of this body—immediately! I knew full well that this guy was committing an illegal act by attempting to shake us down, so he might have been getting nervous by that point. I don't think he ever expected it to turn into such a big deal, and he was caught in a trap of his own making. Next I covered the mouthpiece of my phone and picked up the other phone, with the funeral director on the line, and told him, "Look, I'm speaking with your police major on the other phone. Mexico City has ordered the release of this body, and I'm sending my people in there to collect the body, and you better not do anything to interfere with them, or I'll have you arrested."

While I had the funeral director occupied, my guys walked in, put the casket with Steve McQueen's body on their gurney, and rolled it right out of there with this guy still talking to me on the phone. I finally hung up both phones, and Kathy called the U.S. Border Patrol. They reported that the hearse was rolling past them while the Mexican Border Patrol was standing there flat-footed. The major hadn't had enough time to call them after hanging up with me—even if he intended to. They had no idea what was going on, and when they asked the U.S. Border Patrol what was happening, they simply told them that Steve McQueen's body was being transported back to the United States, and they had already cleared it through channels. Because it was entering the United States, it was our responsibility to clear it anyway.

My phone rang almost immediately. It was the funeral director from El Paso reporting that the U.S. Customs officials had met the body at the airport, inspected it, and cleared it. At the moment, the body was on the Learjet bound for Los Angeles. I thanked them profusely, hung up with them, and promptly got Bill Maher on the line. "He's in the air," I chortled. Bill was literally dumbfounded. He couldn't believe what he was hearing. Over the past twenty years, Maher and I have laughed about this several times. He swears it was only twenty minutes from the time he placed the initial call to me until I called him back to say the body was winging its way to him. I know better. It took at least two hours from start to finish.

I can attest to that because when I hung up from that initial call from Bill, my adrenaline started flowing, the sweat started pouring, and I was like Patton storming his troops. We were engaged in an intense battle for a good two hours. I'm sure I was screaming at Kathy and everyone else in my office. I know how I was then, and I would have been performing just as if I were on a stage. That's what I used to tell people when they would witness one of my confrontations. They couldn't believe how intense, how angry and aggressive I would get during the showdown, and I would just laugh and say, "Hell, I'm just acting. I'm not mad; it's all an act." It was all for effect.

I would have bet you ten to one this wouldn't have worked and that I'd have been on a Learjet on the way to Mexico, where I would have stood toe-to-toe with the officials and demanded the release of the body. They'd have had to lock me up to shut me up. But I remember clearly the intensity of those two hours and the gamble we took in getting the timing of events to work out just perfectly. I was absolutely wiped out after it was over, and I can guarantee I went to Cash McCool's across the street and had a few beers when it was behind me.

But Maher wouldn't let it go. He knew all the movers and shakers in LA, and when I'd be at parties at his house or out and about with him in LA, he always enjoyed telling that story. And through the years it grew and grew, and things got blown out of proportion and embellished quite a bit. Many years after the incident, a journalist in New York was relating the story to me, and the myth had grown to such a point that I was told I went down to Mexico and engaged in a guns-drawn confrontation with the officials, and then kidnapped the body and spirited it across the border, thumbing my nose at the Mexican authorities. It was like I was hearing a tall tale about somebody else; it didn't even resemble the reality of the situation. Even Maher believes today that the events transpired in a way far from the truth. It makes me laugh now when I hear stories of heroics that happened throughout history, and I wonder how much is the absolute truth and how much is legend that has grown distorted through years of embellishment.

This was one of the luckiest things I've ever done. The key to it working was that it took place over such a short amount of time and that we had everything timed just perfectly. But I devised the scheme as I went along, acting on instinct. Plus, I had each of them tied up on the phone at the same time and they were helpless to act. It really was funny how it played out, and at the time I didn't think about the significance of what I had done. I was just doing a favor for a friend. It wasn't until I'd encounter people over the years who had heard the myth that I came to realize what I'd been a part of. I can't imagine my doing anything like that today.

I must say, in relating this story, I struggled about whether to tell the truth or allow the myth to stand.

Chapter 23
Nuclear Disaster in Damascus

CASE THAT DEMANDED my complete attention was the Titan II missile case, which I took on in 1979; it went on for years, and during the first three years I was completely focused on it. I was determined to win. I moved to Nashville in 1981, so I wasn't able to try the case myself. But I believe that my careful preparation allowed Bill Wilson and Kathy Woods to try and eventually win the case. And, I might add, they won a very good judgment for that time.

Let me explain, in the words of Morley Safer, who chronicled the entire Titan II missile disaster on *60 Minutes*, the blueprint for disaster the U.S. government had drawn for three states—Arizona, Kansas, and Arkansas—when they developed a guided missile system to combat the Soviet Union during the Cold War of the 1950s.

The object was to build and put into place in this country a missile that could deal the Soviet Union a devastating nuclear blow. The Titan was such a weapon. Fifty-two of them were built by Martin-Marietta and put in silos in Arizona, Arkansas, and Kansas. They use a very volatile liquid fuel—the best way we had then of reaching the other side of the world with a heavy payload. Designed to last ten years, they were in place for twenty, while new Minute Men missiles, with a safer solid-fuel source, have been developed. The Titans have been kept in once-protective underground silos, which could easily be destroyed by new, sophisticated Russian weapons. When unleashed in anger, the Titan carries with it the biggest nuclear warhead in our arsenal, with a blast 750 times greater than the Hiroshima bomb. It would flatten everything in a circle nine miles across . . . . It is the age of the Titan and the vicious nature of its propellant that makes it so hazardous to us (60 Minutes).

In the *60 Minutes* segment, Sgt. Jeff Kennedy, an Air Force Quality Control Inspector who was involved in a 1980 Titan explosion, explained that it was not uncommon to have three or four Titan missiles leaking at once. These chemicals used to fuel the rocket—nitrogen tetroxide and nitrogen dioxide—were so highly toxic, explosive, and combustible that those handling the fuel had to wear a protective suit with an internal oxygen supply. Ironically, in studying the hazards of the Titan missiles years later, it was determined that these suits were of absolutely no use to the handlers in case of a leak. An Air Force safety study in 1978 showed that it was nine times more dangerous to work in a Titan silo than any other job in the Air Force or Strategic Air Command. From 1973 to 1980, the accident rate due to human error or systems failure had increased ten times.

Not only were the Titans dangerous to the Air Force personnel who worked on the silos, but they also posed a great hazard to the civilians who lived near the silos. Over the years there had been three serious incidents involving civilians, but none of them made much of an impression on me until one such accident brought the dangers uncomfortably close to home.

On the missile site in Damascus, Arkansas, a tanker truck loaded with these deadly chemicals was sitting unattended when it developed a leak, unbeknownst to the Air Force. By the time the nearby farmers saw the toxic cloud over their heads, some had breathed the noxious fumes. They reported the leak to the Air Force personnel who, forty feet underground in the command module, were blissfully unaware of anything going on around them.

The Titan II case came to me because of the farm I owned at Center Ridge, ten miles from the Titan II missile site in Damascus, where I was raising cattle. I was doing business with a fellow cattleman, John Stacks, a young man just in his twenties, who owned a dairy farm that bordered the missile site. Barton Williams was an older man who worked for John on his farm. From John's fence line, I could have thrown a rock over the missile silo.

When the gas leak occurred, John and Barton were out in the field working with a cow and a calf and were exposed to the nitrogen tetroxide. When a person inhales the fumes from nitrogen tetroxide, it scars the lungs to a degree, depending on the strength of the fumes one inhales. It would be lethal if you were too close to it. They immediately developed problems breathing; they also experienced headaches. John called me, and I had them consult a pulmonary specialist, who confirmed that exposure to those fumes had caused their symptoms, and they would be permanently disabled. It affected both men's ability to work.

The Air Force denied it was happening, even while it was happening and even though it was captured on film. I thought when I took the case all I had to do was call the Air Force and say, these guys have been hurt by your gas leak, and you need to compensate them "x" amount of money. I thought they'd come forward and acknowledge that they'd made a mistake, and they were sorry and wanted to take care of these citizens they'd harmed. Instead, the Air Force denied everything.

First they denied that the leak happened; then they denied that the leak would cause any medical harm whatsoever. Yet they'd had these leaks previously and they knew the danger of them. The Surgeon General of the Air Force wrote me a letter saying that "the civilians had breathed a substance no more dangerous than smog." We had civilian doctors and staff from the University of Arkansas Medical School on record as saying there was nothing more dangerous than exposure to nitrogen textroxide. What's really interesting is that later, doctors who worked for that same government department wrote an article for the *Journal of the American Medical Association* saying that exposure to those same substances was potentially lethal.

None of the Air Force men could even be near that site without wearing protective clothing. If there was no danger to humans or livestock, why did they bother with protection? Everything they said was inconsistent with what they did. So I began to gather the evidence against them. I was trying to get information out of the Air Force, but every time I would get too close, they would tell me they couldn't release information because of national security issues. We had filed suit by that time, and I knew I could get their records on discovery—we could get a court order demanding that they release certain information.

Then an interesting thing happened. I got a phone call from a person who would not identify himself, but he wanted to meet with me to discuss the accident. He made it clear that he had to know he could trust me because his life could be in danger. Right away I speculated it was probably someone in the Air Force.

Jacksonville, where the base was located, was about twenty miles from Little Rock, and I suggested meeting at the Chief's Club up there, a place where some of us went to shoot pool and drink beer. He didn't want to meet in Jacksonville, though, and suggested instead some off-the-beaten-path place in Little Rock.

When we met, even though he was in civilian clothes he identified himself to me as an Air Force officer. He told me he was appalled at what he had witnessed in regard to this accident—the Air Force had not only lied, they had destroyed evidence—and while he was proud to serve his country, he was ashamed of the conduct of the Air Force. He provided me with information that I could then ask the Air Force to supply me with. I would probably never have known that this information existed without his assistance. He even arranged for me to gain access to some Air Force medical and maintenance records on leaks—they'd had leaks all over the country at other Titan sites. He was invaluable in developing the case. He became a confidential informant, and I never made mention of his name anywhere in the case file. As far as I know, Kathy never met with him or talked to him. I knew if I ever exposed him, he'd be court-martialed and washed out completely.

I later became friends with a Colonel, Don Hessenflow, who served in a public relations capacity at the Pentagon, and I met a general in England who was commander at the Little Rock base during that time. I told them I was the guy who sued them over the Titan II missile explosion. Don told me that after that case the Air Force held public relations seminars, and the example of what *not* to do was the Little Rock Air Force Base case. The Air Force made every mistake it was possible to make in handling the publicity. But there really was nothing a public relations officer could do when lying and destroying evidence were involved. And the Air Force would never settle that case—it went to trial—and they almost succeeded in bankrupting me because I took the case on contingency and had to finance it myself. I have no idea how much money out-of-pocket I was in that case, but once we received a judgment, they paid me everything. The incident was in 1979 and went to trial five years later, in 1984. The case wasn't tried before a jury, but before a federal judge. There's no doubt if it had been a jury trial, the judgment would have been much larger. The Air Force's conduct was reprehensible.

On September 18, 1980, while I was preparing the case, the missile exploded one night and blew the 250-ton door to the silo a quarter of a mile in the air. Now you were really talking about Keystone Cops. The Air Force lost the atomic warhead that was sitting on top of the missile, and they had to scramble to find it.

I then represented the heroic sergeant who was injured in the blast and also represented another airman who unfortunately was killed. So while my case with John Stacks was still pending, I began talking to the sergeant who was in charge of maintenance at the very site. He confirmed all the leaks, the cover-ups, and how bad the situation truly was. He also confirmed the basis of my case, which was that those leaks were dangerous. A military man can't sue the U.S. government, so we sued Martin-Marietta, the company that manufactured the missile. This is basically the way a rocket works: The hydrazine is fed down to the tubes of the igniters, and the engine is nothing but the fuel tank and a very small unit that ignites when the fuel—the hydrazine and the nitrogen tetroxide—comes together, and then it explodes. When the rocket ignites, the thrust is controlled by the fuel mixture.

On the day of the explosion, the silo already had a leak, and then an airman dropped a nine-pound socket from a wrench down the silo. It dropped sixty-six feet down the silo, hit the floor, and bounced into the very fragile outer covering of the fuel tank, causing a hydrazine leak. There was nothing they could do then unless they could shut off the nitrogen tetroxide flow, because when the two come together, they explode. It was a disaster waiting to happen.

And it happened. At 9:20 p.m. on the eighteenth, Sergeant Kennedy, the quality control inspector on duty at the by-now-abandoned command center, was sent to read the gauges after the socket was dropped. The gauges indicated that a massive spill was occurring below. Kennedy went down to see what damage the socket had done. The interesting thing was that although a catastrophic explosion was a great fear to the Strategic Air Command at this point, that concern was never passed along to the crew at the silo. Even Sergeant Kennedy felt that the 750-ton door would provide adequate protection in the event of an explosion. The Air Force feared the worst, yet little was done in the way of safety precautions in spite of the fact that they had nine hours to prepare after the wrench was dropped.

Six hours after his initial inspection, Sergeant Kennedy and a partner, Airman David Livingston, were ordered down into the complex, now dangerously saturated with highly combustible vapors. The last order sent to them was to turn on the exhaust fans, which they did. A second later, the place was blown to bits. Kennedy was thrown 150 feet away, into a fence. Then pandemonium set in, and many things happened that, when they came to light, had us dazed at the ineptitude of the Air Force. The evacuation of the remaining personnel was anything but orderly. Six airmen were badly injured, and it took three hours to get Kennedy and Livingston to a hospital sixty miles away. Livingston lived only eighteen hours after the explosion. In a perfect example of the dysfunctional and contradictory manner in which the Air Force responded to the incident, Sergeant Kennedy, who became the hero of the night, was first issued a written reprimand by the Air Force for going down into the silo alone. Then later he was awarded the Airman's Medal of Bravery for his conduct. And when it was all finished, the dropped socket cost the military a whopping $225 million. But the worst thing about it was the attitude of the government toward the victims; they used to always say in the military, there's one thing that's expendable and that's the personnel. The government held firmly to that philosophy during the aftermath of the explosion.

I seemed to always take on cases that landed me in the headlines.

Handwritten on photo: June 1970: To the mysterious mouth-piece with fond regards. Bill Alexander MC

2-1. Congressman Bill Alexander (right) and Bill (peering around the seat) on the plane with FedEx founder, Fred Smith.

Stone rolls into court again

Associated Press Wirephoto

Rolling Stones' guitarist Keith Richard (right) enters Provincial Court in Toronto yesterday to face drug charges that could send him to jail for life. Richard's lawyer, L. William Carter, escorts him. The rock star, free on $25,000 bail after his Feb. 28 arrest, was told he might be called for another hearing in about 10 days.

2-2. Newspaper photo of Keith Richards as Bill escorts him into a Canadian court.

2-3. Mick Jagger and Bill in Washington, DC, 1974

2-4. Mick Jagger meets the Chinese Ambassador to the U.S., Chai Zemin. Accompanying him are Congressman Bill Alexander (second from left) and Bill.

2-5. Mick Jagger meets with Senator Ted Kennedy (second from left). Pictured are Kathy Woods, Kennedy, Bill, Jagger and Jane Rose of Rolling Stones Records.

2-6. Visiting with an old friend, the Stones' Ron Wood, backstage during the Rolling Stones show in New York.

2-7. At the same New York show, Bill's daughter Joanna joined Keith Richards and Bill for a backstage visit.

2-8. Tanya Tucker signs her MCA contract as Mike Maitland, head of MCA Los Angeles (left) and Bill look on.

2-9. Country music superstar and actress Reba McEntire with Bill Carter.

2-10. Reba receives a gold record on the set of TNN's *Nashville Now*. For the presentation are (left to right) Red Stegall, MCA Nashville head Bruce Hinton, Reba, Bill and *Nashville Now* host, Ralph Emery.

2-11. From left to right, Bill Carter, Sir David Frost, Michael Merriman.

2-12. From left to right, John Harricharan, Bill Carter, and Kathy Woods.

Chapter 24
I'm a Little Bit Country ... I'm a Little Bit
Gospel ... I'm a Little Bit Rock 'n' Roll

FTER EACH TOUR WITH THE Stones and all the ancillary activities that entailed, I steadfastly returned to Little Rock and tried to practice a little law, but as I've said, I've never planned anything in my life; interesting things just seem to find me.

Take, for instance, how the negotiations on an HBO special for rock legend David Bowie almost cost me a client and caused the futures of a TV producer and a business manager to flash before their eyes, but provided plenty of myth-building material for my growing reputation. I had actually forgotten the experience until Bill Zysblat was laughing not too long ago, retelling it from the perspective of Tony Eaton, a television producer, who was present at the time. Zysblat, the Stones' business manager, who by now had become a really good friend, also represented British rocker David Bowie, and he brought me in to negotiate an HBO special for Bowie. Bowie had a high-powered New York lawyer who resented my being in the picture.

Tony Eaton had done one television special, on the Oak Ridge Boys, who were hot in country music but little known outside that world. But Zysblat knew Tony, and I had met him through the Oaks, so we called him in. This would mean a huge shot to his career. Betty Bitterman was head of music for HBO, and we were pretty far along in the negotiations with Betty when she called a meeting in HBO's conference room at their New York headquarters. Zysblat, Tony Eaton, Kathy Woods, and I were present for the meeting with Betty, and we were talking about money. Betty said she only had something like $650,000 to spend on the special, and that was all she'd pay. I told her we had to have $1 million. She refused. My briefcase was open on the conference table, so I stood up, slammed the lid closed, and walked out of the room without a backward glance, with Kathy trailing behind me. Zysblat laughs that Tony Eaton saw his whole future flash before his eyes as I was leaving. He said he could just see him thinking, *One little incident and my career is over before it really began.* Plus, Zysblat was thinking he had seen the last of David Bowie as a client because he was sure to be fired. They were convinced I had just blown the HBO deal. I had already punched the elevator button, but before the elevator could arrive, Betty Bitterman had run after me, yelling for me to stop. "All right," she said. "You've got the million dollars."

I do stuff like that. I've always said I thought my expertise was shoving some-one right to the edge of the cliff without shoving them over. Maybe I learned that technique as a Secret Service agent—knowing what someone's limit was. When I heard that story retold, I couldn't imagine I would do something like that. What would cause somebody to be that brash? But, hey . . . just because it's business doesn't mean it can't be fun. I've always believed in asking for something. All they can do is say no, and my clients just might get more than they were expecting. You don't know what people are willing to pay, and you can throw them off balance by putting a high figure on the table. If they really want the deal, you'll find out right away. So you always want to go high.

I don't gamble; I'm not a poker player. But I can sure gamble with other people's money.

That episode left the impression among certain New York types that I knew something about television, so MTV asked me to put together a show for them. Of course, they told me they didn't have any budget for it. They wanted to do a show live from Tokyo using the band Asia, a new band made up of members of Yes and several other rock artists, so I asked them if they could raise the money. They suggested I use Allen Branton for lighting and get David Mallet, a famous live director who had done the Bowie special, and I knew they wouldn't come cheaply. So I called Frank Kohler, a friend from LA who had worked with corporations on product placement in movies and television. I suggested he might want to take this idea to some of his clients, which he did. One of his clients, Montgomery Ward, a big department store chain at the time, wanted to do the deal. So I found myself producing the television special, and I brought a fully recovered Tony Eaton in to produce, Mallet to direct, and Branton to light. What was there to do but sit back and take credit? I spent a year putting that project together, and at the end of the year my profit was $27,000. I decided I couldn't afford the TV business; I'd go broke. I didn't know then you could lose just as much money managing artists.

In 1976 I was still practicing law in Little Rock but representing the Stones and Tanya Tucker. Red Stegall, a successful recording artist and songwriter at the time, had discovered a red-headed rodeo barrel racer and big singer in Oklahoma a couple of years earlier named Reba McEntire. Red, who was also involved in Jim Halsey's publishing company in Nashville, had promised Reba's mother, Jackie, to help her children (Reba had three siblings) in the music business. So he invited Reba, who in his opinion had the best shot at a career in country music, to come to Nashville and record some demos, mostly of his songs. Red had Joe Light from the publishing company take those demos to a friend at Mercury Records, and

Reba was signed to a singles deal at Mercury in 1975. In addition to being Reba's mentor, Red was doing a little "unofficial" managing of her career, too.

E.O. Stacey at ICM told Red he should send Reba to see me for career advice. She and her brand-new husband at the time, Charlie Battles, called and came to Little Rock to meet with me. They wanted me to represent Reba, and while I liked both Reba and Charlie, my focus was pretty much on the Rolling Stones, and I didn't know what I could do for Reba. I told her this but also told her if things got further along with her career, she should call me.

I didn't hear from her again, and in the meantime, I moved to Nashville in 1981, after Jan and I divorced. That same year, I was working on the Stones '81 tour and was traveling from Nashville to New York when I bumped into Reba and Charlie at the Nashville airport. By then Reba had recorded three albums for Mercury, which had produced some modest radio hits, and she said she thought it was time for us to get together. When we met at my office in Nashville, she told me her contract was coming up for renewal at Mercury, and she wanted to know what kind of help I could be in negotiating the new contract. I began to work with her immediately as her attorney, negotiating her deal.

Reba was slowly but surely getting better with each single, and by the time we started the contract negotiations, she had scored her first number one record, "Can't Even Get the Blues." In what seemed like a repeat of the Tanya Tucker dealings, Mercury wouldn't meet our demands, so I notified them I intended to shop Reba around. I went to all the labels, and they all made some kind of offer. I had not called MCA yet, because they had apparently passed on Reba once before. Jim Fogelsong was head of MCA Nashville at that time, and while we had nothing but respect for him, the label already had Barbara Mandrell, who was huge at the time.

I actually had a contract on my desk from CBS when I ran into Irving Azoff, whom I knew through the Stones, during one of my frequent trips to LA. The former manager of The Eagles, Irving had taken over at MCA. He asked me to come see him about Reba, so I went by his office before I left LA. I was kind of surprised he knew who Reba McEntire was, but not only did he know who she was, he believed in her voice and recognized what Reba's talent would be worth to a label. "Take the CBS offer and add a figure to it and make me an offer," he stunned me by saying.

I explained that I had deals on the table from several labels already, including the one we were close to signing with CBS, so I said, "You make *me* an offer." He wouldn't do it. I decided to shoot for the moon, so I threw out an enormous amount (for that time, anyway) for an advance and royalties.

I was in Quebec City in July 1983, working on the David Bowie tour, when I got a call from Zack Horowitz, MCA's legal affairs head in LA. He said he was getting on an airplane for London with Irving. "Irving told me to call you and say we have a deal," he explained. I asked him what he meant, and he said MCA was willing to accept my proposal. I explained we were pretty close to signing with CBS, and I was out on tour with Bowie, so I'd need to see something in writing. "I'll wire you a firm offer as soon as I land in London," he promised, and he was as good as his word. As soon as he got to London, he sent me a telegram confirming their interest in signing Reba. All this from a man who had never even seen Reba perform!

I immediately called Reba and Charlie to tell them. The funny thing is that Jim Fogelsong was in Toronto attending a Country Music Association board meeting, and Irving got to him first. So Jim called me to say he understood that they had signed Reba and he didn't know who should congratulate whom. I felt really bad because it looked like I had gone around Fogelsong, and that had not been my intention at all. Reba points out in her autobiography that we were even able to put a clause in her contract that gave her marketing control—a move unheard of in Nashville then.

We then had to decide on producers for the first album. Reba loved Jerry Kennedy, who had produced her six Mercury albums, but he couldn't come over from Mercury and work with her. So we chose Norro Wilson, one of Nashville's great characters, songwriters, and producers, and we made what we felt was a good record with Norro producing.

In the meantime, there was a shake-up at MCA Nashville, and Jim Fogelsong was replaced by Jimmy Bowen, a man with a reputation as something of a maverick. In other words . . . a man after my own heart. Bowen was considered by many to be a brilliant producer, but he had also been a songwriter and recording artist in his early career. He was not a big Reba fan and even told me that he was thinking about dropping "the redhead" because something about her voice bothered him. Bowen took over in May 1984, right after the album with Norro, *Just A Little Love*, was released. For an artist who had just scored her third number one single, "You're the First Time I've Thought About Leaving," the lackluster performance of the album was disappointing. The highest chart position a single reached was number five for the album's title track.

My recollection is that Bowen fired Norro, saying, "I don't like this record, so we're getting a new producer." Reba's contract gave her approval over producers, and we finally settled on Harold Shedd, who was producing the hottest act in country music at the time, the group Alabama. These were the days when country acts were trying to cross over into pop by putting strings and lush arrangements behind the songs, and Reba felt the songs Harold was choosing for her album were too pop for her. She was not at all happy and came to see me.

Reba and I talked about her options. We felt Bowen was an incredible producer and could make a great record on Reba. Plus, we also knew that as both producer and head of the label, he would have an added stake in her career success, and she would be a priority at the label.

Reba and I decided to go out to Bowen's house to have a little meeting of the minds about her career. Reba started the meeting by telling Bowen she didn't like the songs Harold had found. "Fine," he said. "Go find your own songs."

"I want you to produce me," she told him. I think he was totally startled, and he told us he would think about it. He ultimately turned down her request to produce, but he did put her with his trusted A&R guy, Don "Dirt" Lanier, to help her find songs.

I even got into the act. There was a popular watering hole in Nashville at the time—Maude's Courtyard—a spot where songwriters and other music industry types hung out frequently. Harlan Howard—*the* guy at that time, who is still considered the greatest songwriter ever to come out of Nashville—was one of Maude's regulars. I often ran into Harlan and his buddy Chick Rains, holding court in the bar there. He was a true character whose songs, including "I Fall to Pieces," had broken many country careers wide open. During the time we were looking for material for Reba's album, I called Harlan at home and told him we really needed a hit song for this album and asked if he had anything that would be suitable for her. He hesitated and said, "I don't know. She's not selling that many records." I told him she never would sell a lot of records if she didn't record hits. Finally he said, "Send the little redhead out to the house, and I'll see what I've got. I might have something in my dresser drawer." I sent Reba out to Harlan's house to see what he had.

Reba tells the story in her autobiography, *Reba, My Story*, that when she and Charlie were at Harlan's house, Harlan played her several mediocre songs and she passed on all of them. Finally, he popped "Somebody Should Leave" into his tape recorder, and she knew immediately that she had found her hit. She always felt like Harlan was testing her song savvy; if she had gone for songs he knew weren't that good, she never would have been given "Somebody Should Leave" (p. 141).

Reba sold that song on stage like nobody else could have, with real tears shining in her eyes. She even performed it on the CMA Awards Show, and it was a career-maker for her. That song started selling records . . . really selling records, and it earned standing ovations when she performed it on tour. We had her set it up properly by telling what the song was about; then we'd bring the stool out on stage and shine a spot on her. She really sold the song, with tears running down her cheeks as she sang the chorus. It touched a responsive chord in audiences everywhere and made them sit up and take notice of Reba McEntire. It was her second number one song off the album, after "How Blue."

Harold made a pretty good record on Reba, *My Kind of Country*, but it was never a comfortable fit. In keeping with the crossover mentality at the time, and against Reba's objections, Harold had chosen songs that called for all these lush arrangements using violins, and with Reba it was all about fiddle and steel guitar at the time. The title was kind of ironic because she felt it was too pop for her Oklahoma-style country. After that album was released, Reba and I met with Harold in my office, and she told us how she felt about the strings. When Harold told her she didn't have the songs for fiddle and steel, it proved her point that the songs Harold had picked were too pop for her.

Eventually Bowen did end up co-producing Reba's albums with her—I say co-producing because Bowen ceded a good deal of control to Reba over her albums, the first time that had happened to a female in country music. I think that was just one more element that made Reba such a complete entertainer. It's interesting, though, that twenty-one years later, when she had become a huge superstar in music and television, Reba went back to Norro Wilson to make her country comeback record. I think Reba always did like Norro and was disappointed that their album together was not more successful. Certainly he's one of my favorite people.

In the midst of all the producer turmoil, Reba decided to make a management change. Don Williams, one of pop superstar Andy Williams' brothers, had been managing Reba's career from Los Angeles, but she felt she needed a presence in Nashville. She asked if I would consider managing her. My experience with Tanya's career made me realize I didn't really want to manage artists, so I told her I was perfectly happy practicing law. I had managed Tanya with the help of Peter Rudge, but Beau Tucker was actually considered Tanya's manager. I always felt there was a conflict in both managing artists and representing them as their lawyer. Reba dug in her heels and insisted, and, against my better judgment, I became an artist manager.

The first thing we did was chart a course for Reba's career. We developed a plan that included awards, her stage show, and publicity, among other things. We had already hired Network Ink, the best publicity firm in Nashville at the time, to do Reba's publicity. Our first goal was to win the CMA Award for Female Vocalist, the pinnacle for a country female at that time. But she won it—in 1984—when we weren't really expecting it. I don't even remember being at the show; I think I was watching on television at home. I think we were both stunned, frankly.

We always felt like the publicity Reba had received had a lot to do with helping her win that award by painting a picture of her as a bigger star than she actually was at that time. That perception may have been a holdover from the time we were negotiating her contract, and Charlie, Don Williams, and I devised a plan to give the impression that Reba was a major star. Reba still lived on a ranch in Oklahoma, but she was well liked in Nashville because she was so genuine. She was an Oklahoma cowgirl, and that was an attractive image. She wore jeans and a great big silver belt buckle wherever she went. The award may have been a little premature in our minds, but it positioned her as the top female in country music. And she kept winning. She repeated her success by winning the award again in 1985—another building block in the career plan.

Reba's career skyrocketed the next year. Her first album with Bowen was titled *Whoever's in New England* and was released in January 1986. Video was in its infancy, and Reba made her first video ever for the title track. It was directed by Jon Small, a well-respected rock video director, and it was the first time I had seen a video have such an incredible impact on a song and an artist. It premiered on *Entertainment Tonight*, which was huge in itself. HBO had a show called *Video*

Jukebox, which was a fill between the movies on the channel. Through my HBO connections, as well as Jon Small and MCA, we got the video played on that show, which again was huge since only rock and pop artists got on *Video Jukebox*. The sales for the album ballooned, due in large measure to that video. It broke her career wide open. It was her biggest song to date and got everyone's attention. That song eventually propelled her to win Entertainer of the Year at the CMA Awards that October, as well as gave Reba her first Grammy. It also gave her tremendous clout as an artist.

The marketing-control clause in her contract also came into play on that album when MCA's marketing genius, Walt Wilson, and I created a campaign called Country in a Crate. This was in the days when the most popular form of recorded music was the cassette tape, so we arranged for a company to manufacture little crates, especially for us. We put a copy of Reba's tape in the crate but left enough room for the consumer to add future cassettes, so it became a tape case with Reba McEntire on it. The MCA sales force talked smaller retailers, like Camelot, into doing a front-of-the-store display so it hit you in the eye when you entered their stores, which were all in malls. We even won a national retailing award for it.

Reba's career was now soaring, but we still weren't getting the proper national respect we felt she deserved. I had an idea that Reba should play Carnegie Hall, but it's not as simple as that; you don't just decide to play Carnegie Hall. But I knew with my rock-and-roll connections I could get the venue. It holds 2,300 people, so we figured that if we sold out the hall, we'd have to pay about $40,000 more than we'd make in ticket sales. That was *if* it was a sell-out; few people in New York knew who Reba McEntire was. I wanted to do a "paper" campaign, where you put up little posters all over construction walls across the city. It would cost about ten grand just to poster the city. At that time, that was a lot of money for an artist to spend to promote a career, but I took the idea to Reba and Charlie. Reba always had the vision to realize what something like that would do for her, and she was quick to agree to it, but we had to convince Charlie to spend the money. When Charlie agreed to do it, I called Ron Delsener, who was the top rock promoter in the city and who had connections with all the "elements." He got Carnegie Hall. I called Bill Zysblat and got all my old rock-and-roll friends to come. Allen Branton, who lit the Stones tours, among others, did the lights. We went to Carnegie Hall, sold it out, and the publicity was enormous. Reba put on a fabulous show and was a huge success. That show elevated her to a national level and was a turning point in her career.

An interesting sidebar to that show was that Reba had gotten mad at her bank, and back then she didn't have a lot of financial clout. So she wanted to change banks. Mike Vaden was her business manager, and he told us about a young banker at Third National Bank who was running the new music department. Vaden introduced us to Brian Williams, who said he'd like to meet Reba and convince her to let him handle her account. I told him if he'd fly up to New York for the Carnegie

Hall show, I'd introduce him to Reba and she in turn would be impressed that he had flown up for the show. Brian told me later it took a lot of convincing on his part to get his boss to agree to fly him to New York. The department was fairly new and they didn't have the kind of budget for such a trip. In the end his boss agreed to let him go, but with the instruction that he'd better bring back the account. Brian was at the show and he met Reba, but we didn't talk business. He laughs that two weeks went by without a word from us, and he was really sweating it. Finally, I called one day and asked him to come up to the office, without telling him why.

He came right over to my office, and I had Reba waiting in the conference room. We left him dangling for a few minutes with just small talk, but finally I said, in a backhanded manner, "Oh, and Reba wanted to talk to you about opening some accounts." Brian landed the account and launched his career as the most success-ful music industry banker in the South for what is now SunTrust Bank. As far as I know, he's still Reba's banker.

I think one of the other significant developments that happened when I was managing Reba was that we were able to affect the way CMA conducted their press conferences after the CMA Awards. When Reba won Female Vocalist of the Year, CMA was using an archaic system under which they waited until after all the awards were handed out. Then they rushed everyone through the crush backstage to vans that took them up a back driveway to a service entrance at Opryland Hotel, and then they were finally herded up a flight of cement stairs to a backstage holding area. There, along with everyone else who had won an award, they would await a press conference. Since all the artists were arriving at once, it was a madhouse in the little holding area, and depending on how many had already arrived, it could be a long wait before an artist got to the microphone. After the press conference, artists were escorted through the upper hallway at the hotel to do one-on-one interviews with television reporters. All the people who were attending the post-awards party were in the same area, so an artist was stopped at every turn. By the time all the interviews were done, it was after two in the morning, and the artists couldn't even celebrate their victory. Reba absolutely hated it the year we had to go through that process.

By the time that Reba won Entertainer of the Year, some of the record companies had rebelled against the crush of the CMA post-awards party and started having their own private parties for their executives and artists. MCA didn't have a party that year, and because of my friendship with Joe Galante, head of RCA Nashville, Reba and I had been invited to the RCA Party. I attended the show that year and was already in the limousine waiting for Reba. She came out with the escort CMA had assigned to her and said they wanted to take her to the hotel for the press conference. I asked her if she wanted to go, and she said she didn't, so I told her to get in the car, and we went to the RCA party and celebrated her win.

The next year, some of the executives from the CMA took me to lunch at a fancy restaurant and tried to get me to agree that if Reba won again she would do the press conference. I told them that as long as they insisted on treating artists like cattle, Reba McEntire would *not* participate. And she didn't. We even issued a press release to that effect. Not long afterward, they started using the studio in the Opry House as the site of their press conference, and it was a much better system. I was always proud of Reba for taking a stand on behalf of all artists and demanding better treatment.

But all the success as well as the constant touring was taking its toll on Reba and Charlie's marriage. I really liked Charlie, but he was just a rancher and rodeo bulldogger at heart. Reba had outgrown Stringtown, Oklahoma, and was spending less and less time there. I supported Reba completely when she decided to divorce Charlie in 1987, even recommending a divorce attorney in Oklahoma. I went to Oklahoma and testified on her behalf during the divorce proceedings, but when she started seeing Narvel Blackstock in 1988, her steel guitar player who had become her road manager, I knew that my days as her manager were numbered. It was only natural that she would want Narvel to manage her career.

I always viewed my role as manager as coach or teacher and, overall, Reba was the best student I ever had. I tried to teach my clients to accomplish their goals, not impose controls on them. Artists want you to lay out a plan so they can achieve a certain goal, and they have to understand that and cooperate with it. You can get a basketball team together and diagram a play, but it's up to them to carry it out. Reba understood this; she, to me, is the model artist. She was driven—the most important thing to her was her career. Many young artists are pulled in a lot of different directions and have to make a choice to put their careers first. I think Reba's success speaks for itself.

I received a lot of satisfaction from working with Reba because we were able to accomplish all her career goals. She came to me wanting to reach a higher level with her career. All artists want success with their careers. I've never had one come to me and say, "I want to get rich." They all want to achieve recognition for their talent and for what they do. I undertook exposing them to the world. I used to say an artist had succeeded when you could pick up the phone and randomly call somebody in Dubuque, Iowa, and ask if they knew who a certain artist was, and the answer was yes. I think the satisfaction you achieve from working with any artist is seeing that person reach certain levels. It's like the pride a teacher sees when a student graduates with honors. If a manager can contribute something to help artists achieve their goals, that's when you receive your satisfaction.

When Rodney Crowell came to me in the late 1980s, he had already been around for years and was well respected as a songwriter of hits for Bob Seger, Emmylou Harris, Waylon Jennings, Crystal Gayle, and others. But he had yet to break through as a recording artist, in spite of some pretty good records he had put out at Warner Bros., and he had gained a sizable following for having been involved in two of the legendary bands in music, Emmylou's Hot Band and his own, The Cherry Bombs.

In 1988 Rodney signed with CBS Records. He persuaded his old Hot Band and Cherry Bombs piano player, Tony Brown, who had become a record executive/producer at another label, to produce him. Together they created a brilliant record called *Diamonds and Dirt*. I got involved with him about that time and was able to help guide him to the most success he had ever achieved or has since achieved. He was the first artist, and may still be the only one, to have five consecutive number one records off one album. He was nominated for all kinds of awards and won the Grammy for the song "After All This Time." Seeing him garner all that recognition and receive all those awards and plaques made me smile and say, "I'm glad I was able to help him do that." I really love Rodney and respect his talent, which he has in abundance, and am proud to have been associated with him.

I have to say I am also proud of my eleven-year association with Shenandoah. They were a five-man group out of Muscle Shoals, Alabama, who had achieved some early success with singles like "Church on Cumberland Road." They were signed to CBS Records and produced by Rick Hall, a legendary producer out of Muscle Shoals. I was able to guide them during a particularly rough patch in their career when, because of some contractual obligations that threatened to torpedo their fledgling career, they were forced to declare bankruptcy and look for another record label and producer. They landed at RCA Records, where they scored a Grammy Award for a duet they recorded with Alison Krauss, "Somewhere in the Vicinity of the Heart." Although the original band broke up in the mid-'90s, I still hear from their very talented lead singer, Marty Raybon, from time to time. I really liked all those guys and valued my association with them.

Through my friend E.O. Stacey at ICM, I also worked for a short time with Anson Williams, an actor who portrayed Potsie on a hot TV show at the time, *Happy Days*. He wanted to parlay his TV success into a singing career and was represented by Stacey, who asked me to get involved and provide some guidance to Anson. I don't recall how long I worked with him but became friends with him more than anything else. He's now a very successful director in Los Angeles.

I had my disappointments as a manager, though, chiefly Lari White. I got to know her when she was singing back-up on Rodney Crowell's 1992 *Life Is Messy* tour and became her manager and her friend. She is probably the most talented and creative artist I've ever worked with, but we just could not break her, in spite of her working her butt off and the best efforts of RCA Records. I went to a Celine Dion concert years later and called Lari afterward and told her she could sing better than Celine and was a better performer. It just breaks my heart that she's not a big star.

I never felt like I failed an artist or let one down if certain career goals weren't achieved. I know I gave 100 percent; there's often just no explaining why one artist's career takes off and another equally talented artist's doesn't. A manager can guide, offer advice, and fine-tune certain elements, but a manager can't make an artist succeed. One real key in breaking an artist is developing an image, and we did that with Reba before she had the big break-out hits. When she did have the big break-out hits, everything else was in place. We did the same thing with Rodney.

I also believed strongly that if you break artists at the grassroots level, they can sustain a career for years. I did that with several artists I managed, including Reba, Shenandoah, and Lonestar.

Wal-Mart changed our society. I like to use Kennett, Missouri, as an example because I grew up fourteen miles from Kennett. My hometown of Rector probably never will have a Wal-Mart, because there's one in every town surrounding it. But Kennett had the big radio station, KBOA, and when Kennett got a Wal-Mart, it became the center of activity for that whole area. So it occurred to me, if you can get a record played on KBOA and then listeners can go to Wal-Mart and buy the record, you've got a sale. The mentality of the record companies is to get airplay on the stations that then report to the national music trade publications, and those are found mostly in large markets. In Arkansas, the only reporting stations would be in Little Rock, but there's a Wal-Mart in just about every town in the state.

I also believed in servicing the little weekly papers in Kennett, Missouri, and Hope, Arkansas, whenever an artist was touring within fifty miles of those towns because those papers are looking for news to report. They'd jump at a chance of getting an interview with an artist, and it would receive major placement in that newspaper.

Some of my techniques I learned when I was involved with Ralph Emery's radio show for Goody's Headache Powders. It wasn't carried on most of the major reporting stations, but we would saturate a large market with smaller stations. Instead of having one or two of the big reporting stations, we'd have seventeen or eighteen stations across the state carrying the show. People in Kennett don't listen to the station out of St. Louis, they listen to KBOA. Goody's was trying to reach the rural market with their product, and we were able to do that by saturating the markets where folks listened to their local radio station and read their local newspaper.

Another example of grassroots strategy is Bill Gaither, the biggest name in gospel music, who had to find ways other than radio airplay to sell his *Homecoming* videos. I used to tell the Nashville record labels that they took airplay on major radio stations for granted. They knew only one way of doing things, and that was to get airplay. If they couldn't get airplay, they didn't know what to do. Bill Gaither never had the luxury of radio airplay—except on a small number of gospel stations—and he was a role model for me from a marketing standpoint because he succeeded in spite of the lack of airplay. He knew how to work the grassroots marketplace. Today he's one of the biggest artists in the business because he understands the market.

Political campaigns are similar—you've got to start block by block. If you're gonna win an election, you can't just run an ad on television, because that saturates the market; you have to get out and let the people see you and feel you and meet you personally. The more of that you do, coupled with media, the more solid your base. As you develop that base, you're developing your fan base. Shenandoah had one of the strongest fan bases I've encountered, and they developed that through their grassroots following. They may not have a record deal today, but they're still out there touring.

I never practiced law again after I gave it up to manage Reba, although I negotiated deals for all kinds of music industry clients. And one of those was radio/television personality Ralph Emery, whose long-term relationship I treasure. Ralph even made me reconsider my rule not to get involved in television again.

It seems like I've known Ralph forever—even though it's been only since the Tanya Tucker days. His *Nashville Now* show was the flagship show on The Nashville Network (TNN) when it launched in 1983, and when he was negotiating his contract with TNN, he came to see me. I did all his subsequent contracts at TNN, and that evolved into working on his sponsorships as well as other things. I have such respect for him, and I've always enjoyed working with him.

He's truly one of the legends in country music and deserves to be enshrined in the Country Music Hall of Fame. I think every artist who came to town from the '50s through the '90s felt like they knew Ralph Emery and owed him something because he helped so many people in their careers. He was always willing to put them on his shows—whether his long-running show on WSMV-TV, the NBC affiliate in Nashville, which used to give *Today* its highest lead-in numbers of any other affiliate in the country, or his all-night radio show on WSM Radio or his TNN shows. He always made artists feel like stars even when they weren't, so he could call them and get them to do most anything. After *Nashville Now* he hosted other shows for TNN, including a daily morning show from Opryland Hotel and *On the Record*, where he interviewed legendary artists. He hosted a Time/Life compilation called *Classic Country*, which was a huge success, and he's now on PBS with *Ralph Emery's Country Legends* series.

Through my dealings with Ralph and others, I was developing a reputation as a skilled negotiator, going all the way back to the Tanya Tucker contract with CBS. CBS knew they weren't treating Tanya right, but they were so arrogant they couldn't imagine an artist who wanted to be a star would challenge them. When I couldn't get them to compete with the other labels, they took it for granted I wouldn't do anything. I popped them good, and they reeled from that for years; I think Billy Sherrill blames me to this day. And he should, except CBS should have come to the table as I tried to get them to do. I gave them every opportunity short of getting on my knees and begging. They weren't accustomed to dealing with someone like me, who didn't care whether or not I made enemies. I'm sure I could have rolled over with CBS, and they probably would have sent me a lot of business. That wasn't in my make-up; I challenged them instead, got the contract voided, and went on to do business with another company. I think that incident, combined with the Stones at the time, developed my reputation worldwide. People would call me thinking I could work miracles for them.

And sometimes I can . . . it's a matter of knowing the right people. David Hall was the president of TNN, and in late '92 or '93 he had the vision of having a segment on TNN related to country shopping. His idea wasn't fully developed, but he was thinking it could be merchandise associated with the country lifestyle . . . clothes, furniture, music, whatever. He wanted me to ask Ralph Emery to test the concept at Home Shopping Network, and if it worked, then he would put it on TNN. Ralph and I met with HSN, and they loved the idea. They even went so far as to hire somebody to put together products. We pulled out of it at the last minute because of TNN's change of direction, but we had already begun looking around for products to sell.

Both Jerry Crutchfield, who was a friend of mine, and Ken Harding, who had an independent Christian record label, called me about Bill Gaither, who had just begun producing a series of videos called *Homecoming*, spotlighting the pioneers of gospel music. It was a concept that had come about quite by accident. He had been selling the videos through a thirty-minute infomercial and was beginning to have some success. Crutch and Ken wanted to know if they could sell the videos on an HSN segment. I had known who Bill Gaither was for a long time and had actually seen the first video when it ran on *The 700 Club*. The production at the time was bare-bones and the lighting was bad, but the music and the voices were incredible. It was the old-time music I had heard in church all my life that just warms your heart. I asked them to get me a copy of the videos.

I was going to my sister Doris' house in Mountain Home, Arkansas, and I took the videos with me. My brother-in-law, Stan, had a little TV/VCR back in an exercise room, and I took the videos to that room to get away from everyone. My mother came in and joined me, and then some other family member joined us, and before long, everyone in the house was crowded in this little room, watching the videos.

When I returned, I called Crutch and Ken, and they set up a meeting. Bill Gaither and Barry Jennings, who is president of the Gaither companies, came down from Indiana, and we met at Crutchfield's office. Bill Gaither told me there was no gospel music on television at the time and wanted to know if I thought I might get them a slot on TNN. It never occurred to me that there was no gospel music currently on TV, since I had watched shows like *Gospel Jubilee* all my life, but it suddenly dawned on me that he was right. That shocked me. I told him it should be easy since Hall and I were big buddies. So I called David and, not surprising for a Vanderbilt engineering graduate, he had never heard of the *Homecoming* videos. He was at least open to the idea and asked me to meet with Brian Hughes and Paul Corbin, who were responsible for programming the network. We met in Paul's office out at the Opryland complex. Brian later told me that he liked the videos but Paul didn't, and David didn't say anything. They turned me down flat, saying they weren't interested, and ushered me out of the office.

I kept working Hall, though with little success. Tammy Wynette had a show on the network that featured music legends—mostly country. The show seldom scored more than a .7 rating, so I didn't consider it to be really successful. I was watching that show one night, and her guests were Bill Gaither, Vestal Goodman, Jake Hess, and J.D. Sumner—all gospel music legends. Since I got the TNN ratings every week because of my association with Ralph Emery, I looked at the rating for that show, and bam! It came in at 1.3. I grabbed that ratings sheet and hurried out to TNN, pointing out to Hall that Tammy had featured every country legend of any consequence on that show without moving the needle, so what made this show different? He hemmed and hawed, but Hall's not stupid, so when I again begged for him to give us just one shot, he finally agreed to do one show.

One of his main arguments for not airing the *Homecoming* shows was that the production was substandard. So I had to agree to produce a completely new show, using quality lighting and sound, and we chose the historic Ryman Auditorium in Nashville as our venue. Coincidentally, this was where Bill Gaither had seen his first all-night gospel sing. "Ryman Homecoming" aired the Saturday after Thanksgiving in '95 and copped something like a 1.5 rating, which was incredible for TNN. I made a deal with Hall that if we scored as well as Tammy's legends special had done, he had to give me more shows. He kept his promise, and we became a mainstay on the network until it changed formats.

In February 1996 we taped two more shows at the Tennessee Performing Arts Center, and they had even higher ratings than "Ryman Homecoming." We started getting regular time slots on Saturday night on TNN, which was a great night because they aired the Opry, then the Statler Brothers, and then Gaither—great pairings. And it was good for everyone; David said we consistently had the highest- or second-highest-rated show on the network (after the Statler Brothers). As our ratings held steady and our audience grew, we started venturing into some really prestigious venues, like the Kennedy Center in Washington. It was a great match because their demographic was our demographic.

We were doing better shows, but the lighting badly needed upgrading, so I called Allen Branton and told him we needed some help.

I had known Allen since he was just a kid out of Arkansas perfecting the fine art of lighting as a member of the Stones 1981 tour. Allen had started his career as a musician but took a job with ShoCo in Dallas in 1973 and became a lighting director for rock shows kind of by accident. He sought me out in 1979 when he moved back to Little Rock and needed some advice about a TV shoot. We just bumped into each other on the '81 tour without each other realizing the other one was out there. I had taken over writing checks in those days, and knew what he was making. I scolded him unmercifully for cutting himself such a bad deal on that tour, so when he was asked to light Bowie's Serious Moonlight Tour, he asked me to represent him and before long I found myself mentoring him. Allen likes to say that I helped him understand the big picture, so he could realistically assess his value. He told me recently that I helped him improve his production and how he was perceived, basically elevating his craft. Whether I did or not, Allen became the best in the business, and I turned to him when we needed help with Reba, so there was no one else in whom I had more confidence for the Gaither shoots.

Allen wasn't available, so he turned me on to a protégé of his in Chicago. The lighting was better, but I don't think Bill ever saw the difference. Then we were doing Jubilate, a live New Year's Eve show in Charlotte, and the Chicago guy wasn't available, so I called Allen again. Now, Allen makes big money lighting major rock tours, not to mention the MTV Awards and other major network television shows, so I told him this wasn't the money he was accustomed to making. Allen never forgot that I went to bat for him with the Stones to get him more money on the '81 tour, so he told me not to worry about the money. He came to Charlotte and lit Jubilate, and Bill and Gloria Gaither were just blown away. The stage was in the round and they were sitting offstage, so they could see what was happening on the stage. Gaither wanted to meet with Allen after that because he saw the impact the lighting could have on production. We'd slowly bring in better technical people and spend some money on set design, including employing John Caulkin, one of the top set designers in the world. Our budgets grew tremendously, and we taped shows all over the world.

We were on TNN for about five years, until Viacom bought the network and completely turned the programming around, ousting music of any kind. But by then millions of people knew who Bill Gaither was, and he had gained the respect of people inside the TV industry as well. We struggled after TNN, but we were able to maintain on lesser networks. Through our friendship with David Hall, we were able to forge a partnership with PBS through their Memphis affiliate, and they now regularly air Gaither programming, including a multipart series called *Gaither Homecoming Classics.*

I was still doing a little artist management but was at the end of a five-year relationship with Lonestar, a Texas group I had started representing just before they signed a major label deal with BNA Records, a label in the RCA family. During the five years I worked with them, they achieved great country success, but in the last year, they put out an album called *Lonely Grill,* produced by a hot guitar player and heavy metal producer, Dann Huff. They changed their image from cowboy hats and jeans to form-fitting T-shirts and flat-front pants. The first single, which we all believed in, surprised us all by tanking, so we released a big ballad as the second single. We all thought it was a good song but were stunned when "Amazed" shot to the top of the country charts, stayed there for nine record-setting weeks, and then crossed over to the adult contemporary and pop charts. It boosted sales of the album past the million mark and really established Lonestar as a top country group.

But my heart was more and more in gospel music and less and less in artist management, so when I parted ways with Lonestar at the end of their contract, I shuttered the management end of my company and concentrated solely on Gaither Television Productions because I was having such a good time doing their programming. I was doing more than just television production, I was consulting on the marketing and coordinating other activities, and that became pretty much a full-time job. I had lost my appetite for going to showcases and number one parties and such. I had moved to a beautiful farm in Lebanon, about thirty minutes outside Nashville, and when I was finished at the end of the day, I wanted to go home. I loved the Gaithers, I loved the music and the artists, who are so nice and kind, and I loved the challenge.

Since we were always looking for fresh ideas for television programming, we created a separate division of GTP to develop programming outside the traditional Gaither Homecoming concept. A long-time friend, Joe Moscheo, who had been part of a ground-breaking gospel quartet, The Imperials, backing Elvis Presley in the '70s, called me one day and said, "You know, the [Elvis] Estate, has never done anything with Elvis' love of gospel music." Now, Elvis was a contemporary of mine, but I knew nothing about him except his movies and his pop hits. I was certainly aware of his legendary status, but I was shocked to learn that the only Grammy Awards Elvis won were for his gospel albums. Because of Elvis' reputation and the way he died, Joe said that he had been hesitant to approach Bill Gaither about Elvis in spite of the fact that Elvis had been responsible for Bill Gaither's first Grammy nomination for a song he had written, "He Touched Me," that Elvis had recorded in 1969.

Joe wanted to know if I could get Gaither TV Productions to do a show. I thought the story was compelling, so we set a meeting at Graceland, in Memphis. I took it to Barry, who told me to feel out Bill Hearn, head of EMI Christian Music, our distribution company, to see if he could get a videotaped documentary in Christian bookstores. Hearn said if we put Gaither's name on it, we could get it in the stores.

Barry and Joe and I flew to Memphis, not expecting to wrap anything up that day, but we came back with the deal made, and Barry turned it over to me. We needed a director who was a really good editor, so I called my daughter Joanna, who was head of the video department at Capitol Records, and asked her who she would recommend. She gave me the names of two or three people, but the only one I really knew was Michael Merriman; she told me she thought he was one of the best, and that's who we chose. He did a superb job. We also chose Sander Vanocur, the well-respected journalist who had been the White House correspondent for NBC-TV during my Secret Service days, to narrate.

When we started putting the show together, I was totally amazed at the story that was unfolding. I had no idea how Elvis had struggled with his spirituality, and that struggle had eventually led him into drugs and his demise. I must have watched the various edits dozens of times, and the story never failed to move me to tears. I was having dinner with a friend's family one night, and she insisted I bring the three-hour rough show for her family to watch. I felt it would never hold their attention for that length of time, but they were spellbound, and I began to realize that we had something extraordinary on tape. We aired it first on TNN, but they were just changing over their programming at the time, so when it saturated there, we took it to PAX-TV. It showed well there and was still selling, but a typical project tapers off, so we figured we had about run our course of the two years or so since its release.

David Hall had left TNN when the network dropped country music and had been consulting with GTP, so David and I were meeting with WKNO, the PBS station in Memphis, in an attempt to get PBS to air some country legends shows we had done. They didn't take the country shows, but somehow the Elvis project came up in discussion, and they expressed an interest in airing it. They first went out with twenty stations on it during a pledge drive, and it was hugely successful. It's been airing during almost every pledge drive period on PBS for the past three years and is one of their most successful offerings of all time.

We had so much success with the Elvis gospel documentary that it naturally led us to look around for other projects to develop in the same vein. In early 2000 Bill Gaither had taken many of his Homecoming regulars to the Cove, the Billy Graham Training Center, in the mountains around Asheville, North Carolina, to tape a special about the music that had influenced Billy Graham in his ministry. I doubt that there is a person anywhere in the world who has not been aware of Billy Graham over the past half-century. I grew up in a home where a Billy Graham telecast was never missed. To me Billy Graham represented Christianity as it should be. His devotion, integrity, and his simple Christian message appealed to masses as well as world leaders. When I was growing up he was someone I could always turn to for a revival of my faith and hope. When we decided to tape the special, it fell on me to coordinate the production with Dr. Graham's son, Franklin.

The taping was one of the most spiritual events of my life, and after the event was over, Bev Shea, Dr. Graham's Crusade soloist for more than fifty years, came up and put his arms on my shoulders and said, "The spirit of God was in this place tonight." It was that kind of evening. Although Dr. Graham's health prevented him from attending, his wife, Ruth, one of the most beautiful women on earth, was with us, as was Cliff Barrows, also a fifty-plus-year veteran of the Billy Graham Evangelistic Association. And the entire Graham organization seemed pleased with the two-part special that resulted.

In the course of staging the production, we had come to value our relationship with Franklin and his executive assistant, Donna Toney, and have stayed in fairly regular contact with them. The Gaither Vocal Band, Bill Gaither's quartet, appeared on almost all the Billy Graham crusades of the past five years.

Barry and I were meeting one day, and I suggested that we approach the BGEA about doing a documentary on the life of Billy Graham. Although Billy Graham was one of the most recognizable figures on the face of the earth, no documentary on his life had ever been sanctioned by BGEA. We were both aware that Billy Graham numbered several U.S. presidents among his close associates, not to mention world leaders, so he and the association could have their pick of any news organization or production company on earth to record the story of his life. But "can't" is not a word in my vocabulary, so I said, "Why don't we just call and ask them?" Barry gave me the green light to call.

When I presented the idea to Franklin, he asked to be given time to think about it. Within a couple of weeks, Donna Toney called and said that Franklin had approved the idea for us to proceed with the biography on Dr. Graham. After the lawyers from both sides had ironed out the details, I called on Michael Merriman again, and together we visited the Billy Graham Center Archives at Dr. Graham's alma mater, Wheaton College, where the bulk of his papers are stored. It took us four years of sorting through fifty years of footage, then conducting interviews with U.S. presidents; people all over the world; Dr. Graham's official photographer, Russ Busby; his biographer, Bill Martin; and numerous crusade staffers to get the documentary to the stage where we would present it to Franklin. When we did, they asked us to do a separate, expanded piece for BGEA to use for historical purposes.

I first met Dr. Graham backstage at a crusade where I accompanied the Gaither Vocal Band. My old Secret Service buddy, Win Lawson, was on Dr. Graham's security detail at the time, and he introduced us casually. In fact, Win and another former Secret Service agent, Toby Chandler, were both on his security detail for many years. Another time, I flew to a crusade on which the Vocal Band was performing to try to get a sound bite from Dr. Graham for the *Homecoming* special about what music had meant to his ministry. That didn't work out, but Russ Busby was backstage with us, and he pulled me aside to where Dr. Graham was seated. He told Dr. Graham, "I'd like to get a picture of you and Mr. Carter," and Dr. Graham invited me to sit beside him. He took my hand and made me feel like the most special person on earth. He was so kind and generous in spite of the fact that he was concentrating on his sermon. Many of his associate pastors told us, "When you're with Dr. Graham, you're the most important person in the world to him. He always makes you feel you're special."

If I never do anything else in my life, I'll always be grateful that I was given the opportunity to be involved in the making of this documentary. My mother never missed watching Billy Graham whenever he was on TV, so I have admired him my entire adult life but never more so than after delving into the history of his life and ministry. I always thought I knew Billy Graham, but it didn't take me long to realize just how little I really knew. The impression he had made on me was his overriding message to the world: "God loves you." Through the years we spent compiling and then editing the footage, I came to realize his crusades were only a small part of Billy Graham. His real contribution to society was the enormous impact he had on the social issues of the twentieth century, such as civil rights and the fall of Communism. I sincerely hope that the legacy of the documentary, much like Dr. Graham's legacy, will be that viewers will be compelled to become better people. That's certainly the lasting impact Billy Graham has effected on my life.

Chapter 25
The Early Years—Life in Rector

Y LIFE HAS INDEED BEEN an unusual journey. To better understand the man I became, it's important to know the person I was before my days as a Secret Service agent and my time with the Rolling Stones and beyond. Everything I did and everything I became was framed by my early life and later influenced by my belief in psychic phenomenon. To this day I am amazed that a poor farm boy from Rector, Arkansas, was able to travel the road I did.

I was born January 19, 1936, in the Snowden house, in Rector, Arkansas, to Henry Gaston Carter and Essie Faye Richardson. At the time of my birth, I had two older brothers, Donald and Richard, and an older sister, Doris. My father's parents were James Douglas Carter and Sarah Elizabeth Winkleman, whose parents, Jacob Winkleman and Katherine Brewner Winkleman, were German Jews. My mother's parents were William Drewry Richardson & Mollie Henley Balfour.

The Balfours had a history interesting enough to be worthy of description. They came to America from Scotland and settled in North Carolina. Andrew Balfour was a colonel in the Revolutionary War and, we are told, a friend of George Washington. His family apparently had some resources because he bought lots of land in North Carolina after the war. Colonel Balfour, it seems, was antagonistic to the Tories, and in 1780 he and Jacob Shepherd, another prominent Whig, were captured by the Tories. They were being transported as prisoners when the party was attacked by the revolutionaries, and they were freed. Colonel Balfour was at home on his plantation one day in 1782 when a Mr. Fanning and his son, who had plundered the Balfour home three years previously, rode up to the house on horseback. Having already been warned by a neighbor that an attack was imminent, the colonel went onto the porch to greet the men. A member of the raiding party took immediate aim at Balfour, breaking his arm. When he returned to the house, his daughter and sister threw themselves upon him, clinging in despair. Fanning and his son entered the house, tore the women away from Balfour, and shot him through the head. They were apparently never caught.

My father's history was not quite so colorful. He was the youngest boy in his family, born and raised in Nimmons, in Clay County, Arkansas, about ten miles from Rector, where I was born. His father, James, died when my father was fourteen years old, so my father went only as far as the eighth grade. He had to stay home and work the farm. His older brothers, Harry and Jim, and his older sisters, Rose and Ruby, were grown and had moved away. One sister, Renee, who was younger, remained at home. When my father got older, he settled in St. Louis to work for his brother Harry, who owned a business school. While in St. Louis, he eventually met and married my mother, but they were forced to move back to Rector when the Great Depression hit. He worked at a Kroger store in Rector until it was forced to close. After that, he sold Raleigh products, worked at the cotton gin, then the sorghum mill, essentially taking whatever work he could find. He was a laborer.

When I was just an infant, my grandmother, Sarah Winkleman Carter, sold her farm and moved to town, and we moved in with her in 1938. The house on Third Street was a big old house—but not a very good one, even in those days. My dominant memory of the house is how cold it was. It had a wood cook stove in the kitchen and a coal stove in the front room, which heated the whole house. We kept all the bedrooms closed, so all of the kids slept in the living room in the winter to stay warm.

I do remember Grandmother Carter's brother, my Uncle George Winkleman. George lived with his sister, Sarah—my grandmother—all his life. He wasn't retarded, but he had a harelip and was tongue-tied, and because of those impediments he couldn't talk very well. He lived all of his life with people thinking he was handicapped, so he never had any education. I suspect he could neither read nor write. No one went around Uncle George very much, but I used to go in his room on occasion.

Uncle George received bags of oranges from welfare, and he kept them under his bed. Being the kind man he was, he would always give me an orange. He seldom left home, preferring instead to stay in his room. Because of his impediment he drooled, so I suspect people made fun of him all his life, and that's why he didn't go into town very much. I do remember that when he died, Doctor Futrell, the town physician, came to the house to pronounce him dead. It was customary for dead bodies to lie in state in the house, and I have a vivid memory of the casket remaining in the living room until the funeral.

Our neighborhood was full of kids—there must have been twenty or so. For entertainment, we liked to shoot marbles and have rubber gun wars. Back then you could whittle out a gun from a board and notch it. Then you'd stretch the rubber—made out of old, discarded inner tubes from tires—from those notches. When you got ready to shoot somebody, you just took your thumb and flipped the rubber off that notch and knocked the dickens out of whichever kid you hit.

I have few memories of my childhood until I was about five or six years old and started school.

In the '40s, in rural Arkansas, classes were split up so one-half of each grade attended school only half a day. I was in the morning class, so I went home before lunch and could play in the afternoon. My first grade teacher, Mrs. Maude McBride, was a firm disciplinarian, and I got my hand slapped many times for acting up in class. I was always mischievous—forever talking or cutting up.

I think I misbehaved partly because of my size. I was always small, and because we had few material things, I developed an inferiority complex early in life. We had a 1928 Chevy, a cold house, and few clothes, and I always felt inferior because we had so little. Even though no one had much in those days, it seemed everybody else had more clothes than I did. I don't know how old I was before I had more than one pair of shoes—probably in high school. Mostly my clothes were hand-me-downs from my older brothers.

When I was seven years old, Grandmother Carter sold her house and moved to live with her oldest daughter, my Aunt Nellie Raethe, in East St. Louis, Illinois. We rented a house at the edge of town called the Parrish house, which was in a peach orchard. About a month after we moved in, my baby sister, Carol, was born. I walked to school, probably about two-and-a-half miles, but everybody walked to school in those days. We walked to school and then walked home for lunch, hurrying to eat lunch before returning to school.

My best friends up until the seventh grade were Marion Futrell, who was Doctor Futrell's son, Jim Dalton, whose dad, Albert Dalton, had the hardware store in town, and George Barker, whose dad was a cotton broker. Doctor Futrell was probably one of the wealthiest men in town, and since he was a doctor he always had a nice car and house. When I was eight, in April 1944, we moved back into town into a rental house at 308 Dodd Street, known as the Dowdy house. My two older brothers worked for Elsass Creamery, so they went to work about four o'clock every morning. They worked until school time, and then went to school and back to the creamery after school. I looked up to my brothers, but they didn't have much influence on me, because they worked all of the time. Nor did my sisters influence me much. My personality is very different from any of my brothers and sisters, which could be a reason I ended up with such an unusual career path.

During World War II, Rector, like every town across America, was very patriotic. When World War II broke out, all men of draft age were called up, but because my dad was a little over the draft age, he was not affected. Practically every healthy man from eighteen to forty was drafted to serve in one branch of the armed services. It was a big occasion for us to go to the train station to see them off. Sadly, many of them would come back in caskets, and the townspeople would meet the train carrying their remains. But many of them returned as war heroes. I can still remember people dreading to see Henry Alstadt coming to their houses during the war because if he pulled up to your house in his old car bearing a small yellow envelope, you knew that your husband or son or brother had been killed. Everyone who had a relative serving in the war hung a cloth star in their window. My brother Donald joined the Navy in 1944, and I'll always remember the day that we took him to the bus station to leave for Little Rock and then to go to war. He went first to San Diego, but he never did see any combat—thank goodness—because the war was over about a year after he went in.

I wasn't the best student. I was either cutting up in class or talking or something equally as bad. I can't remember when I got my first whipping in school—I got so many, it's hard to identify the first one. I do remember, however, when I first got into serious trouble. I was in the seventh grade, and my teacher was Mrs. Lee See. She was one of my favorite teachers and turned out to be a great friend in later years. Somebody threw a paper wad and hit her while she was writing on the blackboard. Assuming it was me, she came back and hit me upside the head with her paddle. That made me so mad that I took the paddle away from her and threw it out the window. I was immediately suspended from school. My dad whipped me good when I got home. He always chose a leather strap that was used to sharpen a straight razor, and he usually whipped me until my butt was black and blue. Interestingly, when I was allowed back in school, Mrs. See actually apologized to me.

Entertainment was limited in those years. We looked forward to spending Saturday afternoons at Ford Theater, which charged a ten-cent admission for cowboy features starring Roy Rogers, Gene Autry, and Randolph Scott. We would stay at home and listen to *Amos and Andy* and *Lum and Abner* on the radio, but it was usually so hot at night that most people would stay outside on the porch until it was time to go to bed.

Looking back, I think I probably resented my parents then, especially my father. I blamed him because we were so poor, and I didn't understand why that was so. My dad had virtually no education, so he never developed any real communication skills. My parents never sat me down and asked, Can I help you, or Can I give you some advice? My mother got up at five o'clock every morning, fixed a meal, washed, and ironed. My dad was off to work early and came home late and tired. There was never really any communication among any of the seven of us. I wondered many times about that when I was young, and I blamed my parents. But I think I took most of my anger and disappointment out on my father. It was not until I was a young adult that I realized he did the best he could. He was not a learned person, so the only way he knew to deal with anything was to teach us discipline and teach us how to work. I even rebelled against that.

My parents never gave me any money—ever. When she wasn't working in the house, my mother would pick cotton. When I was a baby my mother would take me to the fields with her. I would ride on her cotton sack until I was old enough to have a little sack of my own. Picking cotton was the only way anyone made any money. If you picked cotton in the fall, then you made enough money to last you through the winter. You could also chop cotton or pick up some seasonal farm work and make a little money to get you through the spring. I learned from an early age that if I didn't work at one of those jobs, I wouldn't have any money.

There came a point when I rebelled against working, taking the position that my parents owed it to me to give me some money, which, of course they didn't. I would stage my own one-person strike. It didn't do me any good, though, so I would finally give up and go back to work. If I didn't work, I wouldn't have any money to go to the movies with the other kids. If I didn't work, I wouldn't have any money at all. I could strike all I wanted to, but it wouldn't get me anywhere. Nobody ever paid any attention to my strikes, so I didn't hurt anybody but myself. I finally figured out that you only got new clothes if you worked and made money to buy them.

By the time I was in the ninth or tenth grade in high school, I had become very popular: I guess everybody thought I was cute. I've been told I was a good-looking kid, plus I had a good personality. I was not active in sports, because I was so small; it wouldn't take much for bigger boys to whip me. But I was kind of the cool guy—the ringleader of sorts of whatever mischief was going on in school. The teachers would look to me first when something happened because they naturally assumed I was behind it. Hence: Get Carter!

When I was a sophomore in high school, Larry Elmore moved to town. His mother shipped him down from Detroit to live with his grandparents because he had gotten into some serious trouble up there involving gangs and fighting. About the same time, Jim Parham moved to Rector from California to live with his grandparents. Parham had been born in Rector but moved with his parents to Modesto, California. He wanted to finish school in Rector, so his parents sent him back. I remember him as being a guy nobody wanted to mess with. So two tough guys moved to town, and right away they became my best friends. Elmore was just mean, and both of them would fight anyone. All the guys who had been mean to me through the years now had to answer to Elmore or Parham. So now I was a big part of this bunch of young rebels.

My grades had begun to suffer, and it was about this same time that my older brother Richard had joined the Air Force. I started thinking that all I wanted to do was to get out of high school and join the service—either the Marines or the Army. I wanted to join the service because it was a way out of Rector. People went off to the service and came back dressed in snappy uniforms, and everyone looked up to them.

For the most part, I found my high school years to be fairly boring and uneventful with the exception of a few incidents. The most vivid incident that stands out in my mind today was when the Arkansas Education Commission, which supervised and accredited schools, announced that they were coming to our school to make their annual inspection. Elmore, Parham, and I decided the time was right to create a little havoc. The school janitor had this great big old brass bell down in the furnace room that he would ring when we had fire drills. During these drills, all the students had to evacuate the school. The three of us decided that we needed to set this fire alarm off right when the accreditors were there. Everyone would assume it was a real fire, and pandemonium would break out. We had timed it perfectly. Elmore actually rang the bell, and he, Parham, and I all had different escape routes. I was to go to the band room and act as if nothing had happened. When we set the fire alarm off, everyone thought it was a real fire because no note had been passed around from the superintendent indicating there would be a fire drill that day. Kids were jumping out windows, the superintendent's secretary was throwing records out the window, and it was total pandemonium—just like we envisioned it would be. The volunteer fire department even came. Apparently Elmore was seen by one of the hall monitors, unfortunately, so we were immediately caught and expelled from school.

One of our pranks caused us to be hauled before the entire student body and paddled. Talk about humiliating! Then there was the cherry bomb incident. Jim McKenzie was the superintendent, and every morning when he got to school, he went to the men's room to take a leak before he went up to his office. Just like clockwork—every morning. This bathroom where Mr. McKenzie conducted his business was all concrete, and it echoed so badly that when you peed in there it sounded like a river flowing.

Some of us boys decided to set off a cherry bomb in that bathroom. We experimented for days with a cigarette butt to see how long it would take for the butt to burn down enough to ignite the fuse. One of the guys—we selected the son of the school board chairman; he had never been in trouble so no one would suspect him—put the cherry bomb in the bathroom. I was shooting pool in Gordon's Pool Hall—playing hooky—and the others were somewhere else, but we all had alibis. Well, Mr. McKenzie walked in, and that cherry bomb went off at the exact perfect time. We were the first people they came looking for. Richard Gordon told them that I was down at his place shooting pool, and I, of course, got in trouble for skipping class, but at least I had an alibi. They never found out who was responsible. Twenty years later, the principal asked me about that incident, and I owned up to it and told him how we did it. He really got a charge out of it.

And, of course, there was the time we burned a house down, which I've already described.

I always had a job; I shined shoes, worked at the food market sacking groceries or in the meat department, and I swept out the skating rink. My brothers were great skaters, and by the time I was ten years old, I was also a whiz on roller skates. Of course, back then that was a big deal. Every town had a skating rink, and you would go from town to town skating and trying to impress the girls. Also, if you were really good on skates, nobody could mess with you because you could easily trip someone. I used to do all kinds of tricks on roller skates, but that was about my only real athletic accomplishment.

When I got out of high school, I had not really dated anyone to speak of—I'd never even gone steady with a girl and never thought I was in love. During the '50s, we certainly had not experienced the sexual revolution that would emerge in the late '60s. Most of the nice girls didn't allow you to do anything. So I was still pretty naïve about the opposite sex until much later.

Chapter 26
Dress Blues

AFTER I JOINED THE AIR FORCE, I whizzed through basic training and was assigned to Keesler Air Force Base in Biloxi, Mississippi, to attend electronics school for radar systems. Frankly, I was surprised that I was chosen for that school because my high school grades weren't all that great, especially my math grades. I had a ball in Keesler, though, and I thought I'd died and gone to heaven.

Keesler was down on the Gulf Coast and was a beautiful base. Biloxi was a fun town with great beaches. At least it used to be before Hurricane Katrina virtually destroyed it this year. There was an exclusive girl's college in Gulfport; we'd slip over there occasionally, and we'd go to New Orleans when we had weekend passes. It was really the first time I had been away from home for such a long period, completely on my own. I got three meals and a regular paycheck. I didn't have any expenses to speak of, so I could spend all of my money on entertainment. Right away I was convinced I was going to make a career out of the military—I loved it that much. Since the Korean War had ended, everyone seemed to be breathing a sigh of relief, and there were no other impending crises on the horizon.

In 1954 we were concerned about Russian bomber attacks, so we had an air defense network of radar systems all around the country to protect us against incoming Soviet bombers. The ADC was a new command in the Air Force—it was early warning radar to detect bombers approaching the United States. There were two lines of defense: the DEW line, or distant early warning, which ran across Greenland, Iceland, and northern Canada, and a second defense line that ran across the northern United States and the Canadian border. There were probably 125 men on these little radar sites.

A radar site would be located on about three acres and consisted of a non-commissioned officer's club for entertainment, a chow hall, a couple of barracks and an officers' barracks. Out of the 125 or so men on the site, about half a dozen would be officers. There were two radar towers—one to detect the distance of an airplane and one to detect the height. When I graduated from radar school, I was sent to the radar site in Wadena, Minnesota, and then I was transferred to Iceland.

Before going to Iceland, the Air Force sent me first to the Brighton Beach Naval Station, near New York City, where I spent thirty days for processing—psychological testing and screening. I'd never been in New York City before, and I was awestruck at my initial glimpse of the first really big city—other than St. Louis and New Orleans—I had ever seen. This was the mid-'50s, so the subways were clean and safe, and it was a wonderful place. A bunch of us guys would take the subway down to Times Square where they had those dime-a-dance places. You could buy tickets for ten cents and dance with pretty girls. I loved it. Girls! I'd meet a girl in the park, and I didn't even have to ask her out—they were all so forward. The girls were mostly ethnic—Italian, Polish, or some other European nationality. They weren't looking for sex or a serious involvement, just someone to go with them to the movies or dancing. Boy, I had the biggest time. New York, New York, New York—wow! Then came reality in the form of Iceland.

I left New York and flew to Iceland on an old DC-6, four-engine military transport plane. It was about a twelve-hour flight, and that old plane vibrated so badly that when I got there I could hardly feel the ground. I arrived at Keflovick AFB, near Reykjavik, the capital city, but I was there for only a few days before they put me on a C-47 and flew me to the other side of the island, on the edge of the second largest glacier in the world.

About thirty-five guys worked at this little radar site—there wasn't even a town, but it was our nearest point to the Soviet Union. It sat on a rocky shore on the southeast corner of Iceland, which would have been the most direct line for bombers coming from the Soviet Union. We got our mail, food, and beer by boat or plane. If the weather was bad, a plane didn't always have enough space for everything, so we had to vote whether or not we wanted mail or beer. We always voted for beer. We were totally isolated at this radar site. We'd get off duty and go to the NCO club and drink until it was time to go to bed. Then we'd get up, pull our shift again, and go back to the NCO club.

There was no television because this was in the days before satellites. We weren't allowed off-site. Contrary to what the name sounds like, Iceland has a moderate climate—much like Tennessee. But when it snows, it snows a lot. In the summertime we had six months of daylight, and in the winter we had six months of darkness. In the summertime, we'd have softball games at ten o'clock at night. About twelve-thirty or one o'clock in the morning, dusk would settle in; then the sun would rise again in about an hour. When it was dark, we'd have about an hour of daybreak, and then it was dark again. We were at the very foot of the glacier, but we had to get permission from the Icelandic government if we wanted to explore it, so I never did. One thing I realized while I was in Iceland—I need the presence of women in my life. I don't necessarily mean for sex—because that wasn't an issue at the time—but just the softness a woman's presence brings. If not, I get downright ornery.

On one occasion I was given the responsibility of taking a confidential pouch into Reykjavik, about 150 miles away. It was kind of a reward to get off-site for a few days, but I had a pouch handcuffed to me. I was flying on an old Icelandic Airlines DC-3, and I was the only person on the flight who spoke any real English. We hadn't been in the air long when the pilot announced that we were encountering bad weather and would have to set down in a little village. By the time we landed, we were in the middle of a blizzard. There is so much moisture in the air in Iceland that when it snowed, it would snow three to five feet easily. Well, we were isolated and unable to fly for two or three days. They put me in a little building in the village with only a coal stove for heat and absolutely nothing to do. Hardly anyone spoke English, but the flight attendants would come by to see me, and the village people would bring me food. I hadn't even been able to communicate with the Air Force to let them know where I was. Plus, I had to keep that pouch handcuffed to me the entire time. When the weather cleared and they were able to clear the runway, we flew on to Reykjavik.

Because we were the first line of defense, we used to have our own B-57 spy planes fly over us on occasion; we'd pick them up on radar. The Russians used to bring submarines right up to the radar site and photograph us. They were brazen about it and didn't care if we saw them. The Navy would alert us when a sub would be in the area, and when we'd pick it up on radar, we'd call an alert and issue weapons and have everyone take a defensive position. We never knew what weapon we'd be issued, and half the time we wouldn't have been trained on the weapon we were issued. It was tense when the subs came around, but it was more or less a game to them.

I had been growing physically—putting muscle on bone—and when I got to Iceland I began to work out because there wasn't much else to do. By now I was an Airman First Class and was made NCOIC, or non-commissioned officer-in-charge, of the maintenance section. I really did well in the military, so I was getting promotions on a regular basis. I spent a fairly uneventful year up there, and I remember thinking then that it was a year of my life pretty much wasted. But as I look back on it later, I realize it did two things for me. First, I did make an important decision about my life during that year—I decided a career in the military was not for me.

When I left Iceland, the Air Force sent me to finish out my tour of duty in Yuma, Arizona, where I spent a year. When I arrived in Arizona from Iceland, in addition to being physically stronger, I had shot up to six feet tall and weighed 195 pounds. Being out in the desert in Arizona was another new culture for me. Again, I had never seen anything like the desert, and it was a far cry from Iceland, but I had a great time out there.

During my time in Arizona, someone told me that you could get out of the Air Force ninety days early if you enrolled in college. I was coming up for a promotion to staff sergeant, and my superiors were trying to get me to stay in the service. But

I decided to go back home and enroll in Arkansas State College and forego my promotion, although I was told I could join the reserves and still get my promotion there. I wanted out of the service early, but I never intended to go to college. I was really planning to apply to college, hope to get accepted, and make the Air Force give me a ninety-day early release.

Chapter 27
The College Years

I MUSTERED OUT OF THE SERVICE in 1957 and immediately went to Jonesboro, Arkansas. I had to actually register at Arkansas State—which I did. Then I thought, I'm here, and I'm getting $135 a month from the GI Bill, so I'll just go to class. When I came back from Iceland, my brother-in-law and sister, Stan and Doris King, lived in Detroit, where he was with Ford Motor Company. Stan had arranged for me to buy a used '56 six-cylinder Ford. I started going to class and realized that it wasn't all that bad, and since I was doing all right in my classes, I decided I'd finish the six-week summer term and then I'd split. I thought about going to St. Louis and getting a job with the police department because most of my relatives lived there.

Instead, I stayed the first six weeks at Arkansas State and took English and another course. Imagine my surprise when I made a B in English, and I also made a pretty good grade in the other course. My high school English teacher, Mrs. Castner, had pounded enough English in me that I guess it stuck. And then there were all these girls! I really wasn't dating anybody, but I was a veteran, and at that time that was a pretty cool thing to be. All these guys were coming back from the Korean War, so there was a Veterans Club on campus that later became a fraternity. Veterans were looked up to on campus, so I was a pretty cool dude. Our intramural team used to beat the hell out of the fraternities because we were older and tougher. After doing so well in the first summer session, I decided to go to the next six-week summer session. So I enrolled again, and again made good grades. I was having a good time, so I stayed in college.

In the meantime, I had begun dating a girl in Rector, Jan Hamra, whose dad had a store in town—a dry goods store. She was just finishing high school when we started dating. I was dating other girls, too, but Jan and I settled into a serious relationship, and on July 24, 1959, we were married. We lived in a little duplex in Rector, and I commuted the thirty-nine miles to Jonesboro for classes.

Classes had just ended in May of that year, when Dan McBride, who ran the Irby Funeral Home, called me and said he was short-handed because one of his undertakers had quit. He wanted to know if I would be interested in working for him. I assumed all I'd have to do was drive the ambulance, and I thought that would be pretty cool, so I agreed. Little did I know that I was also going to assist the undertaker.

When Dan hired me, he explained that Doyne "Digger" Webb and I would switch off shifts—twenty-four hours on and twenty-four hours off. I told him I didn't know what that had to do with me, since all I was going to do was drive the ambulance. He quickly set me straight. While that was technically true, if someone died on my shift I had to pick up the body. I guess I hadn't stopped to think about that. The funeral home had two undertakers—Dan and Digger Webb—so when I was on duty or on call and someone died, Dan would embalm the body and I would assist him. I didn't know anything about embalming, although I soon learned. Here I was, twenty-two years old, and I was driving the ambulance for the funeral home. Back then, all the funeral homes operated ambulance services—there were no paramedics or EMTs or ambulances as we know them today. Up to this time, I had only seen a dead body once or twice. I had vague memories of Uncle George lying in state at home when he died, and I remember going to the funeral for my grandmother. But I had never had an up-close-and-personal experience with a corpse. Because I dreaded the thought of that so badly, I remember vividly the first call I got to pick up a dead body. Dan called me about three o'clock in the morning to go with him to Corning to pick up a body. I swear, nobody ever dies during the day. This guy was thrown out of a car during a traffic accident on a bridge over the Black River. His head hit a concrete post on a bridge, and he was killed instantly. We picked his body up at the funeral home in Corning and headed back to the funeral home in Rector. We put him on a slab, and Dan started to embalm him. I was terrified—I was so damn scared of the body and the whole process. The man's head was in pretty bad shape, so I don't think I slept or ate anything for several days after that.

But I finally grew accustomed to working with dead bodies, and it was a good experience for me. I learned about respecting people when they're dead as well as comforting the grieving families. I learned a lot about human nature and the way people deal with the loss of a loved one. It was a maturing experience for me as well as the beginning of the development of a little philosophical bent of mind.

I had an experience that summer that involved a very pregnant woman about my own age. The woman was in labor, and I got the call to take her to the hospital in Paragould. We had just gotten to Marmaduke, which is only about six miles into the almost twenty-mile trip, when she started screaming hysterically, telling me to stop the ambulance, that she was having the baby. I stopped the ambulance and went back to check on her. Her water had broken, and she told me I was going to have to deliver the baby. All she had on was a nightgown with no underwear. She pulled that nightgown up around her waist, and I almost fainted.

I flew back around to the front of the ambulance, jumped in the driver's seat, and tore up the road getting her to the hospital. There was no way I was delivering that baby—I'd never even seen anything like that before. We didn't have radios or cell phones, so I couldn't even let the hospital know we were coming. I pulled up at the hospital yelling for help, and here was this woman, bleeding and screaming with the baby coming any minute. I was white as a sheet. My cousin Nareen Bunch was a nurse at the hospital, and she and the other staff members got a real charge out of that incident.

I hated my job at the funeral home when I took it, but I made the most of it. Over the years I had a number of jobs I didn't like, but I always made the most of every opportunity. I resented my father for making me work, but as I matured I realized that the most important legacy my father left me was a great work ethic. I can do just about anything. To this day, I'm proud of the fact that I never left a job—no matter how bad it was—that they wouldn't have taken me back if need be. I could be on the street tomorrow and get a job doing anything. I ended up having a pretty good time working for Irby's—plus, they were paying me $250 a month, which was good pay for Rector. At the end of the summer, Dan thought I was doing a great job, so he encouraged me to become an undertaker. He really wanted me to go to embalming school and make a career of it, but I passed. I stayed at Irby a year, worked on 110 bodies, and have some vivid recollections of some of them. I remember one lady dying in a church pew down in Marmaduke. She was a really big woman, and it was raining the night she died. I had to get the men in the congregation to help me load her in the ambulance. Well, she was so heavy we all mired up in mud, and it took eight or ten of us to carry the corpse. I got her back to the funeral home about midnight, but at that hour I couldn't find anybody to help me unload her. I got Finis "Fat" Young, the night marshal, to come over and help me, but we couldn't get her out of the ambulance. We had to rally some citizens to come down to the funeral home and help us unload this gal and get her on the slab.

Another time I remember a girl coming into the funeral home to pay on her burial insurance. Digger and I were hanging out with nothing to do but wait for someone to die. This woman had an incredible body, and Digger was a great admirer of female anatomy. After she left, we made some interesting comments to each other about her anatomy and what one might do with that sort of thing. At the time, my sister Doris and her husband Stan were in town and staying at my folks' house. We had planned to make homemade ice cream and cook hamburgers on the grill that night.

This girl, along with her husband and a bunch of friends, was going fishing the afternoon of the day she came into the funeral home. Back in the '50s and '60s, all the businesses in Rector shut down on Wednesday afternoons in the summertime. I was at home when I got an emergency call to get right to the funeral home. I was told to get the ambulance and head toward Boydsville, where there had been a wreck. When I got to the scene, seven people had been killed in a head-on collision, and this girl was one of them. We had to embalm her the same day we were admiring her. I had been there quite a while working on those bodies, and you can imagine that it was a bloody mess. When I got home that night, I still had blood on my shirt, and my family was repulsed. They were put out with me that I came home to get ice cream without washing the blood from my clothes, but I hadn't even noticed. I had gone from being terrified of dead bodies that first day on the job to eating meals in the embalming room while we were working on the bodies.

Digger loved to play tricks on me. I came in one morning and the secretary told me we had gotten a body overnight and asked me to go turn off the light in the embalming room. The bodies were always covered with a sheet, and as I walked into the room, the body rose up and groaned. I nearly fainted. It was Digger lying on the slab.

Eventually I told Dan I didn't want to be an undertaker, but instead I wanted to go back to college. He was disappointed, of course, but understood why I needed to complete my college education. I enrolled back in Arkansas State to finish my two remaining years. I was at the point now where I had to declare a major, and I was thinking about majoring in political science and pursuing a career in politics. But I had an economics professor—he was head of the economics department—who talked me into majoring in economics. This led to the offer of a scholarship in economics at SMU, in Dallas, which then led me to law school and then to my becoming a Secret Service agent.

I could never have planned all the steps that led me in what turned out to be a most unusual direction. But in looking back, it now all seems so natural.

Chapter 28
The Psychic Years

URING THE TIME I WAS IN the Secret Service, in the early 1960s, Ruth Montgomery was a senior White House correspondent for the old Independent News Service. Prior to that she had been the White House correspondent for Knight News Service. She was considered the "dean" of the female press corps and, as such, was highly respected in news circles as well as among the White House staff. I didn't know Ruth personally, but I knew who she was.

A decade after leaving the Secret Service, in 1974, I was in Los Angeles on business for the Rolling Stones. I was staying at the Beverly Wilshire Hotel and was browsing in the lobby bookstore when I noticed a book titled *A Search for the Truth* by Ruth Montgomery. I picked it up and, in reading the dust jacket, found it was a book about psychic phenomenon. I recognized the name of the author and wondered if it was the same Ruth Montgomery from INS. I kept reading and discovered that it was indeed. I remember thinking it odd that such a highly respected newswoman would be writing a book on that particular subject. The two seemed a little incongruous.

I had a strange experience when I was still in elementary school. I was sitting in class one day, daydreaming, when I had the oddest feeling that I had lived before. I had never before experienced anything like that, but from that point on, I felt like I had had another life and I am reincarnated, although at that time I didn't know what that meant. Now, that was a strange experience for a farm boy from small-town Arkansas and not something I could readily share with anyone. We were reared in the Methodist Church. My mother went to church, but my dad hardly ever did. He worked all the time, so if he had any time off, he opted to go fishing rather than to go to church. Even though my mother was a faithful churchgoer, I didn't have any real religious training. Nevertheless, I've almost always enjoyed a healthy spiritual life. Since I knew from an early age that I had lived past lives, I had always had an interest in the paranormal. And because I also recognized the author, I bought the book. That first book intrigued me so much that I bought several more of Ruth's books over the next few years.

In 1982 I was living in Nashville when I received a call from a longtime friend in Arkansas, telling me that an old buddy, Ronnie Hawkins, who was known as the Father of Rockabilly Music, was returning to Arkansas. Ronnie had been living

256

in Toronto for some time and was booked for a gig at a popular Little Rock club, Cajuns' Wharf. He told me that poultry king Don Tyson was throwing a party for Hawkins to celebrate his homecoming and wanted all Ronnie's old friends to show up. I had a trip scheduled to Jamaica for Keith Richards, and it was impossible for me to change my plans.

Not long after that, Hawkins himself called me. There was a possibility, he told me, that he might be coming to Nashville later to play at Cajuns' Wharf there. He said if that happened he'd call me because he had a girl singer from Canada he wanted me to meet. I told him I would really look forward to seeing him and meeting her. I have to admit I was lying to him because after working in the music business for only a short time, I already had absolutely no interest in meeting a female singer.

I forgot about Hawkins until about three weeks later when I noticed he was booked at Cajuns' in Nashville. I knew I'd hear from him sooner or later because Cajuns' owner, Bruce Anderson, was also an old friend from Arkansas, and I always went out to the Wharf when Bruce was in town. Hawk called me as soon as he got to town, but I had a conflict the first couple of nights and didn't go. Then Bruce called me and said he was having a reception for Hawkins before the show and insisted I come because everyone in the music business was invited, and he knew Hawkins wanted me there.

I went to the reception, along with about two hundred other people. I had parked myself in a corner of the room, visiting with my friends Don Light and Jack Brumley. Our corner was the farthest point from the entrance. I happened to look over toward the entrance and saw a young lady enter the room accompanied by a young man. She and I immediately made eye contact, and she walked straight over to me and introduced herself as Amy, from Toronto, Canada. She told us she was singing with the band, so I knew this must be the girl singer Hawk wanted me to meet. When I introduced myself, she said Hawk had told her about me, and I confessed that he had also called me about her.

From that first meeting, it was as if I'd known Amy all my life, and she told me later she felt the same way. We talked for what seemed like a long time before she was dragged away by Hawkins' manager, Steve Thompson, to meet other guests. Amy eventually made her way back to me, but she was getting ready to go on stage. She asked if I would stay so we could visit more between shows.

I stayed, and we spent her break together. She then suggested I stay for the second show, and I agreed. When she finished for the night, I drove her back to her hotel, and the next day we had lunch together. I saw her every day and every night for the length of the engagement. For the next four years, Amy and I were together as often as we could be. I visited her in Toronto, and she stayed with me until she rented an apartment two blocks from me in Nashville. There was a spiritual connection between us that we both recognized. I had never experienced anything like it before.

After completion of the 1981 Rolling Stones tour, Bill Zysblat, who is also David Bowie's business manager, asked if I would assist on some projects for Bowie's 1983 *Serious Moonlight* Tour. I was in New York at the Parker Meridien Hotel for several weeks while I negotiated the HBO Special for the Bowie tour. Amy had come down from Toronto to be with me. Zysblat had also asked me to secure a book deal for Bowie, and I had successfully completed the deal with Jim Fitzgerald, a senior editor at Doubleday. To celebrate the deal, Jim had invited me to have dinner with him, and I invited Amy to come along.

Amy and I already believed we had known each other from previous lives; she had read the Ruth Montgomery books and was infatuated with Ruth and her writings. During dinner, Jim asked me to bring him some other book deals, and I laughed and told him I wasn't a literary agent and didn't know of any other book proposals. Amy spoke up and asked me why I didn't do a book on Ruth Montgomery. I told her I didn't know Ruth and wouldn't know how to reach her, but even if I did I wouldn't have the nerve to contact her.

Jim was aware of Ruth's successful record in selling books and was very interested in having me make contact with her. Amy also kept pushing the idea. The Bowie tour was completed, and Jim and I continued to stay in contact about the Bowie book. Amy kept asking if we had done anything about a book with Ruth because she wanted to meet her and talk with her about psychic phenomenon. Months went by, and in 1984 I would mention Ruth to Jim again, but neither of us knew what to do. Amy's persistence caused me to suggest to Fitzgerald that he get her address from her last publisher and write her, proposing a book deal.

On July 13, 1984, I sent Jim a memo with the following message: *The spirits won't leave me alone until you call Ruth.* On August 24, 1984, I received a copy of a letter Jim had written Ruth:

> In the wake of the recent Shirley Maclaine book, it occurs to me as an editor that the book-buying public is still very intrigued by spiritual contact. Your personal experiences, Ruth, are perhaps the most credible of all those who have made spiritual contact. I guess what I'm trying to say here is that I'd be very interested in a book by you on your personal reminiscences with the spiritual life. As a successful author, you have undoubtedly been approached many, many times to do a similar type of book, but I'd like to throw my hat in the ring and perhaps come to Washington and talk to you about it . . . .

The letter showed a carbon copy to William Carter. I called Jim and said I was surprised he showed a copy to me since Ruth wouldn't have any idea who I was. However, he received a call from Ruth after she received his letter, asking him to come to Washington for a meeting. Jim called and requested that I meet him in DC and accompany him. When I asked if he had mentioned me to Ruth, he said he had not. I pointed out that I felt like a fool going to the meeting with nothing to contribute but agreed to accompany him anyway.

Ruth and her husband, Bob, lived in an exclusive building adjacent to the Chinese Embassy on Connecticut Avenue NW. We arrived and were greeted at the door by Ruth. She shook Jim's hand, and then Jim turned to me and said, "This is Bill Carter." Instead of taking my hand, she hugged me as if we were old friends. I was stunned!

We sat in Ruth's parlor while Jim discussed the book. Ruth then turned to me. "What do you think the book should be?" she asked. I said, "I'm just here with Jim; I don't have anything to do with Doubleday." "But the book was your idea," she replied, "so tell us what you think it should be about."

Since I had been asked directly, I had no trouble voicing my opinion. "I think the book should be about your life and communication with the spiritual world. It could include summaries of your previous books and end with predictions for the coming years." Ruth liked the idea and agreed to proceed to a deal with Doubleday.

We stayed with her for an hour or so and then had a couple of martinis before departing. As we were leaving, Ruth told me she wanted me to handle the contract for her and to coordinate the development of the project with Doubleday. She gave me another big hug as we left. I was shocked by her total trust and acceptance of me.

Upon returning to Nashville, I called Ruth. "I must tell you, I can't get over the trust you've placed in me," I said. "I'm just an unknown lawyer to you; no one trusts lawyers, and here you are turning your business over to me without questions."

She replied, "Oh, honey, I've known you forever—we had many former lives together, and I know you well."

Needless to say, I was taken aback. I couldn't wait to tell Amy, and I promised her I would take her to meet Ruth later.

Over the next few months Ruth communicated with her spiritual guides about me, and I've reproduced some of those reports here. Ruth communicated with her guides and did automatic writing by sitting at a typewriter and going into a trance after typing out questions. In trance, she would receive their answers in typewritten form. In the beginning, I was skeptical and gave her what I thought to be trick questions, intending to mislead the guides to see if they would provide correct information. I didn't tell Ruth about Amy at first but just said I was seeing a girl in Nashville and wondered if it would be a serious relationship. The guides replied that they saw a serious relationship with a girl from the North and that we were soul mates from many former lives together. I later gave them Amy's name and asked for any specific information. I share with you some of their replies. I found all their answers to be accurate, especially since none of the information had been shared with Ruth prior to her trance.

For instance, they told her that I was ". . . an English gentleman in his lifetime in the latter part of the last century." The report continued, "He was Amy's husband then, and they had a country place in Essex where he rode to the hounds and she did also. They were extremely devoted, but he died rather early in that lifetime and she married again, although not as happily as with him. In another lifetime, in early America, they were a frontier couple who moved westward from New England and settled in the territory that now encompasses Oklahoma and Arkansas. They worked hard, had a number of children, and were devoted to each other and to them but were so busy that they had little time to express that devotion outwardly. It was inevitable that they should be drawn together in this lifetime because both felt such strong ties to the other."

Ruth's book was completed in 1985, and *Herald of a New Age* was released by Doubleday in 1986. My friendship with Ruth and her husband continued through the years, and I visited them frequently in Washington and at their other home in Naples, Florida, where they were living when Bob died. I felt a closeness to and love for Ruth that I have rarely experienced. I compare it to the closeness of a mother and son or other close relative or lifelong friend. I am certain we have known each other in past lives and will cross paths again in future lives.

In 1985 I was in my office in Nashville one day when I received a phone call from a young woman in another city, whom I will call Sue. She asked my advice about some personal problems, and after several minutes of intimate conversation, I stopped her and inquired if I knew her. She said I didn't, so I then asked how she came to call me and reveal such intimate, personal problems to me. She said a good friend of hers and mine, Pat Wilson, recommended that she call me. Although I didn't say as much to Sue, I didn't know a Pat Wilson, but Sue and I talked for more than an hour.

As the conversation was coming to a close, I asked when she had spoken with Pat last, and she said she had spoken to her just prior to calling me. I told her that I had misplaced Pat's number and asked her to give it to me so I could call and say hello. It was a 615 area code, indicating it was near Nashville, and I immediately dialed the number. This was well before phones were equipped with caller ID, but when Pat answered the phone, she answered by saying, "Hello, Bill." I asked if I knew her, and she replied with what was becoming a familiar reply, "Yes—not yet in this lifetime, but in many past lives." Pat and I talked at length and continued to talk often on the telephone.

One day she told me she was coming to Nashville on the following Sunday. She would be staying in a hotel and wanted to meet me. I told her I would meet her in the lobby of a large hotel and asked Amy if she would like to go with me. I didn't ask Pat to describe herself, although from her voice I thought she was probably in her fifties. On the way to the hotel, Amy and I tried to guess what she would look like. The one thing we didn't guess was how many women would be in the lobby of that hotel. The hotel was hosting a convention, and there were at least five hundred people in the lobby. I kept looking around for Pat, but I didn't see anyone I thought fit my mental picture of her, until Amy pointed to a woman sitting on a bench in the hallway, surrounded by several people. She had a feeling that was Pat. I laughed, thinking there was little chance that Amy could pick her out that easily without even having spoken to her. But I walked up to the woman, and she immediately said, "You're Bill Carter." It was Pat Wilson, and we renewed a long past-life relationship.

Pat was absolutely tuned into both Amy's and my mental spiritual frequencies. She would call me when she knew I was feeling bad, as well as to tell me what Amy was thinking. I was in a hotel in LA on one occasion when I received a call from Pat wanting to know what was wrong with me; she sensed I had a serious problem. I told her she was mistaken because I was feeling great, was happy, and had no problems to speak of. Pat, however, was convinced that she had not made a mistake and was dumfounded that I was in such great spirits. I assured her I was fine, and I was, until I phoned Amy later, and she told me she was concerned over a lot of personal matters and was a bit depressed. I later told Pat about Amy and she replied, "That's it! I was picking up on Amy instead of you."

When Pat was ill she would call me to talk, saying she needed to feed off my positive energy. She did this regularly until her final days, when she was unable to call. I prayed for Pat through those days and still pray that God has blessed her soul and advanced her to a higher spiritual level.

In the meantime, Amy had decided that in order to realize her ambition of being a successful pop songwriter, she needed to move to LA, where that industry was headquartered. We also had been having serious conversations about my possible conversion to Judaism. That was not something I would consider, nor did I want to move to California. I did a lot of soul-searching during this time, as I'm sure Amy did, but I finally came to the conclusion that I could continue to love Amy without being with her in this lifetime. I did the only thing I could: I told her that I would always love her, but she had to follow her bliss.

After Amy moved to California, Pat called me on a Saturday morning to tell me I would receive a letter from Amy and what it would contain. I received a letter that very afternoon, and it said exactly what Pat predicted it would. It was not a negative letter, but she wrote about problems she was having. She ended the letter by professing her eternal love for me. Pat confirmed what Ruth had already told us—that Amy and I had been together in many past lives and would probably always be together in the lives of our souls. Pat had told me that in this life we had come together to confirm our eternal love for each other but that we would probably not marry this time. She indicated that marriage in every physical life is not necessarily important; that sometimes we make contact, but because of karma we may need to separate in order to overcome a past-life mistake. In my previous life, I had left Amy by death at an early age.

My treasured friend, John Harricharan, a psychic I also came to know during this time, tuned into that lifetime and related the following about Amy:

> It seemed like it was a recent lifetime. When we say "recent," it must be understood that in a timeless Universe, "recent" could be a few hundred years or a few years ago. You were riding into a small town, leading

a band of horsemen. This appeared to be in Europe, perhaps the border area of what is now called France. You are the leader of the group and they followed you without question.

You were passing through that town (actually, it was more of a village than a town) and the inhabitants greeted you with songs and flowers and food. You and your soldiers decided to rest for a day or so. The recent battle had been fierce, but as always, you won a brilliant victory. Now it was time for a short rest as you prepared to march forward into other battles. You were quite a commander—young, strong, handsome, and powerful.

Among the villagers was a beautiful, young woman (this is the person you call Amy in your present lifetime). She brought you food and drink and spent that first night with you. There was an immediate past-life recognition. It was as if you had known each other forever. And, yes, you both knew each other well. You were together for long and short periods through many lifetimes. This may seem strange, but the two of you fell deeply in love. Yet, duty called and you knew you'd have to leave her to go on another campaign in a day or two. You promised to return, but you never did.

Amy was heartbroken because you did not return. She thought you had abandoned her. What she didn't know was that you were killed in battle and would not be able to return, at least, in that lifetime. She was left all alone to give birth to a child—your child. Both mother and child died during childbirth. You came together again in this lifetime because of a deep knowing, strong past-life memories, and a "soul-attachment." Your work together was not done. You had to reassure her in this lifetime that this bond was eternal.

Although I have met many psychics and mediums from all over the world, only a few seemed genuine to me. Psychics may or may not be tuned into your soul frequency. It is my opinion that you have to be very careful when consulting psychics; they could be trying to read you, but are instead picking up the frequency of someone else. This is what happened when Pat called me thinking something was wrong, but she was reading Amy instead. I would caution anyone to be skeptical of such readings and give the psychic a test. You should ask a series of questions to which only you know the answer. Also, base the questions on subjects about which the psychic cannot just hazard a guess.

When I tried to trick Ruth Montgomery's guide, Arthur Ford, he saw right through the camouflage and still gave me the correct answers. I never had to ask Pat Wilson a question; she always told me what would happen before I knew enough to ask.

As I've already mentioned, another interesting person I met during those years was John Harricharan. I met John in 1985, through Ruth, when he was writing his book *When You Can Walk on Water, Take the Boat*. We have remained friends all these years. John also spoke of my past lives. I never once asked John any questions; he would always have a vision and call me. In 1986 or 1987, John called me and told me of a vision he had that I was about to meet three women; however, he said he could see only two of them. The first was a young woman from the eastern part of the United States who would seek me out because she needed to correct a past-life karma. He said it would not be a romantic relationship but one of deep recognition and friendship. Once she connected with me, she would need to reconnect by becoming my friend. It seems I had abandoned her in a past life, and she simply needed to overcome her resentment toward me.

The second woman, he explained, would be an international beauty from Europe, specifically from Paris, and she would seek my advice, but she was actually a mistress from a past life. John predicted that when we met, there would be instant and intense recognition. I laughed and told John I couldn't wait. John had even seen a physical description of the two women; they were both blonde, but one was short with short hair while the other was a tall beauty. But John had no vision of the third person.

Months went by, and I had actually forgotten about his predictions. I'll be honest and say I didn't take them seriously. Then one day I received a call from a young lady in Los Angeles who identified herself as a producer for VH-1. She wanted to come to Nashville and talk to me about Reba McEntire—whom I was managing at the time—doing a VH-1 segment. I agreed to meet with her, and she stopped in Nashville on her way back to New York, where she lived and worked. She was cute, with short blonde hair, and when we met we discussed details of Reba's appearance on VH-1. We hit it off great. I felt comfortable with her, and it seemed we became instant friends.

After her return to New York, she called and suggested she return to Nashville for a few days to work out final details on the segment. I offered to let her stay at my condo and even offered her my pickup truck to drive so she wouldn't have to rent a car. She thought it would be cool to drive around Nashville in a pickup, and she readily agreed. She stayed in my guest bedroom and drove my truck during her trip. I was perfectly comfortable being with her; however, we never had a romantic relationship during our three-year friendship. Sometime during the relationship, I realized that she must be the female from the east of whom John spoke.

One Saturday morning, I was just leaving my condo to run errands when the phone rang. The woman on the phone identified herself as Alexia, an acquaintance of Sharon Osbourne—Ozzy Osbourne's wife. She was calling me for advice, at Sharon's suggestion. She immediately called me Bill and spoke as if she knew me. It was a warm, friendly, and lengthy conversation. When I asked, she said she was calling from London, but she was a model working in Paris, London, and New York. We spoke several times by phone before she finally told me she was coming to New York and wanted me to fly up and meet her. Since I needed to be in New York anyway to meet with Chet Flippo, the *Rolling Stone* author I was representing, I agreed. I was staying at my usual hotel, the Parker Meridien on 56th Street, and she suggested that to avoid any trouble in identifying each other, she would come up to my hotel room. When she knocked on the door, I opened it to find one of the tallest, most beautiful women I had ever met. She smiled and embraced me. We immediately hugged and kissed each other. Unusual, huh? It was as if I'd known her forever as we talked and kissed and touched each other. Actually, it seemed as if I was meeting someone I had loved deeply but who had been absent from my life for a while. She was about six feet tall, blonde, and beautiful. I was as comfortable with her as if I had been married to her for years. We went down to the hotel bar for drinks, and I introduced her to Chet when he arrived for our meeting.

When John predicted my meeting Alexia, he described our relationship so accurately that I felt guilty. Once, on a trip to New York when we were having dinner, I related to her John's prediction about our meeting. I described it like a movie script because I knew in advance how it would play out. She laughed and said the first time she talked to me on the phone, she felt close to me as if she had known me all her life. I told her of a past life we had lived together, and she believed it.

Our relationship was short, but intense. I expect to see her in future lives. I recently received a communication from John in which he describes his vision of the part this international model has played in my past lives:

We will call her Asha-arun because that was her name in a past life. Asha-arun spent many past lives with you. Some of them were short, maybe a period of only a few months. Other lives were for much longer periods. So it was in an Egyptian lifetime. This time you were the commander of the Pharaoh's armies. I get the feeling that it was during the reign of the Pharaoh Amenhotep II, a fierce ruler of the kingdom of Egypt. You are sitting on a horse of enormous proportions. You yourself are a tall, handsome man, somewhere in your early twenties. Your skin, bronzed by the sun, glistened in the sweat of the midday sun.

All around were soldiers waiting to do your bidding. Suddenly, out of nowhere it seems, a woman, riding on a black stallion, comes up to you. In those days this was unusual since this is not the normal thing that anyone would have dared to do. But this woman was unusual in many ways. She dared to go where no one else would. She is tall with raven black hair, beautiful beyond belief. She is Asha-arun, the Magnificent, from the royal house and the line of the great pharaohs of Egypt. She dismounts and walks toward you. You lean down and kiss her hands as she raises them to you. Words are exchanged, but I cannot hear the words. She returns to her horse, mounts and rides away. You wave to her knowing full well you'll see her in the evening time.

And so, through centuries you traveled, meeting for a moment or a lifetime. Down through the ages until one day, this time in the twentieth century, you meet again. She still is tall and beautiful. There is a knowing and a comfort between the two of you that transcend time and place. For the short time you reconnected in this lifetime, there was intensity as well as devotion, joy, and pain—all rolled into one. You are both destined in this dimension and others to always get back in touch. Your agreement with each other spans eternity itself.

Do not be surprised, Bill, if in your dreams, or in other alternate life-times, you find yourself staring into the eyes of the beauty once known as Asha-arun. There will always be the close feeling of other lifetimes and other glorious adventures you've had together. You can call her Alexia if you like. You see, she also lived a few other Egyptian lives as well as a few in Rome and Greece. One of her favorite names was "Alexia."

Pat Wilson is deceased, but I'm sure she is watching over me. I last saw Ruth in 1996, and she too is now deceased. I remain friends with John and talk with him often.

Amy is happily married, has two daughters, and lives in Canada. It's not that difficult to be physically separated when you share eternal love of the soul.

My spirit and attitude remain positive and upbeat. Emotional downs are relatively foreign to me. In my entire life I have never suffered from depression. As a young person, if I suffered any setbacks, I never went into depression. I didn't even know what depression was. Many years ago, during my training for the Secret Service, I was about to undergo a psychiatric exam. The psychiatrist asked me what the longest period of time was that I'd ever suffered from depression. I told him I could not recall ever being depressed about anything. He was shocked that I hadn't suffered from depression at some point in my life. But then he said maybe I was right because, from tests, he didn't see any evidence that I had ever had any sort of depression.

I have always had a very positive attitude. If I am angry, I can still love. I can turn my emotions any way I want to with my mind. If I feel bad, I can start feeling good. I've healed myself; I've made myself feel better. I find it somewhat unusual that I've always had this tremendously powerful positive attitude. Now, there are a lot of things that I can't control, but I can control what I think. I don't have ill feelings toward people, because I realize that when you engage in those feelings, you lose control of your emotions and you can begin to hate. I won't let negative emotions enter my mind. If they try to slip in, I zap them and get them out. I feel the same way about physical illness. I try to control it with my mind.

John Harricharan taught me a most effective way of dealing with unwanted emotions or thoughts. In order to stop thinking about a problem, we must simply change our focus to a pleasant experience and the problem will no longer occupy thinking space. His method of doing this is to visualize yourself pressing an imaginary button to break the focus and disconnect from the problem. I've used that method quite successfully over the past twenty-five years. I can't say enough about the positive influence John has exerted over my life. His books *When You Can Walk on Water, Take the Boat* and *Power Pause* have meant so much to my life, as have his wise counsel and his continuing friendship.

Chapter 29
The View From The Cumberland

𝕴 LOOK BACK AT MY LIFE NOW—from the perspective of distance and age—and I find it hard to believe I did some of the things I did. Was that really Billy Neal Carter or someone who answered to my name? Instead of jetting around the world fixing problems, I can often be found on my 40-acre farm outside Nashville riding my tractor or my bulldozer. Instead of frequenting the backstage areas of stadiums and arenas attending to rock and country stars, I spend most of my time outside the office on my boat on the Cumberland River with my lovely wife, Marlow, a few good friends and my family. There is a peaceful aspect to my life now compared to the turbulence of the first few decades, and I relish that. No question that I enjoy life more now than I've ever enjoyed it.

I owe a lot of that to the last decade of working with the Gaithers as well as the four years we spent working on the Billy Graham project. Bill Gaither entered my life at a time when I was maturing anyway, but the influence he and the Homecoming artists and the music have exerted on my life has been invaluable. The same is true with my association with the Graham organization. We conducted many interviews over the course of four years of preparing the documentary on Billy Graham, and each time when I returned from a taping, my assistant, Darlene Fort, would say to me, "I wish you would wake up every morning and watch a Billy Graham video, because there's such a peace to you when you return from being with them."

If a person lives a perfect Christian life, they would be calm, gentle, patient and kind, and you get that from a Gaither taping. I felt the presence of the Holy Spirit so strongly the very first Homecoming taping I attended, and while there have been times when it was stronger than others, I never fail to feel refreshed and renewed spiritually. The music touches your heart so, it's like going to a revival meeting.

The same is true with my association with people in the Graham organization like Bev Shea and Cliff Barrows. I never have a communication from Cliff that he doesn't include a line of scripture or a word of prayer. Whenever you see them, whether it's at a Crusade, or in a hotel lobby, there is just so much love that radiates from them. It rubs off on you. I have worked closely with Franklin Graham on the Billy Graham documentary and most recently with Franklin and his Samaritan's

Purse staff in South Africa. Franklin, Hans Mannegren, Duane Gaylord, Jim Harrelson, John Lampkins, and Paige Green worked with the Gaithers to distribute Christmas shoe boxes to needy children in South Africa. The dedication and spirit of these individuals is infectious. The Holy Spirit hovers over these special souls, and its influence is overwhelming. I thank God that He has blessed me by knowing such holy people. I am especially grateful that Franklin Graham provided us with this opportunity for additional spiritual development.

I hosted a political event recently at my home, and many of the guests, looking at photos in my office of my career with the Rolling Stones and JFK, wanted to talk about those events. I related stories to them, but it seemed as if I was talking about another person separate from me. The person I am now could never have negotiated the Steve McQueen deal or participated in some of the other showdowns I was involved in over the years. I'm sure there was a purpose in my life then—to help certain people who needed my expertise, but God blessed me with a change of direction and gave me more maturity as well as helping me focus on my love of the Holy Spirit. All this just goes to prove a point I've tried to make throughout this book—I never planned anything in my life. I truly believe God blessed me in everything I've done.

I'm really where I want to be in my life right now. I don't know what the definition of success is in the dictionary, but it should be one word: happiness. Money and power have nothing to do with happiness. When I went to Guatemala to help a young boy have heart surgery, I met some of the poorest people you can imagine, except in one way. They were rich in happiness. They didn't have a lot of "stuff" but they smiled and laughed all the time.

I don't know that I can point to any thing that I've contributed to life, but I can honestly say I'm a happy man. It's been a good life, and I feel enormously blessed by the people who have touched my life throughout that life. I've been fortunate to brush shoulders with some of the giants of the 20th century—Billy Graham, John F. Kennedy, Lyndon Johnson, Harry Truman, Bill Gaither, the Rolling Stones, and Wilbur Mills. I can't explain why I was chosen, but God obviously had a reason. I wasn't from a wealthy family nor did I have a prestigious education, but that made no difference. And there is one thing I've learned along the way: if I don't know anything else, I know that God loves me. What else do I need to know? All the questions have been answered for me.

Bibliography

Arkansas Democrat-Gazette, November 25, 1963.

Bennett, John. *Memphis Commercial Appeal*

Bradford, Sarah. *America's Queen: The Life of Jacqueline Kennedy Onassis.* New York: Penguin Books, 2001.

Bradlee, Benjamin C. *A Good Life: Newspapering and Other Adventures.* New York: Simon & Schuster, 1995.

Brandt, Charles. *"I Heard You Paint Houses": Frank "The Irishman" Sheeran and the Inside Story of the Mafia, the Teamsters, and the Last Ride of Jimmy Hoffa.* Hanover, NH: Steerforth Press, 2004.

Burleigh, Nina. *A Very Private Woman: The Life and Unsolved Murder of Presidential Mistress Mary Meyer.* New York: Bantam Books, 1998.

Flippo, Chet. *On The Road with the Rolling Stones: 20 Years of Lipstick, Handcuffs and Chemicals.* New York: Doubleday, 1985.

"Inside the KGB." NBC-TV, May 25, 1993.

John Kennedy Visit to Arkansas, KATV-TV, Little Rock, AR: Written and Produced by Bill Rogers, 1988.

Lane, Mark. *Rush to Judgment.* Emeryville, CA: Thunder's Mouth Press, 1992.

Mailer, Norman. *Oswald's Tale: An American Mystery.* New York: Random House, 1995.

Manchester, William. *The Death of a President.* New York: Harper & Row, 1967.

McCullough, David G. *Truman*. New York: Simon & Schuster, 1992.

McEntire, Reba, and Tom Carter. *Reba: My Story*. New York: Bantam Books, 1994.

New York Times Press. *Four Days*. Introduction by Bruce Catton. New York: New York Times Press, 1963.

Reeves, Richard. *President Kennedy: Profile of Power*. New York: Touchstone, 1994.

Report of the Warren Commission. New York: Bantam Books, 1964.

Ressler, Robert K., and Tom Shachtman. *Whoever Fights Monsters*. New York: St. Martin's, 1992.

Salinger, Pierre. *P.S., A Memoir*. New York: St. Martin's Press, 1995.

Salinger, Pierre. *With Kennedy*. Garden City, NY: Doubleday, 1966.

Sandford, Christopher. *McQueen: The Biography*. New York: Taylor Trade Publishing, 2003.

Schlesinger, Arthur, Jr. "JFK Revisited. A Noted Historian and Kennedy Administration Insider Refutes The Revisionist Version of JFK's Legacy." *Cigar Aficianado*, December, 1998.

"Secret Service: The Inside Story, 1965 to the Present." VHS. Directed by Benjamin Magliano. New York City: All-American Television and Quorum Communications in Association with The History Channel, A&E Television Networks, 1995.

Sixty Minutes, Morley Safer, CBS, New York City, 1980

RELEASED PER P.L. 102-526 (JFK ACT)
NARA ꙮꙮ DATE 3-26-01

WANTED

FOR

TREASON

THIS MAN is wanted for treasonous activities against the United States:

1. Betraying the Constitution (which he swore to uphold):
   He is turning the sovereignty of the U. S. over to the communist controlled United Nations.
   He is betraying our friends (Cuba, Katanga, Portugal) and befriending our enemies (Russia, Yugoslavia, Poland).

2. He has been WRONG on innumerable issues affecting the security of the U.S. (United Nations-Berlin wall-Missle removal-Cuba-Wheat deals-Test Ban Treaty,etc.)

3. He has been lax in enforcing Communist Registration laws.

4. He has given support and encouragement to the Communist inspired racial riots.

5. He has illegally invaded a sovereign State with federal troops.

6. He has consistantly appointed Anti-Christians to Federal office:
   Upholds the Supreme Court in its Anti-Christian rulings.
   Aliens and known Communists abound in Federal offices.

7. He has been caught in fantastic LIES to the American people (including personal ones like his previous marraige and divorce).

Exhibit 1. Kennedy Treason Poster

272

RELEASED PER P.L. 102-526 (JFK ACT)
NARA ⸏⸏⸏ DATE 3-26-01

United States Secret Service

Chief   12-9-63

SAIC Behn - White House Detail   1-16-611.3

Policy on Special Agents Covering the Presidential
Vehicle

The policy of special agents covering the presidential vehicle is
flexible and is based on the speed of the motorcade; the amount and
type of accompanying escort; the number, enthusiasm, and character
of the people watching the motorcade and how well-controlled they are
by the police; and finally, but certainly not least but perhaps the
dominant factor, the desire or instructions of the President.

There is always an experienced agent riding in the front seat of the
presidential vehicle and there is an experienced agent either riding in
the front seat of our follow-up car or standing on the front right running
board. Either one or both of these agents have the authority, if it becomes necessary, to either motion or tell the agents in the follow-up
car to take their positions around the presidential car at any time.

As stated in the first paragraph the desires and instructions of the
President were a major factor in this policy. On numerous occasions
during motorcades where the pace was slow and crowds were fairly
well-controlled by the police, but the agents were none the less in
position around the presidential car, the President would either tell
me to tell the agents, or he would attempt to tell the agents on his
side of the car, to get back.

In Mexico City in June, 1962, an individual who had the appearance of a
typical beatnik worked his way out into the middle of the street during
the welcoming motorcade and attempted to stop the President's car.
When he found out the driver would not stop, he came around the car
on the President's side and I hit him and knocked him down. The
President immediately told me I should not have done this. This
individual was arrested by the Mexican police, questioned and it was
discovered he was an American citizen who had overstayed his visa
and who had a police record in this country.

1620

Exhibit 2-1. Gerry Behn memo on Covering the Presidential Vehicle

273

RELEASED PER P.L. 102-526 (JFK ACT)
NARA _____ DATE 3-26-01

In West Berlin last June the pace of the motorcade was, for the most of the route, between 10 and 12 miles per hour and the West Berlin police did a remarkable job of controlling the huge crowds. However, there were occasions when individuals would break away from the police lines, evade the motorcycle escort and stand out near the middle of the street waiting for the President's car to reach them. On three occasions the agents on the running boards of the follow-up car would leap off, run forward and push the West Berliners away from the car. Practically every time this happened, the President would either tell me to tell the agents or would attempt to tell the agents themselves not to do this. His feeling was that these people only wanted to shake his hand and should not be pushed away from him.

Shortly after I was promoted to Special Agent in Charge of the White House Detail, and I believe this occurred during the late President's trip in November, 1961, to Seattle, Phoenix, Bonham, Texas, and other stops, he told me that he did not want agents riding on the back of his car. As late as November 18, of this year, he told ASAIC Boring the same thing. He gave me no reason for this. The late President Kennedy believed he belonged to the people. As such, he wanted to see the people and he wanted the people to see him. Perhaps the incidents related above do not belong in this memorandum. However, I believe that they should be included to show that, at times, the President himself was the major factor in determining whether the agents in the follow-up car took their positions around or on his car. It perhaps can be summed up by relating part of a brief conversation between Mr. Kenneth O'Donnell, appointment secretary, and Special Agent Clint Hill, in the Bethesda Naval Hospital. Mr. O'Donnell told Mr. Hill not to blame himself or the Secret Service for what had happened. Mr. O'Donnell went on to say that politics and protection do not mix and that in order to reach a happy medium, both must suffer.

Exhibit 2-2. Gerry Behn memo on Covering the Presidential Vehicle

REPRODUCED AT THE NATIONAL ARCHIVES

RELEASED PER P.L. 102-808 (JFK ACT)
NARA ⟨signature⟩ DATE 3-26-01

CONFIDENTIAL

THE ASSASSINATION OF PRESIDENT JOHN F. KENNEDY
ON NOVEMBER 22, 1963, AT DALLAS, TEXAS

Statement of Special Agent Winston G. Lawson, United States Secret Service,
concerning his activities and official duties on November 22, 1963, and until
his arrival in Washington, D.C., on November 23, 1963:

On Friday, November 22, 1963, I handled general advance details, talked over
final arrangements with Mr. Jack Puterbaugh; Mr. Art Bales, White House
Communications Agency; SAs Hickey and Kinney, and talked to various individuals on the phone before departing the Sheraton-Dallas Hotel. One of those
who contacted me by phone was ASAIC Kellerman in Fort Worth concerning car
seating and instructions as to whether the bubble top on the President's car
was to be used. I also spoke with SAIC Sorrels, Dallas office, on the phone
concerning his taking SAs Hickey and Kinney to the airport. I departed the
Sheraton-Dallas Hotel with SA David Grant.

At about 8:50 a.m. we arrived at the Dallas Trade Mart. I looked over the
security of the parking lot and area where the President was to enter the
building. Inside the building I checked on details of the luncheon, answered
various questions from interested parties, talked with Agent Stewart already
on duty at head table, and left Agent Grant to complete the final preparations
and survey for the President's visit and departed for Love Field.

I arrived at Love Field shortly after 9:30 a.m. and checked to see if police
security was in effect on a special hole cut in fence for our motorcade's
use. I also located the motorcade vehicles and drivers who had been asked
to arrive by 9:30 a.m. I checked with Major Medhal, USAF Advance Officer,
on positioning of airplanes and other information. Questions of various
press, Host Committee, political committee, communications and press
technicians had to be answered. I started forming the motorcade, parking
the vehicles and busses in proper positions, instructed drivers, checked
and gave instructions to police at press area. I answered the security
phone on a number of occasions and talked with Agent Hill in Fort Worth
concerning Dallas weather conditions. The weather cleared and the President's
car was placed in position for departure from airport without the bubble top
covering it. I met some members of Greeting Committee and checked over
flowers to be presented to Mrs. Kennedy and other ladies. I checked with
Chief Curry as to location of Lead Car and had WHCA portable radio put in
and checked. I also checked to see if escort vehicles were in position down
the apron from reception area and checked to see if police were posted for
crowd control.

About this time the press plane arrived and was met by me. White House Press
and Transportation Staff were given instructions. I learned sound equipment,
Presidential Seal, flags and a special chair had been sent by them direct
to Trade Mart from Fort Worth, and so the police escort and vehicles arranged
for these items to be taken to Trade Mart were not needed. Traveling press
were requested to go either to their busses or press area.

Declassified
by A.D. Kelley
Prior To
12/1975

1392

Exhibit 3-1. Win Lawson statement

DUCED AT THE NATIONAL ARCHIVES

RELEASED PER P.L. 102-526 (JFK ACT)
NARA _Soupalluse_ DATE 3-26-01

- 2 -

AF #2 then arrived and I met agents arriving on this plane. Those agents scheduled to be taken by police vehicles to the Trade Mart were shown to these vehicles with instructions to report to Agent Grant at Trade Mart. Agent Bennett was reminded that he would be working Presidential follow-up car on the movement. I then went with those members of AF #2 party who wanted to greet the President's plane and the local Reception Committee to a point near where President's plane would be spotted.

The President's plane, AF #1, was spotted and I positioned myself at bottom of the rear ramp across from Vice President Johnson and others greeting the President. I walked along behind the President as he spoke to this group and continued on to the fence with him. The follow-up car agents and ASAIC Kellerman were with him along the fence and watching the members of the press, so I checked to see if the motorcade was ready to leave when the President was. The motorcade inched forward and many members of it entered their cars. I instructed others to hurry to their vehicles and returned to area where President, Mrs. Kennedy, and others were still proceeding along the fence. The President and Mrs. Kennedy were soon guided towards their car, and after seeing the follow-up car agents were around his car keeping members of press and others out of the way, and doing their other normal functions, I ran to the Lead Car and joined SAIC Sorrels, Chief Curry, and Sheriff Decker.

The motorcade proceeded over the scheduled route from the airport. During the course of the trip I was watching crowd conditions along the route, requesting Chief Curry to give specific instructions to escort vehicles, keeping Lead Car in proper position in front of President's car depending on its speed and crowd conditions, watching for obstructions or other hazards, and in general performing normal duties of advance agent in the Lead Car. Chief Curry was giving instructions at my suggestion to escort vehicles for keeping crowd out of street, blocking traffic in certain areas, requesting pilot vehicle to speed or slow up, and giving orders needed for us to proceed unhampered.

The President's car made one unscheduled stop, apparently at his direction, which was not uncommon. This lasted only a few moments and motorcade proceeded on. On a few occasions I noticed agents leap off the follow-up car to intercept someone or when they thought someone was trying to reach the President's car. They were able to return to positions on the follow-up car.

The motorcade proceeded at about 15-20 miles per hour until the very heavy crowd concentration in the downtown area, when it slowed to approximately 10 miles per hour.

At the corner of Houston and Elm Streets I verified with Chief Curry that we were about five minutes from the Trade Mart and gave this signal over my

1392

Exhibit 3-2. Win Lawson statement

PRODUCED AT THE NATIONAL ARCHIVES

CONFIDENTIAL
- 3 -

portable White House Communications radio. We were just approaching a railroad overpass and I checked to see if a police officer was in position there
and that no one was directly over our path. I noticed a police officer but
also noticed a few persons on the bridge and made motions to have these
persons removed from over our path. As the Lead Car was passing under this
bridge I heard the first loud, sharp report and in more rapid succession two
more sounds like gunfire. I could see persons to the left of the motorcade
vehicles running away. I noticed Agent Hickey standing up in the follow-up
car with the automatic weapon and first thought he had fired at someone.
Both the President's car and our Lead Car rapidly accelerated almost
simultaneously. I heard a report over the two-way radio that we should
proceed to the nearest hospital. I noticed Agent Hill hanging on to the rear
of the President's vehicle. A motorcycle escort officer pulled alongside
our Lead Car and said the President had been shot. Chief Curry gave a signal
over his radio for police to converge on the area of the incident. I
requested Chief Curry to have the hospital contacted that we were on the way.
Our Lead Car assisted the motorcycles in escorting the President's vehicle to
Parkland Hospital.

Upon our arrival there at approximately 12:34 p.m., I rushed into the emergency
entrance, met persons coming with two stretchers and helped rush them outside.
Governor Connally was being removed from the car when the stretchers arrived
and he was placed on the first one. Mr. Powers, myself and one or two others
placed President Kennedy on a stretcher and we ran pushing the stretcher into
the emergency area which hospital personnel directed us to. I remained outside the door where the President was being treated and requested a nurse
to find someone who would know hospital personnel who should be admitted to
the President's room. Other agents, in addition to some members of the
White House staff, then stationed themselves at this door. ASAIC Kellerman
and myself went to an office in emergency area and used a phone to contact
the White House Dallas switchboard, who in turn contacted SAIC Behn, White
House Detail in Washington. Mr. Kellerman informed Mr. Behn what had happened
and we kept that line open to Mr. Behn's office during our stay at Parkland
Hospital. I went outside into a corridor and noticed that agents had
established security to the emergency area then proceeded to rear of hospital
to make sure police security was keeping general public from the immediate
area. Upon returning to the emergency room office, I again assisted in
keeping line to Washington open, talked with Mr. Behn in Washington,
requested the Dallas White House switchboard to contact Austin, Texas, where
the 12 p.m. (midnight) to 8:00 a.m. Secret Service shift was resting and
instruct those agents to take first available plane back to Washington, D.C.
A few minutes later I learned a special Air Force plane would take them
from Bergstrom AFB (Austin, Texas) to Washington, D.C., and requested the
Dallas White House switchboard to notify these agents of this change. It
was then I learned that Mrs. Kennedy wished to return to Washington, D.C.,
with the body of President Kennedy immediately, and I returned to rear of
hospital to see if enough motorcade vehicles remained for transportation of
agents, staff and others needing transportation to the airport.

CONFIDENTIAL

1392

Exhibit 3-3. Win Lawson statement

PRODUCED AT THE NATIONAL ARCHIVES

RELEASED PER P.L. 102-526 (JFK ACT)
NARA _Soup Blue_ DATE 3-26-01

- 4 -

Vice President Johnson had already been taken to Love Field and was aboard
AF #1. The President's car and the Secret Service follow-up car had already
been taken to Love Field for loading aboard the special Air Force plane.

I requested the police to be ready to escort us to the airplanes and drivers
to have their cars ready. Arrangements had already been made by someone
else for a hearse to transport the coffin. Returning inside I learned the
Medical Examiner could not release the body and located Sheriff Decker, who
had returned to his office, by phone. I believe Dr. Burkley, the President's
White House physician, talked with the Sheriff. The President's body was
released and the coffin placed in a hearse from the O'Neill Mortuary. At
about 2:04 p.m. agents accompanied the President's body and Mrs. Kennedy in
the hearse, and other agents rode in a Lincoln automobile behind this
hearse. Other staff members rode in other cars. I rode in a police car
ahead of the hearse, and motorcycles escorted us to Love Field position of
AF #1. We arrived at AF #1 at about 2:15 p.m. I helped remove the coffin
from the hearse and place it aboard AF #1.

I remained outside the airplane until it departed for Washington, D.C., after
Vice President Johnson was sworn in as President by Federal Judge Sarah
Hughes.

Police and agents had removed all general public and press from the immediate
area.

While waiting for the departure of AF #1, FBI Agent Vincent Drain, Dallas
office, told me SAC Gordon Shanklin, FBI, Dallas, Texas, had some information. I spoke with Mr. Shanklin on the phone and he told me that an
individual who had been arrested for the investigation of the killing of a
police officer that afternoon had worked at the Texas Book Depository
Building. I asked Mr. Shanklin to relay this to an agent on duty in the
Dallas Secret Service office and then requested Chief Curry, who was with
me, to speak with Mr. Shanklin on the phone.

After the departure of President Johnson and the body of President Kennedy
aboard AF #1 at approximately 2:47 p.m., I proceeded to Police Headquarters
with Chief Curry and Agent David Grant. En route we learned SAIC Sorrels
was at Police Headquarters. Upon our arrival there I reported to SAIC Sorrels
and remained at Police Headquarters under his direction.

At approximately 11:00 p.m. Inspector Kelley, Chief's Office, United States
Secret Service, arrived and at approximately 1:00 a.m., on November 23, 1963,
he requested me to return to Washington, D.C., on a special plane which was
returning evidence from the Dallas Police in the killing of Police Officer
Tippit and President Kennedy. I went to the FBI Dallas office, met FBI
Agent Drain again, and proceeded with him and the packaged evidence to

1392

Exhibit 3-4. Win Lawson statement

REPRODUCED AT THE NATIONAL ARCHIVES

NARA Sonya Blue DATE 3-26-01

- 5 -

Carswell AFB. I departed Carswell AFB aboard USAF plane #276 at 3:10 a.m., C.S.T., November 23, 1963, and arrived at Andrews AFB at 6:30 a.m., E.S.T.

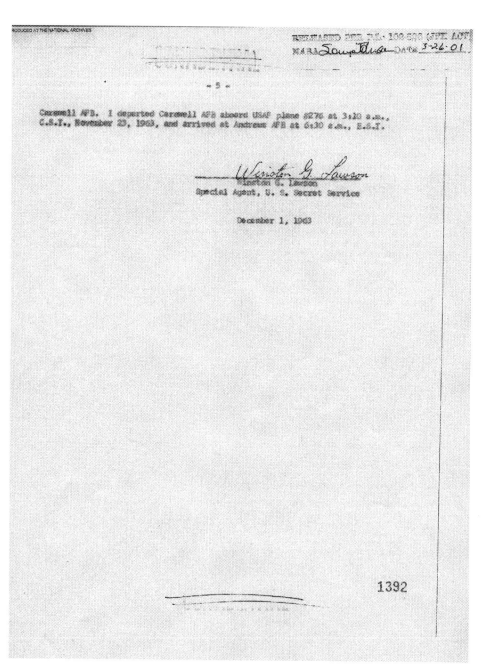

Winston G. Lawson
Winston G. Lawson
Special Agent, U. S. Secret Service

December 1, 1963

1392

Exhibit 3-5. Win Lawson statement

PRODUCED AT THE NATIONAL ARCHIVES

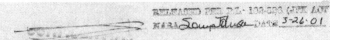

THE ASSASSINATION OF PRESIDENT JOHN F. KENNEDY
ON NOVEMBER 22, 1963, AT DALLAS, TEXAS

Statement of Special Agent Clinton J. Hill, United States Secret
Service, concerning his activities and official duties on November 22, 1963.
Statement dated November 30, 1963.

I, Clinton J. Hill, Special Agent, United States Secret Service,
arrived at Love Field, Dallas, Texas, at 11:40 a.m. on November 22, 1963, from
Fort Worth, Texas, aboard Air Force No. One (USAF #26000) with President and Mrs.
John F. Kennedy. President and Mrs. Kennedy debarked the aircraft first from
the rear ramp followed by Governor and Mrs. John Connally and by three or four
Congressmen and Senators, and then myself and ASAIC Roy H. Kellerman.

Upon alighting, President and Mrs. Kennedy were greeted by a small
reception committee and Mrs. Kennedy was presented a bouquet of red roses. I
ran over to the Secret Service Follow-up car immediately upon my arrival and
placed my topcoat and a small folder containing information on this Dallas stop
of the Texas trip on the floor of the car. I then went back to where the President
and Mrs. Kennedy were greeting an elderly lady in a wheel chair.

The general public was restricted from the ramp area of Love Field by
a permanent chain-link fence. There were a number of photographers and correspondents on the ramp area covering the arrival.

The President noticed the large number of people being restrained by
the fence and walked over to the crowd and began shaking hands. He moved from
his right to his left down the fence. Mrs. Kennedy accompanied him. I remained
very close to Mrs. Kennedy observing the outstretched hands of well-wishers to
make sure no weapons were extended toward Mrs. Kennedy and that nothing was handed
to her. I accompanied Mrs. Kennedy behind the President along the fence and then
to the Presidential automobile which was waiting to take President and Mrs.
Kennedy and Governor and Mrs. John Connally to the Trade Mart for a luncheon,
after a 45-minute motorcade through downtown Dallas.

President and Mrs. Kennedy entered the automobile with the President
getting into the right rear seat and Mrs. Kennedy into the left rear seat. Mrs.
Connally got into the left jump seat and Governor Connally into the right jump
seat. SA William Greer was driving the automobile with ASAIC Roy H. Kellerman
in the right front seat. I went to the left rear side of the Presidential
automobile and stood on the airport ramp along side where Mrs. Kennedy was
sitting.

As the Presidential automobile began to move forward at 11:55 a.m. I
walked along side of the left rear of the automobile for about 150 feet, and since
there were no people at all on the airport ramp I went back to the automobile
immediately behind the Presidential Automobile and mounted the forward portion
of the left running board.

Declassified
by A.D. Kelley
PRIOR TO
12/1975

1392

Exhibit 4-1. Clinton Hill statement

REPRODUCED AT THE NATIONAL ARCHIVES

RELEASED PER P.L. 102-526 (JFK ACT
NARA Soupeliva DATE 3-26-01

Page Two of Statement of Special Agent Clinton J. Hill, dated Nov. 30, 1963:

SA Sam Kinney was driving this Secret Service Follow-up car which was a 1955 Cadillac 9-passenger convertible specifically outfitted for use by the Secret Service. ATSAIC Emory Roberts was sitting in the right front seat and operating the two-way radio. SA John Ready was on the forward portion of the right hand running board; SA William McIntyre on the rear portion of the left hand running board; SA Paul E. Landis on the rear portion of the right hand running board; Mr. Kenneth O'Donnell, Presidential Appointment Secretary, was seated on the left side of the second seat; Mr. Dave Powers, Presidential Receptionist, was seated on the right side of the second seat; SA George Hickey was seated on the left side of the third seat; and SA Glen Bennett was seated on the right side of the third seat.

The Presidential Follow-up car was followed by a 1964 Lincoln 4-door convertible occupied by Vice-President and Mrs. Lyndon Johnson, Senator Ralph Yarborough, with ASAIC Rufus Youngblood in the right front seat. This automobile was followed by a Secret Service follow-up car for the Vice President, and then came automobiles occupied by photographers, correspondents, Senators and Congressmen.

Preceding the Presidential automobile was a Dallas Police Department Lead car in which SA Winston Lawson of the Secret Service was riding. Police motorcycles preceded and flanked the motorcade. There were two police motorcycles on the left side of the President's Secret Service follow-up car running abreast of one another between the automobile and the crowd of people.

My instructions for Dallas were to work the left rear of the Presidential automobile and remain in close proximity to Mrs. John F. Kennedy at all times. The agent assigned to work the left rear of the Presidential automobile rides on the forward portion of the left hand running board of the Secret Service follow-up car and only moves forward to walk alongside the Presidential automobile when it slows to such a pace that people can readily approach the auto on foot. If the crowd is very heavy, but the automobile is running at a rather rapid speed, the agent rides on the left rear of the Presidential automobile on a step specifically designed for that purpose.

As the motorcade moved from Love Field through downtown Dallas toward the Trade Mart, there were four (4) occasions before we reached the end of Main Street where I moved from the forward portion of the left running board of the follow-up car to the rear step of the Presidential automobile. I did this because the motorcycles that were along the left hand side of the follow-up car were unable to move up alongside the President's car due to the crowd surging into the street. The motorcycles were forced to drop back and so I jumped from the Follow-up car and mounted the President's car. I remained in this position until the crowd thinned and was away from the President's automobile, allowing the motorcycles to once again move up alongside of the automobile. When we approached the end of Main Street the crowd was noticeably less dense than had been the case prior to that point.

1392

Exhibit 4-2. Clinton Hill statement

PRODUCED AT THE NATIONAL ARCHIVES

RELEASED PER P.L. 102-526 (JFK ACT
NARA _Sonya Kluge_ DATE 3-26-01

Page Three of Statement of Special Agent Clinton J. Hill, dated Nov. 30, 1963:

The motorcade made a right hand turn onto Elm Street. I was on the forward portion of the left running board of the follow-up car. The motorcade made a left hand turn from Elm Street toward an underpass. We were traveling about 12 to 15 miles per hour. On the left hand side was a grass area with a few people scattered along it observing the motorcade passing, and I was visually scanning these people when I heard a noise similar to a firecracker. The sound came from my right rear and I immediately moved my head in that direction. In so doing, my eyes had to cross the Presidential automobile and I saw the President hunch forward and then slump to his left. I jumped from the Follow-up car and ran toward the Presidential automobile. I heard a second firecracker type noise but it had a different sound—like the sound of shooting a revolver into something hard. I saw the President slump more toward his left.

I jumped onto the left rear step of the Presidential automobile. Mrs. Kennedy shouted, "They've shot his head off;" then turned and raised out of her seat as if she were reaching to her right rear toward the back of the car for something that had blown out. I forced her back into her seat and placed my body above President and Mrs. Kennedy. SA Greer had, as I jumped onto the Presidential automobile, accelerated the Presidential automobile forward. I heard ASAIC Kellerman call SA Lawson on the two-way radio and say, "To the nearest hospital, quick." I shouted as loud as I could at the Lead car, "To the hospital, to the hospital."

As I lay over the top of the back seat I noticed a portion of the President's head on the right rear side was missing and he was bleeding profusely. Part of his brain was gone. I saw a part of his skull with hair on it lying in the seat. The time of the shooting was approximately 12:30 p.m., Dallas time. I looked forward to the jump seats and noticed Governor Connally's chest was covered with blood and he was slumped to his left and partially covered up by his wife. I had not realized until this point that the Governor had been shot.

When we arrived at Parkland Memorial Hospital, Dallas, I jumped off the Presidential automobile, removed my suit coat and covered the President's head and upper chest with it. I assisted in lifting the President from the rear seat of the automobile onto a wheel type stretcher and accompanied the President and Mrs. Kennedy into the Emergency Room. Governor Connally had been placed in an Emergency Room across the hall.

I exited the Emergency Room almost immediately because of the large number of doctors and nurses in the room, which was quite small. I asked a nurse standing outside of the Emergency Room in which the President was lying to please have everyone except those Medical Staff members necessary leave the emergency ward. She immediately began screening medical staff members.

I asked for the nearest telephone. ASAIC Kellerman exited the Emergency Room and told me to contact the White House in Washington and to keep the line open continually. I asked SA Lawson for the telephone number of the Dallas White

1392

Exhibit 4-3. Clinton Hill statement

PRODUCED AT THE NATIONAL ARCHIVES

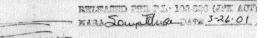

RELEASED PER P.L. 102-526 (JFK ACT)
NARA [signature] DATE 3-26-01

Page Four of Statement of Special Agent Clinton J. Hill, dated Nov. 30, 1963;

House switchboard and he gave it to me. I dialed the Dallas White House operator and told him to connect me with the White House in Washington and to keep this line open continuously. He did so.

ASAIC Kellerman came out of the Emergency Room again and took the telephone and asked for SAIC Gerald A. Behn, Secret Service, The White House, Washington. This was approximately 12:39 p.m. Kellerman told Behn that there had been a double tragedy; that the President and Governor Connally had both been shot and that I would keep him advised. I took over the telephone and told Mr. Behn that the situation was extremely critical. The operator cut into the line and said The Attorney General wanted to talk to me. He asked me what the situation was and I advised him that the President had been injured very seriously and that I would keep him advised as to his condition.

Mr. Kellerman came back out of the Emergency Room and said, "Clint, tell Gerry that this is not for release and not official, but the man is dead." I told that to Mr. Behn and then requested that he immediately contact the Attorney General and other members of the President's family so that he could advise them of the situation rather than having them hear it over some news media.

I then received a request from Mr. O'Donnell to obtain a casket immediately so that we could transport the body back to Washington, D. C., as quickly as possible. I contacted the Hospital Administrator and asked for the name of the nearest mortuary. He said it would be O'Neil, Inc. I telephoned them and identified myself and requested that they bring the best casket immediately available at the mortuary to the Parkland Memorial Hospital Emergency Entrance and deliver it to me. The casket arrived in about twenty minutes at approximately 1:40 p.m. We wheeled it immediately into the Emergency Room where the President's body lay.

I advised the Air Force Aide that we wanted Air Force No. One moved to a different location at Love Field and to have it secured completely away from the view of the General Public. I requested that no press be admitted to the area in which Air Force One was to be placed. I requested SA David Grant to notify the Dallas Police that we did not want to use the same entrance to Love Field that previously had been planned. I then went with the Hospital Administrator and checked the shortest and most direct route from the Emergency Room to the emergency platform where the O'Neil hearse was waiting. I advised ATSAIC Stuart Stout of the route and requested that it be cleared of personnel.

The President's body, accompanied by Mrs. Kennedy, exited the Emergency Room at approximately 1:58 p.m. and proceeded to the emergency entrance platform. The casket was placed in the back of the O'Neil, Inc., hearse and Mrs. Kennedy, Admiral George Burkley (the President's Physician), and I entered the back of the hearse with the casket. SA Andrew Berger drove the hearse; ATSAIC Stuart Stout rode in the center front seat and ASAIC Kellerman rode in the right front seat.

1392

Exhibit 4-4. Clinton Hill statement

REPRODUCED AT THE NATIONAL ARCHIVES

RELEASED PER P.L. 102-266 (JFK ACT)
NARA _Soup Hue_ DATE 3-26-01

Page Five of Statement of Special Agent Clinton J. Hill, dated Nov. 30, 1963:

We departed Parkland Memorial Hospital at 2:04 p.m. SA Lawson rode in the Dallas Police Department Lead Car. A Secret Service follow-up car followed immediately behind the hearse. The motorcade arrived at Air Force One, Love Field, at 2:14 p.m.

At 2:18 p.m. the casket was placed aboard Air Force One with Mrs. Kennedy accompanying it. The casket was situated in the left rear corner of the aircraft where four seats had been removed. Mrs. Kennedy sat in one of the two seats immediately across the aisle from the casket.

The aircraft could not immediately depart because Vice-President Johnson had to be sworn in as the 36th President of the United States and it was necessary to wait for a Judge to arrive to do this. All personnel on Air Force One including Mrs. Kennedy were requested to witness the swearing in ceremony which took place in the Presidential Compartment of Air Force One at 2:38 p.m. I also attended.

I departed Love Field, Dallas, aboard Air Force One at 2:47 p.m. en route to Andrews Air Force Base, Maryland. I arrived at Andrews Air Force Base at 5:58 p.m. I assisted in moving the casket bearing the President's body from Air Force One to a U. S. Navy ambulance. Mrs. Kennedy got in the back of the ambulance with the casket as did Attorney General Robert Kennedy, who had joined Mrs. Kennedy aboard Air Force One upon arrival at Andrews Air Force Base. General Godfrey McHugh also rode in the back of the ambulance. The ambulance was driven by SA Greer with ASAIC Kellerman, SA Landis, and Admiral Burkley riding in the front seat. I followed in the car immediately behind the ambulance with Dr. John W. Walsh, Dave Powers, Kenneth O'Donnell and Larry O'Brien.

The motorcade departed Andrews Air Force Base for Bethesda Naval Hospital, Bethesda, Maryland, at 6:10 p.m. We were escorted by motorcycle police officers. The motorcade arrived Bethesda Naval Hospital at 6:55 p.m. Mrs. Kennedy, the Attorney General, SA Landis and I went immediately inside and via elevator to the 17th Floor of the hospital, the location of the Presidential Suite. Members of the immediate family and close friends were waiting in the suite.

The President's body was taken to the morgue at the hospital, accompanied by ASAIC Kellerman, SA Greer, and Admiral Burkley, for an autopsy. SA Landis and I secured the 17th Floor of the hospital and remained there with Mrs. Kennedy. We established a communications system with the White House and handled all telephone calls both incoming and outgoing, screening each and every call. Any person attempting to reach the 17th Floor was also screened.

At approximately 2:45 a.m., November 23, I was requested by ASAIC Kellerman to come to the morgue to once again view the body. When I arrived the autopsy had been completed and ASAIC Kellerman, SA Greer, General McHugh and I viewed the wounds. I observed a wound about six inches down from the neckline on the back just to the right of the spinal column. I observed another wound on

1392

Exhibit 4-5. Clinton Hill statement

REPRODUCED AT THE NATIONAL ARCHIVES

Page Six of Statement of Special Agent Clinton J. Hill, dated Nov. 30, 1963:

the right rear portion of the skull. Attendants of the Joseph Gawler Mortuary were at this time preparing the body for placement in the casket. A new casket had been obtained from Gawler Mortuary in which the body was to be placed.

I went back to the 17th Floor of the hospital at approximately 3:10 a.m. The President's body was taken from the U. S. Naval Hospital, Bethesda, Maryland, at 3:56 a.m., accompanied by Mrs. Kennedy and Attorney General Kennedy, in the rear of a U. S. Navy ambulance driven by SA Greer. ASAIC Kellerman rode in the right front seat. I rode in the right front seat of a White House limousine immediately behind the ambulance. The motorcade was accompanied by motorcycle police and arrived at the White House at 4:24 a.m. The casket was taken immediately to the East Room and placed in the center of the room on a catephalt.

Clinton J. Hill
Special Agent
U. S. Secret Service

1392

Exhibit 4-6. Clinton Hill statement

285

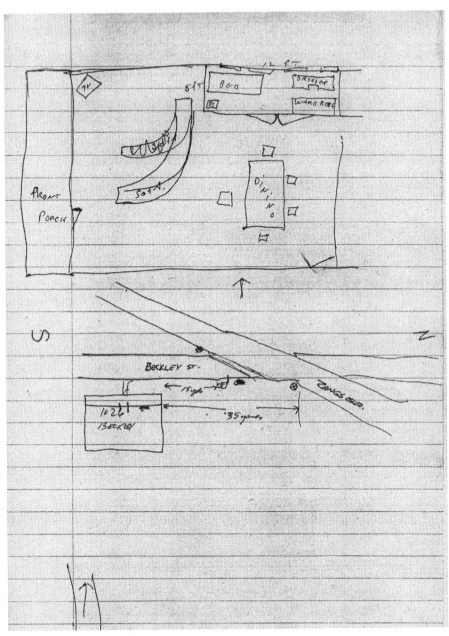

Exhibit 5. Diagram of Oswald's room

DUCED AT THE NATIONAL ARCHIVES

INV. 3

The following typewritten letter was contained in an envelope
addressed to Lee Harvey Oswald, Mail Office, Dallas, Texas,
which was postmarked at Havana, Cuba, on November 28, 1963,
9:30 a.m.

November 10, 1963

Lee Harvey Oswald
Mail Office
Dallas, Texas
U.S.A.

Friend Lee:

One time more I write you since the last
time that we saw each other in Miami. The
Spanish books that you took from the hotel and
I have hardly anything. I told you of the man who
was thinking of visiting here shortly and you ought
to close the business as soon as possible, like I told
you before in Miami, I recommend much prudence and do not
be foolish with the money I gave you. So I hope you will
not defraud me and that our dreams will be realized. After
the affair I am going to recommend much to the chief that
he certainly will have much interest in knowing you as
they need men like you. I told him you could put out a
candle at 50 meters and he did not want to believe me, but
I made him believe it because I saw you with my own eyes and
the chief was astonished. Good Lee, practice your Spanish
for when you come to Habana for Habana is the land of the
free, of the beautiful women and the rich Habana tobacco.
Don't forget to do all I told you to the very letter and
leave nothing that could lead to your trail and when you
receive my letters destroy them as always. After the affair
I will send you the money and we will see each other in
Miami where always.

Sincerely always

Pedro Charles

Peter

CR 205

Exhibit 6-1. Cuban letter

SPRODUCED AT THE NATIONAL ARCHIVES

UNITED STATES DEPARTMENT OF JUSTICE

FEDERAL BUREAU OF INVESTIGATION

WASHINGTON 25, D.C.

January 17, 1964

Com #295

Honorable J. Lee Rankin
General Counsel
The President's Commission
200 Maryland Avenue, Northeast
Washington, D. C.

Dear Mr. Rankin:

     Reference is made to my letter dated December 13, 1963, enclosing a summary of the results of the investigations of several hoaxes and false reports which had arisen in connection with the Oswald case. The following information supplements the data previously furnished to you in this regard.

     The FBI has been furnished four letters written from Cuba indicating or alleging that the assassination of President Kennedy was undertaken by Oswald under the direction of a Cuban agent, one Pedro Charles, who reportedly gave Oswald $7,000 for this mission. Specifically, these letters are as follows:

     (1) A letter dated November 10, 1963, but postmarked November 28, 1963, at Havana, Cuba (six days after the assassination), signed by Pedro Charles and addressed to Oswald, c/o "Mail Office," Dallas, Texas. This letter was intercepted by the Secret Service and was referred to the FBI.

     (2) A letter addressed to the Attorney General postmarked November 28, 1963, at Havana and signed by Mario del Rosario Molina. This letter was referred to the FBI by the Department of Justice.

     (3) A letter postmarked December 3, 1963, at Havana, addressed to the Voice of America and signed by Miguel Galban Lopez. This communication was referred to us by the United States Information Agency.

CR 295

Exhibit 6-2. Cuban letter

REPRODUCED AT THE NATIONAL ARCHIVES

Honorable J. Lee Rankin

     (4) A letter postmarked December 3, 1963, at Havana signed by Miguel Galban Lopez and addressed to the "Editor of the Diario de New York," a Spanish-language newspaper published in New York City. This letter was forwarded to the FBI by an official of the newspaper.

     One copy each of the above-described letters is enclosed herewith.

     As noted above, the first letter received was purportedly written by Pedro Charles, was dated some two weeks prior to the President's assassination, and was designed to give the impression Charles was furnishing instructions to Oswald relative to the assassination. The other three letters purport to be from individuals who have knowledge that Charles conspired with Oswald to kill the President. However, examinations by the FBI Laboratory have shown that all of these communications were actually prepared on the same typewriter and that several of the envelopes used came from the same source. It is, therefore, clear that this represents some type of hoax, possibly on the part of some anti-Castro group seeking to discredit the Cuban Government.

     Sincerely yours,

     J. Edgar Hoover

Enclosures - 4

- 2 -

(R395)

Exhibit 6-3. Cuban letter

REPRODUCED AT THE NATIONAL ARCHIVES

RELEASED PER P.L. 102-526 (JFK ACT)
NARA ⟶⟶ ℒℓⅇⅽ DATE 3-26-01

State of Texas }
County of Dallas } ss:
City of Dallas }

I, Mr. Buell Wesley Frazier, 2439 West Fifth, Irving, Texas, do depose and state:

I work at Texas School Book Depository, 411 Elm Street, Dallas, Texas, and have been employed there since September 13, of this year. I first met Lee Harvey Oswald on his first day at work at the Depository. He told me that he lived in Irving. I told him he could ride home with me since he had stated that he did not have a car. Lee stated that he would ride with me on Friday evenings and Monday mornings since he had an apartment in Oak Cliff. He had very little to say in our first conversation.

I live in Irving, Texas with my sister, Lenny Randall, and she told me that a man by the name of Lee Oswald had come over where I worked for an interview, and he had been hired to begin work on the following Monday. His wife and one child lived in Irving. Mrs. Oswald was expecting another child at the time. Lee Oswald's wife and child lived in the same neighborhood with Ruth Payne. Each weekend on Friday evening, Lee would ride home with me and come back on Monday morning with the exception of one weekend which Lee Oswald stated he was staying in Oak Cliff to take a driver's test. He had previously told me that he was learning to drive.

On Thursday morning, November 21, 1963, Lee asked me if he could ride home with me that night. Lee had never gone home in the middle of the week before so I asked him why and he stated that he was going home to get some curtain rods for his apartment. I asked if he was going home Friday and he said no. On Thursday afternoon, I took him to Irving and let him out in front of Ruth Payne's house.

On Friday morning, the first time I saw him, I was sitting at the breakfast table about 7:00 with Mother and my two nieces. My sister was fixing my lunch. Mother looked up and asked who was at the window. I said that is Lee. At approximately 7:20 I started out to the carport and met Lee there. He was not in the car as yet. He had put a package in the back seat of the car. I got into the car and sort of glanced over my shoulder and saw a package in the seat. The package was approximately two feet in length. It was a brown paper sack and was folded so that the contents could not be seen. I asked Lee about the package, and he said it was curtain rods. He had told me the previous day that he was going to bring some curtain rods. Lee said very little on the way to work and did not speak until a subject was brought up.

When we arrived at work, I parked the car in the parking lot. Lee got out and took the package, and I stayed in the car charging my battery. Lee waited for me by the fence. As I got out of the car, Lee started walking to the warehouse; therefore, he was always a few feet ahead of me.

491

B.W.F.

Exhibit 7-1. Buell Wesley Frasier statement

REPRODUCED AT THE NATIONAL ARCHIVES

RELEASED PER P.L. 102-526 (JFK ACT)
NARA _____ DATE 3-26-01

The package was under his arm lengthwise and the paper was all that could be seen. Lee came in the first door in the back of the depository building. I did not see him when I entered the building after him. Every time Lee rode to work with me he always brought his lunch, but on the day of the assassination he did not bring his lunch.

The only time I went to the sixth floor on Friday was to put up some stock and I didn't see Lee Oswald on that floor. I was standing on the front steps when the parade passed in front of the building. When the shooting occurred, I did not realize the shots were really shots until the second one. At first I thought it was backfire. I did not realize the shots had come from this building but thought they had come from somewhere around the triple underpass or railroad tracks. I returned to the building after the shooting and did not see Lee Oswald.

All I recall about Oswald's clothing on the morning of the assassination was a gray wool jacket. I don't remember what kind of shirt or pants he was wearing.

I have never driven Oswald anywhere other than between the Texas School Book Depository and Irving, Texas, where I live and where Oswald's wife and children were living. I have never driven him to any rifle range.

I have read the above statement consisting of two pages and it is true to the best of my knowledge.

Buell Wesley Frazier
Buell Wesley Frazier

Subscribed and sworn to before me
this 5th day of December 1963
"auth. Title 5, Sec. 93, USC"

William N. Carter
William N. Carter, Special Agent
U. S. Secret Service

Witness: _Ralph W. Blake_

491

Exhibit 7-2. Buell Wesley Frasier statement

291

REPRODUCED AT THE NATIONAL ARCHIVES

RELEASED PER P.L. 102-526 (JFK ACT)
NARA _____ DATE 3-26-01

AFFIDAVIT

State of Texas
County of Dallas
City of Dallas

I, Harold Norman, wish to make the following statement to Special Agents William Carter and Arthur W. Blake, United States Secret Service

I am 25 years of age, and I live at 4858 Beulah Street, Dallas, Texas. I do not have a telephone at my residence. I have been employed as an order filler at the Texas School Book Depository, 411 Elm Street, Dallas, Texas for about three years.

I was acquainted with Lee Oswald during the time that he was employed at this company, but I never did get to know him well. I have spoken to him briefly to say "Hello" or in connection with my work, but I never carried on any conversations with him. He did not mix with the employees and did not appear to want to make friends with me or any of the others. I never saw him at any time other than in the building at work.

On the 22nd of November, 1963, to the best of my memory, the last time I saw him was about 10:00 A. M. when we were both working on the first floor of the building. I did not speak to him at that time.

About 12:15 P. M. on this same date, after I had eaten my lunch, I went to the fifth floor of the bu lding to watch the parade of the President pass the building. Bonnie Ray Williams and James JArman, who also work at this building went with me. We took a position in the south-east corner of the building on the fifth floor and I was looking out the window which is closest to the east end of the buuilding overlooking Elm Street.

Just after the President passed by, I heard a shot and several seconds later I heard two more shots. I knew that the shots had come from directly above me, and I could hear the expended cartridges fall to the floor. I could also hear the bolt action of the rifle. I also saw some dust fall from the ceiling of the fifth floor and I felt sure that whoever had fired the shots was directly above me. I saw all of the people down on the street run toward the west side of the building, so I went to that side with Williams and Jarman, and looked out the west side window. We discussed the shots, and where they had come from and decided we better go down stairs. We walked down the stairs to the first floor and did not see anyone else on the stairway as we went down. From the time of the shots until we started down-stairs was about five minutes.

I have read over the above statement and it is the truth to the best of my knowledge.

Harold Norman
Harold Norman

Subscribed and sworn to before me this 4th day of December, 1963.

William N. Carter
William N. Carter, Special Agent
U. S. Secret Service

Witness: _Arthur W. Blake_
Special Agent, U. S. Secret Service

491

Exhibit 8. Harold Norman, Jr. statement